Adolescent Boys

Adolescent Boys

Exploring Diverse Cultures of Boyhood

EDITED BY

Niobe Way and Judy Y. Chu

FOREWORD BY MICHAEL KIMMEL

New York University Press

NEW YORK AND LONDON

NEW YORK UNIVERSITY PRESS
New York and London
www.nyupress.org

Library of Congress Cataloging-in-Publication Data
Adolescent boys : exploring diverse cultures of boyhood / edited by
Niobe Way and Judy Y. Chu ; foreword by Michael Kimmel.
p. cm.   Includes bibliographical references and index.
ISBN 0–8147–9384–3 (cloth : alk. paper) —
ISBN 0–8147–9385–1 (pbk : alk. paper)
1. Teenage boys—Social conditions.   2. Minority teenagers—
Social conditions.   3. Adolescent psychology.
4. Interpersonal relations in adolescence.
I. Way, Niobe, 1963–   II. Chu, Judy Y.
HQ797.A36   2003
305.235'1—dc22   2003018951

For

Raphael

and

Alexander

Contents

Foreword

The "boy" question burst on the scene a couple of years ago. Suddenly, it seemed, America had "discovered" boys.

A flurry of best-selling titles urged us to "rescue" and "protect" boys. Psychologists like William Pollack, Dan Kindlon, and Michael Thompson described how boys are failing at school, acting out behaviorally, feeling depressed and suicidal, or shutting down emotionally. Most of the better books by these therapists point their finger at what Pollack labeled the *boy code*—the cultural myths of masculinity to which boys try so desperately and so poignantly to adhere, despite their small frames and trembling hearts. They advised anguished parents about boys' fragility, their hidden despondence, and depression, and issued stern warnings about the dire consequences if we don't watch our collective cultural step. Other works by political pundits such as Christina Hoff Sommers and by psychologists like Michael Gurian, sought to rescue boys from feminists, who they claimed were problematizing normal, natural, rambunctious boyhood.

Boys had been "discovered" all right—both as a psychological problem-in-waiting, and as a political football.

Lost in much of the ensuing public conversation were the boys themselves—the richness of their experiences, the texture of their lives. This was to be expected of those who were simply using boys as a foil with which to critique feminism. In fact, the pundits appeared relatively uninterested in boys' welfare; they were simply the latest weapon against feminists.

Yet some of the richness of boys' experiences and lives seemed lost also in the best-sellers by psychologists who had spent their careers listening to boys' voices. The fact that all of their books portrayed white boys on their covers was more than a marketing ploy by their publishers; their books generalized from predominantly middle- and upper-middle-class white boys—who were observed at single-sex prep schools, or were patients of the therapists/authors—to *all* boys. This was an empirical and analytic leap that obscured more than it revealed.

What was missing, then, were all the "other" boys—African American boys, Latino boys, Asian American boys, working-class boys, boys from countries other than the United States. Also missing were gay boys, bisexual boys, boys who didn't yet know their sexual orientation. (Only Pollack included a chapter on homophobia, and it was largely oriented to elicit compassion for homosexual boys.)

But these boys also contend with the boy code—and they do so in different ways, with different social, cultural, and economic resources, as these boys also find their way toward manhood. And it is one of the great strengths of Niobe Way and Judy Chu's remarkable collection *Adolescent Boys: Exploring Diverse Cultures of Boyhood,* that the authors have paid attention to the voices of those other boys. Now we read, for example, of how working-class British lads experience their masculinity; how African American boys construct different definitions of masculinity as they wrestle with racialized definitions of competent manhood; how lower-class Chinese boys experience their relational worlds; or how gay boys come to understand their sexualities. There are even studies that compare boyhoods—internationally, as in the chapter on boys' peer relationships in China and Canada, and across ethnic groups within the United States, as in Way's own work on same-sex friendships among Asian American, African American, and Latino boys.

Through the able (and apparently hands-on) editing by Way and Chu, this anthology minimizes the incoherence and inconsistency that mar many an edited volume: disparate voices, methodologies, empirical objects of scrutiny. The fact that the chapters in this edited volume both stand on their own and cohere into a unitary volume is a testament to judicious editing as well as a well-assembled cast of capable characters.

Having read these empirically rich and theoretically informed chapters, we can no longer pretend that the boy code is the same monolithic and monochromatic entity foisted upon these identical unsuspecting creatures called boys. Rather, we observe different boys developing friendships, negotiating romance, love, and sexuality. Nor can we pretend that boys' lives are the same in every social and structural arena in which they find themselves. There are not only social differences among boys, but differences that are produced by the different types of institutions in which the boys find themselves.

Ignoring the voices of those "other" boys is more than a marketing decision, more than a moment of analytic myopia, more than a problem of simply generalizing from clinical populations in the first place. It is a political problem. For it will inevitably be from these boys' voices—the voices of the others, those marginalized by class, race, sexuality—that we will begin to hear the voices of resilience, of resistance to the boy code, of an understanding of how the boy code works and doesn't work.

After all, it is axiomatic that the marginalized always understand the dynamics of marginalization better than those who are not marginalized. Who better to explore the depths of the boy code than those who have it used against them, who are constantly measured against it and found wanting?

If we want to rescue boys—including those white middle-class boys who grace the covers of the best-sellers—we will need to listen to the voices of the marginalized. As they negotiate their way through boyhood toward different definitions of masculinity, they open doors for the rest of us: doors of resilience and resistance to those very dominant norms.

Thankfully, this superb collection begins that conversation.

MICHAEL KIMMEL
New York City

Acknowledgments

We thank the authors in this book for their effort, patience, and commitment to representing boys' experiences in all their complexity and nuance. On behalf of all of the contributors, we would also like to thank the boys who participated in our studies. In addition, we thank our editor at NYU Press, Jennifer Hammer, for her support of this book and for her dedication to publishing works that reveal the missing voices in the social sciences. Finally, we thank Emily Park for help in editing and organizing the manuscript. The project was supported in part by a Faculty Scholars Award from the William T. Grant Foundation and a grant from the National Science Foundation to Niobe Way, and by a Post-Doctoral Fellowship from NYU and from the Harvard Program in Gender Studies to Judy Chu.

Introduction

This volume brings together current empirical research on the development of adolescent boys from diverse socioeconomic, ethnic, racial, and cultural backgrounds. Recently, there has been a resurgence of interest in boys' lives and experiences. To some extent, this renewed interest has been inspired by the attention given to adolescent girls in the wake of the feminist movement. Through empirical studies of adolescent girls, feminist scholars have highlighted ways in which cultural constructions of gender, as well as biological manifestations of sex, shape girls' development. In turn, this body of work has informed new programs and policies—some at a national level—to help foster girls' sense of agency, broaden the scope of girls' options and opportunities for social engagement and academic achievement, and nurture girls' psychological strength and resilience. As parents, teachers, and health care practitioners have become increasingly aware of how girls' lives and experiences are inextricably embedded within their relationships to other people and to their social and cultural contexts, the question inevitably arose, "What about the boys?" Thus, researchers began to reconsider the relationships and the social and cultural context of boys' lives (Kindlon & Thompson, 1999; Pollack, 1998; Pollack & Shuster, 2000).

The research on adolescent boys' development, however, has been constrained by the same set of limitations as the research with adolescent girls (see Leadbeater & Way, 1996): it has been and is still based mostly on studies with white middle-class populations. Moreover, the findings from these studies are commonly used to generalize to *all* boys rather than serving as a framework for understanding the specific experiences of white middle-class boys. To the extent that white middle-class boys are not viewed as white or middle class but simply "boys," boys who are not white or middle class are regarded as "other," and their experiences tend to be marginalized or neglected altogether. Although the recent discourse on boys claims to consider culture, for instance by evaluating cultural norms and ideals of masculinity, it nevertheless decontextualizes boys' experiences by failing to include the experiences of boys from diverse ethnic, racial, and socioeconomic backgrounds and by ignoring ways in which cultural identities (e.g., race, ethnicity, socioeconomic status, and nationality) and social contexts (e.g., family, peers, and school) shape and are shaped by boys themselves. The few who have studied boys from diverse backgrounds, such as the authors in this volume, suggest that boys' experiences vary within and across cultures and contexts. Like girls, boys influence and are deeply influenced by the environments in which they develop. Thus, understanding how boys respond, experience, perceive, resist, and influence these cultures and contexts is critical to understanding their development.

Another limitation of recent discourse on boys has been the focus on clinical populations and the tendency to pathologize boys. A majority of recent books on boys' development are written by health care practitioners—counselors, therapists, psychiatrists—and focus on the clinical populations with whom they have worked (Garbarino, 1999; Gurian, 1998; Kindlon & Thompson, 1999; Pollack, 1998; Pollack & Shuster, 2000). While this work offers an important perspective on boys' development, there is a tendency in this literature to problematize that development. This pattern is also evident in research with boys of color and with poor and working-class boys, where typically the focus has been on high-risk behavior, gang involvement, and other negative behavior. Starting from the premise that there is something wrong with these boys—either inherent or acquired—research with clinical populations of boys as well as research with boys from low-income and/or ethnic minority families offers a skewed perspective that may help us to understand boys' problems but not boys' strengths, including ways in which boys resist succumbing to negative stereotypes and actively seek out ways to thrive in the midst of great challenges.

One may question the need for empirical studies on boys, given that historically the majority of psychological and developmental research had been conducted almost exclusively with all-male samples. Past studies of human development and psychology missed girls' experiences by neglecting to include females in their samples. However, past studies may have also missed capturing boys' experiences by not only ignoring the relevance of context and culture, but also employing methods of inquiry that do not focus on boys' own perspectives. Thus, whereas girls have been historically under-represented in psychological and developmental theory, boys may have been misrepresented. In order to understand boys' development, it is important to start with boys' own perspectives and to learn what they view as the main issues, key obstacles, and central concerns in their lives. What do they value and hope for? What do they want? What are the sources of pressure and support in their lives? How do they cope with challenges? How do they experience their peers, romantic partners, family members, and school community?

One problem that results from studies that do not take boys' own perspectives into account is that their experiences are often homogenized and stereotyped and, thus, the nuances of boys' lives are not adequately represented. Stereotypes of boys—that they are not interested in intimacy, that they are primarily interested in sex, that they are emotionally stoic, and that they are more interested in autonomy than in relationships—have been repeatedly perpetuated in research on boys' development as well as in the research on adolescents in general. The research presented in this book, however, challenges such common stereotypes by listening to boys' experiences in their own words and on their own terms. Deborah Tolman and her colleagues (Chapter 12), for example, reveal how boys are interested in having close relations with girls and are not simply interested in sex. Way's chapter (Chapter 9) reveals that adolescent boys are emotionally astute and openly vulnerable when discussing their male friends, and also desire intimate male friendships in which friends "share everything." Chu's chapter (Chapter 4) draws attention to the importance of relationships for adolescent boys as they negotiate their senses of self. Each chapter in this volume suggests that boys, even white middle-class boys, may be misrepresented in research that does not take into account the voices of the boys themselves.

Gilligan (1977, 1982) suggests that it is not sufficient simply to add girls to existing paradigms based on boys' experiences, as the inclusion of female voices changes the conversation about human development and psychology in fundamental ways. Likewise, in order to resist the subsequent addition of culturally diverse boys' voices to existing paradigms based on white middle-class boys, we must start from boys' own perspectives. By including boys' perspectives—and especially by including the voices of boys of color and boys from poor and working-class families—the conversation about human development changes once again.

Studying Boys' Experiences in Context

This book presents a collection of new empirical research on adolescent boys' development in the various contexts of their lives. The authors in this book are senior and junior scholars from diverse disciplinary backgrounds, including sociology, psychology, and family studies, who adopt a developmental rather than diagnostic approach to understanding boys' experiences within their immediate relationships and their social and cultural contexts. The chapters in this book focus primarily on exploring the experiences of boys who have been excluded from the research on boys, including poor and working-class boys, ethnic minority boys, homosexual and bisexual boys, and boys who recently immigrated to the United States. The boys in this book also come from a variety of different places in the United States, such as California, New England, Chicago, Wisconsin, and New York, and outside of the United States, including Hong Kong, the United Kingdom, and Canada. The studies described in this book use a range of research methodologies—including qualitative approaches such as case studies, ethnographic observations and interviews, photographic explorations, and focus groups as well as quantitative approaches such as surveys and standardized questionnaires—to investigate boys' lives. While each of these methodological approaches has been criticized for its lack of generalizability or its inability to accurately portray the complexities of individual lives, when considered together, studies employing these methodologies present a nuanced picture of the lives of boys from different ethnic/racial, socioeconomic, and national backgrounds.

This book is divided into five parts, each of which corresponds to a critical aspect of boys' development. Part I focuses on identity development and describes ways in which boys from different backgrounds experience themselves, as males, within the contexts of their relationships and immediate sociocultural contexts. Part II focuses on family relationships with an emphasis on the ways in which they influence psychological health among adolescent boys. Part III focuses on adolescents' friendships and peer relationships with an emphasis on how adolescent boys from different cultural contexts experience their friendships and the impact of friendships on boys' psychological well-being. Part IV focuses on sexuality and romantic relationships and presents research on sexual experiences among heterosexual, homosexual, and bisexual boys. Finally, Part V presents research on adolescent boys' experiences in school with a focus on the daily experiences and meanings of schooling for culturally diverse adolescent boys.

Part I: Identity Development

In Chapter 1, Stacey J. Lee explores the intersection of ethnic and gender identity among Hmong American high school boys. Drawing on ethnographic data—including participant observations in school settings both in and out of the classroom, interviews, observations of local Hmong community events, and analyses of school documents—Lee describes the ways in which Hmong boys construct their masculinities at a public high school in Wisconsin. Lee focuses on the various expressions of masculinity among the boys in her studies that are created in response to the dictates of hegemonic masculinity.

In Chapter 2, Barbara M. Walker presents ways in which four working-class British adolescent boys see themselves, interact with others, and determine their priorities within the communities in which they live. With the aim of giving boys more control over how their lives are depicted, Walker utilizes photographs taken by the boys themselves in combination with data collected through focus groups and interviews in which the boys discussed their photographs and their meanings. The result is a unique account that portrays boys' lives through their eyes, and on their own terms.

In Chapter 3, Howard C. Stevenson explores African American boys' experiences of "hypervulnerability" and how these experiences are linked to identity development. He discusses the Black male experience of being "missed, dissed, and pissed" and the negative consequences of this experience for these boys' development and psychological adjustment. He also explores the association between family socialization experiences and hypervulnerability and suggests that family members can play a significant role in buffering the effects of being "missed, dissed, and pissed."

In Chapter 4, Judy Y. Chu examines ways in which adolescent boys negotiate their senses of self in light of cultural constructions of masculinity that manifest within their interpersonal relationships and social interactions. Focusing on a group of White, middle-class boys attending a private all-boys school, Chu suggests that boys' relational ways of being have been overlooked in recent literature on boys. Based on qualitative ethnographic observations and interviews, Chu presents two case studies to illustrate ways in which boys, as active participants in their development and gender socialization, can mediate the influence of masculine norms and ideals on their self-concepts and subsequently their styles of engaging with and relating to others.

Part II: Family Relationships

In Chapter 5, Elena D. Jeffries examines the experiences of interpersonal trust in relationships with parents in a sample of African American, Latino, and Asian American adolescent boys from low-income families. Based on in-depth qualitative interviews collected longitudinally, Jeffries provides a thematic analysis of the ways in which trust is experienced and defined by youth, and how experiences of trust vary across relationships (i.e., mother vs. father) and change over time. Her findings suggest that the meaning of trust for adolescent boys is deeply embedded in boys' cultural context.

In Chapter 6, Daniel T. L. Shek explores the ways in which family functioning is linked to psychological and social adjustment in Chinese adolescents from poor families. Based in Hong Kong, this study uses measures of family functioning that were specifically created for Chinese samples. The study suggests that while family functioning has similar beneficial effects on mental health for both boys and girls, family functioning is linked to problem behavior only among the boys.

In Chapter 7, Darian B. Tarver, Naima T. Wong, Harold W. Neighbors, and Marc A. Zimmerman investigate the effects of father involvement in preventing suicidal ideation and suicidal risk among African American adolescent boys. The study reveals that father involvement is associated with lower levels of reported suicidal ideation and risk for African American boys, and suggests a need to gain a better understanding of the processes by which father involvement influences the lives of adolescent boys.

Part III: Friends and Peers

In Chapter 8, Niobe Way presents an overview of her qualitative research with African American, Latino, and Asian American adolescent boys. Key themes detected in her interviews revolve around experiences of intimacy, desire, and distrust. She reveals the ways in which these experiences are woven into the fabric of boys' friendships, and suggests that the common stereotypes of boys' friendships, such as their being "activity-oriented," are not accurate representations of the ways in which boys perceive their relationships with other boys.

In Chapter 9, Xinyin Chen, Violet Kaspar, Yuqing Zhang, Li Wang, and Shujie Zheng provide a cross-cultural perspective on Chinese boys' experiences of peer relationships. Based on surveys and qualitative interviews conducted with boys in China and Canada, the authors discuss the role that peer relationships play in boys' social and psychological adjustment and how cultural norms and values and social circumstances may impact the ways in which boys perceive and experience their peer relationships.

In Chapter 10, Michael Cunningham and Leah Newkirk Meunier highlight ways in which perceptions of peers are related to bravado attitudes among African American boys. Based on a survey study set in an urban neighborhood, they explore how boys' experiences of peers in their schools and neighborhoods correspond to bravado attitudes. Their findings suggest a clear need for further exploration of how the multiple contexts of boys' lives in schools, neighborhoods, and home environments can individually and collectively impact how boys feel about themselves.

Part IV: Sexuality and Romantic Relationships

In Chapter 11, Deborah L. Tolman, Renée Spencer, Tricia Harmon, Myra Rosen-Reynoso, and Meg Striepe explore how early adolescents talk about their experiences of romantic relationships. Drawing on longitudinal interview data collected with a socioeconomically diverse group, the authors document the ways in which a heterosexual relational script shapes boys' experiences of sexuality and early romantic relationships. The authors highlight boys' responses to the expectation that males are "naturally" sexual predators. They also explore boys' perceived need to display their heterosexuality publicly and boys' struggles to negotiate the interplay between physical and emotional intimacy.

In Chapter 12, Joseph H. Pleck, Freya L. Sonenstein, and Leighton Ku present data collected longitudinally through the National Survey of Adolescent Males (NSAM) and report how patterns of sexual and contraceptive behavior among 15–19-year-old males living in the United States have changed over time. The authors also highlight ways in which adolescent boys' heterosexual behavior and condom use are linked with issues of masculinity.

In Chapter 13, Ritch C. Savin-Williams explores the first sexual experiences of gay and bisexual boys. Drawing upon case history narratives, Savin-Williams reveals the complexities of gay and bisexual boys' first sexual experiences. His study suggests that the timing of this event (e.g., childhood or adolescence) has a significant impact on its meaning for the young person. His study also underscores the importance of examining the pleasurable aspects of same-sex sex among boys rather than simply the potentially negative consequences of unprotected sex.

Part V: Schooling

In Chapter 14, Carola Suárez-Orozco and Desirée Baolian Qin-Hilliard explore the school experiences and academic engagement of immigrant adolescents coming from China, Central America, the Dominican Republic, Haiti, and Mexico. Drawing from triangulated data that consider the youth's perspective as well as the teacher's and ethnographer's views, the authors consider dimensions of behavioral, social, and cognitive engagement using both qualitative and quantitative data. The authors focus in particular on reasons for the gender differences in school engagement and performance among immigrant boys and girls, with boys often doing more poorly than girls.

Gilberto Q. Conchas and Pedro A. Noguera, in Chapter 15, explore the experiences of academically successful African American students and propose ways to support their achievement. Drawing on qualitative observations and interviews, Conchas and Noguera focus in particular on examining variations in school experiences among high-achieving African American youth at a large urban high school in Northern California. Through focusing on African American male students' own perspectives, Conchas and Noguera begin to unravel what works and what does not work within the school setting.

Michelle V. Porche, Stephanie J. Ross, and Catherine E. Snow, in Chapter 16, explore the role of masculinity as a factor in boys' literacy skills and their subsequent academic achievement. Drawing from observational and interview data collected longitudinally from preschool through middle school with boys from low-income urban families, the authors suggest that boys' gender socialization may be linked to their early literacy training and later literacy practices.

Our Goals for This Book

The overarching aim of this volume is to incorporate the experiences of boys from diverse cultural backgrounds into our current discussions of boys' development. This book is not intended to be an anthology, but rather a focused collection of current research that represents the diversity of perspectives on boys' development. Similar to Carol Gilligan's ground-breaking work on girls, we seek to include the "missing voices" in the literature on boys' development. Rather than offering simple solutions for how to fix boys or quick tips for how to raise boys, this book provides insight into ways in which boys experience and understand their lives and offers ways to move beyond stereotypical representations of them. This book is important for parents and teachers as well as researchers and practitioners who are interested in boys' development and who wish to better understand what is going on for boys so that they can better relate to and support the healthy development of the boys in their own lives.

REFERENCES

Brown, L. M. & Gilligan, C. (1992). *Meeting at the crossroads: Women's psychology and girls' development.* Cambridge, MA: Harvard University Press.

Garbarino, J. (1999). *Lost boys: Why our sons turn violent and how we can save them.* New York: Free Press.

Gilligan, C. (1977). *Woman's place in man's lifecycle.* Harvard Educational Review, 49, 431–446.

Gilligan, C. (1982). *In a different voice: Psychological theory and women's development.* Cambridge, MA: Harvard University Press.

Gilligan, C., Rogers, A. G. & Tolman, D. L. (1991). *Women, girls, and psychotherapy: Reframing resistance.* New York: Harrington Park Press.

Gurian, M. (1998). *A fine young man: What parents, mentors, and educators can do to shape adolescent boys into exceptional men.* New York: Penguin Putnam.

Kindlon, D. & Thompson, M. (1999). *Raising Cain: Protecting the emotional life of boys.* New York: Ballantine Publishing Group.

Leadbeater, B. & Way, N. (Eds.). (1996). *Urban girls: Resisting stereotypes, creating identities.* New York: New York University Press.

Newberger, E. H. (1999). *The men they will become: The nature and nurture of male character.* Cambridge, MA: Perseus Publishing.

Pollack, W. S. (1998). *Real boys: Rescuing our sons from the myths of boyhood.* New York: Random House.

Pollack, W. S. & Shuster, T. (2000). *Real boys' voices.* New York: Random House.

Way, N. (1998). *Everyday courage: The stories and lives of urban teenagers.* New York: New York University Press.

Part I

Identity Development

Hmong American Masculinities
Creating New Identities in the United States

Stacey J. Lee

Asian American men have recently been hailed as "turn of the century American heroes" by the popular press (Pan, 2000). Long stereotyped as passive, effeminate, asexual, and nerdy by the dominant culture, Asian American men are now being described by some journalists and academics as ideal romantic partners for women. According to a February 2000 article in *Newsweek,* hegemonic masculinity as represented by the white male is being challenged by Asian American men. Citing the crossover popularity of actors such as Chow Yun Fat and Jet Li and the growing number of Asian American men marrying outside their ethnic group, the article concluded that "Asian guys are on a roll" (Pan, 2000). The implicit assumption here is that marriage to white women represents an increase in social status for Asian American men. Despite the predictions in the *Newsweek* article, Asian American men as a group have not truly challenged dominant American ideas of masculinity. Although some U.S. communities may be embracing individual Asian American men as symbols of appealing and exotic masculinity, most communities have not embraced Asian American men as ideal symbols of masculinity or as American heroes. In fact, hegemonic masculinity as represented by the white, heterosexual, middle-class, independent, able bodied, Christian man thrives in many public high schools in the United States.

This chapter will examine the way Hmong American boys construct their masculinities at a public high school in Wisconsin. In particular, the focus will be on the various expressions of masculinity that Hmong American boys create in response to messages from their ethnic community and the school community.

As Connell (1995) reminds us, masculinities are culturally constructed by people in everyday life and ideas regarding masculinity are culturally specific. Although there are a variety of masculinities within cultures, there is always a single hegemonic masculinity within a given culture or community. Kimmel (2000) describes the dominant or hegemonic masculinity as "a culturally preferred model against which we are expected to measure ourselves" (p. 4). Boys/men who do not express the behaviors and traits associated with hegemonic masculinity within a given community are identified as possessing deficient masculinities that are subordinate to the hegemonic masculinity. Because whiteness is central to the locally constructed hegemonic masculinity of the school, the Hmong American boys in my study are automatically marginalized because of their race. Most of the Hmong American boys also lack other qualities (e.g., middle-class status, assertive personalities, involvement in school, academic success, etc.) associated with the hegemonic masculinity in school.

The Hmong in the United States

The first Hmong arrived in the United States as refugees from Laos over twenty-five years ago. According to the 2000 U.S. Census, the largest populations of Hmong Americans live in California, Minnesota, and Wisconsin. Much of the scholarship on Hmong refugees has emphasized the differences between Hmong culture—described as preliterate, patriarchal, rural, and traditional—and mainstream American culture (e.g., Donnelly, 1994; Fass, 1991; Rumbaut & Ima, 1988; Sherman, 1988). In fact, cultural differences have been identified as the cause of many of the social and economic problems that Hmong Americans face. According to some researchers, Hmong definitions of success that focus on the family are often in conflict with mainstream American definitions of success which emphasize the individual (Lynch, 1999; Meyer et al., 1991; Trueba et al., 1990; Walker-Moffat, 1995). Several scholars have focused on the cultural differences surrounding gender between mainstream U.S. culture and Hmong culture (Donnelly, 1994; Goldstein, 1985; Scott, 1988; Walker-Moffat, 1995).

Early research on Hmong refugee students discovered that they experienced serious problems in school including high dropout rates from middle and high school (Cohn, 1986; Goldstein, 1985). Limited experiences with formal education, limited English language skills, and cultural differences were identified as the barriers to educational success. Shortly after their arrival in the United States the Hmong refugee community identified education as the key to social mobility in this country. Although the community quickly embraced education for boys and young men, they were more hesitant about the education of girls and women (Rumbaut & Ima, 1988). The Hmong American community supported education for boys because sons were seen as being responsible for supporting their parents in their old age. Thus, the education of sons was seen as an investment for the family. In contrast to sons who remain responsible to their parents for life, daughters become members of their husband's family upon marriage. While education became a new way for Hmong boys and men to gain status in the United States, Hmong girls continued to gain status through early marriage and motherhood as they had in Laos (Donnelly, 1994; Goldstein, 1985). The emphasis on early marriage and motherhood led to high dropout rates among Hmong girls during the 1980s and early 1990s (Donnelly, 1994; Goldstein, 1985; Rumbaut & Ima, 1988).

Within the Hmong American community gender norms and roles have continued to evolve in the last decade. More recent research, for example, highlights the educational achievements of Hmong American girls and women and the changing roles of women in the Hmong American community (Lee, 1997; Ngo, 2000). While a great deal of research has focused on the experiences of Hmong American girls and women, relatively little research has highlighted the gendered experiences of Hmong American boys and men. Some research suggests that Hmong men in the United States are struggling with a loss of status within Hmong families, a result of changing gender roles for women (Donnelly, 1994). Within Hmong families in Laos, for example, male elders were viewed as the undisputed leaders and decision-makers, but in the United States women have gained independence (Donnelly, 1994). In her research on Hmong refugees in Seattle, Donnelly (1994) discovered that many Hmong men dreamed of returning to Laos, but Hmong women preferred life in the United States because they believed the United States offered greater gender equality for women.

Mainstream American ideas regarding masculinity that emphasize the individual have also been identified as a threat to Hmong notions of masculinity that emphasize the family. According to this perspective, the rise of juvenile delinquency among Hmong American young men is due to the abandonment of the Hmong definitions of masculinity (Lynch, 1999; Walker-Moffat, 1995). Lynch explains, "One result of the eroding respect for traditional models of masculinity is that the Hmong American teenage males struggling to define cultural notions of male gender role most often use American models as points of departure. These models stress individualism and are in conflict with traditional Hmong ideals focusing on family-based loyalty and communal definitions of success" (p. 38). Thus, an emphasis on individualism is understood to lead young men away from the control of the family, thereby leaving them vulnerable to the negative influences of the American society. One problem with this argument is that it assumes that the problems within the Hmong American community are simply due to cultural conflict and cultural assimilation, thereby denying the fact that Hmong Americans face racial and class barriers in the United States. Furthermore, it assumes that the maintenance of traditional Hmong culture can protect Hmong American boys from racial and class inequality.

Background of the Study

Data for this chapter were collected as part of a one-and-a-half-year ethnographic study of Hmong American students at a public school I call University Heights High School (UHS) (Lee, 2001a, 2001b, 2002). Located in a mid-sized city in Wisconsin, UHS enjoys an excellent academic reputation in the city and throughout the state. UHS enrolled 2023 students during the 1999–2000 academic year with 29% of these students classified as students of color and 14% identified as receiving free or reduced lunch. According to estimates made by the various school staff, there were 54 Hmong students enrolled at UHS during the 1998–1999 school year and approximately 65 Hmong students enrolled during the 1999–2000 academic year. All of the Hmong American students at UHS are the children of immigrants/refugees. Some students arrived in the United States as young children and others were born in the United States. Although Hmong is the first language in the homes of all of the Hmong American students at UHS and most students' parents speak limited English, all the Hmong American students at the school speak English. Most of the Hmong American students are from low-income families and receive free or reduced lunch. Many live in low-income housing in the poorer sections of the city where lower income African American and Latino families also live.

The fieldwork for the study included participant observation of Hmong American students during lunch periods and study halls, interviews with Hmong American students and school staff, classroom observations, analysis of site documents, observations at school district meetings for Southeast Asian parents and observations of local Hmong community events. My identity, particularly assumptions about my identity, affected the way my informants responded to me. In my first encounters with Hmong American students, I was asked questions about my ethnicity, age, marital status, occupation, and place of birth. As a Chinese American woman, I share race and gender in common with the Hmong American girls, and I believe that this explains why I had an easier time making connections with the girls than the boys. Several girls, for example, asked me about gender roles for Chinese girls and women, specifically my family's ideas regarding gender roles. Significantly, the boys who were most comfortable with the dominant culture were also the ones most comfortable talking to me. By keeping students' secrets and remaining nonjudgmental, I was eventually able to gain the confidence of a range of Hmong American boys.

Hmong American Boys and/versus Hegemonic Masculinity at UHS

UHS prides itself on its racial, ethnic, and social class diversity. Despite the diversity of the student population, a culture of whiteness pervades the school (Lee, 2002). As in many other institutions where whiteness reigns, the culture of whiteness at UHS is shrouded by silence. This virtual invisibility served to normalize whiteness and thereby maintain its dominance (Dyer, 1993). High status extracurricular activities (e.g., music, theater, student government, yearbook staff, etc.) are dominated by white students. Photos of white students engaged in numerous school activities fill the pages of the school yearbook, confirming and reflecting the status of whites in the racial hierarchy of the school.

As in the larger society, whiteness is central to the hegemonic masculinity at UHS. In discussing the historical relationship between whiteness and masculinity, cultural anthropologist A. Ong writes, "white masculinity established qualities of manliness and civilization itself" (1999, p. 266). Similarly, Feagin (2000) argues that "white men have been the standard for male handsomeness, as well as masculinity and manly virtue" (p. 113).

Although whiteness is primary to dominant masculinity, not just any white male meets the standards set by hegemonic masculinity (Lei, 2001). As in the dominant society, boys at UHS gain status by being assertive and demonstrating individual achievement (Kimmel, 1994; Kumashiro, 1999). Although boys at UHS can gain status for athletic achievements, the most honored status at the school goes to white males who are academically successful (i.e., college bound) and involved in one or more high status extracurricular activities. Thus, the hegemonic male at UHS is white, plays on a varsity sports team, and does well in school. It is worth noting that education is central to UHS's definition of hegemonic masculinity because education is valued by the highly educated community in which UHS is located. Higher education is required for the kind of white-collar jobs that middle-class white parents expect their sons to have when they grow up.

Similar to hegemonic males at other schools, boys who embody hegemonic masculinity at UHS express their gendered power by taking up space, both literally and figuratively, in classrooms, corridors, and on playing fields (Orenstein, 1994; Thorne, 1994). These young men garner athletic awards, are elected to the prom court, and are chosen as graduation speakers. They enjoy friendly relationships with teachers and administrators, and are described as "all American boys." Not insignificantly, white males are the only ones honored with this title.

Hmong American boys and girls at UHS are marked as culturally different (i.e., foreign) because they deviate from the white norm (Lee, 2002). Conversations with UHS educators and non-Hmong students revealed that Hmong American boys are viewed as lacking hegemonic masculinity. Teachers remarked that Hmong boys were quieter in class than other boys and were not involved in school activities. Some teachers concluded that the boys were quiet because of language or other cultural issues. Because quietness is associated with femininity, Asian American men have often been constructed as effeminate and therefore not masculine. Cheung (1993) notes, "precisely because quietness is associated with the feminine, as is the 'East' in relation to the 'West' (in Orientalist discourse), Asian and Asian American men too have been 'feminized' in American popular culture" (p. 2). The characterization of Asian and Asian American men as feminine renders them harmless in the eyes of the dominant culture. Seen as too quiet, passive, nerdy, and small, Asian American men fail to exhibit the form of masculinity valued by the dominant American society (Kumashiro, 1999; Lee, 1999; Lei, 2001). Asian American men are thus easily dismissed as inconsequential. At UHS, teachers who assumed that Hmong

American boys are quiet because of language and other cultural differences simply ignored the boys. Although these teachers viewed Hmong American boys as being "different," they noted that they had never had any problems with them in class.

There are other moments, however, when the dominant group views the "quietness" of Asian American men as potentially dangerous and threatening. A few teachers, for example, expressed fears that some Hmong boys were hiding their gang involvement behind their quiet demeanors. One teacher asserted that gang involvement was prevalent among Hmong males.

> I get the feeling that there are, that there are a lot of kids [Hmong boys and other boys of color] who are involved in gangs. And often, it will be, kids will be involved, and then it's just a part of life. You know, it's not even a question, of course you're involved in a gang for protection.

Although this teacher was convinced that many Hmong males were involved in gangs, the teacher admitted to not really knowing many Hmong males at the school. This teacher and others who feared that Hmong American boys were involved with gangs believed that school officials should keep a watch on the boys. Similarly, in her study of race relations at a multiracial high school, Lei (2001) found that the quietness of Southeast Asian American boys was perceived as both "understandable" because they were culturally different and "unsettling" because they might be gangs.

The stereotype of the mysterious Asian American gang member represents the dominant group's fears about Asian American masculinity. The Asian or Asian American gang member represents the alien threat living among "real" Americans (Lee, 1999). Asian American gang members and those assumed to belong to gangs are understood to be dangerous. They express a hyper-masculinity somewhat similar to the hypermasculinity associated with African American men (Kumashiro, 1999; Lei, 2001; Stevenson, this volume). While hypermasculinity is represented as dangerous, hegemonic masculinity is constructed as safe (i.e., man the protector). While men who express subordinated masculinities may have to rely on overt forms of aggression to maintain authority, men who possess hegemonic masculinities do not have to rely on physical power for their authority (Connell, 1995). The characterization of Hmong American boys at UHS as either quiet (i.e., harmless and feminine) or quiet (i.e., dangerous and hyper-masculine) mirrors stereotypes of Asian American men in general. In either case, Hmong American boys are implicitly understood to lack hegemonic masculinity.

Significantly, Hmong American boys at UHS understand that the Hmong are constructed as culturally different and foreign by the dominant culture at UHS. They recognize that white boys/men hold the racialized and gendered power at the school and in the larger society. Furthermore, they realize that as Hmong American boys they lack hegemonic masculinity. Hmong American boys, for example, observed that "Hmong and other Asian guys are short." I heard Hmong American girls complain within earshot of their male peers that "Hmong guys are short." Hmong boys and girls understand that being short is seen as a feminine characteristic by the dominant American society.

The Hmong American boys at UHS express a variety of masculinities in response to the messages about masculinity they learn at school. In addition to negotiating the school's messages about masculinity, Hmong American boys must also negotiate the Hmong American community's messages about masculinity. Some boys attempt to construct a masculinity that reflects, combines, and re-interprets aspects of the hegemonic masculinity valued by the school with aspects of the masculinity valued by Hmong culture. Within the Hmong American community, the ideal man embraces education as a route to social mobility for his family. As noted earlier, this is gender specific because sons (not daughters) are expected to support their parents in old age. Significantly, the younger generation of Hmong American leaders embody this new ideal masculinity. These men serve as a bridge between mainstream American society and the Hmong American community. Although this new ideal Hmong American masculinity represents a cultural transformation, it should not be confused with the hegemonic masculinity of the school or of the larger society because it is also in conversation with the values and beliefs of the Hmong community. At the other end of the spectrum are the boys who express a counter-hegemonic masculinity that resists the hegemonic masculinity advanced by the dominant school culture and the new ideal masculinity of the Hmong American community. These boys reject the authority of the school, question the role of education in social mobility, and reject their responsibilities to their families.

In the next section of this chapter, I will examine examples of masculinity expressed by Hmong American boys at UHS. Although I will present individual portraits of three Hmong American boys, their respective expressions of masculinity should not be read simply as individual accounts. While each boy is a unique individual with a specific history, my position is that each expression of masculinity represents a collective response to larger institutional and cultural forces (Connell, 1993).

Hmong American Expressions of Masculinity

Portrait #1—Cha:
An Expression of Hmong Masculinity from the Past

Sitting with three other Hmong students from the school's ESL (English as a Second Language program), Cha smiled and nodded politely at me when the bilingual resource specialist introduced us. Approximately 5'3" in height and slightly built, Cha is about average in size when compared to his Hmong peers, but is significantly smaller than the non-Hmong males at UHS. Because he fears that his heavily accented English is difficult for others to understand, Cha remains virtually silent in his classes. As a relative newcomer to the United States, Cha is still uncertain about some mainstream cultural practices and this keeps him from engaging in school activities. Unlike the majority of boys at the school, Cha and his friends wear relatively nondescript clothes that are chosen for practicality rather than fashion. In contrast to white boys at UHS who express hegemonic masculinity, Cha and his friends take up little actual or figurative space in the school. Cha occupies the sidelines in the cafeteria, the halls, and classrooms. In many respects, Cha is the quintessential example of the quiet (i.e., harmless) Hmong boys described by some teachers.

Cha has a small circle of Hmong friends that include his girlfriend and two other boys. Significantly, his friends are all relative newcomers to the United States and all are enrolled in the ESL program. Cha regularly eats lunch with this same group of friends and laughs and talks quietly in a combination of English and Hmong when he is with them. He and his friends maintain their distance from the U.S. born Hmong American students at UHS (Lee, 2001b). As immigrants, Cha and his friends are in the minority among the Hmong population at UHS that is dominated by U.S. born Hmong American students. When I asked Cha why he and his friends never associated with the other Hmong American students he explained that he and his friends are "more traditional" and that the U.S. born students are "more Americanized." For their part, the American born Hmong students criticized the newcomers for being "old fashioned."

U.S. born Hmong girls, in particular, mocked boys like Cha for being "nerds."

As a self-described "traditional Hmong," Cha believes that it is important to respect his elders and carry on other Hmong cultural practices. Cha explained that "traditional Hmong sons" grow up and care for their parents in their old age and he intends to live up to this responsibility. Because his father is still in Laos, Cha is already responsible for helping to support his mother. Cha works nearly forty hours a week at a grocery store after school and on weekends in order to help pay the family bills. Because of his work schedule Cha gets home late on most school nights and is often too tired to do his homework. Between a work schedule that prevents him from studying long hours and his difficulties with English, Cha struggles in a few of his classes. Despite his language difficulties, however, Cha receives at least passing grades because of his effort and attitude. Although he would like to pursue a two-year vocational education degree upon graduating from high school, he is afraid that his financial responsibilities for his mother will make it impossible for him to pay for school.

Sometime in the next few years Cha wants to marry a Hmong woman who shares his cultural values. Although he is interested in marrying his current girlfriend, he is not sure that she will want to marry him since she plans to go to college after she graduates from high school. In contrast to other self-described "traditional Hmong men" who do not want to marry educated women, Cha is supportive of his girlfriend's interest in pursuing post-secondary education. Cha is also afraid that his girlfriend's family does not like Cha because he is not from a well-respected and prominent family. Significantly, the fact that his father is still in Laos also leaves his family outside the circle of power in the Hmong American community.

Cha works hard and believes in the achievement ideology, but his limited English language skills will most likely limit his mainstream success. Although Cha has taken on the family responsibilities associated with being a "traditional Hmong son," these very responsibilities interfere with his schoolwork. Since the Hmong American community looks toward the next generation of Hmong Americans to serve as cultural bridges between the Hmong American community and the larger American society, it is also unlikely that Cha will become a leader in the Hmong American community.

Portrait #2—Kao: A New Ideal Masculinity
for the Hmong Americans

Dressed in polo shirts or rugby shirts, jeans, and sneakers, Kao's clothing style sets him apart from most of the other Hmong American boys at UHS. While the majority of his Hmong American peers wear the baggy pants, over-sized t-shirts, and untied sneakers associated with urban youth, Kao's clothes are more like those of the white, middle-class boys at the school. Aware that his clothes make a social statement, Kao shrugged his shoulders as he explained that his brother and many of the Hmong boys at school said that he dressed in a preppy style. Kao's clothes, however, are not the only things that set him apart from most of the other Hmong youth at UHS. Muscular in build, Kao is closer to the physical standards implicit in hegemonic masculinity than any of his Hmong peers. Kao is one of a very small minority of Hmong American boys at the school to participate in mainstream extracurricular activities. In addition to participating in several activities, Kao maintains a "B" average in school. Not insignificantly, Kao is also one of a few Hmong boys who has established comfortable and friendly relationships with both male and female members of the UHS staff. He is even on a first-name basis with the school's head principal. In short, Kao embodies many of the qualities associated with the hegemonic masculinity of the school. One member of the guidance office described Kao as a "good kid" and a "successful student."

Perhaps most significantly, Kao's decisions regarding how and with whom to spend his time set him apart from most of the Hmong American boys at the school. While most other Hmong boys only socialize with other Hmong or Southeast Asian youth, Kao rarely fraternizes with other Hmong boys at UHS. Instead, he associates primarily with white students he knows through participating in school-sponsored sports (e.g., track team) or other extracurricular activities. In addition to his white friends, Kao is friendly with a number of African American and Asian American (non-Hmong) students he knows through his work on multicultural events at the school. Kao explained that he made a conscious decision to separate himself from other Hmong American youth.

> When I was younger, I used to hang out with a lot of Hmong people. And I didn't get much done. I just usually do what they did and just played around a lot. And I guess, now, I just want to better myself, so I

try, try not to hang out with the Hmong people a lot. Just because, somehow, I see them as not trying hard enough, so I try not to hang out with them.

Thus, Kao's decision to distance himself from other Hmong youth was based on his desire to learn about the dominant American culture and to improve his future life chances. He views the adoption of certain aspects of white masculinity as being imperative for mainstream success. Kao asserted that his decision to socialize with white students has allowed him to learn about the larger society, but he also recognized that his choice was not without cost. As a Hmong American student in a largely white social clique, Kao said he is "more accepted than most Hmong people," but he also knows that his race and ethnicity mark him as being different from the rest of the group. There have been occasions, for example, when he has witnessed the way non-Asian students stereotyped Asian students. Although his friends try to reassure him by telling him that he is "different from most other Asian kids," this leaves Kao feeling "good and bad." He realizes that his acceptance by the dominant group is contingent upon his willingness to play by their rules, specifically the rules of white hegemonic masculinity. Significantly, because Kao is not white he can never actually achieve the hegemonic masculinity of the school.

Although Kao distances himself from most other Hmong boys at the school, he does not distance himself from Hmong adults or the Hmong culture. In fact, he maintains a strong Hmong identity. Kao criticizes the Hmong American boys at UHS for being "very nontraditional" in their attitudes toward the Hmong elders in the community. He argues that while most Hmong students isolate themselves socially, they also "try and draw away from Hmong culture." He suggested that most of his Hmong American peers had "Americanized in bad ways." Interestingly, Kao reported that his parents warned him to keep his distance from "Hmong kids who were Americanized in bad ways."

Kao asserted that he was proud to be Hmong and that he tried to make his parents proud by being a "good Hmong son." Kao explained that "good Hmong sons" dress conservatively and specifically not "like a gangster." He went on the explain that Hmong adults assumed that when Hmong kids wore baggy clothes it meant they were involved with gangs. Thus, Kao's relatively conservative clothing style reflects his desires to please his parents and to fit in with the dominant culture. He also explained that "good Hmong sons" are expected to "be respectful of others, elders, get a good education, etc." Interestingly, "good sons" are those who reflect a combination of "traditional" characteristics (e.g., respectful of elders) with acculturated characteristics (e.g., formally educated). Regarding the importance of education for social mobility, Kao explained that his parents want their children "to be in a better position than they are now—financial wise." Kao noted that while his parents encouraged his sisters to do well in school, they have paid particular attention to his education and his brother's education because the sons are expected to remain close to the parents and help them in their old age. Thus, Kao's family, like other Hmong families, views the education of sons as an investment for the family.

Like his older brother, Kao plans to attend a two-year technical college and then transfer to a four-year university. Upon earning his four-year degree, Kao dreams of marrying a Hmong American woman, buying a house and starting a family. In short, Kao's plans bear a resemblance to the "American dream." He believes that associating with white Americans will help him gain access to information and resources necessary for economic and social advancement. Although he seeks individual achievement, he plans to use his achievements to help his parents. In other words, individual achievement in school is understood to be in the service of the extended family.

It is important to note that Kao expresses the type of masculinity expressed by the new generation of Hmong American leaders. Like many of the new generation of Hmong American leaders in communities throughout the United States, Kao views education as the route to social mobility. While this new generation of Hmong leaders has internalized the dominant achievement ideology, they are also committed to maintaining a distinct Hmong identity. In short, these men have adopted the strategy of accommodation without assimilation whereby they adopt aspects of the dominant culture without losing their ethnic identities and cultures. Many of the new Hmong American leaders use their educational backgrounds to work on behalf of Hmong American communities. Similarly, Kao is committed to using his individual success to help his parents. As a "good Hmong son" he believes that it is essential for him to support his parents in their old age. He dreams of raising his children who will be third generation Hmong Americans with a sense of their Hmong heritage and a connection to their paternal grandparents. In short, by being a "good son" Kao is achieving the new ideal masculinity of the Hmong American community.

Portrait #3—Houa: Counter-hegemonic Masculinity

Several UHS educators suggested that I speak to Houa in order to get the perspective of a young man who was disconnected from school. Houa expresses the type of masculinity that teachers associate with gang members. Identified by teachers and administrators as a chronic truant, Houa was difficult to track down. I eventually met him one afternoon when I was interviewing another Hmong American male during study hall. As we neared the end of the interview, Houa walked into the cafeteria with a swagger that exaggerated the masculine conventions of body carriage held by mainstream society. Dressed in baggy pants and over-sized shirt and coat, Houa's clothes are characterized by teachers and Hmong adults as "gang type clothes." When I asked my interviewee about his plans for the future, Houa chimed in with "I'm going to be really rich. I'm going to have my own island named after me." When I asked Houa how he planned to make his money he asserted "I'm going to own a big company, world-wide" and with that he walked away laughing.

After our initial meeting, I didn't see much of Houa again until the following year. I learned that Houa had failed to earn the requisite credits to be promoted and was being forced to repeat his ninth grade year. He spent mornings at the newly created "school within a school" for students who had been retained, and then came back to UHS in the afternoons for a couple of classes. During his afternoon classes, Houa often put his head down on the desk thereby raising the ire of his teachers. When I asked him about school, he simply stated that "school is boring." Like other chronic truants, Houa began skipping school because he was having problems keeping up with the work in his classes. Once he began skipping, his academic difficulties escalated.

One of Houa's teachers reported that although she had repeatedly encouraged Houa to come see her for extra help with his academic skills, he rarely did so. Houa's teacher suggested that Houa was simply "too proud" to seek out help publicly. In my observations, I found that most Hmong American boys rarely approached teachers or other UHS educators for academic assistance or personal support. Their reluctance to go to teachers for help may be related to ideas regarding gender. As mentioned earlier, within traditional Hmong culture men are seen as the ultimate authorities (Donnelly, 1994; Rumbaut & Ima, 1988). Thus, Houa and other Hmong American boys may avoid going to their female teachers for help because they do not recognize female authority. From this perspective, going to female teachers may actually be a threat to their expression of masculinity. Although Houa may be acting out "traditional" ideas regarding gender, his unwillingness to accept the authority of female teachers put him at odds with the school culture. By contrast, young men like Kao have positive relationships with their male and female teachers. Kao's ability to maintain positive relationships with female teachers is an example of the accommodation without assimilation associated with the new ideal Hmong American masculinity.

Although Houa dreams of being wealthy, education does not figure into his plans to achieve mobility. In fact, he does not have any clear ideas about how he might achieve his economic dreams. Inasmuch as education has been embraced as central to the Hmong American community's definition of ideal masculinity, Houa's rejection of school represents a rejection of the new ideal Hmong American masculinity. Houa's problems in school have led to repeated conflict with his parents. He and his friends routinely fight with their parents over issues like school, respect for elders, and clothing styles. Unlike Kao, who hopes that his individual success will benefit his family, Houa dreams of individual success. Houa and his friends dream of being "really rich" so that they can own the consumer goods they covet. In particular, he dreams of having enough money to buy a nice/fast car.

Unlike Kao, who has been able to emulate aspects of the hegemonic masculinity of the school, Houa's academic difficulties prevent him from achieving a central quality associated with the school's hegemonic masculinity. In fact, Houa's academic difficulties and chronic truancy put him in direct opposition to the hegemonic masculinity of the school. Unable and unwilling to achieve masculinity through academic success, Houa has turned to other models of masculinity present at the school and in the popular culture. Specifically, Houa expresses a hypermasculinity, which is a style of masculinity that emphasizes toughness, consumerism, and resistance to authority (see Stevenson, this volume). Houa's choice of clothes and his swaggering walk are also evidence of his hypermasculinity.

School, however, does not view the hypermasculinity expressed by Houa as a legitimate expression of masculinity. Hypermasculinity, in fact, is seen as dangerous and problematic. Adults in the Hmong American community also hold negative opinions about boys who express this form of masculinity. Many Hmong American adults and UHS educators associate hypermasculinity with gang membership. In short, Houa's expression of masculinity is in opposition to both the hegemonic masculinity of the school and the new ideal masculinity of the Hmong American community which requires a level of accommodation to dominant norms without total assimilation. Significantly, the expression of hypermasculinity embodied by Houa is growing at UHS and other U.S. high schools. At UHS, for example, the number of Hmong American boys who dress like Houa and express resistance to school outnumber the boys who exhibit the masculinities expressed by Kao or Cha. Many Hmong American leaders consider the growth of counter-hegemonic masculinity to be one of the biggest concerns within the Hmong American community (Lee, 2001b; Lynch, 1999).

Conclusion

In short, the Hmong American boys at UHS are negotiating new ways of expressing and performing their gendered identities. Viewed as dated and nerdy by the American-born Hmong youth, young men like Cha are increasingly isolated among the younger generation of Hmong Americans. Although he embraces education as the road to social mobility, his limited English language skills and his family obligations limit his educational success. Unable to bridge the gap between the Hmong American community and mainstream American society, young men like Cha are likely to be relegated to the periphery in the Hmong American elite. In short, the form of masculinity expressed by Cha may be dying out within the Hmong American community.

At the other end of the spectrum are young men like Houa who, by expressing a hyper-masculinity, reject both the hegemonic masculinity of the mainstream and the new ideal Hmong American masculinity. The fact that the expression of hypermasculinity appears to be growing more common within the Hmong American community suggests that many young Hmong American men feel trapped by both the larger society and the Hmong American community. A few young men like Kao are negotiating an expression of masculinity that bridges dominant norms and older Hmong norms. Yet these young men are not seen as possessing the qualities associated with the hegemonic masculinity of the school or larger society.

The Hmong American boys in my study are all struggling with how to be men in a larger society that tells them that they are not "real men" and not "real Americans." Their expressions of masculinity are responses to racialized and gendered inequalities at UHS and in the larger U.S. society.

Because whiteness is central to the hegemonic masculinity of the school and larger society, it is impossible for any Hmong American boy to achieve hegemonic masculinity. Thus, Hmong American expressions of masculinity do not challenge the legitimacy of the hegemonic masculinity of the school. In short, none of the Hmong American boys at UHS are seen by the school or by the larger society as "turn of the century American heroes."

REFERENCES

Cheung, K. (1993). *Articulate Silences: Hisaye Yamamoto, Maxine Hong Kingston, Joy Kogawa.* Ithaca: Cornell University Press.

Cohn, M. (1986). Hmong youth and the Hmong future in America. In G. Hendtricks, B. Downing & A. Deinard (Eds.) *The Hmong in Transition.* Staten Island, NY: Center for Migration Studies.

Connell, R. W. (1993). Disruptions: Improper masculinities and schooling. In L. Weis & M. Fine (Eds.) *Beyond Silenced Voices: Class, Gender and Race in U.S. Schools.* Albany: State University of New York Press.

Connell, R. W. (1995). *Masculinities.* Berkeley: University of California Press.

Donnelly, N. (1994). *Changing Lives of Refugee Hmong Women.* Seattle: University of Washington Press.

Dyer, R. (1993). *The Matter of Images: Essays on Representations.* New York: Routledge.

Eckert, P. (1989). *Jocks and Burnouts: Social Categories and Identity in the High School.* New York: Teachers College Press.

Fass, S. (1991). *The Hmong in Wisconsin: On the Road to Self-Sufficiency.* Milwaukee: Wisconsin Policy Research Institute.

Feagin, J. (2000). *Racist America: Roots, Current Realities and Future Reparations.* New York: Routledge.

Goldstein, B. (1985). *Schooling for Cultural Transitions: Hmong Girls and Boys in American High Schools.* Ph.D. Dissertation, University of Wisconsin—Madison.

Kimmel, M. (1994). Masculinity as homophobia. In H. Brod & M. Kaufman (Eds.) *Theorizing Masculinities.* Thousand Oaks: Sage.

Kimmel, M. (2000). Introduction. In M. Kimmel & A. Aronson (Eds.) *The Gendered Society Reader.* New York and Oxford: Oxford University Press.

Kumashiro, K. (1999). Reading queer Asian American masculinities and sexualities in elementary school. In W. J. Letts and J. T. Sears (Eds.) *Queering Elementary Education: Advancing the Dialogue about Sexualities and Schooling.* Lanham, MD: Rowman & Littlefield.

Lee, R. (1999). *Orientals: Asian Americans in Popular Culture.* Philadelphia: Temple University Press.

Lee, S. (1997). The road to college: Hmong women's pursuit of higher education. *Harvard Educational Review,* 67: 803–827.

Lee, S. (2001a). Transforming and exploring the landscape of gender and sexuality: Hmong American teenaged girls. *Race, Gender & Class,* 8(2): 35–46.

Lee, S. (2001b). More than "model minorities" or "delinquents": A look at Hmong American high school students. *Harvard Educational Review,* 71(3): 505–528.

Lee, S. (2002). Learning "America": Hmong American high school students. *Education and Urban Society,* 34: 233–246.

Lei, J. (2001). *Claims to Belonging and Difference: Cultural Citizenship and Identity Construction in Schools.* Unpublished Ph.D. Dissertation, Department of Educational Policy Studies, University of Wisconsin—Madison.

Lynch, A. (1999). *Dress, Gender, and Cultural Change: Asian American and African American Rites of Passage.* New York: Berg.

Meyer, R., Lee, C., Lee, D., Lyfoung, N., Thao, P., Vang, P., Vang, C., Yang, G. H., Yang, T., Vang, V., Lee, V., Her, S. T., Vang, P. & Lenzin, M. (1991). *Hmong Tapestry: Voices from the Cloth.* St. Paul: Hmong American Partnership.

Ngo, B. (2000). *Obstacles, Miracles, and the Pursuit of Higher Education: The Experiences of Hmong American College Students.* Unpublished Master's Thesis, Department of Educational Policy Studies, University of Wisconsin—Madison.

Ong, A. (1999). Cultural citizenship as subject making: Immigrants negotiate racial and cultural boundaries in the United States. In R. Torres, L. Miron & J. Inda (Eds.) *Race, Identity, and Citizenship: A Reader.* Malden, MA: Blackwell Publishing.

Orenstein, P. (1994). *School Girls: Young Women, Self-Esteem, and the Confidence Gap.* New York: Anchor Books, Doubleday.

Pan, E. (2000). Why Asian guys are on a roll. *Newsweek,* Feb. 21, 2000.

Rumbaut, R. & Ima, K. (1988). *The Adaptation of Southeast Asian Refugee Youth: A Comparative Study.* Washington, D.C.: Office of Refugee Resettlement.

Scott, G. (1988). To catch or not to catch a thief: A case of bride theft among the Lao Hmong refugees of southern California. *Ethnic Groups* 7: 137–151.

Sherman, S. (1988). The Hmong: Laotian refugees in the "land of the giants." *National Geographic* 174: 586–610.

Thorne, B. (1994). *Gender Play: Girls and Boys in School.* Rutgers, NJ: Rutgers University Press.

Trueba, H., Jacobs, L. & Kirton, E. (1990). *Cultural Conflict and Adaptation: The Case of Hmong Children in American Society.* New York: Falmer Press.

Walker-Moffat, W. (1995). *The Other Side of the Asian American Success Story.* San Francisco: Jossey-Bass.

2

Frames of Self

Capturing Working-Class British Boys' Identities through Photographs

Barbara M. Walker

With the aim of capturing and portraying adolescents' experiences, researchers have achieved a remarkable degree of intimacy through "shadowing" the private lives of adolescents, or observing adolescents as they engage in their daily routines and interactions. However, such studies are nevertheless limited as they tend to "see" young people through the researcher's eyes and words. Similarly, when photographs are used, the camera is usually operated by the researcher who frames the shot by choosing what to focus on, what to leave out, and when to press the shutter. This chapter presents results from a study in which I privilege adolescent boys' perspectives by handing the camera, and hence more control for what is "seen," over to the boys themselves. The purpose of this study was to understand how working-class adolescent boys see themselves in the world and how they interact with the wider society in which they live.

Challenging Stereotypes

The findings reported in this chapter are primarily based on one of two studies undertaken for the British Economic and Social Research Council between 1995 and 2001. These research projects were stimulated by growing mass media and policy perceptions in Britain that socially dysfunctional behavior by young men, as individuals and in groups, was increasing. Issues of concern included boys' reported under-achievement at school, risk-taking (e.g., drug and alcohol abuse, crime, violence), unemployment, lack of role models, and lack of support networks, as well as the high rate of suicide among boys and young men. Although researchers agree that a degree of risk-taking behavior is normal for young people (Plant & Plant, 1992), others have suggested that accelerated risk-taking may relate to boys' attempts to develop an adult male identity. The task of achieving an adult male identity may be particularly difficult in societies where systems of guidance and support that were available to previous generations of males are disappearing or no longer relevant (e.g., Giddens, 1991; Furlong & Cartmel, 1997).

The two research projects were also a response to the media's tendency to homogenize male "youth" as universally anti-social and problematic. While some have strongly argued against this homogenizing tendency (e.g., Epstein et al., 1998; Martino & Meyenn, 2001), more nuanced understandings of boys' experiences (e.g., Katz, 1997) are rarely heard. Likewise, despite Willis's (1977) influential attempt to redeem white working-class heterosexual young men by means of Marxist cultural analysis, the "moral panic" (Cohen, 1980) at the end of the twentieth century has only reinforced Pearson's (1983) depiction of the post-War working-class young man as an actively dangerous threat to society. On the whole, adolescent boys, particularly working-class boys, continue to raise concerns, especially as their risk-taking behaviors remain one of the few ways for them to establish hierarchy among their peers (Hickey et al., 2000; Mills, 2001).

The Research Program

Much of the popular "Men's Movement" literature (e.g., Bly, 1990; Biddulph, 1994) mourns men's blighted youth, blaming adult male emotional isolation on a range of sources such as mothers, feminists, women teachers, absent fathers (either metaphorically or physically), and urban civilization. The study I present in this chapter aimed to explore the self-perpetuating bubble of isolation that boys are considered to grow up within (e.g., Brannen et al., 1994; Brod & Kaufmann, 1994; Bruckenwell et al., 1995). I sought to discover how boys were experiencing the demands of everyday life and whether they were developing coping strategies. I was interested in taking a closer look at individual boys to see how and in what ways they were influenced by the "script" (Gagnon & Simon, 1973), or sex role stereotype, that men should be powerful, strong, silent and self-sufficient. This stereotype may be particularly influential among teenage boys as they seek to find and define their adult male identities (Moore & Rosenthal, 1993). I was also interested in exploring whether the plurality in current styles of maleness, divided by Harris (1995) into either classical (e.g., adventurer, breadwinner, playboy, sportsman, tough guy, warrior) and modern (e.g., nature lover, nurturer, scholar, technician) (pp. 12–13) meant that adolescent boys were currently experiencing more freedom of choice in building an adult male identity.

The key assumptions of my research were that boys' personal learning is experienced as a staged process involving observation, information processing, reflection, self-critique, reasoning, and theorizing about new ways of being. It is also a cognitively dynamic process in which learners compare new knowledge with existing understandings and evaluate it for its "fit" with their needs and experience (von Glasersfeld, 1991). This approach to learning and development required that I start with how young people see the world and how their own interpretations respond to new information and experiences.

In the first study, I used conventional ethnographic observation and interviewing methods to investigate boys' attitudes regarding their own identity. Seventy-eight boys were interviewed. Their interviews suggested that boys had two aspects to their identity: one that could be characterized as *private*, or more reflective and vulnerable; and a second one that is more publicly visible and could be characterized as *peer* oriented and assertive (Walker & Kushner, 1999). The second study extended the first one, except it also included an exploration of boys' interactions with the wider "society" (Walker, 2001). This addition brought a new methodological challenge in terms of investigating relationships that were less amenable to direct interviewing and where the physical presence of an observing researcher was highly problematic. In an effort to address this challenge, I asked some boys to photograph their worlds so that I might better understand their relationships to the wider society.

One of the most interesting findings from both of these studies was the struggle that boys appear to experience between the private world of their thoughts and feelings and the public pressure to conform to peer norms. In many ways, peer norms were a reflection of the norms of the larger society regarding "appropriate" male behavior. The tension between private thoughts and public action appeared to wax and wane over time but it was never entirely absent from the boys' interviews and was hinted at in their photographs. It was through wrestling with these two aspects of experience that the boys seemed to be developing their own identities. This chapter explores the lives of four boys, told as stories surrounding the photographs they took, focusing on how each boy responds to the tension between private reflection and public pressure to conform to peer norms, and the struggle that emerges from this tension.

Method

Participants

The four boys who are the focus of this chapter live in a northern, de-industrialized, English city. These boys, who had been acquaintances but not friends prior to the study, were chosen by their school's Deputy Principal and represented a range of academic abilities. Uzi[1] was from a Pakistani family and Popeye, Noel, and GB were white. All four boys were from working-class families.

Procedures

I met these boys as a group and individually at their school: a single-sex comprehensive school with an ethnically mixed student body, situated in a catchment area with low socioeconomic status. The part of the city in which the school is located sits between an inner city area with a national reputation for poverty, racial tension, and drug-related violence, and more salubrious suburbs with mostly owner-occupied housing. The school is surrounded by brick, two-story, semi-detached and terraced housing with small gardens. Originally these houses were built by the City Council for a white, working-class population to rent. Many of these houses are currently occupied by families of South Asian origin.

I met with the boys seven times at regular intervals over a two-year period when they were between the ages of 14 and 16. The first six interviews had a focus group format and included group discussions of the photographs. I also conducted final one-to-one interviews with each boy. When I interviewed them for the last time, the boys were about to take examinations to mark the end of compulsory schooling and were beginning to consider the pros and cons of post-secondary education and to think more seriously about their employment prospects.

For logistical reasons, I was unable to visit these boys away from their school. Hence I provided disposable cameras and asked the boys to photograph whatever seemed important to them. Cameras were introduced after the third interview. Disposable cameras were chosen since they are inexpensive and unobtrusive, can be used without fuss and, I hoped, would cause little disruption in the boys' daily routine. No attempt was made to train the boys in photographic technique or aesthetic considerations. I wanted them to feel free to "point and click" whenever they wanted. I found that this approach of having the boys take their own photographs was invaluable in my attempt to explore the fleeting, mobile, and often unvoiced time and energy the boys put into private values and public actions. It allowed access to places and events that a researcher would not necessarily be able to enter, and encouraged reflection and discussion.

Learning about Individuals through Their Photographs

Popeye

Popeye describes himself as confident and sociable. "I like being with people—company." He lives with his mother and his much younger sister. He has an older brother, now in the Army. He emerged as the self-appointed leader of the group and displayed none of the others' occasional physical timidity. At our first meeting, for example, he had two fingers splinted together, an injury acquired "scrapping," he said cheerfully. During a discussion of street violence when Noel was asked what he would do if he were threatened and had no older friend to turn to, Popeye interjected quietly, "Then come to me."

Six of Popeye's seventeen prints featured a red car belonging to an older friend. This car is the focus of much devotion. Three of the prints showed work being carried out on it (Figure 2.1) and two of them showed racing trophies on the roof.

> *Popeye:* There was something wrong with his exhaust so I had to get in the car and like fix his exhaust. It's a fast car, you see, so it gets raced.
> *BW:* How do you learn how to—
> *Popeye:* He tells me and I get under the car.

No one in Popeye's immediate family owns a car, and he is still too young for a driving license. To drive this red car seemed to be his dream.

Figure 2.1: The Red Car

The photographs appear optimistic. The sun is shining, and the setting is a quiet, tree-lined avenue with large houses set back from the road—which is unusual in this area. In addition, the trophies seem to suggest aspirations toward success, perhaps linked to the work being performed on the car.

The photographs of the fast red car, complete with trophies, appear to reinforce the successful hypermasculinity conveyed by Popeye's references in the group interviews to his fighting prowess. Two of his prints are of a girl in profile, sitting on a bed, hiding her face (Figure 2.2). Popeye informed the group, "She didn't want her photograph taken but I took it anyway, didn't I?"

The girl turns out to be his brother's girlfriend, and his comment suggests a macho attitude toward the quiet violation of taking photographs without consent. Again, Popeye's comment seems intended to display an active, assertive masculinity to the rest of the group. The weights stacked below the window denote activity and male strength. As Popeye explains, "I like to keep fit, you see, I do weights in my spare time."

In the one-to-one interview, however, another side to Popeye emerges. Although he has had a girlfriend for some months, she does not appear in his photographs. I only became aware of her existence in our final inter-view. A primary reason for her absence in his photographs may lie with his desire to avoid ridicule from his peers. As Popeye says of his mates:

> Well they haven't got a girlfriend. They're mature but not mature, do you get me? If you talk (about her) it's, "Oh you sissy!" . . . Otherwise my mates, they look up to me. Well they're always phoning me and saying do you want to do this, do you want to do that. And when I go out with my girlfriend its, "Eeew!" Real moan.

He may keep his romantic interests out of his photographs to protect the private side of experience. His public self does not appear to provide room for his private experiences. As a leader among his friends, he feels he has a public hypermasculine "face" to maintain. However, he also seems to feel more "himself" with his friends and distances himself emotionally from his girlfriend.

> Well when you're with your girlfriend you're all loving and affectionate. And with my mates [you] prat around and be yourself. Yeah, you can be yourself much, much more. . . . I've got a load of friends, you see, and I need to keep

Figure 2.2: Brother's Girlfriend

in touch with my mates. . . . I don't know but girls, if they go to see a lad, right, they fall head over heels, right? And as soon as they see you it's love, do you know what I mean? I'm not like that, I hate that. You can't love someone like that, four weeks, as soon as you ask them out it's love. Stupid. And as soon as you say, "I love you," you're trapped aren't you? And if you dump them they throw it back in your face! [Wordless mimicry] So it's best not to say it. [Laughs.]

Although Popeye's perspective here was not typical of older boys in the study, since many believed that their girlfriends were the only person to whom they could really express their "private side," this view is representative of the typical split heard in the interviews between the private emotional life of love and affection and the public persona of being a tough young man who feels "trapped" by love. It is also possible that the romantic private location is fairly new to him and therefore less familiar than the public sphere in which he operates with relative ease.

Yet despite his façade of toughness, Popeye is also affectionate and kind, as indicated in the picture of his dog (Figure 2.3). He was outraged that the dog had been thrown from a car by previous owners. But when the group laughed at the photo, implying that the dog looked "soppy," Popeye bridled saying, "He was only a puppy!" and quickly told a story emphasizing his own courage in removing the dog from its cruel situation, thus reinforcing his tough public persona.

Our last interview took place one to one during the time between the boys' practice examinations and the real thing. Popeye hadn't done as well in the practice examination as he'd expected to. "I didn't revise or anything. I just went in thinking it'd be a doddle." But the bad results had not discouraged him. "Without revising I got two good grades, so I've got to revise." This is typical of Popeye's attitude toward his current and future life. His happy-go-lucky, can-do disposition is evident throughout the transcripts and is echoed in his photographs of smiling people, usually one at a time, in pleasant, sun-lit surroundings. In Popeye's mind there is a clear link between where he is now and where he wishes to be in the future. That link involves some effort, he believes, but is manageable. He is following his slightly older peers who have trod the ground before him. He had thought about following his brother into the Army, but when we last spoke he was hoping to do a carpentry apprenticeship after leaving school or join the police force:

Figure 2.3: Popeye's Dog

Popeye: Well my mate, his brother's in the police. Go to the pub with him
and everything. When you're in uniform you have to have a different
head on but he's still all right. Sounds good. . . .
BW: Where did the idea of the police come from?
Popeye: Driving cars. So, police force, drive cars. Put your foot to the floor,
you know, Vroom!

Fitting into a stereotypic image of a male who loves cars, particularly fast
cars, Popeye discusses his future ambitions of being a policeman. He also
discusses becoming a Physical Education teacher, "but I don't fancy the six
years in college . . . it's like school all over again, isn't it?" He'd also like to
travel: "Fancy living abroad. Like, doing a degree in Sport and Tourism.
Then go, apply abroad and teach over there for a year and then come back
and live here and go somewhere else." But when I remind him that, on our
first meeting, he had said that he wanted to go to America and marry a
rich woman he responds with an ironic, "Oh aye!" and realism takes over
again: "I probably will live at home. It's like, my brother [has left], the last
one home, you feel guilty leaving your mum because it's your responsibility, like, a bit, isn't it?" The apparent conflict between his public persona

of a confident male, driving fast cars, traveling, studying sports, teaching Physical Education, and his private desire to take care of his mother and make sure someone is home for her is readily apparent in his narratives.

Of the four boys whose stories are reported here, Popeye conforms most to the male stereotype. He sees himself as a leader and invests much of his energy in peer relationships, not allowing himself much time for private reflection or love. Although successfully maintaining a romantic relationship, he publicly dismisses this relationship both in his narratives and in his photographs. He seems to feel well in control of his future employment prospects, and his risk-taking is limited—he may be involved in a fight or two, but he always makes sure he has older friends with him.

Popeye is the most confident of the four, and it may be the ease with which he conforms to the male stereotype that makes him appear confident. Yet there is an underlying conflict apparent in his narratives and his photographs (and in the absence of particular photographs). He has a public sense of self and of the future that involves being a policeman, driving fast red cars, and spending time with his friends at the pub, and he also has a private world of his girlfriend and of his mother for whom he feels responsible and wants to take care of. This private world seems to be rarely discussed with his peers or in public. At times he even seems ashamed of this private world. This tension, while not seeming to undercut his apparent confidence, seems to lie at the heart of his identity struggle. Who is he now and who will he be in the future?

GB

GB is the middle child of seven, living with his mother and stepfather. In his interviews, he is friendly and cheerful, not allowing his stammer to inhibit his carefully considered comments. He had the lowest number of successful prints, which disappointed him. The majority of his photographs contained no people although several that had not "come out" were of family pets. Five of GB's photos were of his school—four looking out through barred windows and one of bleak strip lighting. He said he had wanted to emphasize that school was a "prison" (Figure 2.4). His photos seem to speak of private alienation and publicly expressed anger.

GB says he doesn't like going out with mates in the evenings any more "because all we do is cause trouble. That's all we do." This involves vandalism like building roadblocks with builders' rubbish. "And then when the

Figure 2.4: School

drivers come along speeding, they've got to stop and take it apart before they can go on and we're sitting in a bush at the side of the road, laughing!" Sometimes this leads to police chases, which adds to the excitement: "[We're] too fast. And policemen can't climb very well either, so we had to jump over a few walls." However, these activities were beginning to dwindle.

> *GB:* I don't want to get in any more trouble because I've been brought home by the police a few times, about four times, and I just can't do with it at the moment. . . . It's just say like I'm having a laugh, you know, causing trouble and everything, and then a few times I get caught, but when I do get caught I hate it. I don't like it at all. . . . It's just I don't like the feeling of guilt as well, like in my stomach here (rubs stomach). I feel really weird.
>
> *BW:* Do you only feel guilty when you get caught?
>
> *GB:* Er, oh! [Sounds surprised] S'pose so, yeah I do. I feel guilty when I get caught, apart from, I only feel guilty when I get caught, or I know I'm about to get caught, so I try and ease it off a bit. I try and suck up, lessen the punishment.

> BW: So if you didn't get caught, if there weren't policemen out there catch-
> ing you doing it, you'd still be doing it?
>
> GB: Erm . . . probably, yeah.

GB reinforces the common myth that males left up to their own devices will cause havoc. Although he is trying to resist this behavior, he readily acknowledges that he would still participate in this behavior if he were not going to be punished. However, he refers to a feeling of guilt, "like in my stomach," which suggests a conflict regarding his actions. Yet it is unclear what the conflict is for him.

GB is physically a "late developer," which is reflected in his conversations and in his photographs. Girls are not mentioned or photographed, and while other boys talk about pretending to be older in order to visit pubs and nightclubs to meet girls, GB is "not really interested. [It's] daft, that." Nor does he share Popeye's interest in cars—GB talks about riding his bicycle and is more interested in harassing motorists than joining them. Over the two years I knew the boys, only GB remained fixed in his antipathy toward the police. It is possible that privately GB is interested in girls, but his lack of stature, and his family's lack of resources, make the early attainment of a girlfriend unlikely for him. So he invests in an anti-authoritarian, trouble-making public identity as a means of sustaining peer respect and self-esteem.

While school was gradually becoming less important to the other three boys as they turned more thoughts toward their futures, GB was still enmeshed in the small-scale, teacher-versus-pupil power struggles of the classroom. Near the end of our last conversation GB told me that he and a friend were about to be suspended from school. They had started a fire during a Science lesson. School still loomed large in his life, and his photographs reflected this.

GB's identity seems to be linked to his misbehavior and, if he didn't admit to feelings of guilt, one might believe that GB simply fit into the current stereotype of male behavior. Yet this "negative identity" (see Erikson, 1968) seems to stem from his genuine frustration with and anger at the prison-like nature he discerns in his school.

His pictures of his school and his unpeopled photographs reveal quite clearly his sense of alienation and isolation at school and at home:

> BW: Do you talk to your step-dad much?
>
> GB: No. Don't really talk to him much.

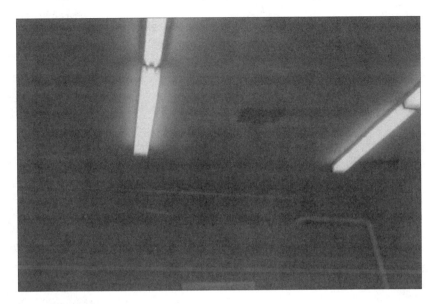

Figure 2.5: School Lighting

BW: How about your mum?

GB: I don't really talk to my mum much either.

BW: Is she too busy, or is it—

GB: —yeah, she's always busy, and I don't feel I can talk to her. I don't feel I can.

BW: So who do you talk to?

GB: Mates. I tell them everything.

BW: Do you tell them about the things that upset you?

GB: Not really no. Nah. I don't. I keep them to myself.

BW: How about your dad, do you see him?

GB: Not often, no. I don't really like him anyway.

BW: . . . So you don't talk to your parents much.

GB: No. If I tried I'd probably get a cup of coffee thrown over me.

It was in the one-to-one interview where GB indicated that privately he is beginning to suspect he has been putting too much emphasis on his peer relationships and that his risk-taking has been getting out of hand. He wants to resist the dictates and actions of his peers but finds it difficult when the context in which he lives doesn't support this resistance by offering positive alternatives. GB is stuck with either following his peers or following the norms of an institution he refers to as a prison. His family does not provide him respite from his conflicts as they don't appear to spend much time talking to him. As others have noted about boys, GB does appear to exist in an emotional "bubble of isolation" (e.g., Lee, 1993; Phillips, 1993; Brannen et al., 1994; Bruckenwell et al., 1995) but at the same time this isolation is reinforced by the familial and institutional context. His friendships, even with their negative peer norms, may provide him with his only sense of connection and pleasure. GB's conflict, like Popeye's, seems once again to suggest a public/private split where the public, which includes his peers as well as his school, is confining him—and limiting his possibilities in the future. In addition, his private world of vulnerabilities and desires is not adequately responded to by his family or friends so he ends up feeling frustrated, alone, and seemingly angry.

Uzi

Uzi's parents came to Britain from Pakistan. He lives with them and his older brother and sister. Uncles, aunts, and cousins live nearby. He was one of the louder, more articulate members of the group. His interjections were not always appreciated by the others, who nicknamed him Mouth.[2] There were, however, gaps in his apparent confidence.

Uzi had requested that he have a camera in time for a school trip to an amusement park. He was delighted with his twenty-three prints, nineteen of which were taken during that trip. Of the others, one is a self-portrait, two are of detached houses belonging to members of his extended family, and one is of a large new truck belonging to a cousin. These pictures indicate family pride and, perhaps, personal aspiration.

Of the photos taken at the amusement park, six are of his friends (see Figure 2.6). Uzi was the only boy to take posed group photographs, and three of these are of groups of up to eight boys. The other three are taken with "trophy" girls[3] that they met that day: one is of a friend with his arm round a girl's shoulders and two are of Uzi and another girl who wears white clothes, their arms around each other as they smile shyly at the camera. Compared with the other boys' photos, Uzi's are crowded. He wants to convey that he is a popular member of his peer group. Uzi's own appearance in three of the prints is an obvious contrast to the other boys' absence in their photos. His representation in his photographs is consistent with

Figure 2.6: Uzi's Friends

the loud, confident, even arrogant public performance he gives in the group interviews. His private insecurities are only voiced in the one-to-one interview. But they are glimpsed in the photo of him with the trophy girl where he looks almost unrecognizably coy and unsure of himself.

The main reason for his delight with the photographs was a chance meeting with the Pakistani national cricket team, in England for a tournament, who were also having a day out at the park. Uzi (a keen cricketer himself) has eight photos of his sporting heroes, mostly posing for his camera, and one of himself with two of them. Uzi's adulation of the cricket team led to a group discussion of sporting role models and also allowed him to explain the importance of cricket in South Asia to three white boys whose major sporting interest was soccer. Britain's Asian population is stereotyped as hardworking and cerebral but physically timid. There have been much-publicized cases where gangs of white youths have indulged their xenophobia through organized "Paki-bashing." The fact that Pakistan's cricketers are easily the equal of English national teams gives boys like Uzi a rare opportunity to display ethnic pride.

It was noticeable that none of the boys took a single photograph of family members. One of Uzi's prints appears to buck this trend: it contains

Figure 2.7: Cricketer and Family

an Asian family picnicking on the grass (Figure 2.7). However, the photo is of a cricketer's family, with the hero-figure sitting in the middle of the group. Perhaps the boys felt that their families are part of their private sides, not to be exposed to public scrutiny.

No white face appears anywhere in Uzi's photographs, which give the impression of a sociable young man firmly embedded in Pakistani culture. However, from the private interview it became clear that he was undergoing an identity crisis. He described his relationship with his parents:

> It's like two totally different people, what I'm doing now and what they've done is totally different. What I do, for them I'm too Westernized. I'm too Westernized to be an Asian and what I'm trying to explain to them, I'm not born in Pakistan, I'm not from the Far East, I'm born in England. . . . I have British nationality and what's here, we can live by the laws here, so there's no point of me living by the laws from there. . . . I'm proud to be Asian, it's just that they're, you see, when I have kids, there's no way I'm going to be like them. . . . To tell you the truth, I do feel sorry for myself. [Pause] I sob sometimes.

When I suggested that most people his age have problems with their parents, Uzi maintained that the problems are greater for Asian young people:

Well you see for English people, it's not that bad. They've got problems with their parents, but on top of that 'cause it's that age, that teenage. We've got that teenage and on top of that we've got that pressure as well, that you're Asian, you can't do this and that, you can't do this, you can't drink, you can't smoke, you can't do this. You can't eat such and such things. We've got these kind of—it's like we're tied up in one circle. If we step out of it we're out of line. We can't do that.

The photographs of himself with the "trophy girl" are evidence of Westernized behavior of which his parents would not approve, as was the story he told the group about giving the girl some cannabis to smoke, making it easier for him to "get into her." Although Popeye, too, was unimpressed by this story:

Popeye: You should have been a gentleman . . . and just left her.
Uzi: Are you stupid?
Popeye: Was she nice?
Uzi: No.
Popeye: I bet she was really nice. You're just saying that now 'cause you regret it!

There was a marked difference between Uzi's story about "ungentlemanly" behavior and his shy demeanor with the girl as shown in the photograph. Perhaps this echoes Popeye's public/private split revealed by the photo of his dog. Popeye, though, is more confident in his public masculinity and uses it here when he takes a moralizing stance with Uzi.

There is also some dissonance between the "aspirational" photographs of a large house together with a new truck, both belonging to older cousins, and Uzi's own immediate future. His cousins and older brother currently make good livings as market traders but warn Uzi that the days are numbered for this type of enterprise. It has been suggested that his future may lie outside family-owned businesses—a prospect he finds privately threatening despite his publicly alleged independent-mindedness.[4]

Uzi's parents were obviously concerned about his future prospects and were, he said, "nagging" him every day to do well in his exams and to take a further qualification exam in Business Studies. But when I asked "Do you see why your parents are anxious?" He responded:

> Yeah I know they mean all good, but they're going a bit too far with it. I know they mean good, by saying study, study, you know what I mean. Get your qualifications, I know they mean good, but it's not the way to push someone. You just stress them. At the end of the day, they're not going to sit in that exam room and do that exam. It's going to be me. The pressure's going to be on me and that way, no one can make me change my mind. It's like when I'm in lessons. I'll tell you the truth. I'm very ignorant at times. When a teacher tells me what to do, if my mind's to it, I'll do the work. Everyone says that, but when I'm ignoring him, and I'll ignore him and I won't do nothing no one tells me to do, no matter what, even the [Principal]. If he tells me to do no matter what I won't do it. I'll just ignore him, it's when my heart says to do something, I'll do it. When I feel like to do it, I'll do it. . . . I'll do what I want, no matter what.

Uzi spends time and effort reflecting on his private identity ("When my heart says to do something, I'll do it"). He is working hard to develop an independent-minded, British-Asian masculinity—perhaps trying too hard for this otherwise white peer group and adult authority figures. Peers and family/school are exerting equal but opposing pressure on his public identity, leaving him feeling alone in his struggle. Looking at Uzi's difficulties, the most obvious split is between his peers and family, which seems less of a problem for the white members of this focus group. Moreover, he is also wrestling in his private sphere, as he tries to work out apparently irreconcilable differences between his Asian identity and English context.

Noel

Noel lives with his mother, father, older brother, and younger sister. Like the others in the group, he was unsure whether to continue with post-compulsory education and has an unskilled Saturday and holiday job that offers only possibilities of low-status employment.[5]

His prints included one (Figure 2.8) that was the most dramatic of the collection. Noel was very excited about it:

> N: That's where some guy got stabbed. That's his blood.
> BW: Is it really?

Figure 2.8: The Blood Stain

> *N:* It is. I swear. Some guy slit his wrists, and this is where we train and play
> football. . . . We were training one day, and some guy, we saw some guy
> lying there and we thought he was just a tramp or something. But he'd
> slit his wrists . . . I thought he was dead at first.

From the conversation, it was unclear whether this had been a suicide attempt, or whether the wounded man had been attacked. His discovery of the man had prompted an immediate dilemma as to whether this was a situation best ignored. However, Noel and his friends had decided to obtain help and the man was taken to hospital. For Noel, this photograph provided evidence of how he and his mates had overcome the challenge of the situation and thus reinforced a heroic public image.

Three photographs of an empty soccer field are taken from an unforgiving angle, but this is Noel's "field of dreams" (Figure 2.9). As he said, "I couldn't take a photo of a match 'cos I was playing in it." Noel's long-cherished ambition was to be a professional soccer player. But this seemed unlikely. Despite the success of his team in local tournaments, the scouts had not spotted his talents. Another possibility was to take a college course, but Noel reflects:

Figure 2.9: Soccer Pitch

> I've been to Stantley College. It's a course for football. And I've asked three
> people that have been there, and they've said it's rubbish. Said you just get
> set up with a rubbish football team, facilities are crap, so I don't think I'll be
> going there.

He was considering another college course, one that combined Sport with
English, but did not sound enthusiastic. He did not equate academic success with high-status employment. "It's like my brother, he's fairly smart.
. . . He's got loads of good grades. He's well more smarter than me and my
sister and he's still working in a supermarket. . . . So that's put me off a
bit." He seemed much more concerned than the others in the group were
about the future. Worries about upcoming exams paled in comparison to
worries about his future.

> But now my bigger worry is what I'm going to do when I leave school. . . .
> That's what I'm most stressed about at this moment of my life. . . . It's just
> like all my mates, they've got something set out that they want to do—and
> some of them haven't got a fantastic thing that they want to do, but most of
> my friends have got something that they want to do and that they're going

to go for. . . . I just want someone to be there and to say, "Right, this is your job, you've got this job. I know what you like, this is your job." I just want someone to say that!

His anxiety about his future emerged in the one-to-one interview, indicating that it is a private worry not to be shared with peers. Talking in the group interviews, Noel preferred to convey the impression of an optimistic, sociable sportsman capable of earning good money in unskilled labor.

A common topic of conversation for all four boys focused on the police. Noel took a photograph of a pub that he and his friends were too young to enter (Figure 2.10), so they "hung about" on the street corner opposite it until the police moved them on. In discussing this photograph, the group complained at length about police harassment. There was a feeling among the boys that they were under constant surveillance. As Noel commented:

I don't like [the police]. I was working yesterday, and we were all in a car—me, him and him (points to photographs)—we sat there 'cos in our dinner break we just go in the car and have some dinner, with the doors open. And

Figure 2.10: Street Corner Opposite the Pub

they just stopped and asked whose car it was. And we went, "It's the manager's." . . . They were watching us to see what we'd do. . . . That's how they are all the time. They see someone on the street and they'll stop you. . . . They think you're going to rob something, probably. As far as they're concerned, if we're not inside of our houses, then we're breaking the law.

The surveillance extended beyond the police. The boys also complained about feeling unwelcome in shops, cinemas, and leisure centers, and being seen as a nuisance by adults in general. GB told a story of a neighbor who called the police when he and a friend were playing soccer in the street. Even the street, the one public area that they might be able to claim, was apparently out of bounds. These feelings were summed up by Popeye's ironic question to me: "Is there a curfew, Miss? I don't know." The police are probably key reinforcers of the male norm but yet they also punish the male norm of misbehavior—a contradiction that appears to irritate the boys greatly.

By the last interview, however, Noel's views of the police had completely changed. His brother had recently been mugged twice by, Noel suspected, the group of friends he had previously "hung around" with:

It can't be no-one else but all them lot. It's like a big gang. It's got to be them. . . . Now I know the police are right, just coming to move them. They should have at least two police cars just patrolling every night, just going round slowly. I think they should always have that.

Noel did not personally feel threatened by this gang because they knew him. However he did feel unsafe in his local streets because, he said, the police had been successful in "cleaning up" a neighboring area that had just displaced the trouble to his own area. "I never feel safe on my own turf," he said, and tried not to be alone on the street. Recently he had adopted the tactic of going by bus to a different area to "hang about" because he felt safer there. However, he believed he would continue to live in the area:

All my family's here, all my friends are here. If I go somewhere else, I could stay in London, what's there to do? Just everyone's here that you know, you know your surroundings as well. And just the little things like your football team, Manchester United, things like that. And it's a good place, but other things are crap.

Like Uzi, there was a marked difference between Noel's public self as evidenced in the group interviews and the anxious, frightened boy revealed when he spoke on his own. Noel appears to be stuck in a blind alley. He sees no way forward. "I just want a flat and a girlfriend," he says, but has no concrete ideas of how to acquire either.

Discussion

The total absence of families, adults in general (except for the cricketing heroes), and the scarcity of girls in all the boys' photographs reinforces stereotypes of adolescent boys as peer focused. When asked about what was important to them, the boys almost invariably mentioned male friendships first. The boys are seemingly trying to rid themselves of family influences, while not yet becoming seriously involved with the opposite sex. They are working out who they are with reference to their male peers.[6] My data indicate that this self-work takes place in two locations—public, peer group situations where "lines" for the male "script" (Gagnon & Simon, 1973) were tested and rehearsed; and private reflections where the boys are trying to make the various influences from peers and adult authority fit with their personal moral code.

The photographs literally allow us to visualize this private sphere as well as the public image these boys want to convey to their peers. Shots of interiors give clues to inner lives and their desired public images of themselves. The "aspirational" images of cars, trophy girls, and large houses give indications of valuing consumer power and status. But it was the one-to-one interviews that illuminated the inner conversations the boys had as they worked out how they should be in the world. Perhaps some aspects of private life are simply too difficult to pin down photographically.

It was noticeable that the stories these boys told the group about their photographs tended to be dramatic and macho, for example the fast car, school as prison, trophy girls, sports, and the rescue of the injured man. More intimate data such as Popeye's girlfriend, GB's feelings about his illegal activity, Uzi's cultural dilemmas, and Noel's fear of street violence and anxiety about future unemployment, only emerged in the private interviews. Perhaps the boys fear that these more tender or anxious feelings would, if publicly revealed, leave them vulnerable to peer ridicule. However, it is the macho public stories that influence the impression boys make in the wider world and exacerbate the tendency of the media and adults in general to think the worst of them—a case of words' speaking louder than actions.

The rules of society are represented in the photographs by the number of barriers depicted. Sometimes these rules are presented overtly (e.g., bars on school windows) and sometimes less obviously (e.g., fences, walls, curbstones, white lines on sports pitches). Authority is ubiquitous and constantly telling these boys where they may and may not go. And, as we have seen, the boys resent the restrictions they feel society places upon them, the surveillance they are under, and the consequent social exclusion and powerlessness they experience. It became obvious while discussing the photographs that the street is a highly contested area (Robinson, 2000). In some sense the boys feel that it is the only public space they are "allowed" to inhabit, and yet adults, police, and other peer groups make rival claims. GB's attempts to reclaim the street from motorists are genuine, if extreme, while Noel's fears of violence illuminate young people's struggle to acquire "street literacy" (Cahill, 2000).

The absence of adult images (cricketers aside) underlines the alienation these boys feel toward adult authority. Rather than being looked up to as role models, for many English boys their parents' generation is regarded, at best, as out of touch with modern issues and, at worst, with disdain. Arguably there is nothing new in this view. But today's boys feel that their parents' limited experience of social contexts and issues—like the clubbing scene, and drug and alcohol use by the young—together with their ignorance of new information technologies means that their advice is irrelevant (Furlong & Cartmel, 1997). Boys look to their peers—which we can stretch here to include those just a few years older—for a steer on life. And the experience of these peers can affect the boys' own confidence and sense of identity.

Conclusion

These boys, three white and one of Pakistani origin, all live in the same working-class area and attend the same school. They were all intelligent and articulate. Yet their photographs and stories showed them to be tackling the demands of everyday life in different ways. As Connell (2000) points out, "[D]iversity is not just a matter of difference between communities. Diversity also exists *within* a given setting" (p. 10). Moore and Rosenthal's (1993) observation that the male stereotype is particularly powerful for adolescent boys was illustrated in this study. Noel and Uzi had trouble adjusting to it and were beset by private doubts. For different reasons these two individuals were struggling to find a role that felt right for them, seeking but not yet finding a comfortable mix of Harris's (1995) multiplicity of acceptable adult masculine styles. GB had, through group vandalism, found an enjoyable way of conforming to peer expectation but it was bringing him into conflict with "society." His behavior could be seen to tally with Giddens's (1991) and Furlong and Cartmel's (1997) arguments that risk-taking can be an attempt to prove masculinity in a world that lacks previous generations' benchmarks and parameters. But although his vandalism gets him noticed by the police, it is lawbreaking of a relatively minor and temporary type and therefore possibly within the continuum of what could be perceived as normal for this age group.

Clearly the well-recorded atmosphere of anxiety and isolation that boys experience growing up pertains to the boys in the present study. The adult world seemed remote for these boys, having little connection with the future they see for themselves. As Furlong and Cartmel (1997) maintain, the world appears to be risky and unpredictable. These uncertainties are being negotiated on an individual level with little assistance from social structures such as families. Peers are more trusted than families. As a result, peer influence is perhaps greater than for previous generations. At the same time, peers do not seem to provide the boys with a sense of security and connectedness. The boys, for the most part, seem to struggle with finding a context in which both their private selves and public images can be consistent and known by others.

The difference between public stories about the photographs, which were told for group consumption, and the private feelings that emerged primarily in the one-to-one interviews exemplified one kind of strategy that these boys undertake to build their masculine identities. The boys appeared to be doing two things simultaneously: they were working to build a public self (or selves) and a private self. There was evidence that these two developmental processes felt very different, although they operated in parallel and the boundaries were fluid. Perhaps it is in the tension between the two, where the barriers come into being and crossovers occur, that attitudes and self-knowledge are formed. Because it is unspoken and yet constant, this self-work is difficult for the young person to explain and therefore for the researcher to pinpoint. This study, however, gave us some clues to the internal dialogue the boys engage in to deal with the ambiguities they experience in their public and private worlds. A similar disjuncture between public behavior and private values and desires has been noticed by writers such as Moore and Rosenthal (1993) and Tolman et al. (this volume).

There are implications from these findings for the public policy debate on young men, risk-taking, alienation, and identity formation. The boys are experiencing a variety of social pressures in their search for an adult male identity that is compatible with real options. By understanding the interaction of aspects of identity experienced as personal, peer, and wider society dimensions, a greater understanding can be gained of how individual boys work in a three-dimensional world. With all four boys, the research was able to show how they were interpreting their experiences and developing identities in a world that, they felt, often showed them hostility, restriction, and a lack of acceptance.

NOTES

1. The boys are referred to by the pseudonyms they chose at the start of the research process.

2. Although, looking at the transcripts, Popeye talked more.

3. I use the term "trophy girls" to denote girls who were relative strangers, photographed almost as an accessory—they looked good on the boy's arm and enhanced the predatory masculine image that Uzi seemed keen to present. These photographs are not reproduced here to maintain anonymity.

4. Family-run businesses are a common type of employment for British Asians.

5. These include building work, catering, and retail.

6. These findings concur with the conclusions of Phoenix et al. (1999) that boys' first concern is popularity. Harris (1998) goes so far as to suggest that peer relationships (and to a lesser extent genetics) are what affect the development of personality: parental influence, she argues, is of little or no importance.

REFERENCES

Biddulph, S. (1994). *Manhood: A Book about Setting Men Free.* Sydney: Finch.

Bly, R. (1990). *Iron John; A Book about Men.* Reading, MA: Addison-Wesley.

Brannen, J., Dodd, K. & Storey, P. (1994). *Young People, Health and Family Life.* Buckingham: Open University Press.

Brod, H. & Kauffman, M. (Eds.). (1994). *Theorizing Masculinities.* Thousand Oaks, CA: Sage.

Bruckenwell, P., Jackson, D., Luck, M., Wallace, J. & Watts, J. (1995). *The Crisis in Men's Health*. Bath: Community Health, UK.

Cahill, C. (2000). Street literacy: urban teenagers' strategies for negotiating their neighbourhood. *Journal of Youth Studies*, 3, pp. 251–277.

Cohen, S. (1980). *Folk Devils and Moral Panics*, 2d ed. Oxford: Blackwell.

Connell, R. W. (2000). *The Men and the Boys*. Cambridge: Polity.

Epstein, D., Elwood, J., Hay, V. & Maw, J. (Eds.). (1998). *Failing Boys? Issues in Gender and Achievement*. Buckingham and Philadelphia: Open University Press.

Erikson, E. H. (1968). *Identity, Youth and Crisis*. London: Faber.

Furlong, A. & Cartmel, F. (1997). *Young People and Social Change: Individualization and Risk in Late Modernity*. Buckingham and Philadelphia: Open University Press.

Gagnon, J. H. & Simon, W. (1973). *Sexual Conduct: The Social Sources of Human Sexuality*. Chicago: Aldine.

Giddens, A. (1991). *Modernity and Self-Identity: Self and Society in the Late Modern Age*. Cambridge: Polity.

Harris, I. (1995). *Messages Men Hear: Constructing Masculinities*. London: Taylor and Francis.

Harris, J. (1998). *The Nurture Assumption: Why Children Turn Out the Way They Do*. London: Bloomsbury.

Hickey, C., Keddie, A. & Fitzclarence, L. (2000*). Regimes of Risk: From Little Boys Big Boys Grow*. Paper presented at the British Educational Research Association Conference, Cardiff, 7–10 September.

Katz, A., in association with Ann Buchanan and JoAnn Ten Brinke. (1997). *Leading Lads*. Working paper published by Oxford University Department of Social Policy and Social Work.

Kenway, J. & Bullen, E. (2001). *Consuming Children: Education-Entertainment-Advertising*. Buckingham and Philadelphia: Open University Press.

Lee, C. (1993). *Talking Tough: The Fight for Masculinity*. London: Arrow.

Martino, W. & Meyenn, B. (Eds.). (2001). *What About the Boys? Issues of Masculinity in Schools*. Buckingham and Philadelphia: Open University Press.

Mills, M. (2001). Pushing it to the max: interrogating the risky business of being a boy. In Wayne Martino & Bob Meyenn (Eds.), *What About the Boys? Issues of Masculinity in Schools*. Buckingham and Philadelphia: Open University Press.

Moore, S. & Rosenthal, D. (1993). *Sexuality in Adolescence*. London: Routledge.

Pearson, G. (1983). *Hooligan: A History of Respectable Fears*. London: Macmillan.

Phillips, A. (1993). *The Trouble with Boys: Parenting the Men of the Future*. London: Pandora.

Phoenix, A., Frosh, S. & Pattman, R. (1999). Boys, masculinities and education. *childRIGHT*, 156, pp. 10–11.

Plant, M. & Plant, M. (1992). *Risk-Takers; Alcohol, Drugs, Sex and Youth*. London: Routledge.

Raphael Reed, L. (1998). "Zero tolerance": gender performance and school failure. In D. Epstein, J. Elwood, V. Hay & J. Maw (Eds.). *Failing Boys? Issues in Gender and Achievement.* Buckingham and Philadelphia: Open University Press.

Robinson, C. (2000). Creating space, creating self: street-frequenting youth in the city and suburbs. *Journal of Youth Studies,* 3(4), pp. 429–443.

von Glasersfeld, E. (1991). Knowing without metaphysics: aspects of the radical constructivist position. In F. Steier (Ed.), *Research and Reflexivity.* London: Sage.

Walker, B. M. (2001). The internal triangle: self, peers and society in boys' identity formation with implications for sexual health education. *Sex Education,* 1(2), pp. 123–136.

Walker, B. M. & Kushner, S. (1999). The building site: an educational approach to masculine identity. *Journal of Youth Studies,* 2(1), pp. 45–58.

Willis, P. (1977). *Learning to Labour: How Working Class Kids Get Working Class Jobs.* Farnborough: Saxon House.

3

Boys in Men's Clothing

Racial Socialization and Neighborhood Safety as Buffers to Hypervulnerability in African American Adolescent Males

Howard C. Stevenson

Being Black and male is surreal. You are desired and you are despised. You are hunted like fox or game and yet idolized for the development of the identity of others. That is, you are imaged as the thing to avoid, to reject, to "not be." Or if you are liked, it is for the sake of having the "taboo" rub off, thus making the other's identity that much more unique and authentic. Your rarity in certain mainstream contexts makes you a marketable commodity worthy of desire and loathing. You are assumed to be hostile and you are assumed to be ignorant. You are followed as often as you are left alone. You want what everybody else wants but it feels as if, when its you who wants it, the thing becomes dirty and undesirable. As Ralph Ellison once quipped, despite its advantages, "[invisibility] is most often wearing on the nerves. Then too, you are constantly being bumped against by those of poor vision. Or again, you doubt if you really exist. You wonder whether you are not simply a phantom in other people's minds." Too often, Black males try to run from police and fight back against these phantom images in themselves and in the "other," sometimes to their own self-destruction. Surrealism then drops off the cliff of tragedy.

The struggle of African American identity or identities in the bodies, souls, and minds of male adolescents is a complex one that involves levels of personal and social vulnerability unprecedented in American human social interaction despite advances in civilization. Hypervulnerability, a term created to describe this intense experience of vulnerability, results from the psychological and physical exposure of one's cognitions, feelings, and actions to annihilation and dehumanization by one's family, friends, neighborhood, society, and the various images that these social institutions blatantly and unwittingly promulgate and manufacture. The internalization of these negative images of black maleness by Black males is the primary motivator for feelings of hypervulnerability. The negative consequences of hypervulnerability include attachment to and acceptance of abusive relationships, failure to expect care or love from others, engagement in dangerous risk-taking behavior, willingness to risk incarceration to demonstrate one's existence, expectation of harm to come from relationships, and acts of hurting others emotionally or physically as a means of self-protection. While Black male youth are "becoming" and developing racial and gender identities, American society represents them in very static ways, and consequently they also present themselves in static ways. This typecasting is what Irving Goffman would call "presented identities," and, for African American males, these public identities are based on feelings of hypervulnerability.

The "Doing" of Black Male Identity

We live in a world where some American citizens are freer than others to express multiple identities. There are some contexts, however, that restrict free expression of identities. Researchers have found, for instance, that living in dangerous neighborhoods affects the emotional experiences of youth (Buka et al., 2001; Osofsky et al., 1993; Richters & Martinez, 1993). Social interactions within particular contexts push all humans, and Black male youth in this instance, to "BE," not "become," and to "DO," not just plan what to do. Black male youth are often pressured to present a static identity, not ambiguous or multidimensional, because the social interactions within a context often demand it. Spencer, Cunningham, and Swanson's (1995) work on reactive coping helps to illuminate this idea of "being" and "doing" as an integral part of one's identity.

Sometimes for poor Black boys, there are serious social and psychological costs to analyzing and critiquing one's existence. Negative images can take control of one's presented identity. As a result, one may face, if only momentarily, the perceptions of animalism and criminality from a Black male–phobic public as well as the abyss of nothingness or nihility within themselves. To critique and change one's presented identity may require some reflection on one's current subordinate status in society as well as one's future. It could also mean a diminution of social status among peers where a change in presentation could give them reason for distrust (Stevenson, 1997). Cunningham and Meunier (this volume) have found that when Black adolescent males are using exaggerated macho identity stances, they are, in fact, coping. This coping is essential in social and ecological environments where danger to personal and familial safety is high. Maintaining a stable identity presentation allows predictability among peers, gives one a set (albeit a limited set) of strategies to manage societal hostility (e.g., "cool pose" and "reactive coping"), and builds a fragile and temporary but demonstrably confident self in socially stressful contexts.

The angst of having to build such identities leaves many Black boys feeling "missed, dissed, and pissed" (Kunjufu, 1985; Stevenson, 1997; Wilson, 1990) or hypervulnerable. They feel "missed" in the sense of feeling misrepresented and misinterpreted, "dissed" in the sense of feeling disrespected and distorted, and "pissed" in the sense of feeling intense anger related to the devaluation experienced since early childhood from societal, familial, and interpersonal rejection. All three of these dynamics are key aspects to the visceral vulnerability or the hypervulnerability that many Black boys experience. Being missed, dissed, and pissed represents the struggle of constructing identity within a quicksand of false Black male images and is as vulnerable as one can get.

Hypervulnerability among African American Boys

Several reasons account for the missed, dissed, and pissed experience of African American male adolescents and how social systems respond to them (Ferguson, 2000).

Racial profiling of Black males while they drive, walk, shop, talk, stand, and gather in groups has reached epidemic proportions (ACLU, 2000). Black males are twice as likely to be arrested and seven times more likely to be held in detention facilities as White youth (Children's Defense Fund, 2000). Black males consistently receive more severe and lengthy punishments than White males who commit the same offenses (Children's Defense Fund, 2000). Black males are over-represented at every level of the juvenile justice system, constituting 70 percent of all juveniles in American correctional facilities. Moreover, Black male young adults report experiencing racial discrimination at higher levels than any other group (Children's Defense Fund, 2000).

The social system has failed to identify adequately the social and mental health needs of African American youth for several reasons. One reason can be found in the insidious nature of racism. Research shows that Black boys are often feared as criminalizing men or animals (Finkelman, 1992; Sampson & Laub, 1993). Sampson and Laub (1993) found through investigation of juvenile court proceedings and records that Black males are perceived as threatening members of society who need to be controlled. Romer, Jamieson, and de Coteau (1998) found that the percentage of crime committed by African Americans in a Northeastern city is significantly lower than the percentage of news coverage of African American crime on three major local news networks. As a result, one gets the impression that African Americans commit crime at higher levels than they actually do. Furthermore, African American males are often targeted as threats and menaces to society by social authority figures ranging from police to school teachers, and this social construction of Black males as "menace" has both public health and economic marketing implications (Gibbs, 1988; McIntyre & Pernell, 1985; Potts, 1997; Rowan, Pernell & Akers, 1996; Sampson & Laub, 1993).

When Anne Ferguson (2000) describes how eleven- and twelve-year-old Black boys are criminalized and expected to land in jail as a group, her findings become even more chilling when she reveals how this perception comes from within schools and from the personnel who run them. The rash of police shootings and killings of innocent, unarmed Black males, the subsequent media white-wash of the social implications of the loss of Black life compared to Whites (West, 1993), and the refusal of major institutions (police) to admit wrongdoing or change their practices in the face of overwhelming statistical or video evidence are just a few of examples of blatant racism that exists in our social structure (ACLU, 2000).

Cornel West discusses the problem of nihilism in poor, minority communities as a danger too often overlooked. Nihility is defined here as the state of or fear of nothingness or nonexistence (West, 1993). I have observed this nihilism in African American boys who have a history of anger- and aggressive-laden social conflicts. The fear of nonexistence often underlies their actions and "presented identities." It is in these complex processes that I am most interested in the present study of hypervulnerability among African American males in high-risk urban contexts. Majors and Billson (1992) have applied Goffman's (1959) notions of "impression management" to Black male identity strivings. They discuss the phenomenon of dramaturgy or the pressure to present and perform one's identity and the stress raised by this process. Unfortunately, false images of manhood perpetuate hypervulnerability.

The more one experiences pressures to "show oneself" and demonstrate masculine competency, the greater the hypervulnerability. The reason is that "showing off" one's manhood is an emotionally immature process. This manhood is insecure and is based on what one does rather than who one is. Insecure masculinity comprises a set of behaviors driven by fear to prove to the world that one's manhood isn't weak, yet these same behaviors can inadvertently increase the feelings of fear they are intended to eradicate. The problem with these dynamics and the drama that accompanies them is that African American boys and men internalize American society's ideas of insecure masculinity that resides in popular icons like the Marlboro Man and James Bond. These are men who are flawed and whose bravado and representation of power covers a multitude of sins. Unfortunately, the tragic reality is that *all* men in America fall short of the masculine images these characters depict. The goal of insecure masculinity is to "look good" regardless of one's internal reality. The fear of failure experienced by men of all ethnic, racial, and socioeconomic backgrounds—evidenced by the power struggles of domestic violence, alcoholism, substance abuse, and child abandonment—only solidifies the futility of placing one's trust in insecure masculinity development (Oliver, 1984, 1989; Stevenson, 2003).

One cannot expect boys to develop into men if the rituals, strategies, communications, and relationships are based upon a historically moribund, culturally enslaving, intergenerational dynamic of insecure masculinity. With the goal to "look good" and BE "The Man," Black youth only add some "cool pose" flavor to the mix of insecure masculinity. However, Black youth do not change the basic nature of insecure masculinity. And yes, other boys and men are emulating these Black youth by buying rap music and borrowing their urban fashion strategies. But this amounts to no more than the blind leading the blind. They are all being led by the simple but life-polarizing mission of insecure masculinity. Here an ongoing identity struggle between life and death rears its ugly head. Childhood should be full of surprises, not solely choices between good and bad. We ask Black boys to become men without experiencing a childhood or shedding a tear and wonder why they die so young. Well, it's hard to be what you don't see, but it's even harder for boys to be men before they finish living or doing boyhood.

For many of the Black male youth I work with, the best they can hope for is to fool most of the people most of the time. They have surmised this over time, often without adult feedback and supervision—but they are pondering how to cope in the world with blinders on, with only limited knowledge. The problem for African American young men is that their access to the tools and resources to look good are limited and, therefore, the cost of pretending is greater and requires greater imagination and ego-boosting psychological resources. To wear cool fashion and to make money by the quickest means possible is not original, individualistic, or entrepreneurial, if the jobs and occupations for Black youth are narrowly scripted. This presents what Stevenson and Davis (2003) have defined as a "Catch 33." They are not "leading a charge" or "making their mark" so much as they are following a script that is not as developed and broad as the scripts that the rest of the adolescent and male world have to follow (Ferguson, 2000; Majors and Billson, 1992; Spencer et al., 1995).

Unfortunately, the script is designed within white society's projected fears of Black manhood, not the self-determined efforts, experiences, and potential of Black manhood. As such, this script is corrupt and any Black male who follows it or lives his life to reject it may be corrupted along with it. To do this script is to self-destruct in the most consistent historical fashion. The vulnerability that African American young males experience is overwhelming and it precipitates violence and negative social interactions. That is, vulnerability at multiple levels and the need to protect oneself from the reality, tragedy, or possibility of one's limitations takes precedence over social etiquette or civility.

The lack of access to the goals and means for men on the periphery of societal existence and on the outskirts of the mainstream experience has been written by sociologists for decades, but often without a contemporary focus on the cultural-ecological implications for Black boys and men. The struggle of African American identity in the bodies, souls, and minds of adolescent boys is unique. The outward appearances of Black male youth are limited and truncated compared to others, and while they can reshape these appearances, true freedom can only come if they recreate their image and redefine the questions for themselves. They must expend most, if not all, of this energy on their own perceptions, not the perceptions of others. History teaches us that it is a huge waste of time and talent to try and reshape the larger societal racist perception.

A lack of trust seems to continually perpetuate Black-on-Black violence. For many boys, the "homies" that they trust the most are ultimately not trustworthy (see Way, this volume). Again, another example of hypervulnerability is when you fear that the friends you "hang with" or your family could betray you. This reality fits with the finding that friend-acquaintance homicide is six times higher for Black youth than for Whites (Children's Defense Fund, 2000). This is likely true for those youth who haven't developed bonding relationships with homies beyond the superficial hanging together types of relationships. Of course, some friendships develop that are closer than family and that have long-lasting and life-supportive characteristics. But where the fear of betrayal or the withholding of trust predominates one's best friend relationships, hypervulnerability is mediating this experience. Hypervulnerability is the flimsy crazy glue that holds this relationship together and fighting against the ultimate death is the cause celebre.

In summary, hypervulnerability is influenced by a lack of awareness of the basic societal structural barriers of racism, internalization of an insecure hypermasculinized social interaction, an overreliance on materialism as a statement of one's identity, a lack of understanding and thus a failure to reject negative Black male imaging, a lack of supportive peer and family relationships, a sense that one is sole protector of emotional and physical existence, and a tendency to engage with peers who are not trustworthy. The fear of rejection in social interactions is a behavioral sign of this hypervulnerability.

Racial Socialization as a Buffer to Hypervulnerability

Racial socialization involves the deliberate and indirect communications and interactions toward others about the importance of one's history, cultural values, and behaviors and about how other persons, social groups, and institutions perceive, challenge, or appreciate one's history, values, and behaviors. Adolescents' experiences of racial socialization have been related to various prosocial behaviors and emotions including academic success (Bowman & Howard, 1985), self-esteem in home, school, and peer contexts reduced anger experience and increased anger control (Stevenson, Herrero-Taylor & Cameron, in press), and reduced fighting behavior (Herrero-Taylor, Mitchell & Stevenson, in press; Stevenson et al., 2002a). In light of these findings, it is conceivable that the socialization of cultural empowerment and social oppression dynamics may be associated with less hypervulnerability or the fear of rejection among Black male youth.

In this study, I ask two basic questions. The first examines whether hypervulnerability (i.e., the experiences of rejection sensitivity) is influenced by neighborhood safety. The second question examines whether racial socialization buffers the experience of hypervulnerability.

Method

Participants and Setting

Participants in this study were 167 African American male adolescents between the ages of 13 and 15 (mean age of 14.1) who had a history of anger and aggression and who were enrolled in a disciplinary school in a Northeastern city in the United States. The boys' referral to the school was based on one or both of the following offenses: weapon violations or a series of aggressive assaults on school personnel or classmates.

Measures

HYPERVULNERABILITY

In order to assess levels of hypervulnerability, I assessed a core component of this concept, namely, rejection sensitivity. The measure of rejection sensitivity that I used is the Children's Rejection Sensitivity Questionnaire (CRSQ) which is based on the work by Downey et al. (1998). The CRSQ measures the extent to which youth anxiously or angrily *expect rejection before* or *react to rejection after* an ambiguously intentioned rejection. The CRSQ has two parts on *rejection expectation* and *rejection reaction*. Part One presents youth with twelve hypothetical interpersonal situations. Six situations pertain to peers and six to teachers. Each vignette presents scenarios, which may be perceived as benign or rejecting, but which have not been resolved. The participant reads (or listens to) the unfinished scenarios and imagines what the characters' motives and scenario outcomes may be.

Each scenario is followed by two questions regarding one's anxiety and anger at the *expectation* of being rejected by the peer or teacher in the scenario. The anxiety and anger responses range from 1, "not nervous" or "not mad," to 6, "very, very nervous" or "very, very mad" and yield scores for anxious expectation and angry expectation. High scores in these two areas represent the anxious or angry expectation of rejection, and low scores indicate the expectation of acceptance. A third question asks how likely it is for rejection to occur in the scenario. Here, the participant indicates the likelihood that the other person will accept or reject them (e.g., "Do you think they were saying bad things about you?"), on a scale ranging from 1, "YES!!!," to 6, "NO!!!" This expectation of rejection is labeled either "Rejection Expectation Anxiety" or "Rejection Expectation Anger" in the remainder of the chapter.

Part Two of the CRSQ restates two of the vignettes from Part One and focuses on the participants' *reaction to* an ambiguously intentioned rejection. Specifically, a measure of the extent to which youth show angry feelings, thoughts, and behavior in *reaction* to rejection was used in this study. In assessing participants' angry reactions to rejection, participants answered how they would respond to scenarios in which a teacher or peer treated them in ways that may be perceived as rejecting. For example, in one scenario, the youth needs help picking up his spilled groceries from the ground. When he sees fellow classmates walking by, he asks them for help. They walk quickly by, as if they don't see him. The respondents are then asked to answer the question, "If this happened to you, how would you feel?" The participants are asked to indicate the degree to which each statement applies to them by answering on a three-point Likert scale ranging from ("Very True," "Sort of True," or "Not True"). Examples of possible angry reactions to perceived rejection included the following: "I would feel like hitting those kids," "I would remember their faces, and next time I see them, I'll find a way to get back at them," and "I would feel mad at those kids because they should have stayed to help me." Given that an angry reaction to rejection involves an emotional reaction and a behavioral plan to respond, it is labeled "Rejection Reaction Anger" for the remainder of this chapter. Downey and colleagues (1998) found that the CRSQ yielded alpha reliability coefficients of 0.72 and above, has strong test-retest reliability, and is reliable for use with urban, low-income, ethnic minority adolescent populations.

RACIAL SOCIALIZATION

A measure of racial socialization (Teenage Experience of Racial Socialization) was used to assess adolescent responses about the frequency of parental racial socialization strategies (Stevenson et al., 2002b). The items assess, on a three-point scale, the frequency of various behaviors. As a result of a factor analysis, five factors were identified. Factor 1 is called *Cultural Coping with Antagonism (CCA)* and includes items that represent messages about the importance of coping with racial hostilities and the role that spirituality and religion play in that coping. Factor 2 includes items that assess exposure to positive attitudes about and knowledge of African American culture and is entitled *Cultural Pride Reinforcement (CPR)*. Factor 3 is called *Cultural Legacy Appreciation (CLA)* and includes items about cultural heritage issues such as enslavement and knowing about the history of African Americans. Factor 4 is called *Cultural Alertness to Discrimination (CAD)* and includes exposure to messages that teach youth to be aware of the barriers of racism in society and the multiple race relation challenges between Blacks and Whites. Factor 5 is called *Cultural Endorsement of the Mainstream (CEM)* and represents messages about the relative importance of majority culture institutions and values and the affective and educational benefits that African Americans can receive by being involved in those institutions.

The mean and standard deviation for the total scale was 85.9 ($SD =$ 14.9), and the Cronbach's alpha for the scale was 0.91 ($n = 260$). The reliability for each of the five factors is good and above an alpha of 0.71. The combination of these five factors makes up a racial socialization scale that appreciates the interrelationship of these varied experiences. A well-rounded understanding of the politics of race and its effects on life, identity, and character requires a knowledge of each of these areas.

For this study, a cluster analytic procedure was conducted using all five factors as key variables. Four meaningful racial socialization clusters were developed: (1) very prepared for coping with the external world, (2) moderately prepared for coping with the external world, (3) underprepared for dealing with the external world, and (4) unprepared. These names were subsequently changed to lots, some, little, and very little experience with racial socialization, respectively, for easier interpretation of results. The cluster identified as "lots" includes individuals who scored high on all five factors, while the "very little" cluster includes individuals with the lowest mean scores on all five factors. For more information on the cluster strategy and analyses, see Stevenson (2002).

NEIGHBORHOOD SAFETY

One question asked "How safe do you feel living on your neighborhood block?" The responses were reduced into groups of three ("Less Than Safe," "Somewhat Safe," and "Safe") or two ("Safe" versus "Less Than Safe") depending upon the type of analysis conducted.

Data Analyses

One-way analyses of variance (ANOVAs) were conducted to assess the effects of either neighborhood safety or racial socialization experiences (RSE) on hypervulnerability (i.e., rejection sensitivity), and a multivariate analysis of variance (MANOVAs) was conducted to assess the joint effects of neighborhood safety and RSE on hypervulnerability.

Results

Findings from a one-way ANOVA indicate that participants who reported living in "safe" neighborhoods showed significantly lower levels of rejection sensitivity (i.e., Rejection Expectation Anxiety and Rejection Expectation Anger) than boys who lived in either "less than safe" or "somewhat safe" neighborhoods (see Figure 3.1). The association between neighborhood safety and Rejection Reaction Anger was not significant.

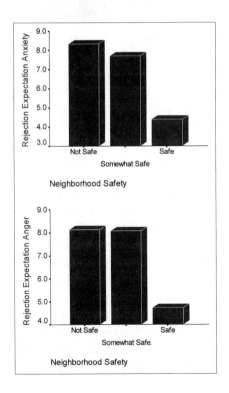

Figure 3.1. Association between Neighborhood Safety and Rejection Expectation Anxiety or Rejection Expectation Anger

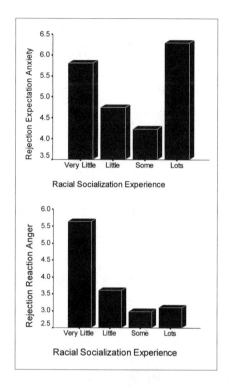

Figure 3.2. Association between Racial Socialization and Rejection Expectation Anxiety or Rejection Reaction Anger

A one-way ANOVA also revealed that higher levels of racial socialization messages were significantly associated with lower levels of Rejection Reaction Anger (see Figure 3.2). It appears that the more parents talk to their children about coping with antagonism, managing mainstream values, and having pride in their cultural legacy, the less boys will feel angry when rejected and perhaps the less likely they will find themselves in self-destructive situations. However, it was also found that those boys who reported the highest levels of racial socialization reported the highest levels of Rejection Expectation Anxiety. This could be a result of a greater level of awareness of the historical, cultural, and complex societal challenges to Black culture, life, and manhood. The association between racial socialization and Rejection Expectation Anger was not significant.

Results from a multivariate analysis of variance analysis[1] indicate in Figure 3.3 that boys with "very little" racial socialization from "less than safe" neighborhoods show significantly higher levels of rejection sensitivity (i.e., Rejection Expectation Anxiety and Rejection Reaction Anger)

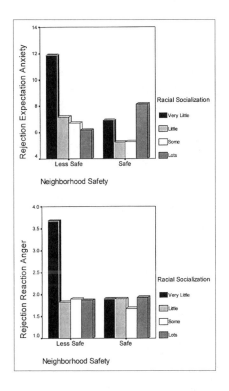

Figure 3.3. Association between Neighborhood Safety and Racial Socialization and Rejection Expectation Anxiety or Rejection Reaction Anger

compared to boys with more racial socialization experience in safe neighborhoods. Figure 3.3 also reveals that boys from safe neighborhoods who receive lots of racial socialization also have slightly elevated levels of Rejection Expectation Anxiety.

Discussion

This study explored the hypervulnerability, as defined by their sensitivity to rejection, of African American boys with a history of anger and aggression. Findings suggested that neighborhood safety was associated with lower levels of anxiety and anger when expecting rejection from peers and teachers. It appears that rejection sensitivity is influenced by residential security. Youth who feel safer in their neighborhoods may be less likely to expect rejection because the systemic dangers that can trigger one's hypervulnerability (e.g., having to fight to prove masculinity, negotiating bullies more frequently, and the increased danger of loss of life) are minimized. In addition, racial socialization was associated with lower levels of anger when rejection episodes occurred. Racial socialization may help youth cognitively and emotionally manage the complexity of negative male images, overmasculinized identity development, and the internalization of insecure masculinity and racist stereotypes. Findings, however, also indicated that those who experience a lot of racial socialization from their families report high anxiety levels in anticipation of rejection. Future research needs to explore why this may be the case. Racial socialization may enhance their awareness of potential rejection and this may increase their anxiety while at the same time decrease their level of anger in response to episodes of rejection.

Implications for Nurturing Boys, Not Men

Professionals and researchers often remain clueless about the social and cultural contexts of Black males, about the functionality of violent behavior, and about how to translate these contexts and experiences into intervention. Ignoring how hypervulnerability reflects a heightened sense of gender and racial identity confusion for boys will only exacerbate the problem of Black male stigmatization. Training professionals to respond to the invisibility of Black male youth is helpful but can't fully address the problem of modern racism. True intervention in this conundrum of "missed, dissed, and pissed" Black youth requires that Black families start the training at home. To expect the mental health establishment to appreciate these larger societal machinations is overly optimistic. Schools are also major socializing agents, but without explicit discussions of the politics of race and gender for Black males, these contexts are unlikely to be safe environments for Black males to find a healthy emotional and cultural identity.

Traditional strategies of psychoeducation, psychotherapy, and intervention are not effective for Black male youth who live in a different world than the one that created these strategies (Lurie, 1999). It is not to say that Black male youth cannot be insightful, cannot appreciate discussing their emotional pain, or cannot learn how to increase self-control through therapeutic challenge of cognitive distortions. On the contrary, African American boys are still boys who desire affection, protection, *and* correction (Stevenson, Davis & Abdul-Kabir, 2001) and this study suggests that when neighborhood dangers are not a threat, they can ponder the deeper meanings of structural racism. However, traditional intervention and research strategies have missed the mark of what is psychologically and dynamically going on for Black boys. Consequently, not only are different and culturally relevant intervention strategies necessary, but without them, traditional approaches are likely to continue to perpetuate the perception that Black male youth require "patrol and control," not caring and prevention.

Given the detrimental effects of societal and institutional racism on Black male youth, culturally relevant interventions must emphasize racial socialization and be relationship-centered. A greater appreciation by the professionals of the real and perceived dangers in the residential and social neighborhoods of Black youth must be developed, yet the structural and invisible dangers of race and gender must not be overlooked as we attempt to "clean up the neighborhoods." Black males must learn that they are not a lost generation. They deserve to be touched emotionally, physically, and intellectually and are capable of learning about and critically outmaneuvering the subtleties of American racism. They need what all boys need—care and compassion.

One project, PLAAY (Preventing Long-term Anger and Aggression in Youth) attempts to address these issues through the novel integration of athletic movement and racial socialization (Stevenson, Hassan, et al., 2001). This project attempts to engage boys in athletic activities such as basketball and martial arts or drama, all activities where the goal is to influence emotional functioning during intense physical activities. The basketball component, TEAM (Teaching Emotional Empowerment during Athletic Movement), allows for multiple interpersonal conflicts within which staff can intervene to maintain the athletic interactions as safe contexts for emotional and physical expression by the boys. Basically, manhood can be challenged and developed "in-the-moment" of vulnerability when insecure masculine tactics are likely to be used by boys unaware of the deeper gender and racial politics. Racial socialization strategies are more directly taught during CPR (Cultural Pride Reinforcement) psychoeducational group therapy sessions where the cultural relevant style of "barbershop debating" is one of several mechanisms to get the boys to think and feel about their racial and gender status in the world. CPR is given such a name because of its importance to life and limb for Black males but it is also the place where strategies to combat insecure masculinity and the internalization of racial stereotyping can be learned. Several other components accompany TEAM and CPR, including parent empowerment sessions (Community Outreach through Parent Empowerment) where parents also receive racial socialization strategies in addition to emotional support for their marginalized positions in society.

It is critical to challenge the exoticization of Black males with a variety of histories and experiences and begin to focus on nurturing strategies instead. This study suggests that context, not image, explains more of their emotional responses within a world still intent on seeing them as something other than who they really are—boys.

NOTE

1. A MANOVA involving the three factors of the rejection sensitivity measure (rejection sensitive anger, rejection sensitive anxiety, and rejection reactive anger) showed significant results for racial socialization experience (Wilks's lambda = 0.82, Multivariate F (3,115) = 2.22, $p < .02$) and for neighborhood safety by racial socialization experience (Wilks's lambda = 0.94, (3,119) Multivariate; $F = 2.62$, $p < .01$). No main effect was found for rejection sensitive anger in any of the analyses involving racial socialization.

REFERENCES

American Civil Liberties Union (ACLU). (2000). *Report/study on racial profiling in Pennsylvania.* http://www.aclupa.org/report.htm.

Bowman, P. J. & Howard, C. (1985). Race-related socialization, motivation, and academic achievement: A study of Black youths in three-generation families. *Journal of the American Academy of Child Psychiatry, 24,* 131–141.

Buka, S. L., Stichick, T. L., Birdthistle, I. & Earls, F. J. (2001). Youth exposure to violence: Prevalence, risks, and consequences. *American Journal of Orthopsychiatry, 71,* 298–310.

Children's Defense Fund. (2000). *Disproportionate minority confinement (DMC).* Available: http://www.childrensdefense.org/ss_violence_jj_dmc.htm.

Downey, G., Lebolt, A., Rincon, C. & Freitas, A. L. (1998). Rejection sensitivity and children's interpersonal difficulties. *Child Development, 69,* 1072–1089.

Ferguson, A. A. (2000). *Bad boys: Public schools in the making of black masculinity.* Ann Arbor: University of Michigan Press.

Finkelman, P. (1992). *Lynching, racial violence, and law.* New York: Garland Publishing.

Franklin, A. J. & Franklin, N. B. (2000). Invisibility syndrome: A clinical model of the effects of racism on African American males. *American Journal of Orthopsychiatry, 70,* 1, 33–41.

Gibbs, J. T. (1988). *Young, black, and male in America: An endangered species.* Dover, MA: Auburn.

Goffman, E. (1959). *The presentation of self in everyday life.* Garden City, NY: Doubleday.

Hawkins, W. E., Hawkins, M. J., Sabatino, C. & Ley, S. (1998). Relationship of perceived future opportunity to depressive symptomatology of inner-city African American adolescents. *Children and Youth Services Review, 20,* 757–764.

Herrero-Taylor, T., Mitchell, E. R. & Stevenson, H. C. (in press). Extending the buffer zone: Further examination of racial socialization, neighborhood risk, and anger expression in African American adolescents. In M. Spencer (Ed.), *Identity in context.* Mahwah, NJ: Erlbaum.

Kunjufu, J. (1985). *Countering the conspiracy to destroy black boys,* vol. 1. Chicago, IL: African American Images.

Lurie, S. (1999). Child psychiatrists address problem of youth violence. *The Journal of the American Medical Association, 28,* 282.

Majors, R. & Billson, J. M. (1992). *Cool pose: The dilemmas of Black manhood in America.* New York: Lexington Books.

McIntyre, L. D. & Pernell, E. (1985). The impact of race on teacher recommendations for special education placement. *Journal of Multicultural Counseling and Development, 13(3),* 112–120.

Oliver, W. (1984). Black males and the tough guy image: A dysfunctional compensatory adaptation. *Western Journal of Black Studies, 8,* 199–203.

Oliver, W. (1989). Black males and social problems: Prevention through Afrocentric socialization. *Journal of Black Studies, 20,* 1, 15–39.

Osofsky, J. D., Wewers, S., Hann, D. N. & Fick, A. C. (1993). Chronic community violence: What is happening to our children? *Psychiatry: Interpersonal and Biological Processes, 56,* 36–45.

Potts, R. G. (1997). The social construction and social marketing of the "Dangerous Black Man." *Journal of African American Men, 2,* 11–24.

Richters, J. E. & Martinez, P. (1993). The NIMH community violence project: I. Children as victims of and witnesses to violence. *Psychiatry, 56,* 7–21.

Romer, D., Jamieson, K. H. & de Coteau, N. J. (1998). The treatment of persons of color in local television news: Ethnic blame discourse or realistic group conflict? *Communication Research, 25(3),* 286–305.

Rowan, G. T., Pernell, E. & Akers, T. A. (1996). Gender role socialization in African American men: A conceptual framework. *Journal of African American Men, 1,* 3–22.

Sampson, R. J. & Laub, J. H. (1993). Structural variations in juvenile court processing: Inequality, the underclass, and social control. *Law and Society Review, 27,* 285–311.

Spencer, M. B., Cunningham, M. & Swanson, D. P. (1995). Identity as coping: Adolescent African-American males' adaptive responses to high-risk environment.

In Herbert W. Harris, Howard Blue et al. (Eds.), *Racial and ethnic identity: Psychological development and creative expression* (pp. 31–52). New York: Routledge.

Stevenson, H. C. (1997). "Missed, dissed, and pissed": Making meaning of neighborhood risk, fear and anger management in Black youth. *Cultural Diversity and Mental Health, 3,* 37–52.

Stevenson, H. C. (1998). Theoretical considerations in measuring racial identity and socialization: Extending the self further. In R. Jones (Ed.), *African American identity development: Theory, research, and intervention* (pp. 227–263). Hampton, VA: Cobb and Henry.

Stevenson, H. C. (2002). *Prepared or not prepared? Cluster analysis of the teenager experience of racial socialization scale.* Unpublished manuscript, University of Pennsylvania.

Stevenson, H. C. (2003). *Playing with anger: Teaching emotional coping skills to African American boys via athletics and culture.* Westport, CT: Greenwood Publishing, Praeger.

Stevenson, H. C., Cameron, R., Herrero-Taylor, T. & Davis, G. (2002a). Mitigating instigation: Cultural phenomenological influences of anger and fighting among "big-boned and baby-faced" in African American youth. *Journal of Youth and Adolescence, 31,* 473–485.

Stevenson, H. C., Cameron, R., Herrero-Taylor, T. & Davis, G. Y. (2002b). Development of the teenage experience of racial socialization scale: Correlates of race-related socialization from the perspective of Black youth. *Journal of Black Psychology, 28,* 84–106.

Stevenson, H. C. & Davis, G. Y. (2003). Racial socialization. In R. Jones (Ed.), *Black psychology,* 4th ed. Hampton, VA: Cobb and Henry.

Stevenson, H. C. & Davis, G. Y. (in press). Applied racial socialization and the catch 33: The meta-art of balancing intolerance, survival, and self-actualization. In R. Jones (Ed.), *Black psychology,* 5th ed. Hampton, VA: Cobb and Henry.

Stevenson, H. C., Davis, G. Y. & Abdul-Kabir, S. (2001). *Stickin' to, watchin' over, and gettin' with: African American parent's guide to discipline.* San Francisco: Jossey-Bass.

Stevenson, H. C., Hassan, N., Lassiter, C., Davis, G., Abdul-Kabir, S., Cassidy, E., Fry, D., Mendoza-Denton, R., Yancy, R., Purdie, V. & Best, G. (2001). *The PLAAY project: Preventing long-term anger and aggression in youth.* In the *Conference Proceedings of the National Men's Health and Fitness Conference.* June 1999. Sponsored by the Philadelphia Department of Public Health.

Stevenson, H. C., Herrero-Taylor, T. & Cameron, R. (in press). Buffer zone: Impact of racial socialization experiences and neighborhood dangers and resources on anger expression in African American adolescents. In D. Johnson & A. Hunter (Eds.), *Racial socialization: Ecologies of child and adolescent development,* part of a series in advances in African American psychology (R. Jones, Series Editor). Hampton, VA: Cobb and Henry.

Watts, R. J. & Abdul-Adil, J. K. (1997). Promoting critical consciousness in young, African-American men. *Journal of Prevention and Intervention in the Community, 16* (1–2), 63–86.

West, C. (1993). *Race matters.* Boston: Beacon Press.

Wilson, A. N. (1990). *Black-on-black violence.* Bronx, NY: African World InfoSystems.

4

A Relational Perspective
on Adolescent Boys' Identity Development

Judy Y. Chu

> This may sound completely absurd but it's questionable
> whether it's right to tell people—it's obviously right, but
> whether it's realistic to tell people that, you know, it
> doesn't matter the way you are, because really, I mean re-
> ally, it does. I mean, that's the way things are.
>   —Taylor, age 15

Much of recent literature on boys has focused on ways in which boys' socialization toward culturally prescribed conventions of masculinity can be
detrimental to boys' development. For instance, clinicians propose that
pressures for boys to accommodate images of masculinity that emphasize
physical toughness, emotional stoicism, and projected self-sufficiency can
diminish boys' sensitivities to people's feelings, including their own (Kindlon & Thompson, 1999), and undermine boys' abilities to achieve intimacy in their relationships (Pollack, 1998). Similarly, researchers suggest
that boys' gender socialization may result in gender role strain, for instance when their failure to conform to masculine standards leads to feelings of inadequacy, when they are traumatized by pressures to conform to
masculine norms, and when they internalize masculine ideals that inherently are not conducive to their overall well-being (Pleck, 1995). Studies
have also shown that adolescent boys who internalize conventional norms
of masculinity tend to exhibit more problem behaviors (Pleck, Sonenstein
& Ku, 1994) and have lower levels of self-esteem (Chu, Porche & Tolman,

in press). In short, this literature suggests that boys' gender socialization may have negative consequences for boys' psychological health, social behaviors, and relationships, despite social advantages of emulating cultural constructions of masculinity.

While these theories and findings have raised important questions about the course and purpose of boys' development, there has been a tendency in this discourse to conceptualize boys' gender socialization as a linear model of cause-and-effect wherein cultural messages about masculinity are introduced and directly impact boys' attitudes and behaviors. In focusing primarily on social aspects, such as the content of the messages boys receive and the sources of pressure in boys' lives to accommodate these messages, this literature tends to objectify boys by depicting them as passive participants in, or even victims of, their gender socialization (e.g., Pollack, 1998). Seldom considered are psychological aspects, such as the ways in which boys experience and make meaning of cultural messages and social pressures to which they are exposed, and how boys are thereby able to mediate the effects of their gender socialization on their developmental outcomes.

With regards to boys' identity development in particular, recent discourse is further limited in its tendency to focus on the extent to which a boy fits a particular construction of masculinity and on the consequences of aligning oneself too closely or deviating too much. As active participants in their identity development, boys are responsive in the sense that they have the capacity to internalize and resist masculine norms and ideals that manifest, for instance, through other people's expectations for and assumptions about them. However, boys are also creative in the sense that they construct their identities, or senses of self, in ways that reflect their individual experiences as well as their cognitive abilities. Therefore, in order to arrive at a more comprehensive understanding of adolescent boys' identity development, it is important to consider how boys are influenced by cultural messages and social pressures but also how boys draw on their continually evolving self-knowledge and conceptions of reality as they develop an understanding of who they are and what they are like.

Examining Boys' Development through a Relational Framework

In this chapter, I present two cases from a larger qualitative study that examined boys' development through a relational framework (Chu, 1998,

1999). Focusing on boys as active participants in their gender socialization, my study investigated how boys negotiate their senses of self, behaviors, and styles of relating in light of cultural constructions of masculinity that they encounter in their interpersonal relationships. Against a backdrop of literature suggesting that boys' gender socialization causes them to become disconnected from themselves (e.g., unable to recognize or articulate their own thoughts and feelings) and disconnected from others (e.g., unable to develop close, mutual relationships), I was interested to learn from boys how their experiences of gender socialization might undermine or lead them to shield their connection to self, connection to others, and genuine self-expression. I was also interested in how boys may preserve their relational ways of being by resisting and/or challenging pressures associated with their gender socialization (Chu, 2000).

While the importance of relationships is widely acknowledged in developmental and psychological theory (Erikson, 1968; Piaget, 1954; Vygotsky, 1978), what distinguishes a relational framework is that it starts from the premise that all humans have a fundamental capacity and desire for close, mutual relationships (Trevarthan, 1979; Tronick, 1989; Tronick & Gianino, 1986; Weinberg & Tronick, 1996), and that our senses of self (e.g., how we see and understand ourselves to be) are inextricably embedded in our interpersonal relationships as well as our sociocultural environments (Gilligan, Brown & Rogers, 1990). In highlighting the centrality of relationships in people's lives (Gilligan, 1996; Jordan et al., 1991; Miller, 1994), a relational framework emphasizes the fact that human development occurs not in isolation with the *option* of having relationships but primarily *through and within* our relationships with other people (Gilligan, 1982; Miller, 1976). Thus, a relational framework calls into question models of development that focus on individuation and separation to determine maturity and health.

With the goal to learn about boys' experiences from boys' own perspectives, I adopted a relational approach to psychological inquiry (Brown & Gilligan, 1992), which conceptualizes the study of people's experiences as a practice of relationships and emphasizes the fact that the nature of data collected depends in part on qualities of the researcher-participant relationship (Brown et al., 1988; Brown & Gilligan, 1990). Given that the boys' willingness to share their experiences with me would be determined by the dynamics of our interactions and also by their perceptions of me, I centered my research methods on developing comfortable and trusting relationships between the boys and myself, and noted how I engaged and responded to these boys as well as how they engaged and responded to me within these relationships. In my study, I also started from a position of not knowing and explained to the boys that, because I am female and therefore do not know what it is like to be a boy, I would be looking to them as my teachers and relying on them to help me understand their experiences.

A School for Boys

The participants in my study were 58 adolescent boys (ages 12–18) attending a private boys' secondary school (grades 7–12) in New England. Of these boys, 82.8% were White, 12.1% African American, and 5.2% Asian American. Most of these boys came from middle- and upper-middle-class families and planned to attend colleges and universities after graduating. Although this population of boys (i.e., predominantly White, middle-class) has been the focus of recent discourse on boys and past psychological and developmental studies, few researchers have investigated boys' experiences from boys' own perspectives among this group (much less other populations of boys). Thus, the complexities and nuances of their lives are seldom represented in the literature.

Over the course of one academic year, I collected data with these boys using qualitative observation and interview methods. I began in the fall by engaging in weekly ethnographic observations that enabled me to establish rapport with potential interviewees through informal contact and casual interactions. In other words, I spent time "hanging out" with these boys so they could inquire about my intentions and get to know me, and so I could get to know them as individuals. Most of my observations took place in common areas at the school during "free periods." However, at the boys' suggestion, I also observed classes in session and attended after-school activities, including sports practices and play rehearsals, in order to develop a fuller sense of these boys' various contexts and relationships at school. In short, I told the boys that I was interested in learning about their lives and experiences and they generously took me under their wing, so to speak, and let me know what I should be sure to see. By the end of the fall semester, the boys had become familiar with me and were accustomed to having me around. For instance, at a sports event when a parent noticed me and asked one of the boys who I was, he casually replied, "Oh, that's just Judy. She's here to study us." As the boys pointed out, my taking the time to develop this sense of comfort and trust with them turned out to be crucial to eliciting their honest thoughts and opinions when it came time for my interviews.

During the spring, I conducted semi-structured, one-on-one interviews while continuing my observations. Interviewees were recruited on a volunteer basis and written consent was obtained from each boy's parent or guardian. Each interview began with a brief explanation of my research interests (e.g., "I'm interested in learning about how ideas about masculinity, like what it means to be a man—being strong, being tough, whatever—how that affects the way you think about yourself and your identity, the way you act, if it affects the way you act, and your relationships") and a question about whether, as males, they have ever felt like they were expected to act or be a certain way. For the most part, I then allowed the boys to introduce topics and issues that they felt were central and/or significant in their lives. As I followed the boys' leads, my questions served primarily to encourage the boys to elaborate on their experiences so that I might better understand their meaning. Given this open-ended format, the boys typically talked about their relationships with peers, friends, family, and other adults (e.g., school faculty and staff), as well as their personal interests and aspirations. Occasionally, if a boy was shy or hesitant, I tried more actively to initiate conversation by asking questions based on topics that other boys had raised, for instance about their relationships and interests in and out of school.

Observational and interview data were analyzed using conceptually clustered matrices (Miles & Huberman, 1994) and also a voice-centered method (Brown et al., 1988; Brown & Gilligan, 1990, 1991; Gilligan et al., in press). Whereas the conceptually clustered matrices were used to identify distinct, recurring, and organizing principles or ideas in the data, the voice-centered method was used to focus this analysis on themes pertaining to the boys' developing senses of self, and to note patterns and shifts in the boys' self-expression around these themes. The creation of conceptually clustered matrices involved organizing excerpts from the boys' interview narratives by boy (columns) and according to themes (rows) to enable comparisons across individuals. The application of a voice-centered method involved multiple readings of the text to highlight the content of what was said (e.g., issues and topics that were addressed) and also ways in which the boys represented themselves and other people in describing their experiences.

Specifically, the first reading of the voice-centered method served to determine the plot (e.g., who, what, when, where, why) of each episode or excerpt and to document the "reader's response," and thereby account for my presence, influence, and reactions as I observed the boys' interactions, engaged them during interviews, and interpreted their narratives. Thus, considerations of how my own identity, biases, and relationships with these boys affected the interpersonal dynamics of my observations and interviews were also integral to this analysis. The second reading involved tracking the boys' modes of self-expression. For instance, when referring to themselves, the boys' use of the first person pronoun "I" was compared with their use of "you," which could extend to people in general (e.g., "you always have to keep up your guard"), and with their use of "we," which indicated a partnership or group of which they felt a part (e.g., "we helped each other a lot"). The boys' use of "they" to refer to a nonspecific group of others (e.g., "kids just attack . . . if they think you're vulnerable") was also examined. The third and fourth readings focused on the boys' perceptions of how other people see them (e.g., adults' expectations and assumptions regarding boys in general and them in particular) and how they see themselves (e.g., the boys' notions of who they are and what they are like) to examine how these perceptions intertwined with and influenced each other, as evidenced in the boys' descriptions.

Selves in Relationship

Contrary to popular discourse that tends to portray adolescent boys as emotionally deficient and relationally impaired, analyses of these data, particularly the boys' interview narratives, revealed these boys to be clearly capable of thoughtful self-reflection and deep interpersonal understanding. These analyses also revealed ways in which the boys' senses of self are embedded in cultural constructions of masculinity, as typically encountered through other people's expectations and assumptions. Consistent with relational theories of development, the boys' senses of self obviously are not self-generated, as though the boys exist in a vacuum. Rather, the boys negotiate their senses of self in light of their experiences in relationships with specific individuals (e.g., friends and family) and with their broader social contexts (e.g., school community).

A pervasive theme in the boys' interview narratives concerned discrepancies that the boys perceived between how other people see them and how they see themselves. The boys were familiar with the masculine norms and stereotypes that influence people's views of boys in general and of them in particular. The boys therefore understood why people might expect them to be rugged and athletic or assume that they are rebellious, disinterested, and oblivious to interpersonal cues. Nevertheless, the boys struggled with the inaccuracies and limitations of these depictions, which seemed to constrain their possibilities of being recognized and valued for the full range of their qualities and abilities. Moreover, the boys' descriptions suggest that the ways in which they reconcile these discrepancies may ultimately shape their senses of self.

An examination of ways in which the boys reconciled discrepancies between other people's views of them and their own views revealed two dominant patterns of response. Both patterns could be seen to some extent in most of the boys in this sample but varied in their prominence across individual boys. One pattern involves internalizing or yielding to other people's views, particularly expectations that reflect cultural norms and ideals, sometimes to the effect of changing how one sees oneself. The other pattern involves resisting or overcoming other people's views, particularly assumptions based on stereotypes and misconceptions, sometimes to the effect of changing how one is seen by others.

These patterns call to mind Piaget's (1954) concepts of assimilation and accommodation, which he used to describe how young children interact with their environmental contexts. Through assimilation, individuals modify environmental input to fit with their existing schemas and conceptions (and thereby resist the imposition of social and cultural constructions). Taken to an extreme, assimilation can result in egocentrism and possibly disconnections from one's relationships and social realities. Through accommodation, individuals modify their existing schemas and conceptions in light of new experiences of their environments (e.g., by internalizing social and cultural constructions). Taken to an extreme, accommodation can result in social conformity and possibly psychological dissociation, or a decreased awareness of one's own thoughts, feelings, and desires. Just as Piaget suggests that healthy development arises through the balanced interplay of assimilation and accommodation, one could define a boy's healthy sense of self in terms of his ability to consider without necessarily succumbing to other people's views of him.

An exploration of differences between boys who were inclined to yield to other people's expectations and boys who managed to resist other people's assumptions indicated that relationships may be key to boys' resilience as they strive to develop a sense of self that feels true to themselves and also grounded in reality. Recent studies have shown that having access to a confiding relationship is the single best protector against psychological and social risks for adolescents (Masten, 1994; Masten & Coatsworth, 1998; Resnick et al., 1997; Rutter, 1990; Wang, Haertel & Walberg, 1994; Werner & Smith, 1982). Findings from this analysis further suggest that, beyond having access to relationships, the ways in which boys experience themselves in their relationships (e.g., as being understood and valued by others) are also crucial to their psychological adjustment and social well-being. For instance, boys who felt misunderstood or misrepresented in their relationships seemed more susceptible to internalizing other people's expectations, even at the cost of discounting their own perspective. In contrast, boys who felt known and validated in their relationships seemed better supported to resist other people's assumptions, perhaps to the effect of preserving their integrity.

In the following sections, I present an example of each of these two patterns (i.e., of internalization and resistance) to offer insight into ways in which adolescent boys' experiences in relationships can support or undermine their resistance and subsequently influence their senses of self. The boys described in these examples are similar in a number of ways. Both come from White middle-class families living in suburban neighborhoods. Both have access to relationships, particularly friendships, in which they feel supported. Both feel that they are regarded within their school community as not fitting conventional norms of masculinity. However, their experiences of self-in-relationships differ such that one struggles despite his friendships to fit in within the school community while the other manages through the support of his friendships to create a niche within the school community where he can fit in and be how he wants to be. Of course, these examples are not intended to represent or be easily generalized to the experiences of all boys everywhere. Rather, they were selected because they point to issues and concerns that were commonly mentioned by the boys in this study and yet seem under-represented in the literature on boys.

Taylor

For Taylor,[1] a 15-year-old sophomore, the process of negotiating his sense of self centers on his efforts to counterbalance his image as an outsider within the school community with his conviction that he is not as deviant as people believe him to be. In terms of his physical appearance, Taylor is lanky without being awkward or clumsy and has straggly blond hair that hits just below his ears. Although his attire conforms to the school's dress code—which requires students to wear a jacket and tie, a button-down shirt (tucked in), and pants (no jeans are allowed)—his appearance departs from its prim and proper image. As we meet at the end of the school day, Taylor arrives with his jacket and tie in hand, the collar of his shirt loosened, and his shirttail hanging loosely outside his pants. His style is effortless; rather than trying to project an image of nonchalance, he seems genuinely comfortable and relaxed.

During our interview, Taylor is articulate and speaks easily and openly about his experiences. While his passionate and persuasive tone indicates that this topic evokes strong feelings for him and that he has given this a lot of thought, his readiness to share his perspective and his responsiveness to my interest suggest that opportunities to express these sentiments beyond his circle of friends (or with an adult) may be rare. With Taylor, my question about whether he has ever felt like he is expected to act or be a certain way prompts a discussion about expectations that he perceives within his school environment and how not meeting these expectations has affected his status and relationships and also his sense of self in this context. As Taylor replies:

> Yeah, there's obviously an expectation for people to act a certain way, especially at an all-boys school, I think. And problems arise when you don't necessarily fall into that category. Like problems have come up, especially with me 'cause I don't necessarily fit into that category very well.

When I ask Taylor about these expectations, he suggests that they involve displaying certain behaviors and attitudes:

> Just in general, things that you would equate with masculinity. . . . It was kind [of an] expectation for kids to, I dunno, pick on each other and have a lack of interest in anything besides, you know, athletics and stuff like that. And I don't know, 'cause it's weird, I used to be a lot like that and I used to be kind of, you know, the all-around normal kind of kid up until 4th and 5th grade and then suddenly I completely changed. And I don't know what it was. I became a lot more intellectual, I guess. And there were problems at [this school] for me, in 7th and 8th grade especially, because I'd kind of look around and I'd see how kids were treating each other and I couldn't, like, relate to it at all because I didn't, you know, I couldn't fit into that.

Consistent with cultural stereotypes, Taylor perceives expectations for boys to be boisterous, indifferent to everything but sports, anti-intellectual, and insensitive. Taylor further suggests that this stereotyped image of boys is perpetuated not only among his peers but within the wider school community as well. As Taylor explains, "It was almost as if the school condoned the way kids treated each other because it was their expectation. Their attitude was, you know, 'That's the way boys act.'" It seems these expectations are not so much ideals for boys to strive toward but assumptions about how boys are and how boys act. All the same, so long as they are a part of the dominant culture of this school and in society at large, there are consequences to not meeting these expectations such that Taylor experiences problems when, as a result of becoming "more intellectual," he finds he can no longer "relate to" and "fit into" that image of being an "all-around normal kind of kid."

Being Marginalized

For Taylor, perhaps the most significant consequence of not meeting his school's expectations for boys is that it becomes difficult for him to be acknowledged within the school community for who he thinks he is. Based on his experience, Taylor suggests that people are often unable or unwilling to see beyond the fact that he does not embody the stereotyped image of boys that pervades the school's culture. As Taylor continues to describe what this image entails, he suggests:

> So much of it has to do with sports. That's almost what it is, but it's more than that. It's the, I don't know, "Boys will be boys" attitude, I guess. You know, like fooling around and, you know, doing stupid things and I feel like so many kids acted, you know—and I could never, I couldn't really act that way. . . . And one of my problems was that from early on I'd try—I was always trying to let people know who I was through doing things like, I dunno, speaking contests and poetry contests and so I kind of got a reputation as like this annoying poetry kid. And so I've had that reputation ever since 7th grade. But I guess that's the price I have to pay for not conforming.

Taylor also finds that people's views tend to be limited by dichotomous conceptions of what a boy can be. As he explains:

> Everything is either black or white. You can't be a good athlete and an actor—'cause I mean, before I came to [this school], I considered myself as

much an athlete as I did in theater, but they don't let you. It's a little as though they can't accept that idea and you either have to be, you know, the jock or you have to be, you know, the fringe, kind of. And I have problems because I'm often seen as being like the fringe of the [school] community. I don't consider myself that. I guess that's life and it's not a big deal for me.

As Taylor cannot bring himself to engage in the rambunctious behaviors and macho posturing that might help secure his masculinity and establish his worth within his school community, and while his athletic abilities are negated by his artistic interests, Taylor becomes marginalized. Moreover, in this context where not fitting "that category" overshadows other aspects of his character, the discrepancy between how others see him and how he sees himself seems inevitable and opportunities to correct other people's misconceptions seem rare. While Taylor portends his resignation to this reality ("I guess that's life") and claims that being seen as "the fringe" is "not a big deal," there is some evidence of his resistance as he continues, at least for now, to hold a different view of himself ("I don't consider my-self that").

Interestingly, in Taylor's case, being marginalized does not imply being isolated. He knows that there are others who also do not meet the school's expectations for boys and who are similarly regarded as outsiders within the school community. In fact, his friends are mostly these boys. However, while Taylor may feel connected to his friends, these relationships do not seem to be sufficient; he nevertheless longs to be accepted and valued within the wider school community. He even makes a point to distinguish himself from those, including his friends, who may feel resentment toward the culture and community that discount their differences. As Taylor ex-plains:

> Unlike a lot of people who are in my situation, I think I have less animosity toward [this school] than a lot of them do because—I mean, I like [this school] a lot more than a lot of my friends do, 'cause most of my friends don't fit that category either, but I respect [this school] because it—you know, for different reasons.

Whereas his friends may shun or rebel against expectations according to which they are deemed deviant and deficient, Taylor harbors a hope of being recognized and validated within this community. Thus, while he is not isolated, he may still feel alone.

BEING EXCLUDED

In addition to having implications for Taylor's status, not meeting his school's expectations for boys also affects how other people relate to him and how he is able (or allowed) to relate to others in this context. As he describes:

> There's a certain feeling of identity between the kids who you call, you know, masculine, you know, like "the guys," I guess. And there's a certain identity that they have that I don't think that I'll ever really have, but I may. I have it with some of my friends, but I can never have it at [this school] 'cause I'm not seen, I guess, as fitting into that category. There's a certain closeness that they have. Although I have closeness with a lot of my friends, I can never be seen with [the guys] in that situation, you know, talking about the Red Sox, even though I would with a lot of my friends.

Again, Taylor's marginalized status does not hinder his ability to have *any* relationships. In fact, Taylor suggests that the feelings of identity and closeness that he shares with his friends are comparable to what he observes among "the guys," or boys who are valued within the school community. Rather than constraining his access to relationships or even the quality of his relationships, Taylor's status mainly limits with whom he can identify and feel close (e.g., not with "the guys" or the school community as a whole). As Taylor explains,

> For instance, I had a speech a few weeks ago. I was talking about sports and stuff like that. And it was almost as if ["the guys"] rejected it, not because they rejected the ideas but they rejected the fact that I was giving it and they saw me as this kid who didn't have the right to talk about the Bruins because, "What does he know? He doesn't play hockey. He's not one of us." And that hurts because that's not really who I am. But I accept the fact and I understand why I've been, you know, put into that category [of not being one of "the guys"] and I guess I don't have any regrets.

What is remarkable about this passage is not Taylor's exclusion by "the guys," which is undoubtedly harsh, but his apparent acceptance and understanding of their rejection. Taylor's hesitation ("*I guess* I don't have any regrets") suggests that he does not fully accept his lot. However, the way in which he soon shifts from expressing his feelings and perspective ("And that hurts because that's not really who I am") to justifying his exclusion by "the guys" ("I accept the fact and I understand why . . .") suggests that his resistance against other people's views of him has begun to waiver.

Furthermore, as Taylor is excluded not only from relationships with "the guys" but from the masculine identity that "the guys" collectively embody, his sense of masculinity is also called into question. Continuing to comment on ways in which he is distanced from "the guys," Taylor describes:

> I guess it's the fact that they are able to be, you know, "guys." It's almost as if just they are able to be that and anyone [else] isn't really allowed to. . . . It's the fact that they have that male identity and they have it with, like, themselves and with the faculty members. It all comes down to, really, athletics 'cause so much of the faculty and the students, that's how they identify themselves and it's hard for someone like me to relate.

As Taylor sees it, involvement in sports not only plays a pivotal role in determining one's masculinity, popularity, and worth, but also serves as a primary means by which "the guys" bond with each other and with the school, including faculty members. Given that only a select few get to be "guys" in this context, Taylor and others like him who are not hearty athletes and thus do not "have that male identity" are left to establish themselves, at best, in opposition or as deficient in comparison to this elite and exclusive group. Likewise, with "the guys" occupying the highest or central positions of status within the school community, Taylor and his friends are relegated to subordinate positions and end up participating from the periphery. To the extent that not fitting "that category" determines who he can be (e.g., not one of "the guys"), with whom he can have relationships (e.g., not with "the guys"), and even how he can act in this context (e.g., not talking publicly about sports), Taylor's exclusion is ensured.

WISHING TO BE TRULY SEEN AND KNOWN

Taylor seems to understand why "the guys" see him as "not one of us," even though he disagrees with their view ("that's not really who I am"). He also acquiesces to the probability that, while he experiences something similar with his friends, he will never be seen as sharing common interests and goals ("a certain feeling of identity") or having an intimate connection ("a certain closeness") with "the guys" and with the school community. However, he struggles with how his alleged deviance stifles his everyday interactions. As Taylor observes:

> It's hard for certain teachers and certain kids to relate to someone like me who doesn't necessarily embody that sort of identity. Although they may respect me, they could never be, like, truly on the same level—they'll never put themselves on the same level because they can't relate to the fact that I don't have this kind of male, generic, you know, idea. Like, for instance, my history teacher I think is a great guy and I like him a lot but he—there's always something about him that's reserved towards me because I'm not a sports hero or whatever. But that's the way it is.

When I ask Taylor how the closeness that "the guys" have with each other compares with the closeness that he has with his friends, he suggests that the main differences between "the guys" and himself are not in their experiences of relationships but in the parameters of their relationships (e.g., with whom they are permitted to be close) and in the value given to their perspectives. As Taylor explains excitedly:

> See there's no difference, but what the difference is—this is so hard to explain—they're allowed to have that closeness in the [school community]. Like I said, they're allowed to be guys in the [school] community and it's just they that are able to do that. No one else is allowed to kind of fit, like, the guy identity, although they may outside of school and with their friends. . . . And it's funny. I always remember, you know, since the earliest days, I'd always say to myself, you know, "I wish they could see me with my friends so they could know that I act just like they do with their friends."

Although Taylor claims complacency ("I guess I don't have any regrets") and acceptance ("that's the way it is"), his desire to be truly seen and known within his school community remains evident throughout his narrative ("I wish they could see"). For now, Taylor remains convinced that his marginalized status and exclusion in this context are based on other people's narrow views of what he is like. Thus, despite feeling oppressed by the cliques within his school's culture, Taylor remains hopeful that, if only people could see him for who he really is, they would see that he is also sociable, worthy of respect, and not as different from "the guys" as they may think.

At the same time, there is some evidence that Taylor is beginning to question his convictions. For instance, when I ask Taylor what it would take for people to be able to see him for who he is, he replies:

> I think that it would take a more, wide acceptance, I guess. But I'm not sure either if it's necessarily—I never really liked questioning, you know, the course of society. I often think the way people are—the way like boys are and men are—is, you know, let it happen. That's why I don't have a lot of dislike about [this school]. I mean, I think that a lot of the reason they are the way they are is, you know, that's the way it is. And I think that I respect [people] for being the way they are, although I wish they would sometimes, you know, at some time see me for who I think I am. I also understand that I may not be who I think I am. I may be a lot more, you know, whatever. I may be what they think I am instead of what I think I am. And so, I dunno. *What makes you say that?*
> I dunno. Well, maybe the fact that I seem to be so universally put into one category, so maybe it may be true.

Taylor's response suggests that he has internalized the notion that there exists a natural state of male being ("the way boys are and men are") and course of male development ("let it happen"). While he recognizes that he deviates from these, he accepts and respects their predominance nonetheless. Perhaps as a result, Taylor's wish to be seen for "who I think I am" becomes linked with doubts that he knows who he is ("I may be what they think I am").

Taylor's confusion is particularly evident when one follows the progression of his thinking by extracting and tracking his "I" statements in this passage:

> I think, I guess, I'm not sure,
> I never really liked questioning,
> I often think,
> That's why I don't have a lot of dislike,
> I mean, I think,
> That's the way it is,
> I think, I respect, I wish,
> Who I think I am,
> I also understand, I may not be,
> Who I think I am,
> I may be, I may be,

What they think I am,
What I think I am,
I dunno,
I dunno, I seem to be,
Maybe it may be true.

In focusing on how Taylor frames his self-expression, one can see his discomfort ("I think," "I guess," "I'm not sure") when my question leads him to critique society ("I never really liked questioning"). As he deliberates his reality ("the way people are," "who I think I am"), one can also see how he begins with his thoughts and feelings ("I think," "I respect," "I wish") and tries to acknowledge other people's views ("I also understand," "I may not be," "I may be") but becomes increasingly uncertain ("I dunno") and ends up questioning his own perspective ("maybe it may be true"). Although Taylor tries to consider other people's views ("what they think I am") and also sustain his sense of self ("who I think I am"), his experiences of being "so universally put into one category" seem to undermine his conviction that he is not the misfit that people suppose him to be.

It seems that Taylor could potentially draw strength to resist this process from the sense of belonging and acceptance that he experiences with his friends. However, the fact that his friends are also marginalized within the school community may ironically lead Taylor to disregard their views. Thus, despite having relationships, Taylor struggles on his own to establish himself in this context. And by cutting himself off from the support of his relationships, Taylor may be especially susceptible to internalizing other people's conceptions of him, including those he previously resisted as misconceptions, to the detriment of his self-concept.

Ethan

For Ethan, an 18-year-old senior, the process of negotiating his sense of self centers on his efforts to be true to himself and to ascertain what that entails as he engages in relationships and social interactions at school and beyond. Like Taylor, Ethan also describes himself as someone who does not fit conventional images of masculinity. However, whereas Taylor's deviance is inadvertent, Ethan's deviance seems more deliberate. One area where this difference is apparent is in how the boys look and dress. Whereas Taylor seems to pay little attention to his appearance, Ethan's style reflects his desire to be different. For instance, Ethan has sideburns at a time when they are not a part of mainstream fashion. And instead of wearing the standard navy blazer with an Oxford shirt and khaki pants, Ethan might wear a tan jacket with a plaid flannel shirt and corduroy pants. While Ethan's style may be considered "alternative," wearing plaid flannel shirts and corduroy pants is not uncommon and there are students who are more outrageous in their dress (e.g., wearing bright green pants or multi-colored checkered jackets). Moreover, Ethan always looks well groomed, not sloppy or grungy, and tends to be soft-spoken and mild-mannered. Thus, Ethan is somewhere in the middle; he manages to distinguish himself but the distinction is subtle and he can easily blend in at this school.

During our interview, Ethan's calm and quiet disposition is evident. He is thoughtful in responding to my questions and occasionally asks for clarification to make sure he understands what I am asking. He becomes slightly timid during pauses in the conversation. However, for the most part, he expresses himself confidently yet modestly and gives the impression of being self-assured but not self-righteous.

Drawing Strength from Relationships

In contrast to Taylor's experience, Ethan emphasizes ways in which his relationships, especially his closest friendship, have helped him to be true to himself and supported his efforts to show others what he is really like. When I ask Ethan whether, as a male, he has ever felt expected to be or act a certain way, he begins by describing how he has fallen short of his dad's notions of how a boy should be:

> I think that I feel pressure to be more masculine, like I feel like my dad sometimes—like when I do things, just the fact that I was never good at regular sports when I was younger, like baseball or whatever. I was never good at that and I could tell, I felt like he was pretty disappointed in me. Or when I didn't want to do work, like yard work or something, he'd always be disappointed. And I felt like, like he's trying to get me to be more like a little boy or like a young boy or something. And I think lately, not really, I think my parents have come to realize that I'm not really like a gung-ho masculine type of guy.

Ethan also describes feeling coerced by his mom's efforts to shape him according to her own ideals:

I think I reached a breaking point when I was about, like, 12 or 13 when—because my mom, *especially* my mom, really tried to get me to be like, I don't know what she tried to get me to be but it was just, I felt like I wasn't being myself at all. . . . It just felt like she was forcing me to try to impress other people and just have me dress the way she wanted me to dress and—I mean, I assume all kids are like that but I just felt like she was really trying to make me be the person that she really wanted me to be. And, um, I suppose I rebelled.

While his dad's disappointment may have undermined Ethan's sense of being sufficiently masculine in the past, Ethan indicates that he has come to accept the discrepancy between his dad's expectations and the reality of who he is, even if his parents have not ("not really"). Likewise, although Ethan may have resented his mom's attempts to foster behaviors that felt contrived and/or uncomfortable to him ("I felt like I wasn't being myself at all"), he has found ways to make his own decisions about who he wants to be and how he wants to act.

Namely, Ethan explains that his relationship with his closest friend has enabled him to resist pressures to accommodate himself, or at least his behaviors, to his parents' expectations and ideals. As Ethan explains:

When I was 13, I met my closest friend right now and he really helped me to become who I want to become. I felt like we both kind of helped each other grow into, like, who we want to be right now. Up until that time, I'd kind of been thinking, "Well, I don't really like this, so why am I doing it?" but continued to do it, like just dressing all neat and trying to impress everyone I met and trying to be like the perfect kid. But in meeting my friend, he really helped—we both helped each other a lot to become who we are right now. And we both like who we are right now, to some extent. . . . But before that, I felt my mom was really pressuring me to be the perfect kid. And I think that's probably why I hate that so much now. Because it really got me mad and it gets me mad now.

When I ask how he and his friend helped each other, Ethan elaborates:

Like, he pointed out all the stuff that my mom was doing to me that I realized, but I never realized that it was there. Like I knew it was happening, but I didn't really. And then he pointed it out to me and I was like, "Hey yeah, that's wrong." And so, we both were like, "Hey, why don't we just be who we want to be."

As Ethan indicates, it is not that his feelings necessarily changed as a result of his relationship with his closest friend. Ethan had disagreed with his mother's expectations ("I don't really like this") and questioned his compliance ("so why am I doing it?"), even before meeting his friend. Rather, talking with his friend has brought to light underlying feelings that Ethan sensed but did not fully realize ("I knew . . . but I didn't really"), and feeling joined by his friend has made the options of resistance and choice seem more viable. Ethan's closest friendship has not negated his parents' influence. Rather, by raising his awareness of how his sense of self is influenced by his parents' expectations, this relationship has enhanced Ethan's ability to consider his parents' wishes without necessarily relinquishing his own goals and desires.

FEELING SEEN AND KNOWN

In addition to helping him resist pressures to accommodate other people's expectations, Ethan's closest friendship fosters a sense of validation and support by providing a space in which he feels truly seen and known. For instance, Ethan describes an intimacy he feels with his closest friend that enhances and is enhanced by their ability each to be themselves in the relationship. As Ethan explains:

> I really feel like he's the person I'm closest with and he really helped me—
> we helped each other a lot through our conversations. . . . It's just like he's
> the person he wants to be and I'm the person I want to be and they're completely different but we're both happy because we both know that we want
> to be that. . . . We're, like, very different. But at the same time, I have a very
> strong bond with him. Every time I see him, it's just the greatest time ever.
> It's just, he's the best.

Ethan seems especially proud of the fact that he and his friend have "helped each other" not to the effect of becoming more alike but of enabling each other to attain their individual goals ("he's the person he wants to be and I'm the person I want to be"). Likewise, Ethan seems empowered by the fact that he and his friend have "a very strong bond" despite being "very different." In other words, the strength of their bond does not depend on their being similar to each other or having the same goals, aside from their shared desire to be true to themselves. Instead, their appreciation and respect for one another has grown from their ability to acknowledge their differences and to accept and support each other nonetheless. Thus, Ethan learns through experience that relationships can withstand and even cultivate differences.

In turn, Ethan's experience of being truly seen and known in relationships seems to shield him from pressures to conform to societal expectations for boys and inspire his confidence to assert himself, especially when people assume him to be less than he is. As Ethan describes:

> I really feel like I can be who I want to be at [this school] and that there's not that much pressure. I mean, I try to be different from other people, in general. I think maybe that's why I don't feel enormous pressure. But I feel like there's not much pressure around the [school] community to be that masculine.

Ethan's perception that there is little pressure within his school community to project a certain image of masculinity is obviously different from what Taylor described. However, it is not that Ethan perceives his school culture and community to be free of expectations; Ethan's very efforts to differentiate himself ("I try to be different from other people") in this context imply the existence of standards and norms. Rather, there is something that protects Ethan from their potentially negative influence that Taylor apparently lacked. It appears that what protects Ethan is the experience of being supported by his teachers and friends to be different and thus true to himself. For instance, when I ask what enables him to be different, Ethan explains:

> It really irritates me when people try to conform and just be who people want them to be. And so that kind of drives me to try to be different, 'cause I hate to see people try to conform and just like give up their own qualities and ideals to be like other people. And all my teachers have always fostered the sense of independence and stuff. And all my friends are pretty supportive of that and all my closest friends are like me and they try to be different themselves and just do what they want to do as opposed to what other people want them to do.

Through nurturing his self-acceptance and self-assurance, Ethan's relationships with teachers and friends make it possible for him to "be who I want to be" despite pressures he may encounter within this context and elsewhere. While Ethan's irritation may motivate his resistance, it is mainly through the support of his relationships that Ethan feels able to act on his feelings.

OVERCOMING ASSUMPTIONS AND MISCONCEPTIONS

Although Ethan associates his efforts to be different with his desire to be true to himself (e.g., by not conforming or otherwise compromising his integrity), these efforts often lead him to feel underestimated and unduly dismissed. For instance, when I ask about difficulties he has encountered, Ethan replies:

> I feel like that's—people look on as just like, "He's being a teenager. He's try-ing to be different. He's trying to be like the generic teenager. He's trying to just get adults angry or whatever and make adults think he's being weird and stuff." Especially during the whole college process when I see other kids trying to really be all perfect and preppy and everything. I feel like I'm really out of place trying to just be myself and stuff. . . . Um, primarily with adults, when I'm with a group of adults and I'm the only teenager or whatever. I feel out of place and like I'm frowned upon and stuff. And I feel like once people get to know me, they realize that I'm not really like a freak or what-ever.

Rather than being defensive or becoming discouraged by these views, Ethan seeks to show people what he is really like ("not really like a freak"), namely through relationships ("once people get to know me"). As Ethan explains further:

> I think a lot of people, when they see my physical appearance, they're like, "Oh, he must be a bad kid," or whatever. And I feel like I have to overcome that through speaking or whatever or talking to them and then, through getting to know them. I feel that, if I get to know a person, I feel like they re-spect me more. But I think that, automatically, people assume that I'm just weird or whatever. I think that, especially with adults, not so much with my peers, but adults, when they initially see me, just assume that I'm not the person I actually am and stuff like that.
> *What do you think that they expect of you?*
> Um, just to be really disrespectful and to be the typical teenager who doesn't care about anything, just stuff like that, to be stupid and to be, like, just re-

ally like, the generic teenager that adults dislike. And I feel like I try to overcome that when I get to know them.

Ethan's optimism that he can change people's views of him by getting to know them and by letting them get to know him is worth noting. For one thing, Ethan's desire to be seen for who he really is challenges stereotypes that depict adolescent boys as indifferent to what other people, particularly adults, think of them. Likewise, Ethan's belief that he can overcome adults' misunderstandings—a belief that may be linked to his experiences of having worked through different viewpoints in his existing relationships—raises questions about how relationships may indirectly shape boys' attitudes and outlooks. Just as Ethan develops his sense of self in light of his parents' expectations, he also comes to understand who he is ("the person I actually am") through reconciling other people's assumptions about him with his own views. Even if he does not always succeed in correcting their misconceptions (e.g., that he is "a bad kid," "just weird," "really disrespectful," "the typical teenager who doesn't care about anything," "stupid," "the generic teenager that adults dislike") the process of trying to counter their views with his own helps him to clarify in his own mind who he thinks he is and how he wants to be.

Discussion

Through framing boys' identity development as a relational process and using a relational approach to learn about boys' experiences from their perspectives, this study highlights ways in which adolescent boys negotiate their senses of self in relationships with specific others (e.g., friends and family) and with their broader social contexts (e.g., peers and adults in their school community). Contrary to popular discourse that tends to depict adolescent boys as disconnected from their emotions (Kindlon & Thompson, 1999) and from their relationships with others (Pollack, 1998), these boys' interview narratives indicate that their relational ways of being, which are detectable in infancy (Trevarthan, 1979; Tronick, 1989; Tronick & Gianino, 1986; Weinberg & Tronick, 1996) and early childhood (Chu, 2000), carry forth into adolescence. Namely, these adolescent boys showed themselves to be (1) keenly aware of their own thoughts, feelings, and desires; (2) sensitive and responsive to the dynamics of their interpersonal relationships; and (3) attuned to the realities of their social and cultural contexts. The boys also indicated ways in which they are able to resist as well as internalize cultural constructions of masculinity that they encounter, for instance, through other people's expectations and assumptions regarding what boys are like and how boys should act. Thus, while boys' gender socialization may influence their senses of self, and also their attitudes and behaviors, boys are able to mediate these effects through the importance they place on adhering to conventions of masculinity and with the support of their relationships to challenge our culture's current portrayal of boys.

The examples presented in this chapter were selected because they underscore discrepancies between how other people see boys and how boys see themselves, as described by the adolescent boys in this study. These examples also highlight ways in which boys may reconcile these discrepancies as they develop an understanding of who they are, of their relationships to others, and of their realities or "the way things are." In particular, these examples illustrate two predominant patterns of response that emerged in the boys' narratives. The first pattern, as exemplified by Taylor's case, emphasizes one's internalization of other people's views, possibly to the detriment of one's own sense of self. The second pattern, as exemplified by Ethan's case, emphasizes one's potential to resist other people's views and thereby sustain, or even strengthen, one's own sense of self. These two patterns also correspond to some extent to Piaget's (1954) conceptualizations of accommodation and assimilation wherein one's accommodation to society involves the internalization of its expectations, one's assimilation implies a degree of self-preservation and thus resistance to prevalent stereotypes and assumptions, and one's self-concept reflects the ability to balance these two processes.

A comparison of boys exhibiting each of these two patterns suggests that relationships can crucially influence whether a boy internalizes or resists societal expectations and assumptions. While most boys are exposed to cultural constructions of masculinity that manifest in other people's views of boys in general and of them in particular, there are differences in how, as individuals, they struggle to define themselves and choose to incorporate other people's views into their self-concept. Although boys' different patterns of response may be partly explained by individual difference (e.g., in age, temperament, attitudes, values, beliefs), what stood out in the boys' narratives were relational differences, particularly in their experiences of self-in-relationship. For instance, while Taylor and Ethan both have friends and they both suggest how their relationships have shaped their senses of self, they do not make meaning of and draw upon their friendships in the same ways. For Taylor, the fact that his friends consider him to be an outsider *like them* may provide him with a sense of belonging. However, as he feels unjustly marginalized within the school community because he does not see himself as being that different from the boys who are valued in this context, Taylor's friendships seem an unlikely source of support. Without the validation he seeks from his friends as well as his school community, Taylor's doubts begin to undermine his conviction that he is not as deviant or misfit as people think he is. Conversely, Ethan's sense of being truly seen and known in his closest friendship enables him to assert himself (e.g., by choosing to be different and trying to show people who he thinks he is) and to feel supported as he resists pressures to conform. That is, beyond having access to relationships, boys' experiences of being validated and valued in relationships appear to be key to boys' resistance and resilience.

Whether boys internalize or resist other people's views as they negotiate their senses of self, they are diligent in striving to understand who they are and conscientious in seeking ways to participate socially while remaining true to themselves. In illustrating how societal expectations and assumptions can infiltrate boys' senses of self, the examples presented in this chapter suggest a complexity to boys' experiences and a breadth and depth to their relational abilities (e.g., skills and strategies for expressing themselves and engaging in their relationships), which are seldom represented in popular depictions of boys. However, this is only a beginning. As these findings are based on a specific group of boys, it will be important for future studies to explore how other populations of boys negotiate their senses of self and reconcile discrepancies between how they are said to be and how they see themselves to be. Given that human development is embedded in interpersonal relationships as well as in society and culture, there are likely to be group differences (e.g., by age, race, ethnicity, socioeconomic status, sexual orientation, and religious faith) as well as individual differences in how boys navigate through these processes. Further research is also needed to examine more specifically how boys' experiences of gender socialization—in conjunction with their experiences in relationships—can hinder and enhance their psychological and social growth. If our goal is to support boys' development in ways that account for their experiences and are relevant to their lives, we must start with their own stories. For it is only by considering boys' perspectives on where they are coming from and what they feel they are up against that we can learn how best to foster their consciousness, awareness, and critical reflection and thus help them to make more informed decisions about who they want to be and how they want to act.

NOTE

1. Pseudonyms are used in place of the boys' real names.

REFERENCES

Brown, L. M., Argyris, D., Attanucci, J., Bardige, B., Gilligan, C., Johnston, K., Miller, B., Osborne, D., Ward, J., Wiggins, G. & Wilcox, D. (1988). *A guide to reading narratives of conflict and choice for self and moral voice.* (Monograph No. 1). Cambridge, MA: Harvard Graduate School of Education, Center for the Study of Gender, Education, and Human Development.

Brown, L. M. & Gilligan, C. (1990, August). Listening for self and relational voice: A responsive/resisting reader's guide. Paper presented at the American Psychological Association, Boston.

Brown, L. M. & Gilligan, C. (1991). Listening for voice in narratives of relationship. In M. B. Tappan & M. J. Packer (Eds.), *Narrative and storytelling: Implications for understanding moral development,* New directions for child development, No. 54 (pp. 43–62). San Francisco: Jossey-Bass.

Brown, L. M. & Gilligan, C. (1992). *Meeting at the crossroads: Women's psychology and girls' development.* Cambridge, MA: Harvard University Press.

Chu, J. Y. (1998). Relational strengths in adolescent boys. Paper presented at the American Psychological Association Conference, San Francisco.

Chu, J. Y. (1999). Reconsidering adolescent boys' behaviors using qualitative methods. Paper presented at the American Educational Research Association Conference, Montreal, Canada.

Chu, J. Y. (2000). Learning what boys know: An observational and interview study with six four-year-old boys. Unpublished dissertation, Harvard University.

Chu, J. Y., Porche, M. V. & Tolman, D. L. (in press). The Adolescent Masculinity Ideology in Relationships Scale: Development and validation of a new measure for boys. *Men and Masculinities.*

Erikson, E. (1968). *Identity, Youth, and Crisis.* New York: W. W. Norton.

Gilligan, C. (1982). *In a different voice: Psychological theory and women's development.* Cambridge, MA: Harvard University Press.

Gilligan, C. (1996). The centrality of relationship in human development. In G. Noam & K. Fischer (Eds.), *Development and vulnerability in close relationships* (pp. 237–261). Mahwah, NJ: Erlbaum.

Gilligan, C., Brown, L. M. & Rogers, A. G. (1990). Psyche embedded: A place for body, relationships, and culture in personality theory. In A. I. Rabin, R. A. Zucker, R. A. Emmons & S. Frank (Eds.), *Studying persons and lives* (pp. 86–147). New York: Springer.

Gilligan, C., Spencer, R., Weinberg, M. K. & Bertsch, T. (in press). On the listening guide: A voice-centered relational method. In L. Yardley (Ed.), *Qualitative research in psychology: Expanding perspectives in methodology and design.* Washington, DC: American Psychological Association Press.

Jordan, J. V., Kaplan, A. G., Miller, J. B., Stiver, I. P. & Surrey, J. L. (1991). *Women's growth in connection.* New York: Guilford Press.

Kindlon, D. & Thompson, M. (1999). *Raising Cain: Protecting the emotional life of boys.* New York: Ballantine.

Masten, A. S. (1994). Resilience in individual development: Successful adaptation despite risk and adversity. In M. C. Wang & E. W. Gordon (Eds.), *Educational resilience in inner-city America: Challenges and prospects* (pp. 3–25). Hillsdale, NJ: Erlbaum.

Masten, A. S. & Coatsworth, J. D. (1998). The development of competence in favorable and unfavorable environments: Lessons from research on successful children. *American Psychologist,* 53(2), 205–220.

Miles, M. B. & Huberman, A. M. (1994). *Qualitative data analysis: An expanded sourcebook* (2d ed.). Thousand Oaks, CA: Sage.

Miller, J. B. (1976). *Toward a new psychology of women.* Boston: Beacon Press.

Miller, J. B. (1994). Women's psychological development: Connections, disconnections, and violations. In M. M. Berger (Ed.), *Women beyond Freud: New concepts of feminine psychology* (pp. 79–97). New York: Brunner/Mazel.

Piaget, J. (1954). *The construction of reality in the child.* New York: Basic Books.

Pleck, J. H. (1995). Gender role strain paradigm: An update. In R. F. Levant & W. S. Pollack (Eds.), *A new psychology of men* (pp. 11–32). New York: Basic Books.

Pleck, J. H., Sonenstein, F. L. & Ku, L. C. (1994). Problem behaviors and masculinity ideology in adolescent males. In R. D. Ketterlinus & M. E. Lamb (Eds.), *Adolescent problem behaviors: Issues and research* (pp. 165–186). Hillsdale, NJ: Erlbaum.

Pollack, W. S. (1998). *Real boys: Rescuing our sons from the myths of boyhood.* New York: Random House.

Resnick, M. D., Bearman, P. S., Blum, R. W., Bauman, K. E., Harris, K. M., Jones, J., Tabor, J., Beuhring, T., Sieving, R. E., Shew, M., Ireland, M., Bearinger, L. H. & Udry, R. (1997). Protecting adolescents from harm: Findings from the national longitudinal study on adolescent health. *Journal of the American Medical Association,* 278(10), 823–832.

Rutter, M. (1990). Psychosocial resilience and protective mechanisms. In S. Weintraub (Ed.), *Risk and protective factors in the development of psychopathology* (pp. 181–214). New York: Cambridge University Press.

Trevarthan, C. B. (1979). Communication and cooperation in early infancy: A description of primary intersubjectivity. In M. Bullowa (Ed.), *Before speech: The beginnings of communication.* Cambridge, England: Cambridge University Press.

Tronick, E. (1989). Emotions and emotional communication in infants. *American Psychologist,* 44(2), 112–119.

Tronick, E. & Gianino, A. (1986). Interactive mismatch and repair: Challenges in the coping infant. *Zero to Three,* 6(3), 1–6.

Vygotsky, L. S. (1978). *Mind in society.* Cambridge: Harvard University Press.

Wang, M. C., Haertel, G. D. & Walberg, H. J. (1994). Educational resilience in inner cities. In M. C. Wang & E. W. Gordon (Eds.), *Educational resilience in inner-city America: Challenges and prospects* (pp. 45–72). Hillsdale, NJ: Erlbaum.

Weinberg, K. M. & Tronick, E. Z. (1996). Infant affective reactions to the resumption of maternal interaction after the still-face. *Child Development,* 67(3), 905–914.

Werner, E. E. & Smith, R. S. (1982). *Vulnerable but invincible: A longitudinal study of resilient children and youth.* New York: McGraw-Hill.

Part II

Family Relationships

5

Experiences of Trust with Parents

A Qualitative Investigation of African American, Latino, and Asian American Boys from Low-Income Families

Elena D. Jeffries

Interpersonal trust plays a critical role in healthy social and emotional development (Bernath & Feshbach, 1995; Erikson, 1963; Rotenberg, 1991), underlies identity formation (Erikson, 1963), and is associated with positive psychosocial adjustment (Doster & Chance, 1976; Hamid & Lok, 2000; Lester & Gatto, 1990; Rotter, 1980; Wilson & Carroll, 1991). An established sense of trust in the world enables one to perceive oneself as predictable, manageable, and secure, and promotes exploration necessary for successful development (Bernath & Feshbach, 1995; Erikson, 1963). Several researchers have also noted that interpersonal trust is crucial for social "survival," paving the way for intimate connection and encouraging interdependence (Bernath & Feshbach, 1995; Omodei & McLennan, 2000; Rotenberg, 1991; Selman, 1980; Stack, 1978).

Despite the important role interpersonal trust plays in healthy development, few studies have directly examined this construct. Remarkably little is known about how children and adolescents experience interpersonal trust in their relationships (Bernath & Feshbach, 1995). We know even less about how boys, in particular, experience trust. Although there has been a growing body of research on girls' experiences of relationships, including the role of trust in their relationships (Brown & Gilligan, 1992), few researchers have focused on such topics with boys. In response to this gap, I sought to explore adolescent boys' experiences of trust in their relationships with their parents.

Background

While there is little empirical literature that explores adolescents' experiences of trust, there exists a rich theoretical literature on the meaning of trust and the ways in which trust shapes the development of relationships. In this literature, Erik Erikson and Julian Rotter's notions of trust are most commonly cited (e.g., see Bernath & Feshbach, 1995; Hochreich, 1974; Imber, 1973; Rotenberg, 1991). Erikson (1963) stated that "basic trust" or mistrust develops in infancy based on the infant-caretaker interaction, and is preverbal, biological, and universal. Rotter (1967), however, argued that trust develops later in life based on numerous interactions, and is mediated through cognitive processes. He defined trust as "an expectancy held by an individual or a group that the word, promise, verbal or written statement of another individual or group can be relied upon" (p. 651). More recently, Selman and his colleagues (Selman, 1980; Selman & Schultz, 1990) explored how trust develops throughout childhood and early adolescence. Based on interviews with predominantly White samples, Selman proposed a five-stage model of interpersonal understanding that centers on children's growing capacity to differentiate and balance perspectives of self and other. His model suggests that trust develops hierarchically in parallel with social understanding.

Despite differences in the conceptualizations of trust, there has been considerable agreement in the research literature regarding the core elements of trust, particularly for adolescents and adults. "Sharing confidences" and/or "dependability/reliability" have been considered the most important components of the experience of trust (Bernath & Feshbach, 1995; Hestenes, 1997; Hestenes & Berndt, 1997a, 1997b; Imber, 1973; Rempel, Holmes & Zanna, 1985; Rotter, 1967). Consequently, research studies examining the concept of trust have relied almost exclusively on measures of shared confidences and dependability to assess the levels of trust in a relationship (Doster & Chance, 1976; Hestenes & Berndt, 1997a, 1997b; Hochreich, 1974; Imber, 1973; Rotenberg & Morgan, 1995). These studies tell us how much children and adolescents are willing to confide in and depend on others. They tell us little, however, about how trust is defined or experienced by the children and adolescents themselves.

The lack of exploration regarding the meaning of trust for children and adolescents is particularly problematic when one considers the ethnic diversity of the current adolescent population (United States Census Bureau, 2002). Since the values and norms of a particular ethnic culture are likely to be a critical part of how youth define and experience trust in relationships, there may be variation in the experience of trust across cultures (Cauce, 1986; Cooper, 1999). The dimensions of shared confidences and dependability may not fully or adequately capture the nuances and variation in the meaning of trust for adolescents from different ethnic cultures. Yet there have been few studies that focus on the meaning of trust in relationships across ethnically diverse youth.

The research literature on interpersonal trust is also limited by its focus on trust within friendships (Bernath & Feshbach, 1995). The few researchers who have examined trust among children and adolescents have almost exclusively focused on trust in friendships (Kahn & Turiel, 1988; Rawlins & Holl, 1987; Rotenberg, 1991; Rotenberg & Morgan, 1995). Researchers have not examined, for the most part, how children and adolescents make meaning of and experience trust with their parents. Some studies, however, have focused on adolescents' willingness to depend on and/or share confidences with their parents (Buhrmester & Prager, 1995; Hestenes & Berndt, 1997a; Rice & Mulkeen, 1995; Youniss & Smollar, 1985). For example, Hestenes and Berndt (1997a) found in their primarily White, middle-class sample that boys were willing to depend on their parents from early to middle adolescence, and they were also equally likely to share their private thoughts and feelings with their mothers and fathers. Their willingness to share their thoughts and feelings with their parents, however, decreased from early to middle adolescence. Youniss and Smollar (1985) found that while boys in their predominantly White sample tended not to share their thoughts and feelings with their fathers, often limiting their discussions to practical issues, they generally confided in their mothers about personal as well as practical issues. In her qualitative study of African American, Latino, and White adolescents from low-income families, Way (1998) found that the boys indicated little willingness to share personal confidences with either of their parents even though they believed their mothers were the most important figures in their lives. These findings not only suggest the importance of exploring the experience of trust more generally, between adolescents and their parents, but also of exploring how experiences of trust may vary across ethnicity and/or context.

The Study

Responding to the gaps in the literature, I explored adolescent boys' experiences of trust with their parents. My colleagues and I conducted semi-structured interviews with an ethnically diverse group of boys with the goal of understanding their own experiences of trust with their parents rather than imposing predetermined categories on their experiences and assessing the frequency of such categories (e.g., shared confidences). Through focusing on the stories of African American, Latino, and Asian American boys, I sought to broaden our understanding of the intricacies, processes, and quality of trust between adolescent boys and their parents, and to examine ways in which trust experiences may vary by ethnicity.

Method

Participants

The findings reported in this chapter are part of a larger longitudinal investigation of the development of peer and parent relationships among poor and working-class, urban, ethnic minority adolescents.[1] The study was conducted at an ethnically diverse public high school in New York City. Ninety percent of students in the high school were eligible for federal assistance through the free or reduced price lunch program. The sample for the present analysis included five African American, five Latino (Dominican or Puerto Rican), and five Asian American (primarily Chinese American) boys (mean age = 16.1 years). These students were randomly selected from the larger study's pool of interviews, with the aim of including members from each ethnic group and of keeping the sample size small in order to allow for in-depth exploration of the interviews.

Procedure

Participants were individually interviewed by one member of an ethnically diverse team of psychology graduate students who were extensively trained in interviewing techniques. The semi-structured interviews were audiotaped and conducted in a private setting within the school. Each interview typically took 1.5 to 2 hours to complete. The interview protocol included such questions as, "How would you describe your relationship with your mother?" "Do you trust your mother/father? Why? In what ways?" "How do you define trust with your mother/father? Give an example of when you trusted your mother/father." In addition, participants were asked to compare their trust experiences across relationships: "Do you trust your mom in the same way that you trust your dad? In what ways? Do you trust your parents in the same way that you trust your friends? In what ways?" Although each interview included a standard set of questions, follow-up questions were based on the interviewee's responses. Throughout the data collection process, the interviewers, along with the larger research team, met weekly to listen to interviews and to provide extensive feedback to one another.

Data Analysis

I used two tools of qualitative data analysis to analyze the interviews: narrative summaries (Miller, 1991) and conceptually clustered matrices (Miles & Huberman, 1994). These methods of analysis enabled me to examine individual differences as well as themes across and within interviews. A "theme" or "pattern" was identified as a repeated phrase, image, or idea present in the interviews. Themes and patterns could occur within or across ethnic/racial groups.

I began the process of analysis by reading through the interviews with the goal of understanding how the boys spoke about trust in their relationships with their parents. I took extensive notes on my initial impressions and referred back to them throughout the analysis. Following this step, I created narrative summaries (Miller, 1991) from the boys' interview data. Narrative summaries, for this study, were summaries of the stories that each adolescent boy told regarding his experiences of trust with each of his parents. The aim of narrative summaries is to capture the essence of the story by sticking as closely as possible to the exact language used by the participant and by condensing the story into more manageable amounts of data (Miller, 1991). Following the creation of narrative summaries, I placed our narrative summaries into conceptually clustered matrices (Miles & Huberman, 1994) to explore themes that were common within and across the boys' interviews. All of the topics in a matrix are conceptually related to each other and present the data in a table format. For example, I created within-subjects matrices that included definitions of trust for mother and father. I then created between-subjects matrices to detect the variations and similarities within each theme. Finally, I re-read the interviews in order to locate where themes appeared within the text. In other words, I attempted to contextualize the themes.

Although each participant had a unique way of describing trust in his relationships with his parents, my intent was not to capture each individual's experience but to identify prevalent patterns that appeared across interviews. From my data analysis, I detected four overarching themes in the boys' interviews: (1) Obligatory Trust, (2) Shared Confidences, (3) Need Fulfillment, (4) "Always Gonna Be There." Some of these themes were only evident for particular groups of boys, while other themes were evident across all of the boys. I will describe the variations and commonalities within and across each theme for the remainder of this chapter.

Patterns of Trust

Obligatory Trust

The boys, predominantly from Latino or Asian American families, conveyed feelings of obligation when discussing experiences of trust with their parents. They stated that they trust their mother or father simply "because" you just "have to" trust your parents. For example, when asked why he trusts his mother, Philip, a Chinese American male, indicated this was a question with only one obvious answer:

> *Do you trust your mother?*
> Yeah I trust her.
> *Yeah. Okay, why do you trust her?*
> Uh, 'cause it's my mom, you know. I can trust her. It's a silly question because you have to.
> *Well not everybody trusts their mother . . .*
> I, I do. Because she's been there every time I needed her.

Philip seems to feel obliged to trust his mother both because she is his parent and because of her reliable and consistent care.

For a few of the boys, the obligation to trust parents seemed to stem from an awareness and appreciation of what their parents have given them. Peter, an African American male, said:

Do you trust your mother?

Sometimes. I mean I have to, she's my mother.

What do you mean you have to?

Everybody should trust their mother and their father. 'Cause sometimes, I don't, I don't know why. . . . Because without your mother and father you wouldn't be here. So you have to trust them to make the right decisions for you. They do whatever they can for you.

Peter conveys an inherent trust in his parents and suggests a feeling of security and confidence in his relationships with his parents.

Like Peter, Juan, a Dominican student, feels obliged to trust his mother. When asked to elaborate on how he defines trust with his mother, Juan stated, ". . . like you should trust your mother and that's your mother. Whether you like it or not she, she gave birth, she went through birth for you, so." Juan's phrasing ("went through birth for you") implies a sense of obligation and gratitude in recognition of what he perceives as his mother's sacrifice.

Miguel—a Puerto Rican student who lost his mother at a young age—feels grateful for all that his father has given him:

Okay, and do you trust your dad?

Yeah, yes, in some things yeah.

Yeah, tell me in, how do and don't you trust him?

Alright, um, yeah, I trust him. I trust him. I trust him. But you know there's, there's like 'cause I don't know. Yeah, I trust him. I gotta trust him. He's my father.

What do you mean you gotta trust him?

'Cause, 'cause, I don't know. He's, he's, he was, 'cause when I was small he was my, he was um and my, when my mother died, he was my mother, you know. He's my father and my mother. So you know, he's both and still is.

Yeah, but what do you mean you gotta trust him?

He's, 'cause I don't know, he's, I mean I feel, I don't know. I just he's my father and he was there when I was small, you know. He brung, he brung me up when my mother wasn't around. And you know he raised me. Everything, mostly things I know, you know, he taught me.

Like Philip, Peter, and Juan, Miguel believes that a key part of his obligation to his father involves trusting him. He is grateful for his father's support and guidance and seems to believe that the acts of his father (i.e., serving as both mother and father) demand that he trusts his father in return. The boys often intermingled their sense of obligation, appreciation, and trust with their parents.

Shared Confidences

The African American and Latino boys' discussions of trust with their mothers and/or fathers were replete with stories of secret sharing with their parents and comparisons of what they tell one parent versus the other. Half of these boys described sharing "everything" with at least one of their parents. Among the boys who distinguished between what they disclose to their mother versus their father, the father was usually the recipient of more shared confidences. None of the Asian American boys reported sharing confidences with their parents.

SHARING "EVERYTHING" AND "ANYTHING"

Parents' ability to listen without criticizing and maintain confidentiality seemed to pave the way for trusting relationships between boys and their parents. The boys appreciated that they could relate to their mother and/or father as both a parent and a friend. When explaining how he trusts his mother with "everything," Chris, an African American male, stated:

> Well you know, it's like sometimes I tell her things and she tells me things. It's like we keep, we're like best friends, me and my mother. We keep things to ourselves, tell each other stuff that we don't tell no one else.

Juan, who holds his father in high esteem, stated that they have both a "father-son" and a "friend-friend" relationship. Because he perceives his father as an "older version" of himself, Juan feels comfortable talking with him about sports, girls, school, and problems with friends. In his interview, Juan linked his trust in his father with his ability to relate to his father:

> *Do you trust your mom in the same way you trust your dad?*
> I find that I have more trust in my father. 'Cause like since he acts the way I do, I feel like I can talk to him as a friend more than a family member. I don't know, he's like a friend and a family member.

So you find it easier to talk to him?

Uh huh. Plus he understands me more, he's a man. Probably been through what I've been through.

Like Juan, Channing, an African American young man, also chooses to share "everything" with his father and talks to him more than his mother because of their "guy-guy" connection.

Other boys described how feeling "understood" by their parents fostered connection and trust in their relationships with parents. For example, Richard, an African American adolescent, described a very close and "tight" relationship with his mother. He believes that the more mutual their understanding of each other, the closer they become in their relationship. His mother's patience, compassion, and acute ability to understand Richard appeared to enhance his trust in her:

Do you trust your mother?

Yeah, yes, yes. I trust my mother a whole lot with everything. Everything. 'Cause she knows how to close her mouth. She don't say nothing to nobody.

What kind of secrets do you tell her? What, what secrets do you tell her about?

Everything, I mainly tell my mother everything. Everything that I do, bad or good, whether I know she ain't gonna approve it or not. I still tell her 'cause we have a tight relationship, understanding.

Unlike many of the other boys, Richard feels comfortable telling his mother things about himself that she might not accept or support. His willingness to take such risks suggests a sense of security and respect in his relationship with his mother.

Selective Disclosure

The boys who were willing to share only partial information with at least one of their parents often drew the line at sharing poor school performance, disobedience, sexual activity, and crushes. In listing common obstacles to open communication with their parents, the boys cited fears of punishment or rebuke, feelings of not being understood, and expectations that their parents would breach confidentiality. Like the boys who confided "everything" with their parents, these boys also equated trusting their parents with sharing confidences. The difference between the two groups was simply the amount of sharing that was actually done with their parents.

Devon, originally from Senegal, shares cautiously with his parents. In the context of describing how he trusts his mother and father, Devon explained how each of his parents has protected him against the other's reprimand. For example, when Devon accidentally broke his mother's glassware, his father took the blame in order to shield Devon from her screams. Devon also stated that his mother keeps the secrets that he "can't tell" his dad, "like if I got left back or like if I'm failing too many classes." In addition, when his mother falsely admitted to breaking his father's radio, he understood that "she didn't want me to get yelled at or something."

Other boys chose not to tell their parents personal information for fear that their parents would betray their confidences. For instance, Orlando, a Dominican student, only shares "some secrets" that he knows his mother will "keep." Similarly when Peter's interviewer asked how he does and does not trust his mother, he stated, "Certain things I won't tell because [my mother] has a big mouth. She likes to tell, and my father's the same way." When asked to elaborate, Peter described other ways in which he limits his conversations with his parents:

> *So what are some examples of what you wouldn't tell your mom?*
> Sex and stuff like that. We don't talk about that.
> *And what about sex do you think prevents you from talking about it?*
> My parents think I'm still a kid, so they don't want me to grow up most of the time.
> *How would they react if you talked to them about sex?*
> They really wouldn't care. They're like, "Do what you want, just make the right decisions. Don't get anyone pregnant, use condoms."
> *And did that ever happen? Did they talk to you?*
> Every once in a while.
> *And would that be you kind of initiating or?*
> It's like, it's most of the times they start talking about things like that and I tell them, "Why am I talking to you about it? Now all of a sudden you want to hear about it?"

While Peter's parents have acknowledged that he is sexually active and discussed safe sex, he believes that part of them wants him to stay innocent. These mixed messages seemed to prevent Peter from initiating conversations with his parents about sex.

All of the African American and Latino boys in the study reported having relationships with at least one parent that involved shared confidences, and repeatedly equated trust with these shared confidences. Trusting their parents involved sharing their personal concerns, worries, and thoughts. These boys commonly identified their father as the typical recipient of these shared confidences, which appeared to be a consequence of gender identity. Each of these boys felt it was easier to talk to his father because "he is a man also." The ability to share personal information with their mother or father, furthermore, appeared to rest on boys' sense of security and confidence in the relationship. The more secure they felt with one of their parents, the more likely it was that they would share their private thoughts and feelings.

SILENCES

In contrast to the African American and Latino boys, the Asian American boys in our study reported minimal communication with both of their parents. These boys were reluctant to discuss such things as their romantic relationships, sexuality, bad grades, and friendships because they believed their parents would not "approve," "understand," or "care." The Asian American boys often connected their lack of shared confidences with their parents to their cultural background. Daniel, a Chinese American boy, stated that unlike American people, "Asian people, right, the kids right, they don't talk to you, their parents about personal stuff that much. Especially girls and stuff." For example, Daniel chose not to tell his parents when he went out with friends that included girls since they "might not approve." He explained that even though he trusts his parents, "you just don't [talk to them]." Daniel suggests that the lack of personal communication with his parents is not related to a lack of trust per se but simply a cultural dictate.

Keith, a Chinese American boy who does not "talk to [his parents] with secrets," offered a reason why Chinese parents and their children might not communicate: "'Cause adults and children, they think differently about . . . stuff. [My mother] might think another way." Keith believes he and his mother are especially likely to disagree about his academic goals and choice of friends. Keith said he trusts his mother and knows she "loves [him] a lot," but "she's just not the person [he] want[s] to talk to." Unlike some of the African American and Latino boys who also worried about what their parents would think if they told them about their personal experiences, Keith did not describe his lack of communication as problematic or indicative of a lack of trust in them.

Philip described what might be a cultural conflict for him between American and Asian norms. When asked how he trusts his mother, Philip initially claimed that he talks to his mother about "anything" and "everything." Later in his interview, he revealed that he keeps virtually all secrets to himself because they are his "own things" and because he "doesn't know how she'd react." Similarly, when asked how he and his father trust each other, Philip stated, "Mmm, same thing [as his mother]. I tell him everything, but not the private stuff. I keep that to myself." These juxtaposed statements ("I tell him everything but not the private stuff") suggest, perhaps, that while he wants to have a relationship with his mother and father in which he could share everything, that is not the norm in his family.

Despite his lack of shared confidences with his parents, Philip asserted that he trusts both his mother and father. Philip's trust in his parents appears to be based on a sense of obligation rather than on shared confidences. Like the other Asian American boys, Philip believes that he trusts his parents because they are his parents and he "should" trust them.

Need Fulfillment

Boys in the study, across all ethnic groups, indicated that trust in their parents was based, at least in part, on the fact that they were dependable caregivers, attending to both their material and emotional needs. They explained how their parents have provided them with shelter and money for both necessities and entertainment and offered effective problem-solving techniques and invaluable advice.

PROVIDING FOR MATERIAL NEEDS

When asked how they trusted their parents, boys referred to their parents' ability to care for their practical needs by providing essentials, carrying out favors, and responsibly handling their day-to-day matters. While a few adolescents offered specific examples, most spoke in global terms about their parents as providers and helpers. They indicated that their parents will "do anything" for them and give them what they "want" or "need." Richard said, "My mother is the greatest woman on earth. Whatever I want, I got it. Whatever I need, she's giving it to me." In a virtually identical description of why he trusts his parents more than his friends, Juan commented, "Whatever, I mean whatever I need they'll [his parents] give it to me." In addition, Peter believes that "without my parents I wouldn't have nothing. My parents find me everything." When asked to discuss his relationship with his mother, Ralph, a Puerto Rican student, described mutual dependability between him and his mother, "I trust her, she trusts me. If I need something I can ask her. If she needs something from me, I'll do it for her. I don't care." In the context of describing what he likes about his father, Ralph also spontaneously mentioned that he can depend on his father. He stated, "If I ever needed something, I come to him and he would do it for me." And Michael, who trusts his mother because of the "person she is," repeatedly mentioned that he trusts her to "do things" for him.

PROVIDING FOR EMOTIONAL NEEDS

Some of the boys also indicated that their parents helped them with problems by intervening, listening, imparting useful advice, and providing comfort. They spoke about the practical solutions and advice they receive from their parents in the face of difficulties. They approach their parents in search of guidance, comfort, and problem-solving tips, and trust them to respond with care and useful suggestions. For example, Ralph, who described a very close and open relationship with his mother, receives "advice" from her about "sex and stuff." Similarly, Orlando often receives valuable advice from his mother about "what to do" when he "likes a girl." Keith "hardly talks" to either of his parents. Nevertheless, he can count on his father to bolster his spirits when he is feeling down:

> *Well how do you trust him? In what ways do you trust him?*
> Probably, probably when I needed his support he give it to me.
> *Like can you give me an example of that? What do you mean by that?*
> Like when I fail a test or I did something wrong, and then when I feel sad and stuff.
> *Uh huh. What would he do?*
> He would just cheer me up.

Chris repeatedly links the experience of trust with emotional support from his parents. When asked how he trusts his mother, he said that his mother comforted him as he dealt with the illness and painful loss of his paternal grandmother. Following his mother's suggestion, they visited his grandmother in the hospital shortly before she passed away. His mother "stood by [his] side" at his grandmother's funeral.

Similar themes are heard in Juan's interview. When asked to provide examples of how he trusts his mother and father, Juan talked about his parents physically being present to support him:

> *Can you give me an example of when you trusted your father?*
> He's been to every last basketball game I have ever played. And I played a lot of games. He's been to every last one. I can trust him to come cheer me on. He gives me pointers. Every last game he has on tape. Everything, everything, everything, everything.

When speaking about how he trusts his mother he stated, "Um, when I was up at Spofford [a juvenile detention facility], she came up every last day I was up there to bring me stuff, bring me clothes. I mean every last thing she did for me." A seemingly important part of Juan's trust in his parents, as well as for many of his peers in the study, is the emotional support they provide during joyous and challenging moments.

"Always Gonna Be There"

For the African American and Latino boys (and not for the Asian American boys), trusting parents was also connected to the belief that their parents have been and were "always gonna be there" in both a psychological and literal sense. For these students, this certainty was an important part of their experiences of trust with their parents. For example, Juan trusts his mother "in every way you could trust a person" because she has "always been there" for him in "every way somebody could ever be there for you." Thus, he draws an explicit link between his trust in his mother and his experience of her as a reliable and stable provider. This history of constancy translates into the belief that his mother (and his father) will continue to be there for him, "Whether you like it or not your parents are always gonna be there."

Each of these students spoke about an important difference between trusting parents and trusting friends. For example, when asked if he trusts his parents in the same way he trusts his friends, Devon told his interviewer:

> It's like if I get in some really, really bad trouble then my friends might get afraid, like you know, and go away. But my parents will always be there. 'Cause it isn't sure that I'm going to be friends with them forever.

In the context of describing why he trusts his parents more than his friends, Channing stated, "You with them [your parents] all your life. They did more things for you and then came the friends." Like Juan, Channing also connects his parents' stable presence in his life to his complete trust in them. Chris makes a similar distinction between friends and family:

> *Do you trust your parents in the same ways that you trust your friends?*
> Well, I trust my friends, I trust, I trust, well I just trust my family more than
>   friends. That's how I see it.
> *Yeah, how come? Why do you think?*
> Well family, you know, they've been around you all your life, you know,
>   they've been with you during the good times, the bad times. And friends,
>   I don't know, they, they, they just know you, you know. They're begin-
>   ning to know how you are and they begin to know about your good and
>   bad times. I would say I trust my family more.

It is especially noteworthy that Chris maintains this belief since he had not seen or spoken with his biological father for two years at the time of the interview. After his parents separated when Chris was four, his father moved down South. Chris and his father spoke and saw each other often, but ". . . every year it started narrowing down smaller and smaller" until he completely lost contact with him. In his effort to "just go on with [his] life," Chris has developed a very close "bond" with his stepfather. Perhaps it is Chris's close relationships with his mother and stepfather that serve to buffer the loss of his father and enable him to maintain faith in his family.

The boys who spoke about their parents "always being there" trusted their parents in a way they did not trust their closest friends. While there is no guarantee that friends will be there "through thick and thin," the African American and Latino boys believed that parents (or in some cases just the mother or father) would never emotionally or physically abandon them.

Discussion

In both popular culture and scholarly literature, males are often thought to have limited capacity for and interest in open expressions of love and intimacy (McAdams, 1989; Pollack, 1998; Prager, 1995). The data from this study challenge this assumption. With compassion and acuity, these boys described their trust in their relationships with their parents. They shared metaphors of connection and used tender language in their narratives of trust with parents.

Consistent with other research (Bernath & Feshbach, 1995; Erikson, 1963; Way, 1998; Youniss & Smollar, 1985), the adolescents in this study indicated that trust with their parents is experienced in a number of ways. Some of the ways in which trust manifests itself in these boys' narratives (e.g., shared confidences and reliability) have been noted in previous research (Bernath & Feshbach, 1995), while other ways (e.g., obligations) have rarely been noted.

The first theme of obligation was heard almost exclusively among the Asian American and Latino adolescents. As several authors note, family obligation is at the center of collectivist Asian cultures (Fuligni, Tseng & Lam, 1999; Huang & Ying, 1989; Sastry & Ross, 1998; Shon & Ja, 1982), and of Latino cultures (Bernal & Shapiro, 1996; Fuligni, Tseng & Lam, 1999; Garcia-Preto, 1996a, 1996b). Therefore, it is not surprising that the experience of trust with parents was associated with obligation for the Asian American and Latino boys. This finding, however, raises questions regarding whether trust is a different experience fundamentally for those who believe that trusting one's parent is an obligation rather than a choice based on, for example, shared confidences, or dependability. Adolescents who believe they have a choice regarding trusting their parents may find the issue of trust more difficult, or challenging, than those who trust their parents simply because that is what one is expected to do. Future qualitative research should explore the issue of choice versus obligation in family relationships and how these two experiences may differentially shape boys' relationships with their parents.

The second pattern that I noted in the interviews related to sharing confidences. As expected based on theoretical and research literature on trust (Buhrmester & Prager, 1995; Hestenes, 1997; Hestenes & Berndt, 1997a, 1997b; Prager, 1995; Rotenberg, 1991), a core element of trust for many of the African American and Latino boys in this study was their ability to disclose their "business," personal information, secrets, thoughts, and feelings to their parents. Their willingness to share their secrets with their parents appeared to depend upon a felt sense of security in the relationship. When they chose to edit their private thoughts and feelings, they often anticipated parental rejection, punishment, or loss of privileges. In addition, they spoke of not feeling fully understood or known by parents, and fearing that their parents would break confidentiality. Sharing confidences, however, was a key component of how and why they trusted their parents.

In stark contrast to these African American and Latino boys were the Asian American boys who indicated that they never or rarely spoke about personal or confidential issues with their parents. They attributed these silences to their ethnic background and claimed that open communication would not be appropriate in their families. Such beliefs have been noted with Asian populations (Huang & Ying, 1989; Shon & Ja, 1982). When asked about trust, the Asian American boys did speak about shared confidences, suggesting that they are aware of the common definition of trust in the United States that equates trust with shared communication. However, these boys made it clear that their disinclination toward sharing confidences with their parents was not due to a lack of trust but simply to a cultural expectation to keep "personal things" to oneself. Their trust in their parents was based on obligations and/or their parents attending to their needs. These Asian American boys challenge us to reconsider our conceptualizations of trust as the experiences of shared confidences and reliability. Their interviews reveal the ways in which the experience of trust is deeply embedded in cultural values.

Need fulfillment emerged as a third theme of trust in relationships with parents. Researchers and theorists have repeatedly recognized need fulfillment as an important aspect of trust among adolescents. Adolescent boys view their parents as important sources of guidance and tangible assistance (Furman & Buhrmester, 1985; Hestenes & Berndt, 1997a; Youniss & Smollar, 1985). This particular theme is evident among boys from diverse cultural backgrounds. It was, in fact, the only theme that was evident across the Latino, African American, and Asian American boys. However, when one compares the present research with previous research on White, middle-class populations, ethnic variations are suggested. For example, Youniss and Smollar (1985) found in their predominantly White, middle-class samples that male adolescents counted on their mothers to fulfill their material and emotional needs, while they relied on their fathers to fulfill their material needs. In this study, participants provided examples of trusting their mothers and fathers to fulfill both their material and emotional needs. Fathers in the current study were described as just as likely to fulfill emotional needs as mothers. Fathers from poor and working-class families and/or from ethnic minority cultures such as African American and Latino cultures may play a more active role in their children's emotional lives than fathers from White, middle-class families (Way & Stauber,

1996). This finding draws attention to the importance of examining not only the construct of trust and its various components but also the nuances in these components of trust with adolescents from diverse ethnic backgrounds.

The fourth theme that I detected in participants' descriptions of trust with parents is the belief that parents are "always gonna be there." The African American and Latino boys indicated confidence that their parents will stick by them and never reject them. Just as Erikson (1963) argued that reliable and consistent care is required to form basic trust in infancy, these adolescents' trust in their parents seemed to grow out of the security of knowing they will invariably be emotionally and physically present in their lives. While no studies have directly examined how this faith in parents stems from and impacts the experience of trust, both attachment (Ainsworth & Bowlby, 1989; Bowlby, 1969) and object relations (Greenberg & Mitchell, 1983) theories posit it is only when children perceive parents as available and dependable that they form secure attachments and a healthy, integrated personality. Knowing parents are "always gonna be there" may help adolescents successfully negotiate the complex developmental tasks of adolescence by providing a secure and trusting base from which to explore the world.

It is unclear why none of the Asian American boys suggested the theme of "always gonna be there." Like the theme of shared confidences, it may be that the belief that one's parents are going to "be there" or the link between trust and "being there" is an American belief not shared by Asian American boys, some of whom only recently immigrated to the United States. Although they may also experience their parents as reliable, their parents' reliability may not be a part of Asian American boys' conceptualizations about trust. It is difficult to know whether this and the shared confidences finding result from the fact that the Asian American boys in the present study are less "Americanized"[2] than the Latino and African American boys in the study, or whether these findings are related to the specific Asian culture from which the boys come. Understanding cultural differences, when culture includes immigrant status and levels of acculturation, as well as race or ethnicity, is a complex but essential goal for future research on adolescent/parent relationships.

My study begins to reveal adolescent boys' own beliefs about trust with their parents. Yet there are many questions that were not addressed in the present study. Does the meaning and experience of trust with friends differ from that with parents? Do these experiences of trust change as adolescents become young adults? How do these experiences of trust change over time? Longitudinal investigations with ethnically and socioeconomically diverse populations (that include immigrants as well as nonimmigrants) are essential to advance our understanding of adolescents' experiences of interpersonal trust in relationships. Researchers should continue listening to the voices of culturally diverse youth so that we can gain a more comprehensive and nuanced understanding of how adolescents experience and make meaning of their social worlds.

1. This larger project focused on urban adolescents is funded by the National Science Foundation and the William T. Grant Foundation and is under the direction of Professor Niobe Way.

2. On average, the Asian American boys in the study had spent less time in the United States than the Latino or the African American boys.

REFERENCES

Ainsworth, M. D. & Bowlby, J. (1989). An ethological approach to personality development. *American Psychologist, 46* (4), 333–341.

Bernal, G. & Shapiro, E. (1996). Cuban families. In M. McGoldrick, J. Giordano & J. K. Pearce (Eds.), *Ethnicity and family therapy* (2d ed., pp. 155–168). New York: Guilford Press.

Bernath, M. S. & Feshbach, N. D. (1995). Children's trust: Theory, assessment, development, and research directions. *Applied and Preventive Psychology, 4*, 1–19.

Bowlby, J. (1969). *Attachment and loss: Attachment (Vol. 1).* New York: Basic Books.

Brown, L. M. & Gilligan, C. (1992). *Meeting at the crossroads: Women's psychology and girls' development.* New York: Ballantine Books.

Buhrmester, D. & Prager, K. (1995). Patterns and functions of self-disclosure during childhood and adolescence. In K. J. Rotenberg (Ed.), *Disclosure processes in children and adolescents* (pp. 10–56). Cambridge: Cambridge University Press.

Cauce, A. (1986). Social networks and social competence: Exploring the effects of early adolescent friendships. *American Journal of Community Psychology, 14* (6), 607–628.

Cooper, C. R. (1999). Multiple selves, multiple worlds: Cultural perspectives on individuality and connectedness in adolescent development. In A. S. Masten (Ed.), *Minnesota symposium on child psychology: Vol. 29. Cultural processes in child development* (pp. 25–57). Minneapolis: University of Minnesota Press.

Doster, J. T. & Chance, J. (1976). Interpersonal trust and trustworthiness in preadolescents. *The Journal of Psychology, 93,* 71–79.

Erikson, E. H. (1963). *Childhood and society* (rev. ed.). New York: W. W. Norton.

Fuligni, A. J., Tseng, V. & Lam, M. (1999). Attitudes toward family obligations among American adolescents with Asian, Latin American, and European backgrounds. *Child Development, 70* (4), 1030–1044.

Furman, W. & Buhrmester, D. (1985). Children's perceptions of the personal relationships in their social networks. *Developmental Psychology, 21* (6), 1016–1024.

Garcia-Preto, N. (1996a). Latino families: An overview. In M. McGoldrick, J. Giordano & J. K. Pearce (Eds.), *Ethnicity and family therapy* (2d ed., pp. 141–154). New York: Guilford Press.

Garcia-Preto, N. (1996b). Puerto Rican families. In M. McGoldrick, J. Giordano & J. K. Pearce (Eds.), *Ethnicity and family therapy* (2d ed., pp. 183–199). New York: Guilford Press.

Greenberg, J. R. & Mitchell, S. A. (1983). *Object relations in psychoanalytic theory.* Cambridge, MA: Harvard University Press.

Hamid, P. N. & Lok, D. P. (2000). Loneliness in Chinese adolescents: A comparison of social support and interpersonal trust in 13 to 19 year olds. *International Journal of Adolescence and Youth, 8,* 45–63.

Hestenes, S. L. (1997, April). *A measure of interpersonal trust for use with adolescents.* Poster session presented at the biennial meeting of the Society for Research in Child Development, Washington, DC.

Hestenes, S. L. & Berndt, T. J. (1997a, April). *Early and middle adolescents' trust in parents and friends.* Poster session presented at the biennial meeting of the Society for Research in Child Development, Washington, DC.

Hestenes, S. L. & Berndt, T. J. (1997b, August). *Adolescents' trust across different types of families.* Poster session presented at the annual meeting of the American Psychological Association, Chicago, IL.

Hochreich, D. J. (1974). A children's scale to measure interpersonal trust. *Developmental Psychology, 9* (1), 141.

Huang, L. N. & Ying, Y. (1989). Chinese American children and adolescents. In J. T. Gibbs & L. N. Huang (Eds.), *Children of color: Psychological interventions with minority youth* (pp. 30–66). San Francisco: Jossey-Bass.

Imber, S. (1973). Relationship of trust to academic performance. *Journal of Personality and Social Psychology, 28* (1), 145–150.

Kahn, P. H. & Turiel, E. (1988). Children's conceptions of trust in the context of social expectations. *Merrill-Palmer Quarterly, 34* (4), 403–419.

Kindlon, D. & Thompson, M. (1999). *Raising Cain: Protecting the emotional life of boys.* New York: Ballantine Books.

Lester, D. & Gatto, J. (1990). Interpersonal trust, depression, and suicidal ideation in teenagers. *Psychological Reports, 67,* 786.

McAdams, D. P. (1989). *Intimacy: The need to be close.* New York: Doubleday.

Miles, M. B. & Huberman, A. M. (1994). *Qualitative data analysis.* Thousand Oaks, CA: Sage Publications.

Miller, B. (1991). *Adolescents' relationships with their friends.* Unpublished doctoral dissertation, Harvard University, Cambridge, MA.

Omodei, M. M. & McLennan, J. (2000). Conceptualizing and measuring global interpersonal mistrust-trust. *The Journal of Social Psychology, 140* (3), 279–294.

Pollack, W. (1998). *Real boys.* New York: Henry Holt.

Prager, K. J. (1995). *The psychology of intimacy.* New York: Guilford Press.

Rawlins, W. K. & Holl, M. (1987). The communicative achievement of friendship during adolescence: Predicaments of trust and violation. *The Western Journal of Speech Communication, 51,* 345–363.

Rempel, J. K., Holmes, J. G. & Zanna, M. P. (1985). Trust in close relationships. *Journal of Personality and Social Psychology, 49* (1), 95–112.

Rice, K. G. & Mulkeen, P. (1995). Relationships with parents and peers: A longitudinal study of adolescent intimacy. *Journal of Adolescent Research, 10* (3), 338–357.

Rotenberg, K. J. (1991). *Children's interpersonal trust: Sensitivity to lying, deception, and promise violations.* New York: Springer-Verlag.

Rotenberg, K. J. & Morgan, C. J. (1995). Development of a scale to measure individual differences in children's trust-value basis of friendship. *The Journal of Genetic Psychology, 156,* 489–502.

Rotter, J. B. (1967). A new scale for the measurement of interpersonal trust. *Journal of Personality, 35* (4), 651–665.

Rotter, J. B. (1980). Interpersonal trust, trustworthiness, and gullibility. *American Psychologist, 35* (1), 1–7.

Sastry, J. & Ross, C. E. (1998). Asian ethnicity and the sense of personal control. *Social Psychology Quarterly, 61* (2), 101–120.

Selman, R. L. (1980). *The growth of interpersonal understanding: Developmental and clinical analyses.* New York: Academic Press.

Selman, R. L. & Schultz, L. (1990). *Making a friend in youth.* Chicago: University of Chicago Press.

Shon, S. P. & Ja, D. Y. (1982). Asian families. In M. McGoldrick, J. K. Pearce & J. Giordano (Eds.), *Ethnicity and family therapy* (pp. 208–228). New York: Guilford Press.

Stack, L. C. (1978). Trust. In H. London & J. E. Exner, Jr. (Eds.), *Dimensions of personality* (pp. 561–599).

United States Census Bureau. (2002). *2001 statistical abstract of the United States.* Retrieved October 3, 2002, from http://www.census.gov/prod/2002pubs/01statab/pop.pdf.

Way, N. (1998). *Everyday courage: The lives and stories of urban teenagers.* New York: New York University Press.

Way, N. & Pahl, K. (1999). Friendship patterns among urban adolescent boys. In M. Kopala & L. Suzuki (Eds.), *Using qualitative methods in psychology* (pp. 145–161). Thousand Oaks, CA: Sage Publications.

Way, N. & Stauber, H. (1996). Are "absent fathers" really absent? Urban adolescent girls speak out about their fathers. In B. J. Ross Leadbeater & N. Way (Eds.), *Urban girls* (pp. 132–148). New York: New York University Press.

Wilson, J. M. & Carroll, J. L. (1991). Children's trustworthiness: Judgments by teachers, parents, and peers. In K. J. Rotenberg (Ed.), *Children's interpersonal trust: Sensitivity to lying, deception, and promise violations* (pp. 100–117). New York: Springer-Verlag.

Youniss, J. & Smollar, J. (1985). *Adolescent relations with mothers, fathers, and friends.* Chicago: University of Chicago Press.

6

Psychological Well-Being, School Adjustment, and Problem Behavior among Chinese Adolescent Boys from Poor Families

Does Family Functioning Matter?

Daniel T. L. Shek

A common theme in family theories is that there is a strong association between family interaction patterns at the dyadic (e.g., parent-child relationships) and systemic (e.g., family cohesion) levels and the adjustment of individual family members (e.g., Beavers & Hampson, 1990). These theories typically assert that positive family interaction patterns will lead to the positive adjustment of family members and vice versa. However, several limitations exist in this literature (Shek, 1997b, 1998). First, there are few empirical studies that assess the association between family patterns and individual adjustment. Second, because indicators of psychiatric morbidity and distress are commonly used to assess adolescent adjustment, studies rarely focus on the association between family functioning and positive mental health. Third, studies have typically employed one or two rather than multiple indicators of adjustment, and therefore a complete picture of the association between family functioning and individual adjustment is not available. Fourth, few studies of family functioning and adjustment have been conducted with poor families. According to the family ecological models (e.g., Ge et al., 1992; McLoyd, 1998), economic stress exerts a negative impact on the psychological well-being of parents, which in turn disrupts dyadic family processes, including spousal and parent-child relationships. It is conceivable that disruptions of these dyadic family processes could negatively influence systemic family functioning as well, which could both, in turn, influence adolescent adjustment.

Another limitation of existing studies is that research has been conducted mainly in Western cultures. Few studies have examined the role of family functioning on adjustment with individuals from non-Western societies such as China (Shek, 2002). According to Yang (1981), familialism and collectivism are basic attributes of the traditional Chinese culture. The importance of the family is reflected in the popular saying of "zai jia qian ri hao, chu wai ban chao nan" (there is no place like home). Hsu (1971) similarly argued that Chinese people are "much more tied psychologically to their kinship base [than are Western people]" (p. 39). Given that families play a particularly important role in Chinese culture, one would expect family functioning to contribute to adjustment in Chinese families.

Furthermore, we know little about the differential effect of family functioning on boys and girls. Given that boys and girls are regarded and treated very differently in traditional Chinese culture, the link between family functioning and adjustment may differ for boys and girls. For instance, there are some beliefs that might lead girls' adjustment to be particularly susceptible to the influence of family interactions. In traditional Chinese culture, girls and women are socialized to have strong attachments to their families. This is reflected in the saying of "zai jia cong fu, chu jia cong fu, lao lai cong zi" (obey the father before getting married, obey the husband after getting married, and obey the son when getting old). Chinese girls and women are also socialized to take care of their families, as is reflected in the saying "nan zhu wai, nu zhu nei" (men are in charge of things outside the family whereas women are in charge of things inside the family). Girls' adjustment may be particularly affected by family processes because the family is considered their "core business" and is often the place where they derive their identity status.

However, there are also beliefs within Chinese culture that might make boys' adjustment particularly susceptible to the influence of the family. In traditional Chinese culture, husbands are regarded as "yi jia zhi zhu" (master of the family) and wives and children are taught to obey the male head of the household. In addition, men are held responsible for maintaining the order of the family. In fact, an ideal family, according to Confucian thought, is one that is characterized by "fu ci zi xiao, xiong you di gong" (the father is affectionate and the son is dutiful, the elder brother is friendly and the younger brother shows respect). As boys are expected to help their fathers regulate the order within the family, one might expect that their adjustment would be heavily influenced by family dysfunction, such as pervasive family conflict and lack of family order (see Shek, 1999).

Some research findings show that male adolescents from Western societies, however, are less susceptible than females to the influences of the family (e.g., Eisenberg et al., 1992; Jaycox & Repetti, 1993). For example, Grossman et al. (1992) found that while family cohesion predicted mood, deviance, self-esteem, and grades in adolescent girls, it only predicted deviance and self-esteem in adolescent boys. Family functioning appeared to be more protective for girls than for boys. Ohannessian et al. (1995) also showed that discrepancies in perceptions of family functioning were more related to depressive symptoms in girls than in boys. It is important to consider whether the association between family functioning and adjustment varies by gender in non-Western societies as well.

This chapter reports findings from a study of perceived family functioning and psychological well-being (i.e., psychiatric morbidity and positive mental health), school adjustment (i.e., perceived academic performance, satisfaction with academic performance, and conduct), and problem behavior (i.e., delinquency and substance abuse) among Chinese adolescent boys from poor families. Specifically, the following questions were addressed: (1) What is the association between perceived family functioning (i.e., Mutuality, Communication, Conflict and Harmony, Parental Concern, and Parental Control) and psychological, academic, and behavioral adjustment in Chinese adolescent boys from poor families?; (2) Are there gender differences in these associations?; (3) Is perceived family functioning in poor adolescent boys different from the perceptions of adolescent boys drawn from a broader community sample? For the latter question, the findings reported in Shek (in press a) will be used as the basis of comparison.

It was hypothesized that those with more positive perceptions of family functioning would report better mental health and school adjustment, and lower levels of problem behavior. It was also hypothesized that adolescent boys from poor families would report poorer family functioning than adolescent boys from a broader community sample. There were no hypotheses regarding gender differences due to the lack of research with Chinese populations.

Method

Measures

ASSESSMENT OF FAMILY FUNCTIONING

Chinese Family Assessment Instrument (FAI): In light of possible cross-cultural variations in the application of Western family measures to non-Western contexts (Morris, 1990), an indigenous measure of family functioning was used. Based on an extensive review of measures of family functioning from Western countries and qualitative analyses of findings based on 412 Chinese adolescents' perceptions of the attributes of happy families (Shek, 2001), an indigenous 33-item Chinese Family Assessment Instrument (FAI) was developed. Shek (in press a) examined the reliability, validity, and factor structure of the FAI in three studies (N = 361, 732, and 3,649, respectively). These studies revealed that the FAI possesses high reliability and validity. Factor analysis suggested five stable dimensions (Mutuality, Communication, Conflict and Harmony, Parental Concern, and Parental Control) of the FAI that served as subscales. The FAI scale and its subscales were found to be internally consistent in this study (alpha = .93, .92, .86, .60, .84, and .63 for the total scale, Mutuality subscale, Communication subscale, Conflict and Harmony subscale, Parental Concern subscale, and Parental Control subscale, respectively). Higher scores on the FAI indicate higher levels of family dysfunction.

ASSESSMENT OF PSYCHOLOGICAL WELL-BEING

Existential Well-Being Scale (EXIST). The Existential Well-Being Scale, which is a part of the Spiritual Well-Being Scale, was constructed by Paloutzian and Ellison (1982) to assess life direction and satisfaction. The scale was found to be internally consistent in the present study (alpha = .80).

Life Satisfaction Scale (LIFE). The Satisfaction with Life Scale was designed by Diener, Emmons, Larsen, and Griffin (1985) to assess an individual's global judgment of his or her quality of life. The Chinese version of this scale was translated by the author and adequate reliability of this scale has been reported (Shek, 1992). The scale was found to be internally consistent in the present study (alpha = .56).

Mastery Scale (MAS). Modeled after the Mastery Scale of Pearlin and Schooler (1978), the seven-item Chinese Mastery Scale was constructed by the author. The scale measures a person's sense of control of his or her life. This scale was found to be internally consistent in this study (alpha = .69).

Chinese Self-Esteem Scale (ESTEEM). The Rosenberg Self-Esteem Scale was designed to assess the self-esteem of high school students (Rosenberg, 1979). The Chinese Rosenberg Self-Esteem Scale was developed by the author and has acceptable reliability (Shek, 1992).

The Chinese Version of the General Health Questionnaire (GHQ). The General Health Questionnaire was developed to measure current nonpsychotic disturbances (Goldberg, 1972). Chan (1985) found that the Chinese GHQ compared favorably with the English version of the scale. There is also evidence suggesting that the GHQ possesses acceptable psychometric properties (Shek, 1989, 1993). Based on Shek's findings (1993), 15 items of the 30-item GHQ that were related to anxiety and depression were used for the present study. Reliability analyses suggested that this abridged version of the GHQ was reliable (alpha = .90). While the GHQ can be regarded as assessing manifested psychiatric symptoms, the other scales can be regarded as tools assessing coping resources (i.e., personal attributes that help individuals to cope with stress: Folkman, Schaefer & Lazarus, 1979) or positive mental health characteristics (Diener, 1984).

ASSESSMENT OF SCHOOL ADJUSTMENT

Three items were constructed to assess school adjustment. The first assesses a respondent's perception of his or her academic performance as compared with schoolmates in the same grade (APC); respondents were asked to give a rating of "Best," "Better than usual," "Ordinary," "Worse than usual," or "Worst" in response to this item. The second item assessed the respondent's satisfaction with his or her academic performance (APS); respondents were asked to give a rating of "Very satisfied," "Satisfied," "Average," "Dissatisfied," or "Very dissatisfied" in response to this item. Finally, the third item was constructed to assess the respondent's perception of his or her conduct in school (CONDUCT); respondents were asked to give a rating of "Very good," "Good," "Average," "Poor," or "Very poor" in response to this item. Shek (1997a) showed that these three items were temporally stable.

ASSESSMENT OF PROBLEM BEHAVIOR

1. Substance Abuse (DRUG1 and DRUG2): Based on a review of the literature, eight items were developed to examine frequency of use

with respect to alcohol, tobacco, ice (methylamphetamine), cannabis, cough mixture, organic solvent, tranquilizers, and narcotics. The items assessing consumption of alcohol and cigarettes (i.e., gateway drugs: DRUG1) and other drugs (DRUG2) were found to be reliable (alpha = .69 and alpha = .65, respectively; in Shek, 2002).

2. Delinquency (DELIN): Based on a review of the literature (e.g., Shek & Ma, 1997), 12 items were developed to examine the frequency of a respondent's engagement in antisocial behaviors, including stealing, cheating, being truant, running away from home, damaging others' property, assaulting others, having sexual relationships with others, gang fighting, using foul language, staying away from home without parental consent, strong-arming others, and breaking into others' places. This scale has been found to have adequate reliability (alpha = .60).

Participants and Procedures

Data were derived from Time 1 of a longitudinal study of the adjustment of adolescents from poor families, in which there were two waves of data collection. Two hundred and twenty-eight Chinese adolescents (106 adolescent boys and 122 adolescent girls) participated at Time 1. The participants were recruited from families receiving Comprehensive Social Security Assistance (CSSA sample, $N = 167$) or full Textbook Allowance from the Government (TBA sample = 62). In Hong Kong, families receiving CSSA or full TBA are regarded as families with financial difficulties.

During home visits, the participants completed an Adolescent Questionnaire, which contains all the instruments described in the previous section. To ensure confidentiality, each participant completed the questionnaire separately. For those who had problems with comprehension, the questions or items were asked in an interview format by a trained interviewer.

Results

Correlation coefficients for the association between family functioning, as indexed by the total scores of the Family Assessment Instrument, and adjustment among the adolescent boys in this study are presented in Table

TABLE 6.1

Correlation Coefficients between the Family Assessment Inventory and
Individual Measures of Adolescent Psychological Well-Being, School Adjustment,
and Problem Behavior in Adolescent Boys with Economic Disadvantage (N = 106)

Variables	FAI
EXIST	−.42*
LIFE	−.13ns
MAS	−.25*
ESTEEM	−.42*
GHQ	.24*
APS	.13ns
APC	.18ns
CONDUCT	.30*
DELIN	.38*
DRUG1	.33*
DRUG2	.11ns

Note: FAI: Family Assessment Instrument. EXIST: Existential Well-Being Scale. LIFE: Life Satisfaction Scale. MAS: Mastery Scale. ESTEEM: Self-Esteem Scale. GHQ: General Health Questionnaire. APS: Perceived academic performance. APC: Academic performance compared with others. CONDUCT: School conduct. DELIN: Delinquent behavior. DRUG1: Smoking and alcohol consumption. DRUG2: Use of narcotics and psychotropic substances.

A two-tailed multistage Bonferroni procedure was used to obtain the data. pFW is based on the familywise Type 1 error rate; pT is based on the Type 1 error rate per test.

* $pFW < .10\ pT > .025$
ns not significant

6.1. Because several correlation analyses were performed, the multistage Bonferroni procedure was carried out to guard against inflated Type 1 error (Larzelere & Mulaik, 1977). In this procedure, a familywise Type 1 error was determined for a family of tests, and the significance of individual tests were then evaluated.

The data revealed that more positive perceptions of family functioning were related to better mental health, better school conduct, and fewer problem behaviors. However, perceived family functioning was not related to life satisfaction, academic performance, or illegal drug use.

Because many adjustment variables were assessed, factor analysis was performed to reduce the data volume. Specifically a principal component analysis followed by a varimax rotation suggested three dimensions or factors that could be meaningfully identified from the large set of adjustment variables. The first factor was labeled Mental Health (MH), and included ex-istential well-being (EXIST), sense of mastery (MAS), life satisfaction (LIFE), self-esteem (ESTEEM), and general psychological health (GHQ) variables. The second factor was labeled School Adjustment (SA), and included perceived academic performance (APS), perceived relative academic performance (APC), and school conduct (CONDUCT) variables. The final factor was a Problem Behavior (PB) factor that included smoking and drinking (DRUG1), psychotropic substance abuse (DRUG2), and delinquency (DELIN). Shek (2002) showed that these factors were highly stable in different samples. Correlations between different dimensions of family functioning and these three factors are presented in Table 6.2.

Correlational analysis suggested that systemic family functioning (i.e., Mutuality, Communication, Conflict, and Harmony) was associated with adjustment for the adolescent boys, while the dyadic parent-child relational qualities (i.e., Parental Concern and Parental Control) were not associated with adjustment (see Table 6.2).

Furthermore, there were no gender differences in the association between the family functioning and mental health (MH) (see Table 6.2). However, a significant association between family functioning and school adjustment (SA) was detected among the girls and not the boys. Finally, there was a significant association between family functioning and problem behavior (PB) for the boys but not for the girls.

Table 6.3 shows that there were no significant differences in most of the dimensions of perceived family functioning between adolescent boys from poor families and adolescent boys from a diverse community sample ($N = 3,649$; Shek, in press a). However, compared with boys in the broader community sample, poor adolescent boys perceived their families to have more conflict.

TABLE 6.2

Correlation Coefficients between Perceived Systemic and Dyadic Family Functioning and the Composite Scores for Adolescent Adjustment

	MH		SA		PB	
	Male	Female	Male	Female	Male	Female
Total	−.31*	−.26*	.23^a	.30*	.34*	.18ns
Mutuality	−.31*	−.24*	.21^a	.25*	.26*	.16ns
Communication	−.29*	−.30*	.25*	.22^a	.40*	.17ns
Conflict and Harmony	−.18ns	−.20^a	.15ns	.31*	.30*	.13ns
Parental Concern	−.21^a	−.09ns	.16ns	.24*	.09ns	.21^a
Parental Control	−.01ns	−.11ns	.05ns	.32*	−.01ns	.05ns

Note: MH: Index of mental health. SA: Index of school adjustment. PB: Index of problem behavior. Total: Total scores of the FAI. Mutuality: Mutuality subscale of the Family Assessment Instrument (FAI). Communication: Communication subscale of the FAI. Conflict and Harmony: Conflict and Harmony subscale of the FAI. Parental Concern: Parental Concern subscale of the FAI. Parental Control: Parental Control subscale of the FAI.

A two-tailed multistage Bonferroni procedure was used to obtain the data. pFW is based on the familywise Type 1 error rate; pT is based on the Type 1 error rate per test.

* $pFW > .10$ $pT > .009$ in the male sample; pFW [less than] .10 pT [less than] .01 in the female sample
^{a} Border significance; $pT > .05$
ns not significant

TABLE 6.3
Differences between Poor Adolescent Boys and Adolescent Boys in the Broader Community Sample on Subscales of the Family Assessment Instrument

| | Present Sample | | Norm | | |
	Mean	SD	Mean	SD	t-value
Total	83.05	18.98	79.77	22.49	−1.46ns
Mutuality	30.14	8.63	29.42	9.07	−0.80ns
Communication	25.38	6.57	25.16	7.55	−0.30ns
Conflict and Harmony	14.99	3.43	12.87	4.33	−4.93*
Parental Concern	5.61	2.36	5.36	2.35	−1.05ns
Parental Control	7.3	2.37	7.07	2.83	−0.81ns

Source: Shek, in press a.
Note: Total: Total scores of the FAI. Mutuality: Mutuality subscale of the Family Assessment Instrument (FAI). Communication: Communication subscale of the FAI. Conflict and Harmony: Conflict and Harmony subscale of the FAI. Parental Concern: Parental Concern subscale of the FAI. Parental Control: Parental Control subscale of the FAI. Norm: findings based on male adolescents reported by Shek (in press a). A conservative alpha level (*p* > .0083) was adopted to evaluate the differences between the two groups.
   * *p* > .001
   ns not significant

Discussion

This study found that adolescent boys who reported better family functioning generally reported better psychological and behavioral health than adolescent boys who reported poorer family functioning. This observation is consistent with previous studies in which a lower level of family competence was related to a higher level of adolescent psychopathology (Martin et al., 1995; McFarlane, Bellissimo & Norman, 1995; Summerville et al., 1994) or a higher level of family dysfunction was positively related to adolescent conduct problems (Frick et al., 1992) and substance abuse (Doherty & Allen, 1994). Academic performance, however, was unrelated to perceived family functioning for the adolescent boys in this study (see Table 6.1). This finding may be explained by the fact that Chinese parents place a very strong emphasis on academic excellence for their children, particularly for their boys. This emphasis is reflected in the cultural saying "wang zi cheng long" (wishing the son to become a dragon). Therefore, the demand for academic excellence may not decrease even though family functioning is poor. In short, the emphasis in Chinese culture on academic excellence in adolescent boys may compensate for the generally negative influence of poor family functioning on academic adjustment.

The findings also suggested that different dimensions of family functioning are differentially related to the adjustment of adolescent boys. While the mental health and levels of problem behavior among adolescent boys were significantly related to the systemic family functioning, none of the psychological, academic, or behavioral adjustment outcomes were related to the dyadic parent-child relational qualities for the adolescent boys. Additional studies are needed to understand the reasons for these findings, and the processes by which different dimensions of family functioning influence adolescent adjustment.

The findings also indicated no gender differences in the association between perceived family functioning and adolescent mental health (see Table 6.2). This observation is not consistent with literature that suggests female adolescents are more susceptible to the influence of family functioning than are male adolescents or that family functioning is more protective for girls than for boys (e.g., Eisenberg et al., 1992; Grossman et al., 1992; Jaycox & Repetti, 1993). This discrepancy between the literature and the current findings may reflect differences in the participants' socioeconomic status and culture. Previous studies have focused almost exclusively on middle-class adolescents. Unlike in middle-class families, healthy family functioning may act as a protective factor in poor families regardless of the gender of the individual family member. Furthermore, healthy family functioning may be particularly protective in cultures such as in China, in which the importance of the family is emphasized. Finally, while there are some beliefs in Chinese culture that may lead girls' mental health to be strongly influenced by the family, there are other beliefs that may make boys' mental health particularly susceptible to the influence of the family. As a result, gender differences in the relationship between family functioning and psychological well-being may not be evident in youth growing up in China.

Gender differences, however, were detected in the association between family functioning and school adjustment, with the association being significant for girls but not for boys. This finding may be explained by the fact that Chinese parents place less emphasis on the importance of academic excellence for girls. This cultural practice is reflected in the saying "nu zi wu cai bian shi de" (it is a virtue for a woman to have no knowledge). Because girls in China are not expected to attain academic excellence, parents tend to support the academic work of girls less than boys. As a result, the negative influence of family dysfunction may spill over to the academic domain for girls but not for boys.

There was also a gender difference in the association between family functioning and problem behavior, which was significant for boys and not for girls. Moreover, the mean value of the correlation coefficients for adolescent boys was nearly three times that of adolescent girls. This finding may be explained by the socialization practices of Chinese parents. Because Chinese parents are very concerned about the chastity of girls, parental control of girls' behavior is generally greater than of boys' behavior (Shek, 2000). Consequently, the opportunity for girls to engage in problem behavior would be less than for boys.

The present findings suggest that the association between family functioning and adolescent adjustment varies across different indicators of adolescent adjustment. For boys, family functioning may influence problem behaviors but that finding may be more the consequence of parental control than of family functioning more generally. For girls, family functioning may influence school adjustment but, once again, the process underlying this finding may have more to do with the value of education for girls than with the level of family functioning per se.

The present study also found that while there were generally no differences between the reported levels of family functioning for boys from poor families and those from a broader community sample, poor adolescent boys did perceive their families to have more family conflict. Low socioeconomic status and the stress associated with that experience may be the primary cause of this latter finding. However, the fact that there were no other differences in family functioning between the two groups may be due to the fact that parents receiving Comprehensive Social Security Assistance (many of the parents in the present study) have been given a longer time to stay at home with their children. This opportunity may enhance family functioning and compensate for some of the more negative effects of the stress of poverty.

Given the correlational nature of the data, one cannot make a causal link between family functioning and adolescent adjustment. Those with mental health problems might perceive one's family in a more negative manner (i.e., perceptual distortion hypothesis). In addition, adolescent adjustment (e.g., distress and lack of life meaning) may be a precursor of poor family functioning rather than vice versa. Longitudinal research, consequently, is needed to assess the direction of effect between family functioning and adolescent adjustment.

Despite limitations of the data, several conclusions can be drawn from the study. First, the findings suggest that positive family functioning is an important correlate of mental and behavioral outcomes for Chinese adolescent boys from poor families. Second, systemic family functioning (i.e., mutuality, communication, conflict and harmony) appears to be a more important correlate of adjustment for adolescent boys than are dyadic parent-child relational qualities (i.e., parental concern and parental control). Third, gender differences in the association between family functioning and adolescent adjustment appear to exist only for academic and behavioral adjustment outcomes and not for mental health outcomes. These latter findings underscore the importance of examining multiple dimensions of adjustment in any study of adjustment. Finally, there were few differences in perceived family functioning between poor adolescent boys and a broader community sample. These findings challenge the common belief that the functioning of poor families is worse than that of non-poor families. Clearly we need to know more about the family functioning of poor adolescents from Western and non-Western cultures and how different aspects of family functioning help adolescents thrive. Longitudinal research with Chinese and non-Chinese populations are needed to address these critical questions.

NOTE

This work was financially supported by the Research Grants Council of the UGC, Government of the Hong Kong Special Administrative Region (Grant CUHK4087/99H).

REFERENCES

Beavers, W. R. & Hampson, R. B. (1990). *Successful families: Assessment and intervention.* New York: Norton.

Bowen, G. L. & Chapman, M. V. (1996). Poverty, neighbourhood danger, social support, and the individual adaptation among at-risk youth in urban areas. *Journal of Family Issues, 17,* 641–666.

Chan, D. W. (1985). The Chinese version of the General Health Questionnaire: Does language make a difference? *Psychological Medicine, 15,* 147–155.

Diener, E. (1984). Subjective well-being. *Psychological Bulletin, 95,* 542–575.

Diener, E., Emmons, R. A., Larsen, R. J. & Griffin, S. (1985). The Satisfaction with Life Scale. *Journal of Personality Assessment, 49,* 71–75.

Doherty, W. J. & Allen, W. (1994). Family functioning and parental smoking as predictors of adolescent cigarette use: A six-year prospective study. *Journal of Family Psychology, 8,* 347–353.

Eisenberg, N., Fabes, R. A., Carlo, G., Troyer, D., Speer, A. L., Karbon, M. &

Switzer, G. (1992). The relations of maternal practices and characteristics to children's vicarious emotional responsiveness. *Child Development, 63,* 583–602.

Folkman, S., Schaefer, C. & Lazarus, R. S. (1979). Cognitive processes as mediators of stress and coping. In V. Hamilton & J. Warburton (Eds.), *Human stress and cognition* (pp. 265–298). New York: Wiley.

Frick, P. J., Lahey, B. B., Loeber, R. & Stouthamer-Loeber, M. (1992). Familial risk factors to oppositional defiant disorder and conduct disorder: Parental psychopathology and maternal parenting. *Journal of Consulting and Clinical Psychology, 60,* 49–55.

Garmezy, N., Masters, A. & Tellegen, A. (1984). The study of stress and competence in children: A building block for developmental psychopathology. *Child Development, 55,* 97–111.

Ge, X. J., Conger, R. D., Lorenz, F. O., Elder, G. H., Montague, R. B. & Simons, R. L. (1992). Linking family economic hardship to adolescent distress. *Journal of Research on Adolescence, 2,* 351–378.

Goldberg, D. P. (1972). *The detection of psychiatric illness by questionnaire.* Oxford: Oxford University Press.

Grossman, F. K., Beinashowitz, J., Anderson, L., Sakurai, M., Finnin, L. & Flaherty, M. (1992). Risk and resilience in young adolescents. *Journal of Youth and Adolescence, 21,* 529–550.

Hauser, S. T., Vieyra, M. A. B., Jacobson, A. M. & Wertlieb, D. (1989). Family aspects of vulnerability and resilience in adolescents: A theoretical perspective. In T. F. Dungan & R. Coles (Eds.), *The child in our times: Studies in the development of resilience* (pp. 109–133). New York: Brunner/Mazel.

Hsu, F. L. K. (1971). Psychosocial homeostatis and jen: Conceptual tools for advancing psychological anthropology. *American Anthropologist, 73,* 23–44.

Jaycox, L. H. & Repetti, R. L. (1993). Conflict in families and psychological adjustment of preadolescent children. *Journal of Family Psychology, 7,* 344–355.

Larzelere, R. E. & Mulaik, S. A. (1977). Single-sample tests for many correlations. *Psychological Bulletin, 84,* 557–569.

Martin, G., Rozanes, P., Pearce, C. & Allison, S. (1995). Adolescent suicide, depression and family dysfunction. *Acta Psychiatrica Scandinavica, 92,* 336–344.

McDonald, L. & Sayger, T. V. (1998). Impact of a family and school based prevention program on protective factors for high risk youth. *Drugs and Society, 12,* 61–85.

McFarlane, A. H., Bellissimo, A. & Norman, G. R. (1995). Family structure, family functioning and adolescent well-being: The transcendent influence of parental style. *Journal of Child Psychology and Psychiatry and Allied Disciplines, 36,* 847–864.

McLoyd, V. (1998). Socioeconomic disadvantage and child development. *American Psychologist, 53,* 185–204.

Morris, T. M. (1990). Culturally sensitive family assessment: An evaluation of the Family Assessment Device used with Hawaiian-American and Japanese-American families. *Family Process, 29,* 105–116.

Murphy, L. B. & Moriarty, A. E. (1976). *Vulnerability, coping and growth from infancy to adolescence.* New Haven: Yale University Press.

Ohannessian, C. M., Lerner, R. M., Lerner, J. V. & von Eye, A. (1995). Discrepancies in adolescents' and parents' perceptions of family functioning and adolescent emotional adjustment. *Journal of Early Adolescence, 15,* 490–516.

Orthner, D. K. (1996). Families in poverty: Key issues for research. *Journal of Family Issues, 17,* 588–592.

Paloutzian, R. F. & Ellison, C. W. (1982). Loneliness, spiritual well-being and the quality of life. In L. A. Peplau & D. Perlman (Eds.), *Loneliness: A sourcebook of current theory, research and therapy* (pp. 224–237). New York: Wiley.

Pearlin, L. I. & Schooler, C. (1978). The structure of coping. *Journal of Health and Social Behavior, 22,* 337–356.

Rosenberg, M. (1979). *Conceiving the self.* New York: Basic Books.

Shek, D. T. L. (1989). Validity of the Chinese version of the General Health Questionnaire. *Journal of Clinical Psychology, 45,* 890–897.

Shek, D. T. L. (1992). "Actual-ideal" discrepancies in the representation of self and significant-others and psychological well-being in Chinese adolescents. *International Journal of Psychology, 27,* 229.

Shek, D. T. L. (1993). The factor structure of the Chinese version of the General Health Questionnaire (GHQ-30): A confirmatory factor analysis. *Journal of Clinical Psychology, 49,* 678–684.

Shek, D. T. L. (1997a). Family environment and adolescent psychological well-being, school adjustment, and problem behavior: A pioneer study in a Chinese context. *Journal of Genetic Psychology, 158,* 113–128.

Shek, D. T. L. (1997b). The relation of family functioning to adolescent psychological well-being, school adjustment, and problem behavior. *Journal of Genetic Psychology, 158,* 467–479.

Shek, D. T. L. (1998). A longitudinal study of the relations of family functioning to adolescent psychological well-being. *Journal of Youth Studies, 1,* 195–209.

Shek, D. T. L. (1999). Marital quality and well-being of Chinese couples in a Chinese context: A longitudinal study. *Journal of Gender, Culture and Health, 4*(2), 83–96.

Shek, D. T. L. (2000). Chinese adolescents' perceptions of parental differences in parenting characteristics, parent-adolescent communication and parent-adolescent relationship. *Adolescence, 35,* 135–146.

Shek, D. T. L. (2001). Perceptions of happy families amongst Chinese adolescents and their parents: Implications for family therapy. *Family Therapy, 28,* 73–103.

Shek, D. T. L. (2002). The relation of parental qualities to psychological well-being, school adjustment and problem behavior in Chinese adolescents with economic disadvantage. *American Journal of Family Therapy, 30,* 215–230.

Shek, D. T. L. (in press a). Assessment of family functioning in Chinese adolescents: The Chinese Family Assessment Instrument. In N. N. Singh, T. Ollendick & A. N. Singh (Eds.), *International perspectives on child and adolescent mental health.* Amsterdam, Netherlands: Elsevier.

Shek, D. T. L. (in press b). Family functioning and psychological well-being, school adjustment, and problem behavior in Chinese adolescent girls experiencing economic disadvantage. *Family Therapy.*

Shek, D. T. L. & Lai, M. F. (2000). Conceptions of an ideal family in Confucian thoughts: Implications for individual and family counseling. *Asian Journal of Counseling, 7,* 85–104.

Shek, D. T. L. & Ma, H. K. (1997). Perceptions of parental treatment styles and adolescent antisocial and prosocial behavior in a Chinese context. *Psychologia, 40,* 233–240.

Summerville, M. B., Kaslow, N. J., Abbate, M. F. & Cronan, S. (1994). Psychopathology, family functioning, and cognitive style in urban adolescents with suicide attempts. *Journal of Abnormal Child Psychology, 22,* 221–235.

Walsh, F. (1993). *Normal family processes.* New York: Guilford Press.

Wynne, L. C., Jones, J. E. & Al-Khayyal, M. (1982). Healthy family communications patterns: Observations in families "at-risk" for psychopathology. In F. Walsh (Ed.), *Normal family processes* (pp. 142–167). New York: Guilford Press.

Yang, K. S. (1981). The formation and change of Chinese personality: A cultural-ecological perspective. *Acta Psychologica Taiwanica, 23,* 39–56.

7

The Role of Father Support in the Prediction of Suicidal Ideation among Black Adolescent Males

Darian B. Tarver, Naima T. Wong, Harold W. Neighbors, and Marc A. Zimmerman

Suicide is a vital public health concern today. The Centers for Disease Control and Prevention (CDC, 2000) report that approximately eighty-six Americans of all ages commit suicide and 1,500 more attempt to commit suicide every day (CDC, 2000). Among youth, suicide is the third leading cause of death for those fifteen to twenty-four years of age (CDC, 2000). From 1980 to 1996 suicide rates in the United States doubled for adolescents ten to fourteen years old (CDC, 2000). According to the National Center for Health Statistics (1997), more young people died from suicide than from cancer, heart disease, AIDS, birth defects, stroke, pneumonia, and influenza, and chronic lung disease combined.

The past two decades have seen a sudden and sharp increase in the suicide rate, specifically among Black Americans. CDC (2000) reports that young Black American males are the fastest growing group at risk for suicide. Between 1980 and 1996, the suicide rate more than doubled for Black American males aged fifteen to nineteen years (CDC, 2000). Although young Black American males are at increased risk for suicide death, few studies on suicidal behavior have included Black adolescents in their samples (Juon & Ensminger, 1997).

Recently, the U.S. Surgeon General proposed that a public health approach be used to address the problem of suicide (Satcher, 1998). A public health approach focuses on those individuals or groups at highest risk and places emphasis on prevention. Research shows that suicidal behavior can be conceptualized on a continuum beginning with suicide ideation (thoughts about intentionally killing oneself), followed by attempts and concluded with completion (Cole, Protinsky & Cross 1992; Paykel et al., 1974; and Dubow et al., 1989 all cited in Marcenko et al., 1999). Therefore, the best way to reduce the incidence of suicide is to prevent suicide ideation. This chapter focuses on understanding suicide ideation in a sample of Black American male adolescents.

The chapter begins with a description of the epidemiology of suicide and a summary of the psychosocial predictors associated with suicidal behavior in Black American male youth. Following this review, the results from a community study are presented and used to explore various risk and protective factors related to suicide ideation. Research has shown that father social support can contribute to adolescent resiliency against a number of precursors for suicide ideation including low self-esteem, substance use, and depression (Grant et al., 2000; Zimmerman et al., 1995). In this study, emphasis is placed on the role of the father and how his support may protect against suicide ideation and its negative correlates. Resiliency theory is used to explain the pathway to suicide ideation for young Black American males. Recommendations for prevention and future research directions are discussed.

Epidemiology

The Youth Risk Behavior Surveillance System (YRBSS), a national survey conducted by the CDC, is one of the few data sources that provide an epidemiologic description of the prevalence of suicide ideation among the general adolescent population. The YRBSS reported that 19.3% of high school students indicated that they seriously considered suicide and 8.3% attempted suicide in 1999. Other studies suggest that 8–11% of all adolescents attempt suicide (Adcock et al., 1991; Walters et al., 1995). One study suggested that up to 60% of youth have experienced some degree of suicide ideation (Smith & Crawford, 1986 cited in DiFilippo & Overholser, 2000). Unfortunately, the national data that are available and many of the studies that use community samples do not report prevalence of suicidal behavior (i.e., suicide ideation and attempt) by race or gender and those that do have limited generalizability (Joe & Kaplan, 2001). It is also possible that the suicidal behavior rates are even higher than those reported because of underreporting due to the sensitive nature of the topic (Joe &

Kaplan, 2001; Gibbs, 1988). Marcenko et al. (1999) suggest that research on suicidal ideation is typically the study of the respondent's willingness to admit suicidal thoughts versus actual assessment of suicide ideation prevalence. Even though the rates for suicide ideation and attempts may be unclear, the fact remains that the suicide mortality rate for young Black American males is steadily on the rise and requires attention (CDC, 2000).

Psychosocial Predictors of Adolescent Suicide

Father Support

Social support has been identified as a factor that fosters resilience in youth (Grant et al., 2000; Zimmerman, Ramirez-Valles, 2000; Zimmerman et al., 1998). Overall, adolescents tend to rate parent support the highest among the various sources of social support (e.g., peers, teachers) (Rigby & Slee, 1999). Adolescent males, in general, are more likely to seek help from their parents and less likely to seek support from their peers than adolescent females (Boldero & Fallon, 1995). Researchers have found that support from parents is a critical factor in buffering the effects of suicidal ideation, depression, and stress (Harris & Molock, 2000; Hollis, 1996 cited in Rigby & Slee, 1999). Other research has found that among Black American males, parent support protects against depression, which is a major risk factor for suicide ideation (Zimmerman, Ramirez-Valles, et al., 2000). These findings suggest that parent support may also play a critical role in protecting against suicide ideation.

It is important to recognize that parent-youth relationships are characterized differently for fathers and mothers and their sons and daughters during adolescence. Some research suggests that mothers and daughters have more intimate relationships than mothers and sons, and that sons and fathers have more intimate relationships than daughters and fathers (Clark-Lempers et al., 1991). Others have found, however, that males and females do not differ in their relationships with their mothers, but females tend to see fathers as less central in their lives (Blyth & Foster-Clark, 1987; Youniss & Smollar, 1985). Overall, mothers are disproportionately more often the focus of parental support research than fathers (Zimmerman, Salem & Notaro, 2000). For instance, Juon and Ensminger (1997) conducted a longitudinal study of Black suicide in the United States that included measures of mother involvement, but they did not include data on father involvement. Typically fathers are not included in studies and if they are, it is usually from the perspective of father absence (i.e., nonresidential) (Levine & Pitt, 1995). Although most research related to fathers focuses on father absence, father absence should not be equated with uninvolvement. Researchers have suggested that nonresidential fathers often provide support to their children regardless of their custodial status and that their absence from the home does not necessarily ensure a poor relationship with or negative behaviors for sons or daughters (Levine & Pitt, 1995; Salem et al, 1998; Way & Stauber, 1996; Zimmerman, Salem & Notaro, 2000).

Interest in fathers' influence on child development is growing. Only a handful of studies, however, consider the role of fathers when assessing factors that contribute to the psychological and social adjustment of youth (Zimmerman, Salem & Notaro, 2000). Grant and colleagues (2000), for example, conducted a study that included 224 Black American male and female middle school students to assess how protective factors like parent support and religious involvement moderated the effects of stressful life experiences (e.g., death of friend, transportation problems). They found that father support reduced experiences of stress and substance use among the Black adolescent males. Phares and Compas (1992) also report strong evidence that father support is associated with lower levels of substance use. Zimmerman, Salem, and Maton found that father support was related to higher self-esteem and less depressive symptoms in a sample of 254 Black American male adolescents. Salem, Zimmerman, and Notaro (1998) replicated these results in a larger sample of Black American youth that also included females. These studies suggest that father support may protect against suicide ideation and related negative behaviors. In contrast, McCabe, Clark, and Barnett (1999) found no relationship between father support and substance use in Black American youth. However, their sample included only sixty-four male and female participants and may not have had adequate power to detect any existing effect.

Depression, Depressive Symptoms, and Depressed Mood

Major depression and previous suicide attempts are two of the most consistent predictors of suicidal behavior among adolescents regardless of demographic characteristics (Shaffer, Garland, Gould, Fisher & Trautman, 1988 cited in Adock et al., 1991). Heightened levels of depression and other psychological conditions have been identified as risk factors among ethnic minority youths. Summerville, Kaslow and Doepke (1996) found minority youth who attempt suicide compared to those who do not are more likely to report depression. In their longitudinal study of 953 Black Americans, Juon and Ensminger (1997) found that depressive symptoms in Black male children were associated with suicide ideation. In their follow-up, depressed mood was a risk factor for suicide ideation and suicide attempt for Black male adults (Juon & Ensminger, 1997).

In general, researchers suggest different trajectories of suicidal behavior for Black and White Americans. Suicide rates for Black males and females tend to peak during adolescence and young adulthood, whereas the rates for Whites increase with age. Little is known, however, about possible explanations for these differences (Joe & Kaplan, 2001; Gibbs, 1997; Spaights & Simpson, 1986). A significant proportion of the suicide literature focuses on clinical samples of youths that have attempted suicide. More research is necessary to understand how depression is exhibited in nonclinical representative community samples to further our understanding of what is predictive of suicide before it reaches the clinical level. There are few studies of nonclinical samples of Black youths and even fewer that solely concentrate on Black males (Juon & Ensminger, 1997).

Substance Use

The relationship between alcohol use and suicidal behaviors has been well-documented (Reifman & Windle, 1995; Langhinrichsen-Rohling et al., 1998). Adolescents who engage in substance use have been identified as having higher levels of suicide ideation than those who have not (Cohen, 2000; Juon & Ensminger, 1997; Jones, 1997). Some researchers have examined suicidal behaviors and drug and alcohol use among Black adolescents (Marcenko et al., 1999; Jones, 1997; Juon & Ensminger, 1997; Vega et al., 1993). In a study of 120 students equally distributed between male and female Black, Hispanic, and White Americans, Marcenko and colleagues (1999) found that substance users were more likely to report ideation regardless of race or ethnicity. Some researchers, however, found alcohol and substance use among males did not predict suicide ideation (Juon & Ensminger, 1997; Vega et al., 1993). The findings from these studies are restricted by small sample sizes and varied measurement of substance use, which may explain the inconsistency between results. Studies that include multiple measures of substance use with larger samples of Black American male adolescents may help to clarify the equivocal nature of this literature.

Resiliency Theory

Resiliency theory provides a useful model for understanding the link between risks (e.g., depression and substance use) for suicide ideation and the role fathers may play to reduce the effects of those risks. Resiliency refers to those factors and processes that interrupt the trajectory from risk to problem behaviors or psychopathology (Garmezy, 1991; Masten, 1994; Rutter, 1987; Werner, 1993). Garmezy and Masten (1991) defined resilience as "a process of, or capacity for, successful adaptation despite challenging and threatening circumstances." Researchers have described several mechanisms by which environmental and individual factors helped to reduce or offset the adverse effects of risk factors (Zimmerman & Arunkumar, 1994). Garmezy, Masten, and Tellegen (1984) have proposed two resiliency models: (1) the compensatory model and (2) the protective model.

Compensatory factors are variables that neutralize exposure to risk or operate in a counteractive fashion against the potential negative consequences introduced by a risk (Garmezy et al., 1984; Masten et al., 1988). An example of compensation is when depression is found to be a risk factor for suicide ideation, but father support helps to counteract the effects of depression. Compensatory factors are hypothesized to have the opposite effect of a risk factor, but both have direct effects on the outcome. Protective factors, unlike compensatory factors, modify the effects of risks in an interactive fashion (Rutter, 1985). An example of a protective factor is the effect father support may have on the association between substance use and suicide ideation. The association between suicidal ideation and substance use would differ for youth with high levels of father support as compared to youth with low levels of father support (e.g., the association would be diminished with high levels of support and remain strong with low levels of support).

This study uses resiliency theory as a framework for studying the effects of father support on Black male adolescent suicide ideation. A compensatory effect is supported if father support has a negative effect in predicting suicide ideation after controlling for depression and substance use. In other words, if father social support is associated with less suicide ideation even after accounting for depression and substance use, then a compensatory effect is detected. A protective effect is supported if father support modifies the association of depression or substance use for predicting suicide ideation. That is, if the relationship between substance use and ideation is different for different levels of father support, then a protective effect is detected. The idea behind a protective model is that the relationship between a risk factor such as depression or substance use and suicide ideation will be reduced by father support. The protective model differs from the compensatory model in that the protective model suggests that the relationship between the risk and outcome depends on the level of father support. In a compensatory model, however, father support simply reduces the impact of a risk factor such as depression on suicidal ideation.

Methods

Sample

Our study sample was from a larger longitudinal study of 850 ninth-grade adolescents selected from the four main public high schools in the second largest school district in Michigan. Students enrolled in the school system at the start of the fall of 1994 with grade point averages (GPAs) of 3.0 and below were selected. This grade cutoff was used because one goal of the larger project was to study youths at risk for leaving school before graduation. Students who were diagnosed as being either emotionally impaired or developmentally disabled were not included in the study. The original sample included 679 Black youths (80%), 145 White youths (17%), and 26 mixed Black and White youths (3%) and was equally divided by sex. Youths were followed for 6 years. The data reported in this study come from Black males in Wave 4 (12th grade). The twelfth-grade sample consisted of 292 Black males. This constituted an 87% response rate from year 1 to year 4.

Procedure

Trained Black and White male and female interviewers conducted face-to-face interviews. Interviewers were not matched to respondents by race or sex because the school wanted the data to be collected as efficiently as possible to minimize disruption. Students were called from their classrooms and taken to select areas within the school for the interviews, which lasted between 50 and 60 minutes. Youths who could not be found in school were interviewed in a community setting (e.g., home or Urban League office). Students were informed that all information was confidential and subpoena protected.

Measures

Table 7.1 reports the means, standard deviations, and skewness for the independent variables.

Suicide Ideation

Suicide ideation was assessed with a single-item measure that asked "During the past week, including today, please tell me how uncomfortable you felt because of the following problem: Thoughts of ending your life." Answers were scored on a 5-point Likert scale that ranged from 1 = "Not at all" to 5 = "Extremely." This item was taken from the Brief Symptom Inventory depression measure (Derogatis & Spencer, 1982).

Depressive Symptoms

Using a 5-point Likert scale, five items were used to assess depressive symptoms. These five items were taken from the Brief Symptom Inventory (Derogatis & Spencer, 1982), and asked students to indicate the frequency during the past week, including today, of various feelings (e.g., "feeling lonely," "feeling no interest in things," feeling hopeless about the future"). Notably, the suicide ideation item from the measure was excluded. Higher scores represented higher levels of depressive symptomatology. The Cronbach alpha for the depressive symptom scale was 0.85.

Substance Use

Substance use included two variables: alcohol use and marijuana use. Alcohol and marijuana use were measured by a sum of last year and last month use on a 7-point Likert scale (1 = 0 times to 7 = 40 or more times). Participants answered these questions in a pencil and paper format following the face-to-face interview. These items were the same as those used in the Monitoring the Future study (Johnston, O'Malley & Bachman, 1988).

Father Support

Father support was assessed using four items that measured emotional and school support. Emotional support was included because conceptu-

TABLE 7.1
Descriptive Statistics for Independent Variables

Variable	Number of Items	N	Mean	SD	Skew
Depressive Symptoms	5	291	1.79	0.95	1.45
Substance Use	6	283	4.56	3.77	.87
Father Support	4	335	2.86	2.14	−.43

ally it is a form of support most closely related to psychological well-being. School support was included because it is a particularly relevant form of support for high school aged youth due to the fact that school can be a significant source of stress for high school youth and may contribute to mental distress for this population. These two forms of support were combined into one measure to increase reliability of the measure (the Cronbach's alpha for this measure was 0.98) and simplify the analysis. For the purposes of this study, we were more interested in father support generally than in specific components of it. Sample items include, "I rely on my father for emotional support" and "My father encourages me to stay in school." The items used a 5-point Likert scale (1 = not true, 5 = very true). Youth ($n = 65$) who responded to the item, "How often do you speak with or see your father?" with "no contact" or "never" were re-coded with zero for the father support variable.

Data Analytic Strategy

First, we conducted an attrition analysis with the youth excluded from the study due to missing data ($n = 43$) to determine if they differed from the youth included in the study. We conducted independent sample t-tests to compare these two groups on all the study variables collected at Time 1. Next, we conducted a point biserial correlation analysis to determine whether the identified risk factors (i.e., depressive symptoms and substance use) and protective factor (i.e., father support) were associated with suicide ideation among Black males. The variables that were related to suicide ideation were included in a hierarchical regression analysis. Hierarchical regression analysis allows for the assessment of the effect that each variable has on the outcome variable. This analysis included entering depressive symptoms (risks) as Step 1, substance use (risks) as Step 2, and father support (asset) as Step 3 (test of compensatory effects). Suicide ideation was the outcome variable. This sequence of steps allows us to examine the effects of father support on suicidal ideation over and above the effects of depressive symptoms and substance use, thereby allowing us to assess the compensatory effects of father support. Separate equations were also run after Steps 1–3 were entered to test for interactions between father support and depression, and between father support and substance use. This series of tests allows us to assess the protective effects of father support. The sample used for these analyses consisted of 292 Black male adolescents out of the possible 335 (87%).

Results

Attrition Analysis

Wave 3 data were used to determine whether the 43 students eliminated from the analysis differed from the 292 students on the study variables. The independent *t*-tests indicated no differences between these two groups on any of the Time 1 study variables (e.g., depression, alcohol and substance, father support).

Prevalence of Suicide Ideation

Based on the 292 students who responded to the suicide ideation question, 80.5% ($n = 235$) reported that suicide ideation was not a problem, while 4.5% ($n = 13$) reported that it was a little problem, 4.5% ($n = 13$) reported that it was a moderate problem, 2.7% ($n = 8$) reported that it was a problem pretty often, and 7.9% ($n = 23$) reported that it was an extreme problem. Due to the skewed nature of the responses to the suicide ideation question, the data were re-coded into two categories—no suicide ideation and suicide ideation—for data analytic purposes. Students who responded "not at all" were re-classified as "no suicide ideation," and those who were in all of the other categories were reclassified as "suicide ideation." Almost 20% ($n = 57$) of the sample reported ideation, while the remaining reported no ideation. Within the sample that reported ideation, 68% of them reported contact with their father compared to 81% of those who did not report ideation. Results from the Mantel-Haenszel chi-squared test showed that those who did not report ideation had significantly more contact with their fathers than those who did report ideation.

Point Biserial Correlations

Table 7.2 reports the correlation among all study variables. The table indicates that depressive symptoms, substance use, and father support are all related to suicidal ideation. The more likely respondents are to feel depressed and use illicit substances, the more likely they are to experience feelings of suicide. Furthermore, father support was significantly associated with suicidal ideation. That is, as support from fathers increases, sons' suicide ideation decreases. Since these data are cross-sectional, no causal inferences can be made from these results. Nevertheless, the findings presented in Table 7.2 suggest that father support is associated with mental health. Subsequent regression analysis included the depressive symptoms, substance use, and father support measures.

Hierarchical Regression

Due to the fact that suicide ideation was re-coded into a dichotomous variable, logistic hierarchical regression was employed for the remaining analytic procedures. Only the variables that were significant in the correlation analysis were included in the regression analysis. The final odds ratios (*OR*), adjusted R-squared values, and change in R-squared values from the

TABLE 7.2
Point Biserial Correlation Matrix of All Observed Variables

Variables	1	2	3	4
Suicide Ideation	—	—	—	—
Depressive Symptoms	.58**	—	—	—
Substance Use	.18**	.23**	—	—
Father Support	−.14*	−.09	−.07	—

* Correlation is significant at the 0.05 level (2-tailed).
** Correlation is significant at the 0.01 level (2-tailed).

TABLE 7.3
Final OR, Adjusted R², and Change in R² for Compensating and Protective Effects

Variable	Final OR	Adjusted R²	Δ R²
Depressive Symptoms	4.62	.44	.44**
Substance Use	1.27	.44	.00
Father Support	.65	.46	.02*
Interactions			
Substance Use/Support	.63	.48	.02*

* $p > 0.05$
** $p > 0.01$.

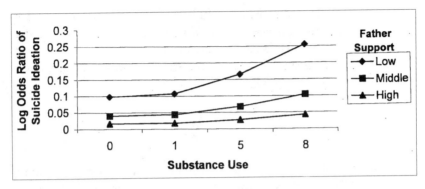

Figure 7.1. Interaction Effect of Father Support and Substance Use for Predicting Suicide Ideation

logistic regression analysis are reported in Table 7.3. Depressive symptoms (Step 1) predicted 44% of the variance in suicide ideation. Step 2, substance use, did not contribute additional variance for predicting suicide ideation. The independent effects of father support (Step 3) contributed an additional 2% of the variance. This finding suggested that father support did have a compensatory effect on suicidal ideation. Father support was a significant predictor of suicidal ideation over and above the effects of depression and substance use. The interaction effect of substance use and father school support (Step 4a) also added 2% of the explained variance in the model. The association between substance use and suicidal ideation varied according to levels of father support. This latter finding suggested that father support was a protective factor in the association between substance use and suicidal ideation. The final model explained 48% of the variance in suicide ideation.

Decomposition of Interaction Effects

We decomposed the interaction effect of substance use and father support following the procedure described by Aiken and West (1991). We computed separate equations to examine the association between substance use and suicide ideation at different levels of father support. Father support was classified into low, middle, and high (where one standard deviation below the mean was classified as low; the mean was classified as middle; and one standard deviation above the mean was classified as high). The lines in Figure 7.1 represent the linear relationship between substance use and suicide ideation at the different levels of father social support. Figure 7.1 indicates that the effects of substance use on suicidal ideation diminish as the level of father support increases. It also indicates that effects of substance use on suicidal ideation are strongest at the lowest levels of father support.

Discussion

We found suicide ideation to be a fairly common phenomenon among Black adolescent males as one out of every five Black males in our sample reported some degree of suicide ideation. This finding is consistent with Vega et al.'s (1993) finding that adolescent Black males had high prevalence of suicide ideation (20.5%) compared to Hispanic (17.8%) and White (19.3%) male adolescents. It should be noted that due to the sensitive nature of the question, it is conceivable that the 20% prevalence rate found in the present study may be an underestimate of the true prevalence level. Nevertheless, this finding illustrates that suicide ideation is a significant issue among adolescent Black males and highlights the need for prevention efforts for this population.

Furthermore, we found father support to be both a compensatory factor and a protective factor for the risk of suicide ideation associated with substance use. The compensatory model of resiliency was supported by the finding that father support predicted less suicide ideation after controlling for both depressive symptoms and substance use. The protective model of resiliency was supported by the interaction effect of father support and substance use for predicting suicide ideation. The interaction effect suggested that, although substance use is associated with suicide ideation, this association is reduced as father support increases. Interestingly, the effects of substance use for predicting suicide ideation are most dramatic at the lowest levels of father support, but these effects are virtually absent at the highest levels of father support. These results are consistent with previous research that the negative effects of problem behavior and psychological distress may diminish as father support increases (Zimmerman, Ramirez-Valles, et al., 2000; Zimmerman, Salem & Notaro, 2000). Our study, however, does not inform us about the characteristics of the relationship that may be beneficial. Future research that includes in-depth interviews with both fathers and their sons may help to identify what factors in father/son relationships help reduce risks associated with suicide ideation.

Researchers have noted that depressive symptomatology is the single best predictor of suicide. Our results also indicated that depressive symptomatology was the most consistent predictor of suicide ideation in our sample. Other researchers have noted that substance use also predicts suicide ideation among Black male adolescents (Vega et al., 1993; Juon & Ensminger, 1997). The results from this study, however, are somewhat inconsistent with these previous findings. Our results indicated that although substance use was correlated with suicide ideation, it was not associated with suicide ideation once depressive symptomatology was accounted for (i.e., controlled statistically). One possible explanation for this finding is that depressive symptoms may mediate the relationship between substance use and suicide ideation. Research that examines the effects of substance use on depression and, subsequently, on suicidal ideation may be particularly helpful for understanding how substance use may be indirectly related to suicide ideation.

Researchers have largely neglected the role that fathers play in the development or prevention of suicidal ideation and behavior. The virtual absence of fathers in the suicide ideation literature highlights the often-implicit belief that support given by fathers, other than financial support, is irrelevant for healthy adolescent development. This study provides evidence that father support may be important for their sons' psychological well-being. Most researchers have focused attention on the role of mothers, but we have little information about how mothers and fathers have differential effects on adolescent development. Future research that examines how father support may be similar to and different from mother support will enhance our understanding of the role that parents play in healthy adolescent development.

Several study limitations should be noted. First, the data used in the present study were cross-sectional. Using data at only one point in time limits one's ability to infer causation. Future studies that use longitudinal data can help to determine whether father support is, in fact, decreasing the risk for suicidal ideation or if those at low risk for suicidal ideation are simply more likely to report higher father support. Second, suicide ideation was measured with a single item that was further limited by recoding it to be dichotomous. Thus, we may have both reduced the variance available to explain and missed capturing a more nuanced assessment of suicide ideation. Nevertheless, we found theoretically consistent relationships even though we had limited variance to explain. Thus, our study may have been a conservative test of resiliency theory and father support. Finally, it is likely that the relationships found would be stronger with more in-depth measures for both suicide ideation and father support. Yet, the fact that effects were found with somewhat limited measures suggest that focusing on father support as an asset in the prevention of suicidal ideation is a valuable direction for future research. Future research that uses a qualitative approach may provide a more in-depth inquiry into adolescent suicide ideation and the mechanism by which assets in their lives may help them overcome the effects of risks.

These limitations notwithstanding, this study builds upon the burgeoning research literature documenting the vital role fathers play in healthy adolescent development. Our results provide additional evidence that Black fathers' support may help their adolescent children to be resilient against the risks they face for harmful outcomes. This study is also significant because it conceptualized fathers as an asset in adolescents' lives. Research on fathers often focuses on the negative effects of their absence from the home and assumes that not being present in the home is the same as being absent from their children's lives. This study is also noteworthy because it examines the role of fathers in adolescent resiliency in a sample and on a topic that has not been widely studied. Suicide ideation among Black adolescents is understudied and the focus on assets in the youths' lives (i.e., father support) is even more uncommon. We hope that this study motivates future research that focuses on fathers, assets in youths' lives, and understudied populations to build knowledge about positive youth development.

NOTE

This study was supported by grants from the National Institute on Drug Abuse, Grant number DA07484 and from the Centers for Disease Control funded Youth Violence Prevention Center, Grant number CCR518605. Support was also provided by The Center for Research on Ethnicity Culture and Health and W. K. Kellogg Foundation. This chapter does not necessarily represent the views of the National Institute on Drug Abuse, The Centers for Disease Control, The Center for Research on Ethnicity Culture and Health, or the W. K. Kellogg Foundation.

REFERENCES

Adcock, A. G., Nagy, S. & Simpson, J. A. (1991). Selected risk factors in adolescent suicide attempts. *Adolescence, 26* (104), 817–828.

Aiken, L. S. & West, S. G. (1991). *Multiple Regression: Testing and Interpreting Interactions.* Newbury Park, CA: Sage.

Bettes, B. & Walker, E. (1986). Symptoms associated with suicidal behavior on childhood and adolescence. *Journal of Abnormal Psychology, 14,* 591–604.

Blumenthal, S. J. & Kupfer, D. J. (Eds.). (1990). *Suicide Over the Life Cycle.* Washington, DC: American Psychiatric Press.

Blyth, D. A. & Foster-Clark, F. S. (1987). Gender difference in perceived intimacy with different members of adolescents' social networks. *Sex Roles, 17* (11/12), 689–718.

Boldero, J. & Fallon, B. (1995). Adolescent help-seeking: What do they get help for and from whom? *Journal of Adolescence, 18,* 193–209.

Brook, J. S., Brook, D. W., Gordon, A. S. & Whiteman, M. (1990). The psychosocial etiology of adolescent drug use: A family interactional approach. *Genetic, Social, and General Psychology Monographs, 116,* 111–267.

Bush, J. A. (1976). Suicide and Blacks: A conceptual framework. *Suicide and Life Threatening Behavior, 6,* 216–222.

Caldwell, C. H., Zimmerman, M. A. & Isichei, P. A. C. (2001). Forging collaborative partnerships to enhance family health: An assessment of strengths and challenges in conducting community-based research. *Journal of Public Health Management and Practice, 7* (2), 1–9.

Carnetto, S. S. (1997). Meanings of gender and suicidal behavior during adolescence. *Suicide and Life Threatening Behavior, 27* (4), 339–351.

Centers for Disease Control and Prevention (CDC) (2000). Suicide in the United States. [Online]. Available: http://www.cdc.gov/ncipc/factsheets/suifacts.htm.

Centers for Disease Control and Prevention (CDC) (2001). Fact Sheet: Youth Risk Behavior Trends. [Online]. Available: http://www.cdc.gov/nccdphp/dash/yrbs/trend.htm.

Clark-Lempers, D. S., Lempers, J. D. & Ho, C. (1991). Early, middle, and late adolescents' perceptions of their relationships with significant others. *Journal of Adolescent Research, 6* (3), 296–315.

Cohen, E. M. (2000). Suicidal ideation among adolescents in relation to recalled exposure to violence. *Current Psychology: Developmental, Learning, Personality, Social, 19* (1), 46–56.

Curran, D. K. (1987). *Adolescent Suicidal Behavior.* New York: Hemisphere.

DeJong, M. L. (1992). Attachment, individuation, and the risk of suicide and women's suicidal behaviors. *Journal of Youth Adolescence, 21,* 357–373.

Derogatis, L. R. & Spencer, P. M. (1982). *The Brief Symptom Inventory (BSI): Administration and scoring procedures.*

DiFilippo, J. M. & Overholser, J. C. (2000). Suicide ideation in adolescent psychiatric inpatients as associated with depression and attachment relationships. *Journal of Clinical Child Psychology, 29* (2), 155–166.

Garmezy, N. (1991). Resilience and vulnerability to adverse developmental outcomes associated with poverty. *American Behavioral Scientist, 34,* 416–430.

Garmezy, N. & Masten, A. S. (1991). The protective role of competence indicators in children at risk. In E. M. Cummings, A. L. Green & K. H. Karraker (Eds.), *Life-span Developmental Psychology: Perspectives on Stress and Coping.* pp. 151–174. Mahwah, NJ: Lawrence Erlbaum.

Garmezy, N., Masten, A. S. & Tellegen, A. (1984). The study of stress and competence in children: A building block of developmental psychology. *Child Development, 55,* 97–111.

Gibbs, J. T. (1988). Conceptual, methodological, and sociocultural issues in Black youth suicide: Implications for assessment and early intervention. *Suicide and Life Threatening Behavior, 18* (1), 73–89.

Gibbs, J. T. (1997). African-American Suicide: A Cultural Paradox. *Suicide and Life Threatening Behavior 27* (1), 68–79.

Grant, K. E., O'Koon, J. H., Davis, T. H., Roache, N. A., Poindexter, L. M., Armstrong, M. L., Minden, J. A. & McIntosh, J. M. (2000). Protective factors affecting low-income urban African American youth exposed to stress. *Journal of Early Adolescence, 20* (4), 388–417.

Harris, T. & Chris L. (1993). Suicide and adolescence. *International Journal of Offender Therapy and Comparative Criminology 37* (3), 263–270.

Harris, T. L. & Molock, S. D. (2000). Cultural orientation, family cohesion and family support in suicide ideation and depression among African American college students. *Suicide and Life-Threatening Behavior: Special Issue, 30* (4), 341–353.

Joe, S. & Kaplan, M. S. (2001). Suicide among African American men. *Suicide and Life Threatening Behavior, 31 (Supplement),* 106–121.

Johnston, L. D., O'Malley, P. M. & Bachman, J. G. (1988). *Illicit drug use, smoking, and drinking by America's high school students, college students, and young adults, 1975–1987.* Rockville, MD: National Institute of Drug Abuse.

Jones, G. D. (1997). The role of drugs and alcohol in urban minority adolescent suicide attempts. *Death Studies, 21* (2), 189–202.

Juon, H. & Ensminger, M. E. (1997). Childhood, adolescent, and young adult predictors of suicidal behaviors: A prospective study of African Americans. *Journal of Child Psychology and Psychiatry, 38* (5), 555–563.

Langhinrichsen-Rohling, J., Lewinsohn, P., Rohde, P., Seely, J., Monson, J., Meyer, K. A. & Langford, R. (1998). Gender differences in the suicide-related behaviors of adolescents and young adults. *Sex Roles, 39* (11–12), 839–854.

Levine, J. A. & Pitt, E. W. (1995). *New Expectations: Community Strategies for Responsible Fatherhood.* New York: Families and Work Institute.

Marcenko, M., Fishman, G. & Friedman, J. (1999). Reexamining adolescent suicidal ideation: A developmental perspective applied to a diverse population. *Journal of Youth and Adolescence, 28* (1), 121–138.

Marciano, P. & Alan, K. (1994). Self-esteem, depression, hopelessness, and suicidal intent among psychiatrically disturbed inpatient children. *Journal of Clinical Child Psychology 23* (2), 151–160.

Masten, A. S. (1994). Resilience in individual development: Successful adaptation despite risk and adversity. In M. Wang, E. W. Hetherington & P. H. Mussen (Eds.), *Handbook of Child Psychology Vol. 4. Socialization, Personality, and Social Development.* pp. 1–101. New York: John Wiley.

Masten, A. S., Garmezy, N., Tellegen, A., Pelligrini, D. S., Larkin, K. & Larsen, A. (1988). Competence and stress in schoolchildren: The moderating effects of individual and family qualities. *Journal of Child Psychology and Psychiatry, 29,* 745–764.

McCabe, K. M., Clark, R. & Barnett, D. (1999). Family protective factors among urban African American youth. *Journal of Clinical Child Psychology, 28* (2), 137–150.

National Center for Health Statistics (1997). CDC unpublished mortality data from the National Center for Health Statistics (NCHS) Mortality Data Tapes. [Online]. Available: http://www.cdc.gov/ncipc/factsheets/suifacts.htm.

Nisbet, P. A. (1996). Protective factors for suicidal black females. *Suicide and Life Threatening Behavior, 26* (4), 325–341.

Phares, V. & Compas, B. E. (1992). The role of fathers in child and adolescent psychopathology: Make room for daddy. *Psychological Bulletin, 111* (3), 387–412.

Prinstein, M., Boergers, J., Spirito, A., Little, T. & Grapentine, W. (2000). Peer functioning, family dysfunction, and psychological symptoms in a risk factor model for adolescent inpatients' suicidal ideation severity. *Journal of Clinical Child Psychology 29* (3), 392–405.

Procidano, M. E. & Heller, K (1983). Measures of perceived support from friends and from family: Three validation studies. *American Journal of Community Psychology, 11,* 1–24.

Reifman, A. & Windle, M. (1995). Adolescent suicidal behaviors as a function of depression, hopelessness, alcohol use, and social support: A longitudinal investigation. *American Journal of Community Psychology, 23* (3), 329–354.

Rigby, K. & Slee, P. (1999). Suicidal ideation among adolescent school children, involvement in bully-victim problems, and perceived social support. *Suicide and Life Threatening Behavior, 29* (2), 119–130.

Rutter, M. (1985). Resilience in the face of adversity: Protective factors and resistance to psychiatric disorder. *British Journal of Psychiatry, 147,* 598–611.

Rutter, M. (1987). Psychosocial resilience and protective mechanisms. *American Journal of Orthopsychiatry, 57,* 316–331.

Salem, D. A., Zimmerman, M. A. & Notaro, P. C. (1998). Effects of family structure, family process, and father involvement on psychosocial outcomes among African-American adolescents. *Family Relations, 47,* 331–341.

Satcher, D. (1998). Bringing the public health approach to the problem of suicide. *Suicide and Life Threatening Behavior, 28* (4), 325–327.

Spaights, E. & G. Simpson (1986). Some unique causes of black suicide. *Psychology, A Quarterly Journal of Human Behavior, 23,* 1–5.

Strauss, J., Birmaher, B., Bridge, J., Axelson, D., Chiapetta, L., Brent, D. & Ryan, N. (2000). Anxiety disorders in suicidal youth. *Canadian Journal of Psychiatry, 45* (8), 739–745.

Summerville, M. B., Abbate, M. F., Siegel, A. M., Serravezza, J. & Kaslow, N. J. (1992). Psychopathology in urban female minority adolescents with suicide attempts. *Journal of the American Academy of Child Adolescent Psychiatry, 31* (4), 663–668.

Summerville, M. B., Kaslow, N. J. & Doepke, K. J. (1996). Psychopathology and cognitive and family functioning in suicidal African-American adolescents. *Current Directions in Psychological Science, 5* (1), 7–11.

Vega, W. A., Gil, A. G., Warheit, G. J., Apospori, E. & Zimmerman, R. S. (1993). The relationship of drug use to suicide ideation and attempts among African American, Hispanic, and White non-Hispanic male adolescents. *Suicide and Life Threatening Behavior, 23* (2), 110–119.

Victor, F., Mikulincer, M. & Bucholtz, I. (1995). Effects of adult attachment style on the perception and search for social support. *The Journal of Psychology, 129* (6), 665–676.

Vilhjalmsson, R, Krisjansdottir, G. & Sveinbjarnardottir, E. (1998). Factors associated with suicide ideation in adults. *Social Psychiatry and Psychiatric Epidemiology, 33* (3), 97–103.

Walters, H. J., Vaughan, R. D., Armstrong, B., Krakoff, R. Y., Maldonado, L. M., Tiezzi, L. & McCarthy, J. F. (1995). Sexual, assaultive and suicidal behaviors among urban minority junior high school students. *American Academy of Child and Adolescent Psychiatry, 34* (1), 73–80.

Way, N. & Stauber, H. (1996). Are fathers really absent? In B. Leadbeater and N. Way (Eds.), *Urban Girls.* New York: NYU Press.

Werner, E. E. (1993). Risk, resilience, and recovery: Perspectives from the Kauai Longitudinal Study. *Development and Psychopathology, 5,* 503–515.

Wunderlich, U., Bronisch, T. & Wttchen, H. U. (1998). Comorbidity patterns in adolescents and young adults with suicide attempts. *European Archives of Psychiatry and Clinical Neuroscience, 248* (2), 87–95.

Youniss, J. & Smollar, J. (1985). *Adolescent Relations with Mothers, Fathers and Friends.* Chicago: University of Chicago Press.

Zimmerman, M. A. & Arunkumar, R. (1994). Resiliency research: Implications for schools and policy. *Social Policy Report, 8,* 1–18.

Zimmerman, M. A., Ramirez-Valles, J., Zapert, K. M. & Maton, K. I. (2000). A longitudinal study of stress-buffering effects for urban African-American male adolescent problem behaviors and mental health. *Journal of Community Psychology, 28* (1), 17–33.

Zimmerman, M. A., Salem, D. A. & Maton, K. I. (1995). Family structure and psychosocial correlates among urban African-American adolescent males. *Child Development, 66,* 1598–1613.

Zimmerman, M. A., Salem, D. A. & Notaro, P. C. (2000). Make room for daddy II: The positive effects of fathers' role in adolescent development. In R. Taylor and L. Wang (Eds.), *Resilience across Contexts: Family, Work, Culture, and Community.* Mahwah, NJ: Lawrence Erlbaum.

Zimmerman, M. A., Steinman, K. J. & Rowe, K. J. (1998). Violence among urban African American adolescents: The protective effects of parent support. In X. B. Arriaga & S. Oskamp (Eds.), *Addressing Community Problems: Psychological Research and Interventions.* pp. 78–103. Thousand Oaks, CA: Sage Publications.

Part III

Friends and Peers

Intimacy, Desire, and Distrust in the Friendships of Adolescent Boys

Niobe Way

At a conference for the Society on Research on Adolescence a few years ago, I was approached by a well-known and respected researcher of friendships who asked me about my research on friendships among adolescents. He wanted to know about my qualitative findings since he had yet to use such methods in his own research. As I was describing some of my preliminary findings, I indicated who my research participants were—urban, poor and working-class, ethnic minority adolescent boys. He interrupted me by saying: "Oh, so you study gangs." I clarified that I do not study gangs but rather the friendships of urban youth.[1] He seemed confused by my distinction.

The conflation of friendships among urban adolescent boys with gangs represents a troubling and harmful stereotype that is pervasive in the social sciences and the larger culture. Relationships between male teenagers from the "inner city" are assumed to be problematic, dangerous, and fraught with violence. This stereotype has led to the exclusion of urban adolescent boys from the developmental literature, which results in an incomplete, reductive, and thus inadequate understanding of adolescent development. Urban, low-income, ethnic minority adolescent boys, like their suburban, middle-class, and White peers, provide information not only about what it means to be an adolescent in a particular environment and from a particular culture, but also what it means to be an adolescent.

For almost a decade, the goal of my research has been to understand the experience of friendships among adolescent boys from urban, low-income neighborhoods. I focus on same-sex friendships because my early qualitative research indicated that male friendships are key relationships in the lives of urban adolescent boys (Way, 1998). Friendships constituted the relationships in which the boys experienced the most joy, but also the most difficulty. In their interviews, the boys spoke of struggling more with finding and maintaining close friendships, for example, than with separating from their parents. Although my early research was originally focused on boys' experiences of peer and family relationships, same-sex friendships repeatedly consumed the boys' interviews.

African American, Latino, White, and Asian American boys from poor and working-class urban families have been telling me and other researchers who focus on similar populations (e.g., Cunningham & Meunier, this volume; Stevenson, this volume) stories that often challenge the most fundamental beliefs about boys' development. Yet, few developmental researchers seem to be listening, believing perhaps that these predominantly ethnic minority boys from urban low SES families are not good representations of what it means to be a boy or to have friends. Their stories are perceived as relevant only for the study of Black, Latino, or poor communities and not relevant for the study of boys, friendship, or adolescence. Those of us who have been listening for many years to boys from the "hood," however, strongly disagree.

Previous Research on Boys' Friendships

Although the research on friendships does not, for the most part, include the voices of urban youth (boys or girls), such research is important to review because it forms the base of what we know about boys' friendships. The research on adolescent boys' friendships[2] has predominantly focused on dimensions of friendship quality (e.g., intimacy, affection, companionship, conflict) and has typically assessed, for example, the levels of intimacy in boys versus girls' friendships or in adolescent friendships more generally (Bukowski, Newcomb & Hartup, 1996; Furman, 1996; Furman & Buhrmester, 1985; Sharabany, Gershoni & Hoffman, 1981; Savin-Williams & Berndt, 1990). Research has repeatedly found that adolescent girls are more likely than boys to experience intimacy in their friendships, while adolescent boys are more likely to have activity-oriented friendships (Belle, 1989; Buhrmester & Furman, 1987). This particular finding has, in some respects, dominated the field of adolescent friendships with textbook after textbook repeating this finding of sex difference in their discussion of adolescent development. Recent research suggests, however, that this sex difference declines over time as adolescents begin to rely on each other for processing, among many topics, romantic relationships (see Azmitia, Kamprath & Linnet, 1998; Rawlins, 1992). Yet despite these newer findings, the belief that adolescent boys have activity oriented rather than intimate male friendships continues to pervade the research literature and popular culture. Research has also suggested that loyalty, as well as feeling understood and being able to truly be oneself in the relationship, is a key component in close friendships for girls and boys (Savin-Williams & Berndt, 1990). These features of close friendships (i.e., intimacy, loyalty, acceptance) are considered critical aspects of adolescent friendships and distinguish adolescent from childhood friendships (Savin-Williams & Berndt, 1990).

Research with ethnic minority youth suggests that friendship qualities, such as patterns of intimacy, may be shaped by culture (Cauce, 1986, 1987; Dubois & Hirsch, 1990; Gallagher & Busch-Rossnagel, 1991; Hamm, 1994; Jones & Costin, 1997; Way & Chen, 2000). In their study of friendships among 240 sixth and ninth graders, Jones, Costin, and Ricard (1994) found that African American males were more likely to reveal their personal thoughts and feelings to male friends than were European American males. Furthermore, European American adolescents were the only ones who revealed significant sex differences in levels of self-disclosure in their friendships. Similarly, DuBois and Hirsch (1990) found, in their study of 292 Black and White junior high school children, that White girls reported having significantly more supportive friendships than White boys. However, no sex differences were detected among the Black students. They also found that Black boys were more likely to have intimate conversations with their best friends than were White boys, whereas no differences were found between Black and White girls. Finally, Gallagher and Busch-Rossnagel (1991) found, in their study of relationships among 311 adolescent girls, that middle-class White and Black girls were more likely to disclose their beliefs and attitudes to their friends than were White or Black girls from low-income families. My survey-based research with adolescents indicated ethnic differences with African American and Latino adolescents reporting more positive and satisfying friendships than Asian American adolescents. In addition, sex differences in perceived quality of general friendships were detected only among the Latino adolescents and not among the African American or Asian American adolescents (Way & Chen, 2000).

While this body of research underscores the importance of culture in understanding friendship processes, a limitation has been its tendency to compare ethnic minority or low SES adolescents with White or middle-class adolescents. Implicit in this research is the premise that White and/or middle-class populations are, or should be, considered the norm against which to compare ethnic minority and/or low-income populations. The experiences of ethnic minority and/or low-income populations, however, should be researched and understood in their own right (see Gaines, 1997). There has also been a tendency in the friendship research with White, ethnic minority, middle-class, and low SES adolescents to study gender differences rather than how boys, or girls, specifically experience their friendships over time. This skews the findings so that the only elements of boys' friendships that are understood are those that appear to be distinct from girls' friendships.

There have, however, been studies that focus exclusively on boys' development. This body of work, primarily focused on White middle-class boys, has emphasized the detrimental impact of conventional masculinity on boys' relationships (Kindlon & Thompson, 1999; Pollack, 1998). In order to conform to conventional masculinity, it is argued, boys cover up their emotions, feelings, and vulnerabilities. Accommodating the norms of masculinity, in essence, forces boys to give up their intimate relationships with other boys in the name of autonomy, strength, independence, and heterosexuality (Kindlon & Thompson, 1999; Pollack, 1998). Yet as Chu (this volume) indicates, this work on boys presents the boys as "passive participants or even victims" of this process rather than as active agents in their socialization and development. There is no room, in these depictions of boys, for boys' responses to these cultural mandates much less boys' resistance to, or at least a conscious engagement with, these norms of masculinity. The boys are presented as if they have little or no agency, and as if their experiences are independent of race, ethnicity, or social class. These limitations result in a series of questions with respect to my own work: Do these arguments have relevance for diverse populations of boys who have not necessarily experienced the benefits of accepting, whether unconsciously or explicitly, a conventional stance of autonomous masculinity? Do boys from urban, low-income families also cover over their emotions, thoughts, feelings, and vulnerabilities in their relationships with other boys? Do they forego intimate relationships with other boys for the sake of maintaining a masculine pose?

In response to these questions and gaps in the research literature, my studies with predominantly ethnic minority adolescent boys from urban, low-income neighborhoods sought to explore how boys experience their friendships with other boys, and how these experiences of friendships change as they go through adolescence.

Method

Participants

Since 1989, I, with the assistance of colleagues and graduate students,[3] have been conducting a series of longitudinal studies of boys and girls from poor and working-class urban environments (Way, 1995, 1998; Way & Chen, 2000; Way & Pahl, 1999, 2001). These studies have focused primarily on the development of friendships and have included, in sum, approximately 200 adolescent boys who have been interviewed each year for a 3–5 year period from early adolescence through late adolescence. The ethnic composition of each study included African American, Puerto Rican, and Dominican youth. Some of these studies have also included Asian Americans who primarily identify as Chinese American and a few White boys. All of the youths in my studies come from poor or working-class families and attend neighborhood schools that are struggling to keep their doors open despite the chaos and dysfunction that permeate their buildings.

Research Orientation

My approach to research is voice-centered, relational, and grounded in feminist theory. Based on women's experiences, a voice-centered, relational approach to research aims to listen closely to the subtleties of human voices and stories. The approach underscores the complexity of development, the "nonlinear, nontransparent orchestration of feelings and thoughts" (Brown & Gilligan, 1992, 3).

A relational approach to research assumes that the patterns that are "found" by researchers are products of what occurred between two or more people—the researcher and the researched. The narrative in an interview or the responses in a survey are never a pure or "innocent" representation of the "Other" (see Fine, 1991), but are jointly constructed. In my research with boys, this relational assumption led me to allow for both stability and spontaneity. Although a specific set of interview questions was posed to each boy, room was given during the interview for the adolescent and the interviewer to follow new and unexpected pathways. This semi-structured approach to interviewing explicitly acknowledges both the interviewer's agenda (e.g., to understand a particular topic from the boy's perspective) and the adolescent boy's agency (e.g., to introduce important new knowledge that the interviewer had not anticipated).

Understanding and attuning oneself to the power dynamics within the research relationship is an additional goal in relational and voice-centered research. What is said as well as what remains unspoken by both the interviewer and interviewee is determined, in part, by the inevitable power dynamics within the research relationship. The research might be empowering and/or disempowering for the interviewee and interviewer depending on the specifics of the interview protocol, context, and goal. Although as an interviewer and principal investigator, I exercise the authority to phrase and select the questions and to interpret the adolescents' responses, the adolescents have the power of knowing, interpreting, and phrasing their own experiences and deciding what to tell me and what not to tell me. Attuning myself to who is speaking and from what vantage point, without pretending to understand another's position completely, strengthens the rigor of my research because it encourages me to see and hear the unexpected.

A relational approach also assumes that an individual's words cannot be separated from the cultural context in which they are embedded. To examine how a person speaks about her or his world is to understand that these experiences are intimately connected to her or his specific location in the world. Holding such assumptions, I am consistently searching and probing during and after the interviews to understand what types of cultural expectations, hopes, desires, and stereotypes are influencing the stories of the participants as well as my own questions, thoughts, interpretations, and comments. Reflections on this process are then incorporated into the findings of the research.

Procedure

The boys in each of my studies have been interviewed by me, one of my colleagues, or a graduate student. These interviewers are ethnically diverse and come from various socioeconomic backgrounds. Often, they have had extensive experience working as counselors or teachers in urban settings.

Although I originally thought that most of the boys should be interviewed by male interviewers, many boys over the years have expressed a preference for a female interviewer. Consequently, most of our interviews have been conducted by women who have had extensive experience working with adolescent boys. The boys were often interviewed by the same interviewer each year for 3–5 years in order to enhance, to the greatest degree possible, the quality of the interviews and to create a safe space for the participants.

The semi-structured interviews in each study have typically been one-to-one interviews that last two to three hours. The interview protocol (similar across all of the studies) focuses on how adolescent boys experience and describe their friendships, what makes them feel close to their close male friends, what they value about their friendships, and how they see their friendships changing over time. Although each interview included a standard set of questions, follow-up questions were open-ended in order to capture the adolescents' own ways of describing their relationships. All interviews were audiotaped and transcribed.

Data Analysis

The data analysis of the interview transcripts has included two techniques: narrative summaries (Miller, 1988) and a variation of a data analytic technique called the Listening Guide (Brown & Gilligan, 1992). The intent of narrative summaries is to condense the stories told by each participant, quoting the participant extensively in order to maintain the flavor of the discussion (Miller, 1988). In the analyses presented in this chapter, my research team and I created brief summaries of each discussion of friendship in each interview. Next, we identified themes across and within these narrative summaries. Then we read the interviews for each theme, which involved highlighting each passage, sentence, or word in the transcription that suggests the particular theme in question. This process of highlighting helps to create a trail of evidence for the themes one is following. My technique of listening for themes is based on the Listening Guide (Brown et al., 1999), which encourages the listener to pay close attention to the form (i.e., how the story was told) and content of the interview, and to follow one's own process of interpretation. Both of these data analytic techniques encourage the listener to attend closely to the voices of the adolescents and to attune oneself to the relational elements of the research process.

Through this analysis, my research team and I were able to identify distinct patterns that revolve around the experiences of intimacy, desire, and distrust and are intricately woven into the fabric of boys' friendships. These patterns are evident, within any one year as well as over time, in the interviews of the boys in my studies over the past decade. The remainder of this chapter focuses on the ways in which these patterns are experienced in the context of male friendships.

Patterns of Friendships among Boys

Intimacy

SHARING SECRETS

James, a 15-year-old African American who spends most of his free time writing plays with his best friend, tells his interviewer that he has satisfying and trusting relationships with other boys. He believes that they know him well and that they can relate to him emotionally:

> *Interviewer:* OK, can you tell me things that you like about your friends who are guys?
> *James:* They understand how I am. They know how to make me feel better whenever I am feeling down. We all understand each other's feelings and, you know, if there's a home problem, we understand that.
> *Interviewer:* How do you know that somebody else understands you?
> *James:* They show it by their feelings, like, expressions.

Although James is an unusually creative boy, who does improvisational theater with his best friend on a regular basis, his sense of intimacy with his friends and the language he uses to describe it are not atypical for the boys in my studies. Boys tell me and the other interviewers that their best friends are their confidantes, their partners, their "deep depth" friends, and those people in their lives without whom they would feel "lost." Boys report sharing their most "private secrets" and firmly believe that they can trust their closest friends to keep them confidential. Boys speak about other boys with great warmth and affection, setting a tone that conveys an emotional depth and intensity to their friendships.

Talking together and listening to each other's problems is a critical part of these boys' friendships. Asked what he does with his best friend, Julio, a sensitive 15-year-old from Puerto Rico, tells his interviewer: "we hang out, we talk to each other about serious things, share some deep secrets." For Julio, whose mother was dying of AIDS at the time of the interview, it seems particular important to be open with his best friend. Fortunately, his friends are quite empathic.

> *Interviewer:* Do you think this [best] friendship has changed since you were younger?
> *Julio:* It changed a lot. Just like my other friends changed a lot.
> *Interviewer:* Like how?
> *Julio:* When we were younger, it used to be like not so tight as we are now. It was not like if something goes wrong, like one of us would shed a tear, the other one will cry.

Johnny, a 14-year-old Chinese American boy, tells his interviewer about his friend comforting him when he was sad: "I had this goldfish for a long time and it died. So I started crying and crying, I don't know why but I went [to my best friend] and I was crying and . . . you know, he comforted me, he talked to me." Although the severity of the loss that Julio and Johnny were experiencing is not the same, the empathy and concern that their friends showed them were similar. Crying along with a friend and comforting him are acts of feeling for and with a friend, defying stereotypes of adolescent boys as lonesome cowboys who prefer to keep their feelings to themselves.

Brian, an African American 15-year-old says about his best friends: "I tell them anything about me and I know they won't tell anybody else unless I tell them to." A key part of Brian's friendship is the mutuality: "He could just tell me anything and I could tell him anything." When asked to define a best friend, Justin, a 16-year-old Puerto Rican, says: "Like I always know everything about him. . . . We always chill, like we don't hide secrets from each other." When asked what he likes about his friend, Justin says: "If I have a problem, I can go tell him. If he has a problem, he can go tell me." Steven, a 16-year-old African American, says about his best friends: "We share secrets that we don't talk about in the open." When asked to explain why he feels close to his friends: "If I'm having problems at home, they'll like counsel me, I just trust them with anything, like deep secrets, anything." When Jerome, a 16-year-old West Indian boy, is asked to describe his best friend, he says:

> He's like a brother, I could tell him anything, anything. If I ask him to keep
> it a secret, he will keep it a secret. If he tells me something, he tells me not to
> tell nobody. I keep it a secret. If I need him, I know he's going to be there . . .
> When I talk about problems . . . he'll tell me or give me ideas or things
> to do.

Shawn, a 15-year-old African American student, says that his best friend has "privileges like you can do things with him or talk about things, anything like you can't with somebody else, [you can] talk about . . . private stuff, secrets."

Malcolm, a 16-year-old African American adolescent, suggests a strong sense of intimacy in his friendships when he speaks about the difference between his best friend and his girlfriend. "Cause if you have a best friend you know, you express yourself more and you like—you feel lost without them. So you know with her it's really just we have a close relationship where we can express things." Expressing one's thoughts and feelings, "deep depth secrets" and "private stuff" is a central part of the friendships of the boys in our studies. Adolescent boys, who have been described in the literature as activity oriented rather than relationship-oriented (see Belle, 1989; Kilmartin, 1994), carefully described the emotional nuances of their friendships and the importance of shared secrets in their friendships.

SHARING MONEY

Intimacy was experienced through shared secrets but also through borrowing and loaning money to each other. Like a mantra, the boys repeated that they trusted their best friends to "keep [their] secrets" and "to hold [their] money." When Randall, a 14-year-old Dominican teenager, is asked: "In what ways do you trust your friends?" He responds: "I trust them to hold my money, and I trust them to, if I lend them money they'll pay me back." When Nathan, a 16-year-old African American adolescent, is asked the same question, he says:

> I could leave any amount of money with him. He gave me money, I give
> him money. If I need something, he gives it to me, I give it to him [if he
> needs something] . . .
> *Interviewer:* Can you tell me about a time that you trusted your best friend?

Nathan: [On Friday] he asked me if he could borrow fifty dollars and he
gave it back to me by Monday. He gave me back seventy-five, he was like,
thanks for lending it to him. He gave me back extra.

Mark, a Puerto Rican boy in his sophomore year, knows he can trust his
friends because if: "I give them a stack of money to hold, they wouldn't be
like 'oh well I lost it.' Or 'somebody took it from me' or something like
that. They would like keep it in a safe spot and wouldn't tell anybody that
they are holding that money for me." When Mike, another Puerto Rican
boy in his junior year, is asked in what ways he trusts his friends, he says:
"If I lend them money, I usually don't have to ask them for the money,
usually get it back, I don't even have to ask for it." In addition to knowing
that friends would pay them back, the boys emphasized their willingness
to loan their friends money when they needed it. Sharing, borrowing, and
lending money were critical elements of intimacy among these boys.

PROTECTION FROM HARM

In addition to experiences of shared secrets and shared money, protection
from harm was another way in which boys expressed intimacy with each
other. Raphael, a 17-year-old Dominican boy, is asked by his interviewer:
"How do you trust your friends?" He says: "Let's just say I had a big fight, I
got beat up, I had like five guys against me, they'll come and they'll help
me out." When Akil, an African American boy in his junior year, is asked
why he trusts his best friend, he says: "You get into a fight with somebody
else, [my best friend] will tell me to calm down, chill . . . like when someone jumps me, he will help me." He also claims that he feels close to his
best friend because he knows that his friend would protect him in a fight.

Armando, a Dominican young man in his freshman year, discusses the
bonds between him and his friends being enhanced through the protection of each other in fights. He describes a time when he and his three
male friends were confronted by another group of boys who wanted to
fight. He explains how it was up to him to protect his friends: "And I'm behind my friend . . . if something happened to him where it was like he
couldn't react fast enough and I was behind him, it would have been up to
me to . . . protect him and help him out." Armando explains that had he
not protected his friend, he would have been isolated by his friends:

If something had happened and I didn't do anything, I'm just standing like
a big dummy, you know, I mean, none of them would ever want to hang out

with me again, and it would be the same with any of them. So, it's a trust thing.

As a result of this incident, he and his friends felt closer to each other knowing each would protect the other.

Like Armando, the boys in my studies repeatedly indicate that if they discover that their friends do not protect them, the friendship is terminated. Mark, a Dominican adolescent in his sophomore year, says:

> One month ago I happened to be in a fight. I was getting jumped and one of my friends, who's supposedly my friend, he didn't come to try to help me. I was like "yo I was getting jumped why didn't you help me?"
> *Interviewer:* What happened to the friendship?
> *Mark:* There was no friendship simple as that. There was no friendship.
> *Interviewer:* And there was a friendship before?
> *Mark:* There was a friendship before but now there is no friendship.

Protecting each other was not only about "backing each other up" in fights, but also about helping each other calm down, thus preventing a fight. Chris, a Puerto Rican student who was 16 at the time of the interview, emphasizes how his best friend, Scott, helps him stay out of trouble. For him, this is a crucial aspect of their friendship.

> *Interviewer:* Why do you think your friendship with Scott is better than with other friends?
> *Chris:* Well with him when I'm in an argument with somebody that disrespected me and he just comes out and backs me up and says, "yo, Chris, don't deal with that. Yo let's just go on, you know," 'cause I could snap.

Another way the boys protected each other was by showing concern about harmful behaviors such as smoking, selling drugs, and cutting class. Jorge, a 14-year-old Dominican who is trying to help his best friend change, tells his interviewer that his best friend is like a little brother to him. However, Jorge is trying to change his friend's behavior.

> *Interviewer:* What do you not like about this friendship?
> *Jorge:* That he smokes weed and that he sells drugs.
> *Interviewer:* Is there something you would like to change about Benny?
> *Jorge:* That! That's about it . . . Well I'm trying to change him. He's, you

know, trying to stop cause I told him. I be talking to him and he's trying to get off drugs and smoke.

A similar relationship is described by Jonathan, a 14-year-old African American adolescent. With his best friend, Jonathan is the "little brother" whereas his friend, who is almost the same age as Jonathan, acts like a protector. Jonathan says about his best friend: "He's honest, he never lets nobody try to harm me, and he's like a big brother that I never had. So we've become closer than we ever have been." When asked what makes his friend like an "older brother," Jonathan answers: "He's taking care of me, he buys me what I need. Like if I need stuff for my birthday, or need something to go out, he'll buy me an outfit or some sneakers or whatever I'll need, he'll try his best to give it to me." The nurturing quality of his friend's protection is readily apparent. Not only does his friend protect him against potential attackers, but he also provides for his friend.

These stories from boys about being protected by their friends and protecting their friends were striking in their apparent vulnerability. The boys wanted to believe, and did believe, that their best friends would protect them from harm and that they would also protect their friends. However, they did not emphasize, as one may expect based on stereotypes of boys, the protection of their friends but rather their friends' protection. They openly referred to and seemed proud of their interdependent, sensitive, and caring relationships with other boys.

FAMILY CONNECTIONS

An additional way in which intimacy was expressed among the African American and Latino adolescents exclusively (and not by Asian American boys) was by considering their male friends as "like brothers" or "like family." African American and Latino boys made such references to fictive kin when asked to describe the quality of their friendships with other boys. In addition, these boys often claimed that they are close to their friends *because* they know each other's families. Anthony's aunt (who is his primary caretaker) used to babysit Pedro who is his best friend. His other best friend's mom is the best friend of his aunt. Michael says about his best friend: "Since we were real small I have known his whole family, he knows everybody in my house, we just walk over to his crib, open his fridge without asking or something, that's how long we've known each other." Ken, a 15-year-old Puerto Rican young man, says he's close with his best friends' family and that is a large part of what makes the friendship "special."

When asked to define a best friend, Ken says: "Like I always know everything about him, I'm close with his family, he is close to my family, we always chill." Farouk, a 14-year-old African American boy, says when asked what makes him close to his best friend: "Um basically 'cause he knows my family, he knows my sisters, my mom, my dad. I know his mom, his dad. We know where each other live." In his interview the following year, Farouk says he is close with his best friend Scott because he knows Scott's parents. Armando says: "if you know somebody's parents, then you know how far the trust can be stretched."

Some boys gave family status as a reward to those who have been most loyal to them. Jonathan says about his closest friends:

> They are there for you. Even though your family can be there for you too, your family got to be there for you. Your friends, they don't have to be there, but they choose to be there and since they choose to be there for you, they make you want to accept them into your family . . . so you make your family bigger and bigger.

These boys expressed love and concern for each other by bringing their friends into the fold of their families.

Desire

With a clarity that is striking in light of the dominant beliefs about boys' friendships, the interviews consistently have suggested a strong yearning for intimate friendships among the boys who do not have close male friendships. Albert, a Puerto Rican boy in his junior year, says to his interviewer:

> *Albert:* I got friends and everything but I don't consider them as close friends, not now.
> *Interviewer:* Why is that?
> *Albert:* No 'cause it's like I haven't known them that good. I know them this year and a part of last year, you know so I don't know them good . . . I would like a friend that if I got anything to say to him or like any problems or anything I'll tell him and he'll tell me his problems . . . Some friends be your friends when you're not in trouble, when you have money or something. Once you don't have a lot of money or something

they'll back off. But a real friend will stick right there with you. He won't back off.

In contrast to what the research literature suggests, Albert does not claim to want friends with whom to "do things," but to discuss personal problems. Victor, an African American student, suggests a similar theme in his junior year:

> *Interviewer:* Do you have a close or best friend this year?
>
> *Victor:* I wouldn't say, I don't say I would. 'Cause I feel that a friend is going to be there for you and they'll support you and stuff like that. Whether they're good and bad times, you can share with them, you would share your feelings with them, your true feelings . . . that's why I don't think I have any real close friends. I mean, things can travel around in a school and things would go around, and the story would change from person to person. Yeah, basically, I hate, it, I hate, it, 'cause you know I couldn't mind talking to somebody my age that I can relate to 'em on a different basis.

Boys, like Albert and Victor, yearned for friends who "would really be there" and with whom they could share their "true feelings." They feel betrayed by the gossip of their peers and they sought refuge from the rumors.

When asked what he would like to change about his friends, Michael says: "everything. I would like to have better friends . . . that I could trust as family." Scott says: "I would like one that I could trust. 'Cause then I could be able to talk to him about things or talk with him about things that I can't even talk to my family about." These boys stated that although they valued their relationships with their families, they still desired close male friendships. Carlos, who says that he does not have a close or best friend because he can't trust "nobody these days," would still like to have such a friend: "Yeah as long as like, you know I could talk to them about anything and if I tell them to keep a secret, to keep it, like I been telling you." Alberto wants a best friend who "doesn't talk nothing behind my back, tell my personal problems to . . . not leaving me for another . . . You know a friend that would be real tight to me, close, that I could tell him just anything." These boys spoke of not having but yearning for intimate male friends who don't "leave [each other] for another."

These stories of yearning for intimate friendships with other boys are not stories revealed exclusively by acutely sensitive boys who are isolated in school. They are stories told by popular boys in the school who are members of athletic teams as well as boys involved in theater arts. They are told by straight "A" students as well as by students who are struggling to get by in school. The language of yearning for intimacy is used by boys looking hip hop, cool, laid back, and macho in their low riding pants, Walkmen around their necks, baseball caps drawn low over their brows, sneakers untied. Boys who have been portrayed in popular culture as more interested in shooting each other than in sharing their thoughts and feelings spoke to us about male friendships that "you feel lost without," about "deep depth" friendships, and about wanting friends with whom you "share you secrets," "tell everything," and "get inside."

Distrust

The context of this world of intimacy, however, was a world of distrust of peers who will "try to take over you and take you for everything you've got and step on you." Comments such as "you can't trust anyone" are heard alongside comments about love for their male friends. In response to a question about his male peers in general, Anthony, a 17-year-old African American young man, says: "I don't trust [them], I trust me, myself, and I. That's the way I am. I trust nobody." Although he has a best friend during all four years of the study, a friend in whom he confides and to whom he feels close, he expresses strong distrust of others. Richard, a 16-year-old Puerto Rican young man, says about his male peers: "Can't trust anybody nowadays. They are trying to scam you, or scheme, or talk about you." Richard admits that although he has never directly experienced these types of betrayals from his male peers, he "know[s] what most of [them] are like." At times, this theme of distrust seemed to be a cliché that the boys perpetuated among themselves. I often wondered whether the boys truly believed these assertions or whether they simply repeated statements of distrust because that is what their peers were saying.

Yet by their junior and senior years, the boys' feelings of distrust were increasingly based on actual experiences with friends. While the affection for their close male friends was still heard in the boys' interviews in these latter years of high school, the stories of distrusting peers and even close friends began to dominate their interviews. Boys spoke of trusting neither their peers nor their friends due to experiences of betrayal. Joseph, a Dominican student, tells me in both his freshman and sophomore years that he has a best friend with whom he had been friends for ten years. In his junior year of high school, however, the situation has changed.

> *Interviewer:* Do you have a close or best friend?
> *Joseph:* No. I don't trust nobody.
> *Interviewer:* You don't trust nobody? How come?
> *Joseph:* (Pause) Can't trust nobody these days.
> *Interviewer:* Have you had bad experiences with people?
> *Joseph:* Yeah, especially this year.
> *Interviewer:* Can you tell me about one of them?
> *Joseph:* Yeah, okay. Me and my friend got, you know, in trouble at school 'cause we broke the elevator. . . . Don't say nothing about it. And he went and told Mr. Talcott that I was the one who did it . . . nobody knew that we did it. So he just went and told him. He went ahead and told and I got in trouble. I got suspended for five days.

Experiences of betrayal do not register lightly for the boys in my studies. The boys' sensitivity to betrayal seems acute and dramatic. Boys who are actively discouraged in homophobic mainstream culture to have intimate, close male friendships appear to become particularly intolerant of maintaining such friendships when they entail betrayal and loss.

In his senior year, Albert explains:

> Can't trust people no more. Before you could, but now, you know when you got a girl, and they think that she's cute, they still might go try to rap to her and everything. You can't trust 'em like before that they will be serious. Like that friend I had in New York, my best friend [the friend he referred to in his sophomore year], I could trust him with my girl, you know, and he could trust me with his girl. People ain't like that no more . . . back then you could trust.

Albert believes that when he was younger, trusting others was easier than it is now. He remembers his former best friend from junior high school (whom he mentions each year) as someone he could trust and whom, he says later in his interview, he could "talk to and he would talk to me, too."

Albert's "back then" seems to indicate less "the good old days" than simply a younger age.

Many of the boys in our studies refer to junior high school as a time in which they could have close friendships with other boys. A few boys, in fact, made links between having friendships and the junior high school itself. Justin says:

> That's why in this school I can't be friends with like a lot of people 'cause you can't trust nobody. 'Cause in this school you say one thing and it's all over the school in two days. Nobody here got their own mind. . . . In junior high it was better because everyone knew each other so there was more trust. . . . now that you in a new area, you gotta maintain yourself and make sure you don't blab at the mouth.

While many of the boys continued to have close friendships during high school, they often believed, as did Justin, that it was easier to have close male friendships when they were younger.

When Marcus, from El Salvador, is asked about his close friends in his freshman and sophomore years, he discusses his close friends in great detail. However, by his junior year, he says he doesn't have a close friend.

> *Marcus:* I don't trust trust nobody. You know I have just a little trust.
> *Interviewer:* Why is that?
> *Marcus:* I don't know. I just think I always think that [my friends] won't be there when I probably need them a lot.

The fear of betrayal deeply influenced boys' experiences of intimacy. Marcus says in his junior year that while he has friends who protect him, he does not have friends whom he trusts. When the interviewer voices confusion regarding why this may be the case, he responds:

> I believe that, I mean all I know is that, say if I was with these guys and these guys didn't get along with the other guys. But I'll have his back, and he'll have my back, you know. We know that already. If my friend was in trouble, I'll be there, backing him up, or if I was in trouble, he'll be backing me up. But that's not being trustful.
> *Interviewer:* Why?
> *Marcus:* 'Cause maybe the next day, he might be the one that's joking and making fun of you.

In this revealing description of friendship and trust, Marcus suggests that someone who "backs you up" may not necessarily be trustworthy. He implies that although a friend may "be there" when he is in danger (i.e., he may protect Marcus when he is physically threatened), this type of dependability may not last, or may not ensure that this friend will respect him or protect him from embarrassment or feelings of vulnerability ("he might be the one that's joking and making fun of you"). Marcus appears to be drawing a distinction between physical and emotional protection. The boys' experiences of physical protection from their friends did not necessarily mean that they trusted their friends to protect their feelings.

The fear of betrayal, the distrust of peers (and sometimes close friends), and the loss of close friendships during the latter years of high school have each been themes in the boys' interviews. Like the themes of intimacy and of desiring intimate close male friendships, the themes of distrust, betrayal, and loss are heard in the interviews of a diverse set of boys: boys who are popular, boys who are alienated, and boys who are star athletes. They are themes that weave in and out of the boys' narratives of male friendships and seem to have a profound influence on boys' experiences of relationships. However, these themes of distrust are embedded in a world of intimacy and desire. The boys may distrust their peers, and have "lost" many close friends due to experiences of betrayal, but they often continue to have or desire close intimate friendships with other boys. Even in a context of distrust, many of the boys resist these dictates to distrust by maintaining close friendships with other boys. It is this juxtaposition of feelings of intimacy, desire, and distrust that seems most remarkable and poignant in the boys' stories of friendships.

Discussion

Listening to African American, Latino, and Asian American boys from poor and working-class families, we hear old and new stories about boys' friendships. As many other researchers have heard, my research team and I hear similar themes of loyalty and acceptance in close friendships. We also hear, however, themes of intimacy that involve shared secrets, shared money, protecting one another, both physically and emotionally, and family and friend connections. We hear boys discuss their loyalty and love for, their desire to share "everything" with, and their trust in their close male friends. In some cases, we also hear boys' longing for intimate friendships. In addition, we hear themes of distrust, fears of betrayal, stories of deceit that lead to loss, and reluctance to find new friends based on experiences of betrayal. Adolescent boys, who have so often been portrayed in the research literature as having friendships that are emotionally flat and that focus predominantly on physical activities rather than on sharing thoughts and feelings (see Hartup, 1993; Kilmartin, 1994; Savin-Williams & Berndt, 1990), were typically found to have or want friendships that involve shared secrets, emotional commitment, as well as physical and emotional protection. Activities (i.e., playing video games or basketball) were a part of boys' friendships, but sharing secrets, shared money, protection, and, for the African American and Latino boys, familial connections appeared to be particularly important aspects of boys' friendships throughout adolescence.

Why haven't we heard these patterns of intimacy before in studies of boys' development? Why haven't we heard, for example, the emphasis on "sharing everything" and "deep depth" friendships or the emphasis on desiring intimacy? Friendship research has suggested that African American adolescent boys report higher levels of self-disclosure in their male friendships than White adolescent boys (Jones, Costin & Ricard, 1994). Furthermore, gender differences in levels of intimacy are often not found among African American adolescents (DuBois & Hirsch, 1990). These studies suggest that the emphasis on shared secrets heard among the boys in the present sample may lie with the cultural context. The beliefs and values maintained at home and in the larger community in which adolescent boys reside most likely influence the ways in which boys befriend each other. In White, middle-class communities where values of independence are often emphasized, boys might have more difficulty expressing emotions and vulnerabilities in their relationships due to their desire to seem emotionally autonomous and stoic. In African American, Latino, and Asian communities, however, where community and "brotherhood" are strongly emphasized, boys might have less difficulty expressing vulnerability, emotional complexity, and sensitivity within their close male friendships. The interdependent value system that is typical of many African American, Latino, and Asian American families (Chao, 2000; Fuligni, Tseng & Lam, 1999; Townsend, 1998; Hines & Boyd-Franklin, 1990; Nobles, 1974) might enhance the likelihood of intimacy and self-disclosure between male friends.

Another reason for these patterns of intimacy may stem from urban adolescent boys' responses to conventional notions of masculinity. The dictates of traditional masculinity—the imperative to be autonomous, independent, to take oneself out of relationships with other boys, and to be emotionally neutral—may be resisted by ethnic minority adolescent boys from urban low-income families because, quite simply, they don't benefit from adhering to these dictates. The benefits that are reaped by White, middle-class males for playing by the rules, for privileging autonomy over relationships, are great—they gain positions of power and prestige and are taken even more seriously in the wider society. Urban boys of color from low-income families, however, do not typically experience such benefits. The attraction, therefore, of following the autonomous trajectory inherent in mainstream masculinity may not be as great as it is for White, middle-class boys.

Urban boys of color living in urban, low-income communities, particularly African American and Latino boys, may also be more socialized than White middle-class boys to resist certain components of mainstream masculinity. Boys from poor urban environments are often raised by their mothers and/or grandmothers. These women, by virtue of being raised as women in Western culture and in African American or Latino cultures (Anzaldúa, 1990; Bell-Scott et al., 1991), may reinforce the importance of relationships and encourage boys to experience the full range of their emotions.

By the latter years in high school, however, the boys became more pessimistic about finding and maintaining intimate relationships with other boys. At the edge of adulthood, when relationships with women often become more central, the demands of a homophobic culture may begin to consume boys, and they become less able to resist the demands of heterosexual masculinity. However, the emotional expressiveness and sensitivity heard in the boys' interviews were evident in each year of our studies. While friendships with other boys were often abandoned during late adolescence, the boys' resistance to emotional neutrality or stoicism in their language seemed to be maintained throughout adolescence.

The difference in findings regarding intimacy in my studies and the studies of White, middle-class youth may also be due to the methodology used. What would White, poor, working-class, or middle-class adolescent boys say about male friendships if they were included in a voice-centered, relational research study that emphasized close listening? Perhaps they, too, would reveal a desire for intimate male friendships, for shared secrets, for protection, and emotional commitment from their male friends. Chu's work (this volume) with White, middle-class adolescent boys suggests that the differences between the present study and previous studies with White, middle-class boys is based, at least in part, on the methodology used. When Chu, using a voice-centered, relational approach to research, listens to White, middle-class boys, she hears similar themes regarding the desire for genuine relationships with other boys.

In addition to sharing secrets, knowing one could borrow from or lend money to one's friend was an important component of intimacy in boys' friendships. It is unclear whether this pattern is unique to those adolescents from low-income communities, where money and material items are not as readily available as in more affluent communities. The emphasis on knowing that their friends "would pay them back" is likely influenced by the extent to which one needs the money or worries about being paid back (see Grant, 2003). It may be that borrowing money is intimately linked to the belief that boys protect one another. Loaning or borrowing money is another way perhaps, in addition to physical protection in fights, to be protected or to protect their friends in need. The free exchange of money may be experienced, furthermore, as consistent with the belief that their friends are "there" for them when they need them.

Protection from physical and emotional harm was also a critical element of intimacy in boys' friendships. Unlike sharing secrets and sharing money, however, the theme of protection has been noted as an important aspect of childhood and adolescent friendships in previous research (Azmitia, Kamprath & Linnet, 1998), and as a more important element of boys' friendships than of girls' friendships (see Youniss & Smollar, 1985). Yet the ways in which protection is experienced (i.e., as an interdependent process) has been rarely noted. The boys in the current study repeatedly expressed their desire to be protected by their friends, both physically and emotionally. Their friends' protection is what, in fact, made them feel close to their friends. They openly described the ways in which their friends took care of them and they, in turn, took care of their friends. Communities that emphasize interdependency may produce adolescent boys who are able to freely discuss their ways of relying on each other. In addition, survival for poor and working-class youth of color in poor urban areas may be based precisely on boys' ability to depend on each other for both emotional and physical protection. Protection may serve as a way to maintain relationships as well as a way to cope with the real challenges of living in dangerous urban neighborhoods.

Family connections were an important aspect of intimate friendships among African American and Latino boys as well. This theme has also been noted in previous research (Kerns, 1994; Kerns & Stevens, 1996; Armsden & Greenberg, 1987; Greenberg, Siegel & Leitch, 1983). Adolescents from ethnic minority communities have often described links between family members and friends (Stack, 1974; Townsend, 1998; Hale-Benson, 1986; Hines & Boyd-Franklin, 1990). However, when the links between family and friends have been examined in the friendship research, the focus has been on the ways in which attachment styles are similar between family and friends or the ways in which parental monitoring influences children friendships (see Parke & Ladd, 1992; Patterson, Pryor & Field, 1995; Snyder, Dishion & Patterson, 1986; Mounts, 2001). These studies have neglected to examine how family connections or knowing each other's families enhance the intimacy of friendships among boys. The association between friendship and family relationships, however, appears to be culturally based, with none of the Asian American boys describing such a link. Other researchers have also detected cultural variations in the association between family relationships and friendships (see Cooper & Cooper, 1992). Understanding why and how these patterns may vary across cultural contexts is an important direction for future research.

Strikingly, intimate friendships for the boys existed within a context of extreme distrust. Although most of the boys had intimate friendships at some point during the study, especially during their freshman and sophomore years, they typically described their peers as untrustworthy and deceitful. These beliefs seemed to stem from parental warnings that one should be wary of trusting others and should always "watch their backs" in any situation. Ken says in his freshman year: "can't trust nobody. That's what my mother always used to say. Can't trust nobody." In his sophomore year, Ken repeats the same theme: "Can't trust everybody . . . basically my mother always told me 'you gotta watch out who you hang out with.'" These types of messages may reflect a belief system, common within many close-knit, oppressed communities, that those who are not part of one's immediate or extended family should not be trusted (Stack, 1974).

Reasons for high levels of distrust might also lie with the experiences of racism and harassment that adolescent boys of color experience regularly. The African American and Latino boys in our studies frequently spoke of harassment from the police, of being watched carefully in stores, on the street, in the subway stations and school buildings, and in their own neighborhoods. They are watched by adults both outside and inside their own communities. When an entire auditorium of students in one of the high schools where I conducted research was asked if they had ever been stopped by the police, approximately 90 percent of the boys raised their hands. These adolescent boys repeatedly told stories of being strip-searched, asked for their identification, and questioned by police. They receive clear messages that they are not being trusted by many of the adults in their lives. This lack of trust experienced on a daily basis is likely to have an effect on these boys' ability to trust each other (Epstein & Karweit, 1983).

The Asian American boys also spoke of racism and harassment but these experiences primarily took place in school with their peers rather than outside of school with adults. The Asian American boys often spoke of being victimized in school by their African American, Latino, and Asian American male peers. Some of the African American and Latino males in our studies, who often resent the Asian American males who are regularly and openly treated preferentially by teachers and principals, taunt and harass their Asian American peers. Asian American males, wanting to "be cool," also pick on their Asian American male peers who are smaller and less able to defend themselves. These difficult experiences may lead the Asian American boys to distrust their peers as well.

The types of school where the studies have taken place may further explain the pervasiveness of distrust among the boys. All of the boys attended large, underfunded, and chaotic inner-city schools that lacked any real means to create a community within the school. The rates of suspension and dropout were high in the high schools in which we have conducted research. Epstein and Karweit (1983) state: "Negative features in a school environment—ridicule, discrimination, low expectations, stereotypes, repressions, punishment, isolation—may increase the dissociative quality of the setting and affect the thought processes and social behaviors of the students" (p. 60). The social relations and behavior of the adolescents who participated in my studies may be deeply influenced by their school. The school in which they spend a substantial part of their day conveys to them that they are not trustworthy, and these messages of distrust may influence their interpersonal relationships.

Nevertheless, these feelings of distrust did not prevent close, trusting, nonfamilial friendships from flourishing, at least during the freshman and sophomore years of high school. The context of friendships was one of mistrust but the close friendships themselves were often trusting and intimate. It may be that considering friends as "fictive kin" or as family members allowed adolescents to cross the barrier created by feelings of distrust (Rotenberg, personal communication). Furthermore, the mistrust of peers may enhance the closeness experienced between best friends. An antagonistic "other" may lead adolescents to appreciate their close friendships even more than if the contrast did not exist. However, not trusting peers also made it more difficult for some of the adolescents to make and maintain friends, and by their senior year, close friendships with other boys were no longer possible. This shift suggests that boys are falling out of relationship with other boys right at the point in their lives when the messages about the presumed link between manhood and heterosexuality are at their peak. Raymond (1994) notes that "intense same-sex friendships that continue after adolescence—particularly those between men—are often discouraged, judged immature, and occasionally severely punished" (120). Not trusting other boys, and choosing not to maintain close relationships with other boys during late adolescence, might allow boys to distance themselves from their own potentially risky desires for close, intimate relationships with other boys.

My studies over the past decade have sought to understand the experience of friendships among ethnic minority boys from low SES families living in urban areas. The findings draw attention to the ways in which the friendships of boys are deeply embedded in the culture in which they are a part. Understanding those cultures and exploring how cultural beliefs and values shape and are shaped by boys' perceptions of their friendships seem to be particularly important directions for future research. If our understanding of adolescent boys is going to be more comprehensive and meaningful, it is essential to explore longitudinally and through the use of voice-centered, relational methods the ways in which adolescent boys from diverse cultures experience their relationships. From these studies, theories can then be generated about the ways in which cultures and contexts shape and are shaped by boys' relationships, and practices with boys (i.e., teaching, counseling, parenting) can be more responsive to and nurturing of boys' development.

NOTES

Parts of this article have been previously published (Way, 1998; Way & Pahl, 1999; Way, 2001).

1. The term "urban youth" is used in this chapter to refer to low-income adolescents from urban areas.

2. While there is a large body of research on peer relationships, the focus of the literature reviewed here is on dyadic friendships.

3. Colleagues include Michael Nakkula and Helena Stauber. Graduate students include Tine Pahl, Rachel Gingold, Susan Rosenbloom, Mariana Rotenberg, Geena Kuriakose, Lisa Chen, Vivian Tseng, Kirsten Cowal, Esther Marron, Melissa Greene, and Joanna Sattin. Postdocs include Judy Chu. Thank you to all!

REFERENCES

Anzaldúa, G. (1990). *Making face, making soul: Creative and critical perspectives by women of color.* San Francisco: Aunt Lute Foundation.

Armsden, G. C. & Greenberg, M. T. (1987). The Inventory of Parent and Peer Attachment: Individual differences and their relationship to psychological well being in adolescence. *Journal of Youth and Adolescence, 16,* 427–454.

Azmitia, M., Kamprath, N. & Linnet, J. (1998). Intimacy and conflict: The dynamics of boys' and girls' friendships during middle childhood and early adolescence. In L. Meyer, H. Park, M. Genot-Scheyer, I. Schwarz & B. Harry (Eds.). *Making friends: The influences of culture and development.* (pp. 225–241). Baltimore: Paul H. Brookes Publishing.

Bell-Scott, P., Guy-Sheftall, B., Royster, J., Sims-Wood, J., DeCosta-Willis, M. & Fultz, L. (1991). *Double stitch: Black women write about mothers and daughters.* Boston: Beacon Press.

Belle, D. (1989). Gender differences in children's social networks and supports. In D. Belle (Ed.). *Children's social networks and social supports.* (pp. 173–188). New York: John Wiley & Sons.

Brown, L. M. & Gilligan, C. (1992). *Meeting at the crossroads: Women's psychology and girls' development.* Cambridge, MA: Harvard University Press.

Brown, L. M., Way, N. & Duff, J. (1999). The others in my I: Adolescent girls' friendships and peer relations. In N. Johnson, M. Roberts & J. Worell (Eds.). *Beyond appearances: A new look at adolescent girls.* Washington, DC: American Psychological Association Press.

Bukowski, W. M., Gauze, C., Hoza, B. & Newcomb, A. F. (1993). Differences and consistency between same-sex and other-sex relationships during early adolescence. *Developmental Psychology, 29* (2), 255–263.

Bukowski, W. M., Newcomb, A. F. & Hartup, W. (Eds.). (1996). *The company they keep: Friendship in childhood and adolescence.* Cambridge: Cambridge University Press.

Buhrmester, D. & Furman, W. (1987). The development of companionship and intimacy. *Child Development, 58,* 1101–1113.

Cauce, A. (1986). Social networks and social competence: Exploring the effects of early adolescent friendships. *American Journal of Community Psychology, 14,* 607–628.

Cauce, A. (1987). School and peer competence in early adolescence: A test of domain-specific self-perceived competence. *Developmental Psychology, 23,* 287–291.

Chao, R. (2000). Cultural explanations for the role of parenting in the school success of Asian American children. In R. Taylor & M. Wang (Eds.). *Resilience across contexts: Family, work, culture, and community.* (pp. 333–363). Mahwah, NJ: Lawrence Erlbaum Associates.

Clark, M. L. (1989). Friendships and peer relations in black adolescents. In R. L. Jones (Ed.). *Black adolescents.* Berkeley, CA: Cobb & Henry.

Connolly, J., Furman, W. & Konarski, R. (2000). The role of peers in the emergence of heterosexual romantic relationships in adolescence. *Child Development, 71,* 1395–1408.

Cooper, C. R. & Cooper, R. G. (1992). Links between adolescents' relationships with their peers: Models, evidence, and mechanisms. In R. Parke & G. Ladd (Eds.). *Family-Peer Relationships.* (pp. 135–158). Hillsdale, NJ: Lawrence Erlbaum Associates.

Crick, N., Bigbee, M. & Howes, C. (1996). Gender differences in children's normative beliefs about aggression: How do I hurt thee? Let me count the ways. *Child Development, 67,* 1003–1014.

DuBois, D. L. & Hirsch, B. J. (1990). School and neighborhood friendship patterns of blacks and whites in early adolescence. *Child Development, 61,* 524–536.

Epstein, J. L. & Karweit, N. (1983). *Friends in school: Patterns of selection and influence in secondary schools.* New York: Academic Press.

Fine, M. (1991). *Framing dropouts: Notes on the politics of an urban high school.* Albany: State University of New York Press.

Fuligni, A., Tseng, V. & Lam, M. (1999). Attitudes toward family obligations among American adolescents with Asian, Latin American, and European backgrounds. *Child Development, 70,* 1030–1044.

Furman, W. (1993). Theory is not a four-letter word: Needed directions in the study of adolescent friendships. In B. Laursen (Ed.). *Close friendships in adolescence.* (pp. 89–104). San Francisco: Jossey-Bass.

Furman, W. (1996). The measurement of friendship perceptions: Conceptual and methodological issues. In W. Bukowski & A. Newcomb (Eds.). *The company they keep: Friendships in childhood and adolescence.* (pp. 41–65). New York: Cambridge University Press.

Furman, W. & Buhrmester, D. (1985). Children's perceptions of the personal relationships in their social networks. *Developmental Psychology, 21,* 1016–1024.

Gaines, S. (1997). *Culture, ethnicity, and personal relationship processes.* London: Routledge.

Gallagher, C. & Busch-Rossnagel, N. A. (1991, March). *Self-disclosure and social support in the relationships of black and white female adolescents.* Poster presented at Society for Research on Child Development, Seattle, WA.

Grant, K. (2003, June). The experiences of stress and coping among urban adolescents. Talk given at the William T. Grant Faculty Scholars Retreat. Charlottesville, Virginia.

Greenberg, M. T., Siegel, J. M. & Leitch, C. J. (1983). The nature and importance of attachment relationships to parents and peers during adolescence. *Journal of Youth and Adolescence, 12,* 373–385.

Hale-Benson, J. E. (1986). *Black children: Their roots, culture and learning styles.* Baltimore: John Hopkins University Press.

Hamm, J. (1994). Negotiating the maze: Adolescents' cross-ethnic peer relations in ethnically diverse schools. In L. Meyer, H. Park, M. Genot-Scheyer, I. Schwarz & B. Harry (Eds.). *Making friends: The influences of culture and development.* (pp. 225–241). Baltimore: Paul H. Brookes Publishing.

Hartup, W. (1993). Adolescents and their friends. In B. Larsen (Ed.). *Close friendships in adolescence.* (pp. 3–22). San Francisco: Jossey-Bass.

Hines, P. & Boyd-Franklin, N. (1990). Black families. In M. McGoldric, J. McPearce & J. Giordano (Eds.). *Ethnicity in family therapy.* (pp. 84–107). New York: Guilford Press.

Hogue, A. & Steinberg, L. (1995). Homophily of internalized distress in adolescent peer groups. *Developmental Psychology, 31,* 897–906.

Jones, D. C. & Costin, S. E. (1997, April). The friendships of African-American and European-American adolescents: An examination of gender and ethnic differences. Paper presented at the Society for Research on Child Development, Washington, DC.

Jones, D. C., Costin, S. E. & Ricard, R. J. (1994, February). Ethnic and sex differences in best-friendship characteristics among African American, Mexican American, and European American adolescents. Poster session presented at the meeting of the Society for Research on Adolescents, San Diego, CA.

Kerns, K. A. (1994). A longitudinal examination of links between mother-child attachments and children's friendships in early childhood. *Journal of Social and Personal Relationships, 11,* 379–381.

Kerns, K. & Stevens, A. C. (1996). Parent-child attachment in late adolescence: Links to social relations and personality. *Journal of Youth and Adolescence, 25,* 323–342.

Kilmartin, C. (1994). *The masculine self.* New York: Macmillan.

Kindlon, D. & Thompson, M. (1999). *Raising Cain: Protecting the emotional life of boys.* New York: Ballantine.

Leaper, C. (1994). Exploring the consequences of gender segregation on social relationships. In C. Leaper (Ed.). *Childhood gender segregation: Causes and consequences.* San Francisco: Jossey-Bass.

Miller, B. (1988). Adolescent friendships: A pilot study. Unpublished qualifying paper, Harvard Graduate School of Education, Cambridge, MA.

Mounts, N. (2001). Young adolescents' perceptions of parental management of peer relationships. *Journal of Early Adolescence, 21,* 92–122.

Nobles, W. W. (1974) Africanity: Its role in black families. *Black Scholar, 5,* 10–17.

Parke, R. & Ladd, G. (1992). *Family-peer relationships.* Hillsdale, NJ: Lawrence Erlbaum Associates.

Patterson, J., Pryor, H. & Field, J. (1995). Adolescent attachment to parents and friends in relation to aspects of self-esteem. *Journal of Youth and Adolescence, 24,* 365–375.

Ping, Y. & Berryman, D. L. (1996). The relationship among self-esteem, acculturation, and recreation participation of recently arrived Chinese immigrant adolescents. *Journal of Leisure Research, 28,* 251–273.

Pollack, W. (1998). *Real boys.* New York: Random House.

Rawlins, W. K. (1992). *Friendship matters: Communication, dialectics, and the life course.* Hawthorne, NY: Aldine de Gruyter.

Raymond, D. (1994). Homophobia, identity, and the meanings of desire: Reflections on the culture construction of gay and lesbian adolescent sexuality. In J. Irvine (Ed.). *Sexual cultures and the construction of adolescent identities.* (pp. 115–150). Philadelphia: Temple University Press.

Savin-Williams, R. C. & Berndt, T. J. (1990). Friendship and peer relations. In S. Feldman & G. R. Elliot (Eds.). *At the threshold: The developing adolescent.* (pp. 227–307). Cambridge, MA: Harvard University Press.

Sharabany, R., Gershoni, R. & Hoffman, J. E. (1981). Girlfriend, boyfriend: Age and sex differences in intimate friendship. *Developmental Psychology, 17,* 800–808.

Snyder, J., Dishion, T. J. & Patterson, G. R. (1986). Determinants and consequences of associating with deviant peers during preadolescence and adolescence. *Journal of Early Adolescence, 6* (1), 29–43.

Stack, C. (1974). *All our kin: Strategies for survival in a black community.* New York: Harper and Row.

Strauss, A. & Corbin, J. M. (1990). *Basics of qualitative research: Grounded theory procedures and techniques.* Thousand Oaks, CA: Sage Publications.

Townsend, B. L. (1998). Social friendships and networks among African American children and youth. In L. Meyer, H. Park, M. Genot-Scheyer, I. Schwarz & B. Harry (Eds.). *Making friends: The influences of culture and development.* (pp. 225–241). Baltimore, MD: Paul H. Brookes Publishing.

Way, N. (1995). "Can't you see the courage, the strength that I have?" Listening to urban adolescent girls speak about their relationships. *Psychology of Women Quarterly, 19,* 107–128.

Way, N. (1998). *Everyday courage: The lives and stories of urban teenagers.* New York: New York University Press.

Way, N. & Chen, L. (2000). The characteristics, quality, and correlates of friend-ships among African American, Latino, and Asian American adolescents. *Journal of Adolescent Research, 15,* 274–301.

Way, N. & Pahl, K. (1999). Friendship patterns among urban adolescents boys: A qualitative account. In M. Kopala & L. Suzuki (Eds.). *Using qualitative methods in psychology.* (pp. 145–162). Thousand Oaks, CA: Sage Publications.

Way, N. & Pahl, K. (2001). Individual and contextual predictors of perceived friendship quality among ethnic minority, low-income adolescents. *Journal of Research on Adolescence, 11,* 325–349.

Youniss, J. & Smollar, J. (1985). *Adolescent relations with mothers, fathers, and friends.* Chicago: University of Chicago Press.

9

Peer Relationships among Chinese Boys
A Cross-Cultural Perspective

*Xinyin Chen, Violet Kaspar, Yuqing Zhang,
Li Wang, and Shujie Zheng*

> One cannot herd with birds and beasts. If I am not to be
> among other men, then what am I to be?
> —Confucius, *Analects, xviii*

Peer interactions and relationships constitute an important social context
for human development (Hinde, 1987; Piaget, 1932; Sullivan, 1953). During peer interactions and affiliations, children learn social and cognitive
skills in solving interpersonal problems and achieving personal and social
success. Peer relationships may also be a source of social and emotional
support for children in coping with adjustment difficulties. Experiences
with peers may become increasingly important during childhood and
adolescence, when children strive for social recognition and social status
beyond the family (Harris, 1995).

Cultural influences on children's peer relationships have received an increasing amount of attention from developmental and cross-cultural researchers in recent years (e.g., Chen & Kaspar, in press; French, et al., 1999;
Krappman, 1996). Cultural norms and values may serve as a basis for social interpretations and evaluations of behaviors in peer interactions and
thus determine behavioral correlates and predictors of peer acceptance
and rejection. Culture may also provide guidelines for the establishment
and maintenance of specific dyadic relationships and affect the nature,

function, and significance of the relationships. Finally, cultural context may affect the structure and organization of peer social networks and groups.

Whereas there is increasing interest in cultural influences on social functioning and relationships in general, little research has been conducted to examine peer relationships of boys from a cross-cultural perspective. As a result, it is largely unknown how boys experience peer relationships in different cultural contexts. In this chapter, we examine peer relationships and friendships among Chinese boys. We focus on boys in particular because in Chinese culture they have been traditionally expected to be more active than girls in engaging in social interactions and establishing social relationships with peers outside of the family.

Cultural Background and Socialization of Boys

In Western cultures, a primary socialization goal is to help children achieve psychological autonomy and individuality (Larson, 1999; Triandis, 1990). This individualism is reflected in the cultural expectation for increasing emotional separation from parents and "becoming one's own person" during development (Larson, 1999). Peer relationships may be a source of emotional support and "stimulation" that facilitate the process of separating from the family and achieving personal autonomy (e.g., Rubin et al., 1998). Since the experience of being rejected by, or isolated from, the peer group is likely to be associated with negative feelings about one's own competence and self-worth, peer relationships are important for the development of self-confidence and emotional well-being. Accordingly, achieving individual social status, such as popularity in the group, and developing assertiveness, confidence, and feelings of self-worth in peer relationships are considered major indexes of accomplishment in social development (Hartup, 1992; Rubin et al., 1998).

Whereas North American culture represents a typical individualistic culture, collectivism is a major characteristic of Chinese culture (see Hofstede, 1980; Kim et al., 1994; Oyserman et al., 2002). Collectivism, as a value system, emphasizes the welfare and interests of the group, especially when they are in conflict with those of the individual. The dominant tasks of socialization in Chinese culture are to help children develop collectivistic ideologies, to become a part of the group, and to make contributions to the well-being of the collective (Chen, 2000a). The expression of one's needs or striving for autonomous behaviors is often considered socially unacceptable. Behaviors that may threaten the group functioning and the well-being of the collective are strictly prohibited.

Consistent with the socialization goals of Western culture, Chinese culture appreciates and emphasizes the functional role of peer relationships in socialization and child development in a broader manner (King & Bond, 1985; Luo, 1996). There is rich literature in China on how to interact with other people including parents, friends, and other significant figures, and how to coordinate different types of social relationships in one's life. Proverbs such as "Relying on your parents at home, and friends outside" reflect the significance of social relationships in Chinese society. There are systematic rules and principles concerning social interactions and relationships in different groups. For example, whereas "filial piety" is a Confucian doctrine dictating that children pledge obedience and reverence to parents (e.g., Hsu, 1981), loyalty and trust have been considered fundamental principles in interactions and relationships between friends (Chen et al., 1990).

Interestingly, the Chinese literature on peer relationships has traditionally focused on boys and men. This may be due to the fact that during hundreds or even thousands of years in Chinese history, social contacts for girls from early adolescence to adulthood are limited to family members (parents, siblings, husband, and children). Girls are typically encouraged to help parents with household chores, whereas boys are encouraged to go out and interact with peers and adults. Traditional Chinese families are authoritarian and hierarchical, with men being dominant (Lang, 1968). The hierarchy in the family is backed by legal and moral rules, such as the "three rules of obedience" for women (an unmarried girl should obey her father, a married woman—her husband, and a widow—her son). Men have the responsibility to maintain and enhance the status and reputation of the family (Ho, 1987). Given the importance of social relationships (*guan xi* in Mandarin) for men in Chinese society, it is not surprising that boys are taught the social skills necessary for interactions with people outside of the family. In the famous novel *Three Kingdoms*, three friends were described as so dedicated and loyal to each other that they wished to die on the same day. In the story, the old "brother" told others that his wife was his clothes but his friends were his arms. Boys in China are often expected to appreciate the value of "true" friendship from this type of story.

The traditional ideologies concerning the status of men in the society and boys in the family have changed dramatically in the past century, largely due to the introduction of Western cultures into the country and the feminist movement. Since the late 1970s, China has implemented the one-child-per-family policy. This policy has been highly successful, especially in urban areas. As a result, over 95% of all children in urban areas are "only" children. It has been found that the only child, either a boy or a girl, in a family which often has the "four-two-one" (four grandparents, two parents and one child) structure, is likely to receive much attention and even be "spoiled" by adults (Jiao et al., 1986). Nevertheless, some traditional values such as relatively higher expectations for boys, especially in the area of social skills and status, remain evident in contemporary China in both rural and urban areas (Chen & He, in press). Despite the social and cultural changes, traditional cultural beliefs and practices still play a significant role in the lives of Chinese boys.

In the following sections, we explore peer relationships among Chinese boys. Our exploration will be based on findings from four studies that we conducted in recent years. The first study focused on the associations between peer acceptance/rejection and social and psychological adjustment, and compared samples of Chinese boys with Canadian boys. The second study focused on exploring underlying beliefs, motives, and feelings that are involved in peer acceptance and rejection among Chinese boys. The third study compared the major functions of friendship, such as the provision of emotional intimacy, companionship, instrumental assistance, and enhancement of self-worth, between Chinese and Canadian boys. Finally, to acquire a more in-depth understanding of the significance and meaning of friendships among Chinese boys, the fourth study explored the ways Chinese boys perceive and interpret their friendships. In each of these studies, we gathered information from multiple sources through "standardized" measures, interviews, naturalistic observations, and archival data, and used integrative strategies in data analysis. Moreover, to maintain ecological validity of the assessments, we engaged in informal communications and discussions with children, parents, and local experts to search for culturally appropriate explanations of our findings.

Peer Acceptance and Rejection

Since the early 1980s, research on peer relationships in North America has focused mainly on peer acceptance and rejection (Rubin et al., 1998). Researchers have been interested in whether a child is popular, rejected, neglected, controversial, or "average," and how sociometric status is linked to individual adjustment such as self-regard and feelings of loneliness (e.g., Asher et al., 1990). Substantial evidence has indicated that children who have difficulties with peer acceptance are at risk for maladaptive outcomes including academic problems, delinquency, and psychopathological symptoms (see Rubin et al., 1998).

Peer acceptance is based on social perceptions and evaluations concerning how peers accept the child, that is, the collective attitude and affect toward the child. Due to the emphasis on the socialization role of peer relationships, it is the social-evaluative nature of peer acceptance, rather than personal popularity or salience, that is often stressed in Chinese cultures. The social-evaluative nature of peer acceptance and rejection suggests that peer evaluations may play an important role in child development. Specifically, peer acceptance carries with it the prescription of behaviors that are considered appropriate and acceptable in the society, and thus, is an indicator of cultural norms and values. Moreover, social evaluations and responses direct and regulate children's behaviors according to socialization goals of the culture, as children seek social recognition and acceptance (Sullivan, 1953).

Peer Acceptance and Social and Psychological Functioning—Study #1

An important question in the research on peer relationships concerns how social, behavioral, and psychological factors may be related to peer acceptance and rejection. Researchers in North America have paid particular attention to how social behaviors in peer interactions may predict peer acceptance and rejection in boys (e.g., Cillessen et al., 1992; French, 1988; Hinshaw & Melnick, 1995). In general, the findings suggest that sociability and assertiveness are associated with peer acceptance and that aggression and disruption are associated with peer rejection. Thus, whereas sociable and cooperative boys tend to be popular among peers, aggressive, impulsive, and disruptive boys are likely to be rejected in the peer group (e.g., Cillessen et al., 1992). In addition, it has been found that shy, anxious, and submissive boys may experience problems in peer acceptance (French, 1988). Regarding psychological adjustment, the findings indicate that rejected boys are likely to report negative self-perceptions of self-worth and social competence and high levels of loneliness and social dissatisfaction (e.g., Cillessen et al., 1992).

Yet it is unclear how social behaviors such as sociability-cooperation, aggression, and shyness-anxiety are associated with peer acceptance and rejection in Chinese boys. Are patterns of associations between emotional functioning such as feelings of loneliness and depression and peer acceptance/rejection similar in Chinese and North American boys? To address this question, we conducted a cross-cultural study in samples of Chinese and Canadian boys on the social and psychological correlates of peer relationships. Based on the argument that peer acceptance may reflect cultural norms and values, we expected that social and psychological functioning would be associated with peer acceptance in similar as well as different ways across cultures. For example, since sociable and prosocial behaviors are generally encouraged and aggressive and disruptive behaviors are discouraged in both Chinese and North American cultures, we hypothesized that, in both samples, sociability would be positively associated with peer acceptance whereas aggression would be positively associated with peer rejection. However, given that shy-anxious behavior is often considered an index of social maturity in Chinese culture and that children are encouraged to be cautious and restrained in social situations in Chinese culture (e.g., Chen, 2000b; Ho, 1987), we expected that unlike their counterparts in North America, shy-anxious Chinese boys might not experience difficulties in peer interactions. Indeed, we expected that whereas shyness-anxiety would be positively associated with peer rejection in Canadian boys, it would be positively associated with peer acceptance in Chinese boys.

PARTICIPANTS, PROCEDURES, AND MEASURES

The Chinese sample consisted of 284 boys in Shanghai, People's Republic of China, and the Canadian sample consisted of 249 boys in Southern Ontario, Canada. They were in grades 3 to 7. The boys were mainly from middle-class families in terms of social, educational, and economic status according to the standards in the country. Peer acceptance and rejection were assessed based on *sociometric nominations* ("Nominate up to three classmates with whom you like to play, and up to three classmates with whom you would rather not play"). The nominations received from all classmates were totaled and then standardized within each class to permit appropriate comparisons. Positive and negative nominations by peers provided indexes of peer acceptance and rejection. Data on children's social functioning were obtained from peer assessments (based on the measure of *Revised Class Play,* Masten et al., 1985). In the *Class Play,* children were requested to nominate up to three classmates who could best play each of the 30 roles (e.g., "Someone who is a good leader"). Subsequently, nominations received from all classmates were used to compute each item score for each child. Factor analysis revealed three orthogonal factors in this measure: sociability-cooperation, aggression-disruption, and shyness-sensitivity in each sample. Sociability-cooperation included items tapping several aspects of social competence (e.g., "makes new friends easily," "helps others when they need it," "is a good leader"). Aggression-disruption included items assessing overt physical and verbal aggressive behaviors (e.g., "gets into a lot of fights," "teases others too much," "picks on other kids"). Shyness-sensitivity consisted of items assessing shy-inhibited behavior in social context ("very shy," "feelings get hurt easily," "usually sad").

Teachers completed, for each participant, a *Teacher-Child Rating Scale* (*T-CRS*, Hightower et al., 1986). Items in the scale tapped school-related competence, including frustration tolerance, assertive social skills and task orientation, and learning problems. Teachers were asked to rate, on a 5-point scale, how well each of these items described each child, ranging from 1 ("not at all") to 5 ("very well"). The students were asked to complete a self-report measure on *loneliness and social dissatisfaction* (adapted from Asher et al., 1984). They were requested to respond to 16 self-statements (e.g., "I have nobody to talk to," "I am lonely," "I don't have anybody to play with at school") on a 5-point scale (1 = not at all true; 5 = always true). In addition, data on leadership and academic status were obtained from the school records for the Chinese sample. The Western-based measures were translated and back-translated to ensure comparability with the English versions. These measures have been used and proven reliable, valid, and appropriate in Chinese cultures (e.g., Chen et al., 1992; Chen, Rubin & Li, 1995).

RESULTS

The results concerning the associations between social behaviors and peer acceptance and rejection are presented in Table 9.1. The relations between sociability and aggression and peer acceptance and rejection were largely similar in the two samples. A careful examination of the results, however, indicated that the associations between sociability and peer acceptance and rejection were stronger in the Canadian boys. In contrast, the association between aggression and peer rejection was somewhat stronger in the Chinese boys. The differences between the samples may reflect differential

TABLE 9.1

Correlations between Social, School, and Psychological Adjustment and Peer Acceptance and Rejection in Chinese and Canadian Boys

| | Peer Acceptance | | Peer Rejection | |
	Chinese	Canadian	Chinese	Canadian
Sociability	.51***	.76***	.05	−.43***
Aggression-disruption	−.04	−.05	.78***	.52***
Shyness-sensitivity	.14**	−.43***	.23***	.27***
Teacher-rated competence	.23***	.30***	−.22***	−.45***
Teacher-rated learn. prob.	−.18**	−.10	.37***	.30***
Loneliness	−.27***	−.24***	.19***	.28***
Leadership	.31***	−.03		
Distinguished studentship	.22***	−.04		

$N = 284$ and 249 in Chinese and Canadian samples, respectively.
** $p > .01$
*** $p > .001$.

emphasis on social initiative and self-control in individualistic and collectivistic cultures. According to the cultural model developed by Chen (2000b), social initiative or level of social participation represents the tendency to initiate and maintain social interaction, whereas self-control or self-regulation serve to regulate or modulate behavioral and emotional reactivity in order to perform in social situations in an appropriate manner. Since sociability is based on a relatively high level of social initiative, it may be more valued in Western cultures than in Chinese culture. As a result, sociable boys are more likely to be accepted by peers in Canada than in China. Moreover, since aggressive-disruptive behavior is based on relatively low self-control or regulation, this behavior may be more strictly prohibited in Chinese culture than in Western cultures and thus more strongly associated with peer rejection in Chinese boys.

The results regarding the association between shy-sensitive behavior and peer rejection and acceptance suggested cultural differences as well. As expected, shy-sensitive behavior among the Canadian boys was positively associated with peer rejection. However, shy-sensitive behavior was positively associated with both peer acceptance and peer rejection among Chinese boys. A further analysis based on sociometric classification revealed that shy-sensitive Chinese boys were "controversial" among peers, that is, they were liked and disliked by peers at the same time. The controversial status of shy-sensitive Chinese boys may be related to the recent "psychological health education" in Chinese schools. According to Chen and Su (2001), China has been experiencing rapid changes toward the "market economy" system. During this process, Western values and ideologies have been introduced into the country. Many schools in China, especially in urban areas, have started to include psychological health classes in which students are encouraged to develop "better" social skills such as social assertiveness. Perhaps the mixed attitudes of peers toward shy boys in China today indicate the cultural conflict between imported Western values on social initiative and assertiveness and traditional Chinese values on shyness and social restraint. Our results suggest that how children's social behaviors are perceived and evaluated by others may be influenced by these societal and cultural changes. It is important for future research to examine the long-term effects of the influx of Western values on individual development in Chinese children.

The patterns of relations between school performance and psychological adjustment and peer acceptance and rejection were largely similar in Chinese and Canadian children. However, teacher-rated learning problems were found to be negatively associated with peer acceptance in Chinese boys, but the association was not significant in Canadian boys. The results suggest, perhaps, a greater emphasis on academic performance in the friendships of Chinese boys (e.g., Stevenson et al., 1990).

Underlying Motives for Peer Acceptance and Rejection—Study #2

The study described above was based largely on a Western conceptual framework, using "standardized" measures such as the *Revised Class Play* (Masten et al., 1985), to address the research questions. Whereas the results are interesting, it is possible that the behavioral dimensions in the Western measures are not particularly relevant to peer interactions and relationships among Chinese boys. There may be social and behavioral characteristics that are important in Chinese culture but are not tapped in Western measures. Moreover, "standardized" assessments and conventional quantitative analyses that often require adequate variability of responses may not be sensitive in detecting behaviors that may be low in prevalence in Chinese culture but culturally relevant.

To achieve an in-depth understanding of peer acceptance and rejection in Chinese boys, we conducted in-depth interviews with a sample of adolescent boys in China. The purpose of the study was to investigate why a child likes or dislikes another child, without placing any restraint on the child's responses. The information obtained from these interviews may help us understand the nature of peer relationships from an "insider's" perspective.

PARTICIPANTS AND PROCEDURE

A random sample of 67 boys in grades 4, 6, and 8 from three schools in Beijing, People's Republic of China, participated in the study. They were individually interviewed by trained research assistants who were graduate students or senior undergraduate psychology students at a Chinese university. During the interview, after two "warm-up" questions about his extracurricular activities, the participant was asked to describe who he would like to play with and who he would rather not play with in the class and why. He was asked to provide specific reasons for his acceptance and rejection of a particular child. The interviewer attempted to obtain as many responses as possible by continuing to ask "Are there other reasons?" until the child said no. Clarification was sought when any of the child's statements were unclear to the interviewer.

The interview data were first coded by using a coding scheme developed specifically for the study. The coding scheme tapped various aspects of social, academic, and personal characteristics.

RESULTS

It was found that main reasons for "why do you like to play with or be with that person" include (1) high academic achievement (e.g., "he is smart," "working hard on schoolwork," "having good grades") (24%); (2) cooperative and prosocial behaviors (e.g., "helping me with assignments," "polite," "helping others when they have difficulties") (30%); (3) common interests and mutual understanding (e.g., "both like to play with computers," "get along with each other") (22%); and (4) desirable personal qualities (e.g., "always nice to me," "funny") (9%). In contrast, reasons for "why would you not like to play with or be with that person" mainly included (1) poor academic achievement (e.g., "very poor in academic performance," "not interested in schoolwork") (19%); and (2) aggressive-disruptive behaviors (e.g., "fighting with others," "hitting me," "disturbing others in class") (72%).

The main themes in the boys' interviews were academic achievement and prosocial and aggressive behaviors, which was consistent with the emphasis on social-behavioral qualities and academic achievement in Chinese culture (Chen, 2000a; Stevenson et al., 1990). The primary goal of education in Chinese schools is to help students develop in three aspects: moral-behavioral, intellectual, and physical. Interestingly, however, few of the boys in our sample indicated physical ability as a main reason for either liking or disliking a peer. In addition, inconsistent with the results based on the Class Play in the previous study, few boys mentioned shyness, reticence, or sensitivity as reasons for peer acceptance or rejection. The results suggest that whereas shy-sensitive behavior may be interesting in cross-cultural comparisons, especially between Chinese and North American children, its significance for peer relationships may be somewhat limited within Chinese culture from boys' perspectives.

Friendship

In Chinese culture, friendship (*you yi* in Mandarin) has traditionally been regarded as one of the five most important social relationships in human life (the other four relationships are between ruler and minister, father and son, husband and wife, and elder brother and younger brother). Friendship is often viewed as a phenotype of the sibling relationship (King & Bond, 1985). "Having a true friendship" is ranked as a number one value by contemporary Chinese children and adolescents (Sun et al., 1989). As indicated earlier, traditional Chinese culture emphasizes the importance of friendship for the development of social competence and adaptation, particularly in boys.

Nevertheless, little empirical research has been conducted on the significance and functions of friendship in Chinese boys. As a result, it is virtually unknown how friendships play a role in individual social and psychological adjustment in Chinese boys. For example, what functions do friendships serve in Chinese boys? Are there cross-cultural differences in the functions of boys' friendships? To address these questions, we conducted a cross-cultural study of friendship in China and Canada.

Functions of Friendship—Study #3

According to the ecological view of social support (e.g., DeRosier & Kupersmidt, 1991; Tietjen, 1989), the functional roles that children's social relationships fulfill may vary across cultures. It has been argued that the main functions of friendship include companionship, intimate disclosure, and enhancement of self-worth (e.g., Bukowski et al., 1996; Rubin et al., 1998). Among these functions, the enhancement of self-worth is regarded as particularly important for individual social and emotional development (e.g., Furman & Buhrmester, 1985). This function has been viewed as deriving from human social and psychological needs, and reflecting a high level of social development (e.g., Weiss, 1974). Since individual psychological well-being has often been considered relatively unimportant in Chinese culture, the function of friendship in the enhancement of self-worth may not be highly appreciated among Chinese boys. In contrast, given that the primary task of socialization in Chinese culture is to help children become part of the group and to integrate into the collective, social relationships including dyadic friendship may be valued mainly in terms of their functions to help children cooperate with others. Thus, mutual understanding and care may be a more important function of friendship than the enhancement of self-esteem in Chinese children. We attempted to test these hypotheses in a friendship study.

PARTICIPANTS, PROCEDURE, AND MEASURES

Participants in the friendship study were 248 boys in Shanghai, People's Republic of China, and 178 boys, in Southern Ontario, Canada, in grades 3 to 7. In the study, the boys completed a friendship function measure, which consisted of sets of statements about the functional roles of friendship. The statements tapped six typical functions of social relationships including security-protection (e.g., "I would like to be with this person when I feel uncomfortable or scared in a new place"), instrumental assistance (e.g., "I can count on this person when I need help"), companionship (e.g., "When I want to do something for fun, I can usually find this person"), intimacy (e.g., "I share my secrets and private feelings with this person"), understanding and care (e.g., "This person cares about me"), and enhancement of self-worth (e.g., "This person makes me feel important and special") (Furman & Buhrmester, 1985; Weiss, 1974). To avoid problems that often exist in rating scales, such as high overlap among different functional dimensions (Furman & Buhrmester, 1985), and to reduce the influence of "response style" on cross-cultural comparisons (Chen, Lee & Stevenson, 1995), an "ipsative" approach was used (i.e., the descriptiveness of the items were evaluated relative to each other *within* the particular individual) in this measure. The participants were requested to select and rank three statements in each set that were most descriptive of their friendships. Total scores for each function were computed based on the selection and ranking ("most descriptive" = 3; "second most descriptive" = 2; "third most descriptive" = 1) of corresponding statements.

RESULTS

A repeated-measure MANOVA first revealed a significant interaction between cultural groups and the within factor of the friendship function variables, *Wilks* = .86, F (5, 457) = 14.33, p < .001. Follow-up univariate analyses were conducted to detect cross-cultural differences and within-cultural patterns. The descriptive data and t-tests are presented in Table 9.2. It was found that, in general, the boys in both Chinese and Canadian samples selected companionship and intimacy as primary functions of friendships. Scores on companionship and intimate disclosure were significantly higher than those on other variables within each sample. Canadian boys, however, had higher scores than Chinese boys on companionship, and no differences were found between the samples on intimacy. Consistent with our expectations, Canadian boys had significantly higher scores on enhancement of self-worth, and lower scores on understanding and care than Chinese boys.

In addition, the Chinese boys had significantly higher scores than the Canadian boys on instrumental assistance, suggesting that Chinese boys were more likely than Canadian boys to appreciate the instrumental value of their friendships. Relative to scores on companionship and intimate disclosure, however, scores on instrumental assistance were significantly lower in both Chinese and Canadian samples. This later result was clearly *inconsistent* with Smart's (1999) argument that, in general, the Chinese tend to stress the instrumental or "mutual usefulness" rather than expressive or emotional facets of friendship. Regardless of the cross-cultural differences, both Chinese and Canadian boys indicated that playfulness and emotional intimacy were more important than the instrumental "usefulness" in their friendships.

TABLE 9.2
Functions of Friendship in Chinese and Canadian Adolescents

| | Chinese (N = 242) | | Canadian (N = 221) | | |
	M	SD	M	SD	t value
Security-protection	2.33	1.91	1.64	1.84	4.47***
Instrumental assist.	3.33	1.98	2.42	2.13	5.25***
Companionship	6.64	2.44	7.46	2.92	−3.59***
Intimate disclosure	4.71	2.23	4.78	2.58	−.38
Understanding and care	3.22	2.22	2.53	2.12	3.88***
Enhancement self-worth	2.58	1.74	3.04	2.43	−2.71**

** p < .01
*** p < .001.

Finally, security-protection was considered the least important by both Chinese and Canadian boys. However, Chinese boys emphasized this function more than their Canadian counterparts in friendships. This may be due to the fact that Chinese children including boys may be more likely than their Western counterparts to feel insecure and anxious in unfamiliar and challenging situations (e.g., Chan & Eysenck, 1981; Chen et al., 1998; Kagan et al., 1978).

Descriptions of Friendship—Study #4

Developmental and gender-related patterns concerning children's understanding of friendship have been revealed in Western children (Aboud & Mendelson, 1996; Biglow, 1977; Selman & Schultz, 1990). During childhood, children's descriptions of friendship often focus on physical proximity, common activities, and instrumental help. From late childhood to adolescence, youth pay more attention to a friend's behavioral and psychological characteristics and to the relationship itself. Similarity in personality, intimate feelings, and mutual support are the common descriptive features of adolescent friendships. Compared with girls, boys' friendships appear to be focused more on agentic needs such as self-esteem, self-actualization, power and control, achievement and autonomy, and less on communal needs such as affection and intimacy (see Buhrmester, 1996).

Yet we know little about the experience of friendships among Chinese boys. What does friendship mean to Chinese boys? How are cultural values and customs reflected in their conceptions of friendships? To explore these questions, we conducted interviews with Chinese boys about their understanding of friendships. The participants were the same 67 boys in Beijing, People's Republic of China, who participated in the interview study of peer acceptance and rejection. Similar to the interviews on peer acceptance and rejection, we asked the children to describe how they formed close relationships with their best friends and why they wanted to be friends with them.

The descriptive data first suggest that, largely similar to findings in the West, there were clear age/grade differences in the understanding of friendship in Chinese children and adolescents. Descriptions of friendships were mainly concerned with specific activities and physical proximity in the lower grades, but changed to concerns related to more social and psychological characteristics such as modesty and moral character in early adolescence. The focus of friendship conception also appeared to shift with age from salient behavioral characteristics of the friend and benefits that friendship can provide (e.g., "He is good at math, and he often helps with my homework") to more internal and less observable personality characteristics and relationship qualities (e.g., "He is an easy-going and straightforward person, and we get along with each other very well"). The differences were particularly salient between elementary school boys (grades 4 and 6, $n = 42$) and junior high school boys (grade 8, $n = 25$), with mean proportion scores of .89 and .29 ($SD = .24$ and .33) on concrete, activity-related reasons [$t(65) = 7.88, p < .001$] and .09 and .62 ($SD = .20$ and .38) on psychological, relationship-oriented reasons [$t(65) = -6.51, p < .001$] respectively.

Several themes emerged in the content analysis of the friendship descriptions of Chinese boys. First, similar to the responses on the peer acceptance and rejection task from Study 1, most of the descriptions concerning why the child wants to be friends with another child were related to academic achievement (18%), prosocial behaviors (24%), common interests and mutual understanding (31%), and desirable personal qualities (14%). The results indicate that school achievement and cooperative activities provide an important context for the organization and development of close relationships among Chinese boys, which is likely to be due, at least in part, to Chinese collectivistic culture. Nevertheless, compared with the results concerning peer acceptance, there were significantly higher percentages of responses involving common interests, mutual understanding, and desirable personal qualities in the friendship interviews. The results suggest that Chinese boys are more attentive to factors that are relevant to the maintenance of close relationships such as mutual understanding, care, and trustfulness in friendships than in overall peer acceptance. The relationship-oriented features may represent the distinct nature of friendship, which may be similar across cultures (e.g., Bukowski et al., 1996; Rubin et al., 1998).

The instrumental aspect of friendship (i.e., how friendship may be helpful or useful in a concrete manner) was evident in Chinese boys' descriptions (over 50% of the responses involving academic achievement were related to "usefulness" of the relationship). However, the descriptions need to be understood in context. For example, the "instrumental" statements were not necessarily associated with selfish motives. On the contrary, they often reflected collectivistic or cooperative values. Some examples of this type of friendship descriptions are as follows:

Li Jun[1] and I each have some strengths and weaknesses in different areas. I can learn from him in the areas where I am poor, and he can learn from me in the areas where I am good. This way, we can both make progress in school and enhance our achievement. This is why I would want to be a friend with him.

One day, I was working on my math assignment in the classroom. I had been working on it for a long time because I could not figure out the answer to a question. Most of my classmates had left because it was late in the afternoon. Then, Xiang Shi came to my table and asked me whether he could help. Very soon, he solved the problem. After that, we found that we could get along with each other very well and have a lot of things in common. We became good friends.

I remember in one afternoon last term, I was watching a group of students playing on the playground. I was feeling lonely because no one was playing with me. Zhang Cheng was in that group. He came to me and invited me to play with them. This was how we became friends.

In Western cultures, friendship is often regarded as personal, private, and affective (Krappman, 1996). In China, however, parents, teachers, and other adults are encouraged to be involved in children's and adolescents' peer relationships and to exert supervision and control. This control is often due to Chinese parents and teachers being highly concerned with the consequences of children's associations with "bad" friends. Moreover, it is believed that adults are more knowledgeable and competent than children in selecting "right" friends. Although several boys expressed their dissatisfaction with adult intervention, or even defiant attitudes (e.g., "What is important in selecting your friends is how you feel about them, not what your parents or teachers say"), the majority of Chinese boys suggested an understanding and acceptance of adult control over their relationships with their friends.

Conclusions

Peer relationships are an important component of social development in both individualistic and collectivistic cultures. Since social relationships and socialization ideologies and practices are culturally bound, however, boys' experiences in the peer context are likely to be different across cultures. The results of the studies described in this chapter suggest that peer acceptance and rejection reflect cultural values such as the encouragement of behavioral control and academic achievement in China. Findings from all four studies suggest that cultural norms and beliefs are involved in organizing social-ecological settings for child development and serve as guidance for social judgments of specific behaviors and impart "meanings" to the behaviors.

At the same time, however, our results indicate similar features and functions of peer relationships in Chinese and North American boys. The associations between peer rejection and feelings of loneliness in both samples suggest that, regardless of the culture, children who experience difficulties in peer relationships are vulnerable to developing emotional problems. Moreover, both Chinese and Canadian boys emphasize the functions of companionship and intimate communications in their close friendships. It has been argued that feelings of belonging and acceptance in the peer group and intimate mutual communications and exchanges in close dyadic relationships or "chumship" are derived from basic social needs in childhood and adolescence (Sullivan, 1953). Our results suggest that these basic needs may play a significant role in social interactions and relationships across cultures.

Finally, influences of cultural values and developmental tendencies on peer relationships are likely to occur in changing social contexts. Our results concerning the "controversial" status of shy-sensitive boys in the peer group and the small number of "deviant" responses such as dissatisfaction with adult control in China provide initial evidence of the role of societal changes in children and adolescents' experiences and adjustment. Like many other countries in the world, China is currently undergoing major social and cultural changes toward the market economy. Western values and ideologies have been introduced into the country along with advanced technology. The "westernization" may become more dramatic in the near future since China has recently joined the World Trade Organization (WTO). It is reasonable to expect that the social, political, and economic changes may affect socialization patterns including parental expectations of boys' behaviors and social relationships. It is important that future researchers investigate how Chinese boys adjust to their social circumstance during the transitional period.

NOTES

The preparation of this chapter was supported by grants from the Social Sciences and Humanities Research Council of Canada and Canadian Institutes of Health Research, and by a Faculty Award from the William T. Grant Foundation and a Health Career Award from the Canadian Institutes of Health Research.

1. The names in the descriptions are not real, to protect the confidentiality of the participants' identity.

REFERENCES

Aboud, F. E. & Mendelson, M. J.(1996). Determinants of friendship selection and quality: Developmental perspectives. In W. M. Bukowski, A. F. Newcomb & W. W. Hartup (Eds.), *The company they keep: Friendship in childhood and adolescence* (pp. 87–112). Cambridge: Cambridge University Press.

Asher, S., Hymel, S. & Renshaw, P. D. (1984). Loneliness in children. *Child Development, 55,* 1456–1464.

Asher, S., Parkhurst, J. T., Hymel, S. & Williams, G. A. (1990). Peer rejection and loneliness in childhood. In S. R. Asher & J. D. Coie (Eds.), *Peer rejection in childhood* (pp. 253–273). New York: Cambridge University Press.

Biglow, B. J. (1977). Children's friendship expectations: A cognitive developmental study. *Child Development, 48,* 246–253.

Buhrmester, D. (1996). Need fulfillment, interpersonal competence, and the developmental contexts of early adolescent friendship. In W. M. Bukowski, A. F. Newcomb & W. W. Hartup (Eds.), *The company they keep: Friendship in childhood and adolescence* (pp. 1–18). New York: Cambridge University Press.

Bukowski, W. M., Newcomb, A. F. & Hartup, W. W. (1996). Friendship and its significance in childhood and adolescence: Introduction and comment. In W. M. Bukowski, A. F. Newcomb & W. W. Hartup (Eds.), *The company they keep: Friendship in childhood and adolescence* (pp. 158–185). New York: Cambridge University Press.

Chan, J. & Eysenck, S. B. G. (1981). *National differences in personality: Hong Kong and England.* Paper presented at the joint IACCP-ICP Asian Regional Meeting, National Taiwan University, Taipei, Taiwan, August.

Chen, C., Lee, S. Y. & Stevenson, H. W. (1995). Response style and cross-cultural comparisons of rating scales among East Asian and North American students. *Psychological Science, 6,* 170–175.

Chen, H. & Su, L. (2001). Child protection and development in China. *International Society for the Study of Behavioral Development Newsletter, 38,* 7–8.

Chen, M., Cheng, G., Zhou, Z. & Li, H. (1990). Psycho-social development in junior high school students and education. In Z. Zhu (Ed.), *Mental development in childhood and adolescence and education in China* (539–579). China: Zhou-Yue Publication House.

Chen, X. (2000a). Growing up in a collectivistic culture: Socialization and socio-emotional development in Chinese children. In A. L. Comunian & U. P. Gielen (Eds.), *International perspectives on human development* (pp. 331–353). Lengerich, Germany: Pabst Science Publishers.

Chen, X. (2000b). Social and emotional development in Chinese children and adolescents: A contextual cross-cultural perspective. In F. Columbus (Ed.), *Advances in psychology research, Vol. I* (pp. 229–251). Huntington, NY: Nova Science Publishers.

Chen, X., Hastings, P., Rubin, K. H., Chen, H., Cen, G. & Stewart, S. L. (1998). Childrearing attitudes and behavioral inhibition in Chinese and Canadian toddlers: A cross-cultural study. *Developmental Psychology, 34,* 677–686.

Chen, X. & He, H. (in press). The family in mainland China: Structure, organization, and significance for child development. In J. L. Roopnarine (Ed.), *Families in global perspectives.* Boston: Allyn and Bacon.

Chen, X. & Kaspar, V. (in press). Cross-cultural research on childhood. In U. P. Gielen & J. L. Roopnarine (Eds.), *Childhood and adolescence in cross-cultural perspective.* Westport, CT: Greenwood Press/Ablex.

Chen, X., Rubin, K. H. & Li, Z. (1995). Social functioning and adjustment in Chinese children: A longitudinal study. *Developmental Psychology, 31,* 531–539.

Chen, X., Rubin, K. H., Li, B. & Li. Z. (1999). Adolescent outcomes of social functioning in Chinese children. *International Journal of Behavioural Development, 23,* 199–223.

Chen, X., Rubin, K. H. & Sun, Y. (1992). Social reputation and peer relationships in Chinese and Canadian children: A cross-cultural study. *Child Development, 63,* 1336–1343.

Cillessen, A. H. N., van Ijsendoorn, H. W., van Lieshout, C. F. M. & Hartup, W. W. (1992). Heterogeneity among peer-rejected boys: Subtypes and stabilities. *Child Development, 63,* 893–905.

Coie, J. D., Dodge, K. A. & Coppotelli, H. (1982). Dimensions and types of social status: A five-year longitudinal study. *Developmental Psychology, 18,* 557–570.

DeRosier, M. E. & Kupersmidt, J. B. (1991). Costa Rican children's perceptions of their social networks. *Developmental Psychology, 27,* 656–662.

French, D. C. (1988). Heterogeneity of peer-rejected boys: Aggressive and nonaggressive subtypes. *Child Development, 59,* 976–985.

French, D. C., Setiono, K. & Eddy, J. M. (1999). Bootstrapping through the cultural comparison minefield: Childhood social status and friendship in the United States and Indonesia. In W. A. Collins & B. Laursen (Eds.), *Relationships as developmental contexts: The Minnesota symposia on child psychology, Vol. 30* (pp. 109–131). Mahwah, NJ: Erlbaum.

Furman, W. & Buhrmester, D. (1985). Children's perceptions of the personal relationships in their social networks. *Developmental Psychology, 21,* 1016–1024.

Harris, J. R. (1995). Where is the child's environment? A group socialization theory of development. *Psychological Review, 102,* 458–489.

Hartup, W. W. (1992). Social relationships and their developmental significance. *American Psychologist, 44,* 120–126.

Hightower, A. D., Work, W. C., Cohen, E. L., Lotyczewski, B. S., Spinell, A. P., Guare, J. C. & Rohrbeck, C. A. (1986). The Teacher-Child Rating Scale: A brief objective measure of elementary children's school problem behaviours and competencies. *School Psychology Review, 15,* 393–409.

Hinde, R. A. (1987). *Individuals, relationships and culture.* Cambridge: Cambridge University Press.

Hinshaw, S. P. & Melnick, S. A. (1995). Peer relationships in boys with attention-deficit hyperactivity disorder with and without comorbid aggression. *Development and Psychopathology, 7,* 627–647.

Ho, D. Y. F. (1987). Fatherhood in Chinese culture. In M. E. Lamb (Ed.), *The father's role: Cross-cultural perspectives* (pp. 227–245). Hillsdale, NJ: Erlbaum.

Hofstede, G. (1980). *Culture's consequences: International differences in work-related values.* London: Sage.

Hsu, F. L. K. (1981). *Americans and Chinese: Passage to differences* (3rd ed.). Honolulu: University Press of Hawaii.

Jiao, S., Ji, G. & Jing, Q. (Ching, C.C.). (1986). Comparative study of behavioural qualities of only children and sibling children. *Child Development, 57,* 357–361.

Kagan, J., Kearsley, R. B. & Zelazo, P. R. (1978). *Infancy: Its place in human development.* Cambridge, MA: Harvard University Press.

Kim, U., Triandis, H. C., Kagitcibasi, C., Choi, S. C. & Yoon, G. (1994). *Individualism and collectivism: Theory, method, and applications.* Thousand Oaks, CA: Sage.

King, A. Y. C. & Bond, M. H. (1985). The Confucian paradigm of man: A sociological view. In W. S. Tseng & D. Y. H. Wu (Eds.), *Chinese culture and mental health* (pp. 29–45). New York: Academic Press.

Krappman, L. (1996). Amicitia, drujba, shin-yu, philia, Freundschaft, friendship: On the cultural diversity of a human relationship. In W. M. Bukowski, A. F. Newcomb & W. W. Hartup (Eds.), *The company they keep: Friendship in childhood and adolescence* (pp. 19–40). New York: Cambridge University Press.

Lang, O. (1968). *Chinese family and society.* New Haven, CT: Yale University Press.

Larson, R. W. (1999). The uses of loneliness in adolescence. In K. J. Rotenberg & S. Hymel (Eds.), *Loneliness in childhood and adolescence* (pp. 244–262). New York: Cambridge University Press.

Luo, G. (1996). *Chinese traditional social and moral ideas and rules.* Beijing, China: The University of Chinese People Press.

Maccoby, E. E. (1990). Gender and relationships. *American Psychologist, 45,* 513–520.

Maccoby, E. E. (1995). The two sexes and their social systems. In P. Moen, G. H. Jr. Elder & K. Luescher (Eds.), *Examining lives in context: Perspectives on the ecology of human development* (pp. 347–364). Washington, DC: American Psychological Association.

Masten, A., Morison, P. & Pelligrini, D. (1985). A revised class play method of peer assessment. *Developmental Psychology, 21,* 523–533.

Oyserman, D., Coon, H. M. & Kemmelmeier, M. (2002). Rethinking individualism and collectivism: Evaluation of theoretical assumptions and meta-analyses. *Psychological Bulletin, 128,* 3–72.

Piaget, J. (1932). *The moral judgment of the child.* Glencoe: Free Press.

Rubin, K. H. & Asendorpf, J. (1993). *Social withdrawal, inhibition, and shyness in childhood.* Hillsdale, NJ: Erlbaum.

Rubin, K. H., Bukowski, W. & Parker, J. G. (1998). Peer interactions, relationships, and groups. In N. Eisenberg (Ed.), *Handbook of child psychology: Vol 3. Social, emotional, and personality development* (pp. 619–700). New York: Wiley.

Ruble, D. N. & Martin, C. L. (1998). Gender development. In N. Eisenberg (Ed.), *Handbook of child psychology: Vol. 3. Social, emotional, and personality development* (pp. 933–1016). New York: Wiley.

Selman, R. L. & Schultz, L. H. (1990). *Making a friend in youth: Developmental theory and clinical analyses.* New York: Academic Press.

Smart, A. (1999). Expressions of interest: Friendship and *guanxi* in Chinese societies. In S. Bell & S. Coleman (Eds.), *The anthropology of friendship* (pp. 119–136). Oxford, UK: Berg.

Stevenson, H. W., Lee, S., Chen, C., Stigler, J. W., Hsu, C. & Kitamura, S. (1990). Contexts of achievement. *Monographs of the Society for Research in Child Development, 55* (Serial no. 221).

Sullivan, H. S. (1953). *The interpersonal theory of psychiatry.* New York: Norton.

Sun, Y., Chen, X. & Peterson, C. (1989). A survey on value systems of contemporary Chinese adolescents. *Youth Study, 1,* 58–61.

Thorne, B. (1993). *Gender play: Girls and boys in school.* New Brunswick, NJ: Rutgers University Press.

Thorne, B. & Luria, Z. (2001). Sexuality and gender in children's daily worlds. In J. M. Henslin (Ed.), *Down to earth sociology: Introductory readings* (11th ed.) (pp. 156–167). New York: Free Press.

Tietjen, A. M. (1989). The ecology of children's social support networks. In D. Belle (Ed.), *Children's social networks and social support* (pp. 37–69). New York: Wiley.

Triandis, H. C. (1990). *Individualism and collectivism.* Boulder, CO: Westview.

Way, N. & Pahl, K (1999). Friendship patterns among urban adolescent boys: A qualitative account. In M. Kopala & L. A. Suzuki (Eds.), *Using qualitative methods in psychology* (pp. 145–161). Thousand Oaks, CA: Sage.

Weiss, R. S. (1974). The provisions of social relationships. In Z. Rubin (Ed.), *Doing unto others* (pp. 17–26). Englewood Cliffs, NJ: Prentice-Hall.

Zarbatany, L., McDougall, P. & Hymel, S. (2000). Gender-differentiated experience in the peer culture: Links to intimacy in preadolescence. *Social Development, 9,* 62–79.

10

The Influence of Peer Experiences on Bravado Attitudes among African American Males

*Michael Cunningham and
Leah Newkirk Meunier*

Developing an identity, or a sense of self, becomes more salient during adolescence than during the childhood years. African American males—like all males—develop a heightened awareness of adult male role expectations during this period. They also look to their peers for social acceptance and popularity relative to the peer group. Their development of self-understanding is, therefore, influenced by larger cultural expectations of what it means to be a man and also their perceptions of themselves in relation to their peers. This normative developmental process occurs within a social environment, with each adolescent boy addressing questions of identity in ways that respond to his immediate surroundings (e.g., home, school, peers, neighborhood). Among African American males living in high-risk neighborhoods, research has found that such males often develop an identity that can be characterized as "bravado" (i.e., hypermasculine or macho) (Cunningham, 1999, 2001; Spencer, 2001; Spencer, Cunningham & Swanson, 1995). However, few researchers have empirically examined this process of developing such an attitude or identity. It is unknown, for example, how peers shape the development of this type of attitude. It is also unclear whether this attitude is a coping strategy or is simply a sign of vulnerability. In this chapter, we explore the role of peers in the bravado attitudes of adolescent African American males who live in high-risk neighborhoods. We also explore the meaning of bravado attitudes among these young men.

The chapter is organized in four sections. First, we define bravado attitudes and review the small but extant literature on the association between bravado attitudes and various types of psychological and behavioral outcomes. Second, we discuss a theoretical framework used to examine how perceptions of peers are associated with bravado attitudes among African American males. Third, we present findings from our empirical study of this topic. Finally, we discuss the meaning of our findings and suggest that bravado attitudes may be both a coping strategy and a sign of vulnerability for African American males.

Bravado Attitudes

Researchers examining bravado attitudes in males have used varying definitions of the construct. It has been referred to as an expression of stoicism (Pollack, 2001; Pollack & Schuster, 2000, p. 18; Taubman, 1986) and objectivity of women (Serniak, 1992). Although these definitions might transcend racial groups, the examples given in the research often exclude the experiences of males of color. Discrimination and racism influence the identities of males of color (Garcia Coll et al., 1996; Spencer & Dornbusch, 1990) and this experience needs to be taken into account in any formulation of identity development. Researchers who have examined identities in males of color have often found that an identity that is common among this broad population, particularly among African American males, is one that is characterized by bravado attitudes or "cool pose." This "cool pose," they argue, is a response to feelings of invisibility and discrimination in the United States (Majors, 1991; Majors & Billson, 1992). Majors and Billson (1992) claim: "Black males, especially those who are young and live in the inner cities of our nation, have adopted and used cool masculinity—or as we prefer to call it, 'cool pose'—as a way of surviving in a restrictive society" (p. 2).

Although the research on bravado attitudes and cool pose are useful in helping us to understand the experiences of males of color, the research rarely attempts to connect bravado attitudes to normative processes of identity development. Additionally, the definitions of bravado attitudes often suggest that they are simply displays of emotional weakness (Pollack, 2001). What is generally missing in the research is an empirical examination of the precursors of bravado attitudes and an exploration of the ways in which bravado attitudes may serve different purposes, including assuring survival, for males of color growing up in high-risk neighborhoods.

A few researchers have made an explicit link between bravado attitudes and other variables. For example, Cunningham (1999) conducted a longitudinal examination of how community factors impacted bravado attitudes in African American adolescent males. The results indicated that bravado attitudes were linked to perceptions of hassles associated with being a teenager (e.g., parents interrupting and monitoring phone conversations and whom teens hang out with or where they go). Adolescents who perceived their parents as constantly hassling them were more likely to express a bravado attitude than those who did not have such experiences with their parents. Additionally, negative neighborhood experiences such as being followed in public places (e.g., shopping malls) or perceptions of being harassed by police while "hanging out" with friends were linked to bravado attitudes. The longitudinal results (two years later) indicated that the adolescent perceptions of parental hassles *did not,* however, have a long-term impact on bravado attitudes. Instead, only the negative experiences in public places continued to be significantly associated with bravado attitudes over time.

In another study of African American males and females (see Stevenson, 1997), the anticipation that one might be a victim of community violence was significantly associated with stoic responses such as bravado attitudes. However, bravado attitudes were only evident among African American males who lived in high-risk urban neighborhoods. Spencer (2001) expanded on this research and also found that living in high-risk neighborhoods was associated with bravado attitudes. In contrast, however, to previous research on bravado attitudes that presents this construct solely as a negative outcome, Spencer describes bravado attitudes as "a reactive coping style" that is not only a normal part of identity development among some youth living in high-risk environments, but is also necessary for psychological survival. She argues, further, that bravado attitudes are linked to experiences in the home, school, and neighborhood. Within these environments, the peer group is especially salient.

Peer Influences

While peers are considered critical to healthy adolescent development, little is known about the influence of peers or peer groups on the development of African American males (Way & Chen, 2000). Peer groups during adolescence are rewarding because of the opportunities that they provide for social comparisons (Erwin, 1993). Similarities between group members are seen as providing a consensual validation of the adolescent's thoughts, feelings, and behavior. But groups not only validate the individual's identity, they also tend to make their members more similar to each other and different from the out-group. In order to be accepted by the group, there is pressure to conform to group expectations and standards (Brown, 1999). Even though research has suggested that the development of antisocial behavior may be closely linked to peer group processes or to peers in general (Poulin, Dishion & Haas, 1999), the role of peers in the development of bravado attitudes specifically is unclear.

Phenomenological Variant of Ecological Systems Theory (PVEST)

Our theoretical framework for investigating the influence of peers on the development of bravado attitudes is Spencer's (1995) Phenomenological Variant of Ecological Systems Theory (PVEST). This perspective integrates Erikson's theory of identity formation, Piaget's notion of formal operations, and Bronfenbrenner's (1989) ecological perspective, with emphasis placed on the self-appraisal process (Swanson, Spencer & Petersen, 1998). Specifically, the PVEST framework suggests that identity processes, especially for people of color, are linked to risk experiences, stresses encountered, coping methods employed, adaptive identity processes, and patterned outcomes (e.g., good mental health or school engagement versus compromised mental health or school dropout) (Spencer, 1995). The model takes into account structural and contextual barriers to identity formation and their implications for psychological processes such as self-appraisal. This model is particularly appropriate for examining adolescence because it helps us understand how the neighborhood or community context influences adolescents' self-perception and attitudes.

Although many have argued that adolescence is a particularly difficult period in the lifespan (Arnett, 1999; Erikson, 1959), this period may be even more difficult for African American male adolescents from poor families living in high-risk environments. Being an economically disadvantaged minority group member, he may find it difficult to achieve positive developmental outcomes because of prejudice, discrimination, or barriers to full opportunity for personal growth (Cunningham, 1999; Cunningham & Spencer, 1996, 2000; Gibbs et al., 1989). In general, issues not faced by majority youth complicate the life experiences of minority adolescents in the United States. Political, cultural, economic, and social forces interact in complex ways with identity development, self-image, relations with peers, school achievement, and career goals (Garcia Coll et al., 1996; Spencer & Dornbusch, 1990). These interactions all occur within specific neighborhood and community contexts in which the peer group plays a significant role. The current study uses the PVEST framework to investigate the association between perceptions of peers and bravado attitudes.

Method

Participants

The sample consisted of 356 adolescent African American boys aged 11–15. Respondents were sixth, seventh, and eighth graders who attended public schools in a large urban Southeastern American city. Although these boys were middle school students, their ages ranged from eleven to fifteen at Time 1 of data collection (*M* age = 13.22, *SD* = 1.09). Some of these adolescents have been retained in school once, twice, and in some cases three times (e.g., 30% have been retained at least once in their school career).

The boys were part of a larger cross-sectional longitudinal study, Promotion of Academic Competence (Project PAC) (Spencer, 1989). This research project was concerned with the development of competence and resilience of African American youth. The students were randomly selected from four middle schools and were given informed consent forms to obtain permission from their parents. Out of the four schools, over 80% of consent forms were returned at two of the schools and the other two schools had return rates above 70%. At three of the four schools, 80–90% of the students received free or reduced lunch support. At the fourth school, approximately 70% of the students received free or reduced lunch. The sample is representative of African American families living under impoverished conditions.[1]

Procedures

As a part of the Project PAC sample, students were seen in small groups at their respective schools; they completed survey instruments about peers and about bravado attitudes during one of three sessions. The majority of the researchers were the same race of the participants. All researchers were well-trained graduates, undergraduates, or older adults who were hired specifically as adolescent interviewers.

Measures

PEER INFLUENCE

The Peer Factors scale (Cunningham, 1994) was used to assess adolescents' perceptions of their peers. The scale was taken from items from the Project PAC survey (Spencer, 1989). The scale was confirmed with principle components analysis followed by varimax rotation. Nine factor groups were developed with factor loadings of .60 or greater. The resulting factors assessed perceptions of peers in the immediate contexts of the adolescents (for a detailed description of the method see Cunningham, 1994). The factors are described as perceived peer factors because they are based on the boy's own view of his experience. In accordance with the PVEST perspective, the emphasis of the scale is on self-appraisal processes as they relate to interactions with peers. The participants answered the questions about themselves and their perceptions of their peer relationships. For example, in the first factor named *Negative Self Perceptions,* students were asked how they felt when they were with their peer groups. This factor has four items and a Cronbach's alpha of .74. An example item is, "I am not much good at anything." The second factor was named *Necessary to Talk About Problems.* It has five items and a Cronbach's alpha of .76. The items describe behaviors or attitudes that facilitate mental health such as, "It is necessary to talk to someone about your problems." This theme of self in relation to peers continued with the third factor, which was comprised of four items and described a *Sense of Alienation* (e.g., "Others don't understand my problems" $\alpha = .70$). The fourth factor was similar to the third; however, the three items described *Feelings of Unpopularity* within a school context (e.g., "This school is too big and other kids do not know me" $\alpha = .76$). In contrast to factor four, the fifth described positive interactions within one's school context. It has three items and was labeled *Good Self and Context Match* (α = .77). The items were, "I feel comfortable in a mixed race class, all African American class, and an all White class." The sixth factor tapped into adolescent experiences of increased self-awareness. It has two items and was labeled *Worry About Acceptance* (e.g., "I worry about being liked" "I worry about having friends" α = .71). The seventh peer factor was concerned with *School Popularity*. It has three items and α = .73 (e.g., "The girls or boys like me at school"). The eighth factor focused on a physical comparison of one's self to one's peers and it was labeled *Self is Better Than Peers*. The students were asked to describe their physical maturation as compared to their same aged peers. For example, "Compared to your peers, are your physical changes early, about the same time or later?" (α = .80). The last factor described dangerous situations in the neighborhood. It has two items and is labeled *Peer/Gang or Turf Hassles* (α = .80) (e.g., "I often avoid turf wars" and "I am often hassled by gangs").

BRAVADO ATTITUDES

To assess bravado attitudes, the modified Machismo Inventory (Mosher & Sirkin, 1984) was used. This protocol was administered as part of a one-on-one interview. The *Machismo Inventory* consists of 30 forced-choice items designed to measure the three components of the macho personality constellation (i.e., callous sex attitudes toward women, violence as manly, and danger as exciting), with ten items assessing each component. Examples of items from each component, with the macho response indicated first, are as follows: For "callous sex attitudes toward women," students were asked a set of items such as "When you are at a party, it is ok to get a girl drunk, high, or hot and she'll let you do whatever you want?"; or, "It's gross and unfair to use alcohol or drugs to convince a woman to have sex." An example of a "violence as manly" item was "I still enjoy remembering my first real fight"; or, "I hope to forget fights I've been in." A "danger as exciting" item was "I like to drive fast, right on the edge of danger"; or, "I like to drive safely, avoiding all possible risks." The Cronbach alpha coefficients for the current sample were .75 for overall Machismo scale (or bravado attitudes), .77 for Callous Sex attitudes subscale, .77 for Violence as manly subscale, and .71 for Danger as exciting subscale.

Results

To examine adolescents' perceptions of their peers, the Peer factors were converted to standardized scores (i.e., Z-scores). As such, the mean for each factor was centered at zero. The means in Figure 10.1 suggest that boys typically thought that it was *not* necessary to talk to others about their problems ($M = -.14$, $SD = 1.39$). Other researchers have linked this lack of openness to receiving help from others to bravado attitudes (Pollack, 2001) and emotional vulnerability (Spencer, 2001; Spencer, Cunningham & Swanson, 1995). Additionally, boys commonly perceived that they have to deal with gang or turf hassles in their respective neighborhoods ($M = .17$, $SD = 1.21$), which has been reported as common experiences for adolescents who live in high-risk neighborhoods (Aber et al., 1997).

The next set of analyses examined the relations between the perceptions of peers and bravado attitudes (i.e., believing that violence is manly, believing that dangerous situations are exciting, and having callous attitudes toward women). Pearson bivariate correlations (see Table 10.1) suggested that there was an inverse relation between age and negative self-perceptions, feelings of unpopularity, and low physical maturation. Younger teens were more likely than older teens to have negative self-perceptions, to feel unpopular, and to report low physical maturation. There was also a significant correlation between the "Necessary to talk about Problems" factor and each dimension of the bravado attitudes scale. When adolescents reported that they believed it was necessary to talk about their problems with peers, reports of bravado attitudes were low. In addition, there was a significant association between "Good self and context match" and each dimension of bravado attitudes. Feeling comfortable in the classroom context with peers was associated with low scores on bravado attitudes. Furthermore, there was a significant correlation between "A sense of alienation from peers" and two of the dimensions of bravado attitudes—"danger as exciting" and "callous sex attitudes toward women." Strong feelings of alienation from peers were associated with beliefs that dangerous activities were exciting and negative attitudes about women. Reports of frequent peer/gang or turf hassles were also significantly associated with two dimensions of bravado attitudes, namely, believing that dangerous activities were exciting and having negative attitudes about women.

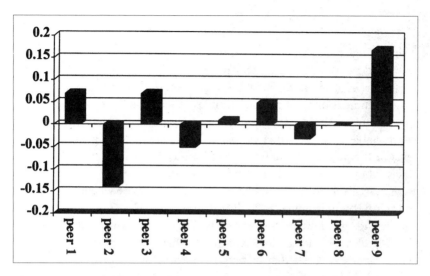

Figure 10.1 Means of Perceived Peer Factors

Note: Peer 1 = Negative Self Perceptions, *Peer 2* = Necessary to Talk About Problems, *Peer 3* = Sense of Alienation, *Peer 4* = Feelings of Unpopularity, *Peer 5* = Good Self and Context Match, *Peer 6* = Worry about Acceptance, *Peer 7* = School Popularity, *Peer 8* = Self is Better Than Peers, *Peer 9* = Peer/Gang or Turf Hassles

TABLE 10.1
Correlations between Perceptions of Peers and Bravado Attitudes

	Age	Bravado Attitudes	Danger as Exciting	Violence as Manly	Callous Sex Attitude
Peer1	−.10*	.06	.04	−.05	.17**
Peer2	.01	−.19***	−.14**	−.14**	−.19***
Peer3	−.04	.10*	.10*	.00	.17***
Peer4	−.22**	.04	.05	−.01	.06
Peer5	.02	−.23***	−.22***	−.16**	−.18***
Peer6	−.08	−.05	−.02	−.07	−.02
Peer7	.06	−.02	−.00	−.04	−.02
Peer8	−.13**	−.05	−.01	−.07	−.03
Peer9	−.02	.17**	.12*	−.07	.23***

Note:[+] = *p* < .10
* = *p* < .05
** = *p* < .01
*** = *p* < .001
Peer 1 = Negative Self Perceptions, *Peer 2* = Necessary to Talk About Problems, *Peer 3* = Sense of Alienation, *Peer 4* = Feelings of Unpopularity, *Peer 5* = Good Self and Context Match, *Peer 6* = Worry about Acceptance, *Peer 7* = School Popularity, *Peer 8* = Self is Better Than Peers, *Peer 9* = Peer/Gang or Turf Hassles

Discussion

The findings suggest that different aspects of peer experiences were related to bravado attitudes for African American males. Specifically, peer experiences in school and in the neighborhood were significantly associated with various dimensions of bravado attitudes. Alienation from peers, not feeling willing or able to speak with someone about problems, not feeling comfortable with peers in a classroom, and experiencing gang/turf problems in the neighborhood were all related to dimensions of bravado attitudes. Those males who seem more at risk interpersonally with their peers were more likely to report bravado attitudes than those who are less at risk in their peer environments. Poulin, Dishion, and Haas (1999) have found that friendships low in trust and satisfaction were associated with delinquent behaviors among adolescent males. This finding, along with the current findings, suggests that helping males develop positive peer relationships should be the focus of prevention and intervention programs serving adolescent male populations. Furthermore, adults working with youth should pay attention to the neighborhood context from which the youth come. Turf wars and gang struggles may pose a particularly difficult obstacle for many African American males living in high-risk environments. These experiences in the neighborhood, as suggested by our data, may play a large role in explaining why these males maintain bravado attitudes.

These findings have implications not only for practice but also for research. Based on the current findings, there is a clear need to further explore how multiple contexts, such as schools, neighborhoods, and the home environment, impact (separately and simultaneously) adolescent attitudes about themselves. How does school, for example, shape adolescent males' attitudes about themselves? Researchers have noted that African American males are strongly influenced by negative school environments that disproportionately place them in special education courses, do not consider them for gifted programs, and have low educational aspirations for them in general (see Ford & Harmon, 2001; Ford & Harris, 2000; Garibaldi, 1992, 1997). Our findings suggest that not feeling comfortable in class relates to bravado attitudes. These findings imply that the experience of school for African American youth makes a difference in their development (see Way & Robinson, 2003). Supportive school environments that do not perceive African American males as threatening and problematic might facilitate positive identity development among these males.

The finding regarding the association between turf wars and gang problems and bravado attitudes supports Spencer's argument that bravado attitudes are coping strategies based on perceptions of safety in the environment. Bravado attitudes may be adaptive, or at least necessary for survival, in high-risk communities. However, bravado attitudes may also be associated with vulnerability, as suggested by the fact that such attitudes have often been found to be associated with negative outcomes. For instance, Swanson, Cunningham, and Dottererr (2002) found that bravado attitudes mediated the relation between stressful life events and depression in African American males. In other words, the negative effects of stressful life events on depressive symptoms were heightened when there were strong endorsements of bravado attitudes. Therefore, bravado attitudes may be necessary for survival or indicative of a coping strategy but, at the same time, linked to vulnerability such as depression, alienation, and/or not being able to ask for help from others. Yet it is unclear whether these adaptive and maladaptive responses continue to be both adaptive and maladaptive over the long term. Perhaps as African American adolescent males become young adults, what was once adaptive and maladaptive becomes simply maladaptive.

Although the present research suggests that peers influence bravado attitudes among African American males, caution should be taken when interpreting the findings. Because the study is correlational, there is no way of determining the direction of effect between peer influences and bravado attitudes. It is plausible that maintaining bravado attitudes leads to alienation from peers, not believing that one should talk about problems with others, and not feeling comfortable in the classroom with peers rather than vice versa. Furthermore, there may be other aspects of peer relationships that were not investigated in the current study, such as feeling trusted and secure in one's relationship with one's closest friends, that may be an important predictor and/or outcome of bravado attitudes. Finally, our research did not address the mental health and behavioral consequences of bravado attitudes. While previous research, for example, has suggested that bravado attitudes have negative effects on mental health outcomes, it is unclear how or in what ways such attitudes negatively affect mental health outcomes or whether these effects are long-term. Future research needs to explore more fully the acquisition, maintenance, and consequences of bravado attitudes for African American males.

NOTES

The research reported is a portion of work conducted in the first author's doctoral dissertation at Emory University. The research was supported by funds awarded to Dr. Margaret Beale Spencer from several sources: The Commonwealth Fund, Spencer, W. T. Grant, and Ford Foundations. In addition, supplemental support from the Children's Trust Fund of Georgia, Social Science Research Council, and Annenberg Foundation were provided.

1. The parents also completed an extensive in-home interview. From self-report family income information, it was determined that 58% of the students' families met federal poverty guidelines (i.e., for a family size of four, an annual family income of $13,950). All of the in-home parental interviewers were same-race examiners.

REFERENCES

Aber, J. L., Gephart, M. A., Brooks-Gunn, J. & Connell, J. P. (1997). Development in context: Implications for studying neighborhood effects. In J. Brooks-Gunn, G. J. Duncan & J. L. Aber (Eds.), *Neighborhood poverty: Context and consequences for children.* New York: Russell Sage Foundation.

Arnett, J. J. (1999). Adolescent storm and stress, reconsidered. *American Psychologist, 54,* 317–326.

Bronfenbrenner, U. (1989). Ecological systems theory. In R. Vasta (Ed.), *Annals of Child Development* (pp. 187–248). Greenwich, CT: JAI Press.

Brown, B. B. (1999). Measuring the peer environment of American adolescents. In S. L. Friedman & T. D. Wachs (Eds.), *Measuring environment across the life span: Emerging methods and concepts* (pp. 59–90). Washington, DC: American Psychological Association.

Cunningham, M. (1994). *Expressions of manhood: Predictors of educational achievement of African American adolescent males.* Unpublished dissertation submitted for Ph.D., Emory University, Atlanta, GA.

Cunningham, M. (1999). African American adolescent males' perceptions of their community resources and constraints: A longitudinal analysis. *Journal of Community Psychology, 27,* 569–588.

Cunningham, M. (2001). African American males. In J. Lerner & R. Lerner (Eds.), *Adolescence in America: An Encyclopedia* (pp. 32–34). Santa Barbara, CA: ABC-CLIO Publishers.

Cunningham, M. & Spencer, M. B. (1996). The Black male experiences measure. In R. L. Jones (Ed.), *Handbook of tests and measurements for Black populations* (pp. 301–307). Hampton, VA: Cobb and Henry Publishers.

Cunningham, M. & Spencer, M. B. (2000). Conceptual and methodological issues in studying minority adolescents. In R. Montemayor, G. R. Adams & T. P. Gullotta (Eds.), *Adolescent diversity in ethnic, economic, and cultural contexts* (pp. 235–257). Thousands Oaks, CA: Sage Publications.

Erikson, E. H. (1959). Identity and the life cycle. *Psychological Issues, 1,* 1–171.

Erwin, P. (1993). *Friendship and peer relations in children.* New York: Wiley.

Ford, D. T. & Harmon, D. A. (2001). Equity and excellence: Providing access to gifted education for culturally diverse students. *Journal of Secondary Gifted Education, 12,* 141–147.

Ford, D. Y. & Harris J., (2000). A framework for infusing multicultural curriculum into gifted education. *Roeper Review, 23,* 4–10.

Garcia Coll, C., Lamberty, G., Jenkins, R., McAdoo, H., Crnic, K., Wasik, B. H. & Garcia, H. V. (1996). An integrative model for the study of developmental competencies in minority children. *Child Development, 67,* 1891–1914.

Garibaldi, A. M. (1992). Educating and motivating African American males to succeed. *Journal of Negro Education, 61,* 4–11.

Garibaldi, A. M. (1997). Four decades of progress . . . and decline: An assessment of African American educational attainment. *Journal of Negro Education, 66,* 105–120.

Gibbs, J. T., Huang, L. N. & Associates (Eds.). (1989). *Children of color.* San Francisco: Jossey-Bass.

Majors, R. (1991). Nonverbal behaviors and communication styles among African Americans. In R. L. Jones (Ed.), *Black psychology* (pp. 269–294). Hampton, VA: Cobb and Henry Publishers.

Majors, R. & Billson, J. M. (1992). *Cool pose: The dilemmas of Black manhood in America.* New York: Lexington Books.

Mosher, D. L. & Sirkin, M. (1984). Measuring a macho personality constellation. *Journal of Research in Personality, 18,* 150–164.

Pollack, W. S. (2001). "Masked men": New psychoanalytically oriented treatment models for adult and young adult men. In G. R. Brooks & G. E. Good (Eds.), *The new handbook of psychotherapy and counseling with men: A comprehensive guide to settings, problems, and treatment approaches,* 2 (pp. 527–543). New York: Wiley.

Pollack, W. S. & Schuster, T. (2000). *Real boys' voices.* New York: Penguin Books.

Poulin, F., Dishion, T. J. & Haas, E. (1999). The peer influence paradox: Friendship quality and deviancy training within male adolescent friendships. *Merrill-Palmer Quarterly, 45,* 42–61.

Serniak, D. (1992). Epistemic bravado attitudes and the problem with objectivity. In L. T. Winegar & J. Valsiner (Eds.), *Children's development with social context,* 1 (pp. 39–61). Hillsdale, NJ: Erlbaum.

Spencer, M. B. (1989). *Patterns of developmental transitions for economically disadvantaged Black male adolescents.* Proposal submitted to and funded by the Spencer Foundation, Chicago, IL.

Spencer, M. B. (1995). Old issues and new theorizing about African American youth: A phenomenological variant of ecological systems theory. In R. L. Taylor (Ed.), *Black youth: Perspectives on their status in the United States* (pp. 37–70). Westport, CT: Praeger.

Spencer, M. B. (1999). Social and cultural influences on school adjustment: The application of an identity-focused cultural ecological perspective. *Educational Psychologist, 34*, 43–47.

Spencer, M. B. (2001). Resiliency and fragility factors associated with the contextual experiences of low-resource urban African-American male youth and families. In A. Booth & A. C. Crouter (Eds.), *Does it take a village? Community effects on children, adolescents, and families* (pp. 51–78). Mahwah, NJ: Erlbaum.

Spencer, M. B., Cunningham, M. & Swanson, D. P. (1995). Identity as coping: Adolescent African American males' adaptive responses to high-risk environments. In H. W. Harris, H. C. Blue & E. H. Griffith (Eds.), *Racial and ethnic identity: Psychological development and creative expression* (pp. 31–52). New York: Routledge.

Spencer, M. B. & Dornbusch, S. (1990). American minority adolescents. In S. S. Feldman & G. R. Elliot (Eds.), *At the threshold: The developing adolescent* (pp. 123–146). Cambridge, MA: Harvard University Press.

Stevenson, H. C. (1997). "Missed, dissed, and pissed": Making meaning of neighborhood risk, fear and anger management in urban Black youth. *Cultural Diversity and Mental Health, 3*, 37–52.

Swanson, D. P., Cunningham, M. & Dottererr, A. (2002, April). *Beneath the surface: Alternative determinants of aggressive attitudes among African American males.* Poster presentation at the 2002 Biennial Meeting of the Society for Research in Adolescence, New Orleans, LA.

Swanson, D. P., Spencer, M. B. & Petersen, A. (1998). Identity formation in adolescence. In K. Borman & B. Schneider (Eds.), The adolescent years: Social influences and educational challenges. *Ninety-seventh Yearbook of the National Society for the Study of Education—Part 1* (pp. 18–41). Chicago: University of Chicago Press.

Taubman, S. (1986). Beyond the bravado attitudes: Sex roles and the exploitive male. *Social Work, 31*, 12–18.

Way, N. & Chen, L. (2000). Close and general friendships among African American, Latino, and Asian American adolescents from low-income families. *Journal of Adolescent Research, 15*, 274–301.

Way, N. & Robinson, M. (2003). A longitudinal study of the effects of family, friends, and school experiences on the psychological adjustment of ethnic minority, low-SES adolescents. *Journal of Adolescent Research, 18, 4*, 324–346.

Part IV

Sexuality and Romantic Relationships

11

Getting Close, Staying Cool

Early Adolescent Boys' Experiences
with Romantic Relationships

Deborah L. Tolman, Renée Spencer, Tricia Harmon, Myra Rosen-Reynoso, and Meg Striepe

"Just wait 'til they're teenagers." This ominous warning surfaced one evening during a middle-aged man and woman's conversation about their young boys' relationships with their peers. While their mother was waxing poetically about their sweet and loving ways, their father was quick to remind her of the inevitable changes ahead. He asserted that the empathic and emotionally intelligent boys of today will become the hormone-possessed teenagers of tomorrow, eager only to find ways to get as much sex as they can, without regard for the (presumed) girls whom they manage to persuade to meet their persistent sexual urges. At that moment, the boys' interest in relationships or intimacy with friends or romantic partners will either evaporate or never evolve, eliminating the chances that anyone will know about their vulnerabilities, hopes, or fears. To turn a phrase, she should not be so foolish as to think that somehow her boys will avoid becoming "boys." The assumption that pubertal changes drive adolescent boys to be single-minded in their sexual aggressiveness prevails as a given principle of adolescent life. The mother in the story may be hoping that her boys will remain "sweet," emotionally sensitive, and generous with their future girlfriends, but the father, speaking from the other side of male adolescence, predicts and expects what is to his mind inevitable.

Working backwards from the burgeoning literature on the psychology of men, it would seem that the father is predicting the future. Bursting

with descriptions of emotionally stunted adult men, this literature consti-
tutes a retroactive search for understanding how and why men's relationships became what are described as emotional wastelands (Bergman, 1995;
Kindlon & Thompson, 1999; Real, 1997) and offers prescriptions for how
men can alter ingrained behaviors and attitudes by developing the requisite skills to match their long dormant and repressed yearnings for intimacy (Brod & Kaufman, 1994). Several explanations of what happens, or
will happen, to boys as they enter the arena of impending adult masculinity and begin engaging in heterosexual romantic relationships have been
proposed. They include the assertion that boys' desire for emotional intimacy is already thwarted by the time they reach adolescence by the lack of
encouragement for the development of empathy and relational skills in
childhood (Kindlon & Thompson, 1999). Coupled with their exploration
of their sexuality through the isolated but highly pleasurable and controllable activity of masturbation, they are thus sexually and emotionally ill-
prepared for developing a relationship with a "real-life girl" (Kindlon &
Thompson, 1999, p. 196). It has also been suggested that boys take a "de-
fensively macho" approach to sexuality to protect themselves from inherent vulnerabilities and fears, and potential shame and humiliation, associated with having to perform with girls (Bergman, 1995; Pollack, 1998). Yet
another perspective holds that biological substrates anchor boys' disinclination toward relationships (Gurian, 1996).

One common characteristic of most explanations for boys' development into sexually aggressive and emotionally off-limits men is an absence
of a wider sociopolitical analysis of the (re)production of dominant or
hegemonic forms of masculinity (Connell, 1995, 2000; Kimmel, 1994,
1996). Identifying the social processes by which "boys learn to fashion particular forms of gendered subjectivity that are policed within regimes of
compulsory heterosexuality" (Martino, 2000; see also Connell, 1995; Rich,
1980), these analyses position masculinity as a kind of quicksand of practices that boys begin to engage with as they experience new thoughts, feelings, responsibilities, and relationships with the onset of adult sexual feelings and heterosexual expectations in adolescence. Boys' behavior in heterosexual relationships becomes a primary site for demonstrating the
"menacing, predatory, possessive and possibly punitive" sexuality (Kimmel, 1994, p. 121) that proves one's manhood primarily to male peers.

This behavior is undergirded not only by the social imperative to
demonstrate successful heterosexuality, but also to deny any possibility of
homosexuality and reject thoughts, feelings, or behaviors that may be

tainted with any hint of femininity. Intimacy, vulnerability, and connection are not only suspicious but potential signifiers of failed masculinity, which may elicit possible rejection or retribution from an ostensibly privileged brotherhood of men to which boys learn to aspire. Thus it is not surprising that Mandel and Shakeshaft (2000), in their study with 7th–9th grade students, found that if a boy is not "overtly or obviously heterosexual, students believe that something is wrong with him" (p. 90). Majors and Billson (1993), in describing the culture of "cool pose" among some African American young men, identify the compulsive quality that efforts toward masculinity can have—suggesting that it is always at risk and must be constantly reconstructed (see also Epstein & Johnson, 1998; Kimmel, 1996; Martino, 2000).

The literature on the development of romantic relationships in adolescence, while significant (e.g., Furman, Brown & Feiring, 1999; Shulman & Collins, 1997), tends to overlook gender as a key dynamic by which the meaning of relational processes is constructed (for an exception, see Feiring, 1999). However, research examining the relational lives of younger and older boys illuminates the importance of gender as a vector of meaning in boys' experiences of relationships. Judy Chu (2000) has observed how young primarily White boys actively engage with expectations that they behave in gender-appropriate ways if they want to be liked and accepted. In in-depth case studies of several 4-year-old boys, she noted that, while these boys show relational abilities and desires, they also begin "to compromise this ability as they learn what it means to be a 'real' boy and become more savvy about how they express themselves and strategic about how they engage in their relationships" (p. 174). Niobe Way (1998) described urban high school boys' experiences of wanting closeness and trust in their same-sex friendships while feeling unable to speak honestly, fearful of making themselves vulnerable to hurt and betrayal. Focusing on the relational needs and constraints that their social location puts at odds and looking for patterns across multiple relationships in these boys' lives, Way suggests the potential role of masculinity in the service of establishing and solidifying heterosexuality in this phenomenon.

These sociological and psychological insights lay the groundwork for considering what the actual experiences of boys who are entering adolescence and having their initial romantic relationships with girls might be. In the current chapter, we explore how early adolescent boys talk about their initial experiences in heterosexual relationships. Turning to in-depth qualitative interviews with a group of 8th-grade boys, we pursued the following questions: How do early adolescent boys describe their early experiences in romantic relationships? How do these boys understand and experience sexual and emotional intimacy and the ways in which these two forms of intimacy connect and do not connect for them? How do these boys negotiate cultural scripts associated with masculinity and compulsory heterosexuality as they enter into these new forms of relationship? We foreground sexuality as a key facet of masculinity as it is encountered by boys in early adolescence, when they are experiencing significant bodily and hormonal changes which will mark them as men in the context of friendships with male peers, burgeoning identity, and new types of intimacy with girls.

Collectively, the experiences of these adolescent boys move us beyond the popularized notion of pervasive and relentless "raging hormones" and provide a survey of the uncharted terrain of boys' experiences in romantic relationships. Revealing the contradictory realities of desiring, actively seeking, and experiencing intimacy in heterosexual relationships, their narratives challenge the assumption that all boys are unquestionably consumed only by desire for easy sex. As they describe their experiences with romantic relationships, these boys reveal, both straightforwardly and more subtly, the different sites of pressure associated with demonstrating or embodying masculinity, as well as refuges from it.

Study Description

As part of a longitudinal study of male and female adolescent sexual health, we conducted individual, semi-structured clinical interviews with a group of 25 ethnically and socio-economically diverse 13- to 15-year-old boys in the 8th grade of a school district serving contiguous urban and suburban communities in a single city. These boys were selected from a larger group of male and female early adolescents who were surveyed ($n = 244$, 133 boys), which included White (52%), Latina/o (23%), and biracial (17%) adolescents from poor, working-class, and middle-class families (26% reported their families currently received public assistance). Of the entire sample, 85% of the boys reported having had some dating experience by the 8th grade and that their dating relationships lasted, on average, more than 2 months. The boys we interviewed were selected from among those surveyed who had reported some experience with dating relationships and who indicated that they were willing to be interviewed.

The interviews were conducted during the spring of their 8th-grade year by male and female project staff (11 of the interviews were with male and 14 with female interviewers). The interviews took place in a private room at the middle school and were audiotaped, transcribed, and verified. The participants chose their own pseudonyms. The interviewers were guided by a protocol designed to elicit narratives that would generate an understanding of the parameters of early adolescent sexuality and relationships. The protocol included open-ended questions about their experiences in dating relationships, such as how these relationships began and ended, reasons for wanting or not wanting a girlfriend, particularly memorable times with girls they liked, who they talked to about their dating experiences, and their experiences with physical intimacy within and outside the context of a romantic relationship. They were also asked to describe their friendships and their understanding of, and experiences with, the larger school culture as one potential, and in hindsight successful, way of eliciting narratives about masculinity ideologies. Interviewers asked questions from the protocol such as "Could you tell me a story about something that's happened in your relationship [or about how it started or a special time] that can help me understand what it's like for you?" They were then asked follow-up questions in response to the stories told, yielding co-constructed narratives about these boys' experiences with romantic relationships (Silverman, 2000). The boys reported finding the interviews interesting, noting that they found themselves considering aspects of their lives that they had not given much thought to in any previous context.

The conceptual anchor of our analyses weaves together one of the prominent frameworks in sexuality research, scripting theory (Simon & Gagnon, 1986), with feminist theory that has articulated "compulsory heterosexuality" (Rich, 1980) as the centerpiece of patriarchy, and recent theory and research on masculinity ideologies and boys' development (e.g., Lesko, 2000). Rich (1980) conceived of heterosexuality as a universally pervasive *institution* comprised of unwritten but clearly codified and compulsory conventions that organize the ways in which males and females join in romantic relationships. Utilizing these theoretical lenses as organizing principles, we examined how these boys negotiated culturally scripted beliefs and behaviors associated with masculinity and compulsory heterosexuality, such as boys only want "one thing" (i.e., sex), as they were beginning to engage in romantic relationships. We conducted standard content and narrative analyses of each of the transcribed interviews by evaluating how culturally scripted beliefs and behaviors appeared, were absent from, or were resisted in the narratives told by these boys. We identified the specific themes of emotional intimacy, sexual intimacy, public performance of heterosexuality and hegemonic masculinity, and tensions between boys' private and public experiences that were used in the content analysis. In this analysis we focus on what was common across the boys' narratives in light of our conceptual emphasis on hegemonic forms of masculinity.

Forays into Intimacy

Emotional Intimacy

Contrary to the popular characterization of boys as only wanting "one thing" from girls, meaning sex, we found that the reach of most of these boys' desires was not confined to the sexual arena. Rather, expressions of desire for emotional connections were predominant in the interviews, with most of the boys expressing interest in having a girlfriend for the potential companionship, openness, trust, closeness, and emotional connection these relationships were thought to offer.

For example, when Sam, a 13-year-old bicultural (White and Native American) boy, was asked why boys his age want to have a girlfriend, he replied, "I want a girlfriend mostly just 'cause of companionship and stuff like that. . . . Like just friends, like not friends but I mean like being able to talk to each other openly and stuff like that." Skater, also 13 years old and bicultural (White and Native American), positioned his desire for companionship and closeness against his awareness that all he is expected to want in a girlfriend is a "make-out body." When he actually had a girlfriend, he discovered that he wanted "[s]omeone with the same interests as me and like, some of the, not just like, [a] make-out body, you know what I mean, like you don't just hang around them to make out, you just hang around them like regular friends, just as regular friends." But he adds the relationship would be different than other friendships "'cause it would be more open, we'd . . . we'd feel closer and I don't know. I don't know how to explain it." Frank, a 14-year-old White boy, echoed the theme of finding a different kind of emotional intimacy with a girlfriend than with his other friends. Girlfriends are fun to be around, he states, because "It's just different than being with your best friend. So you can talk about different things not what you talk about with your best friend." Frank elaborated by saying that with a best friend he might talk about "cars and bikes and blading and sports" whereas with a girlfriend he would "talk about life," or "about days at school and like bad days and good days and like that." Frank signified his desire for intimacy and his understanding that this kind of connection takes time in his stated preference for longer relationships (months as opposed to days or weeks) "because you don't really get to know the person if you're in a short relationship." For these boys, at this point in their relational development, emotional honesty, more than physical intimacy, seemed to be the basis for fostering feelings of openness and closeness.

Not only did these boys' stories provide evidence of emotional connection and mutuality, it is this quality that most of them said they liked most about their relationships. Boo, a 13-year-old White boy, who had been with his girlfriend for "maybe a year and 8 months," said that the relationship was important to him "because she's like one of the few people that actually like cares about me." Although Boo has close male friends, his relationship with his girlfriend was different, he explained, because "I'm more able to tell her things." He narrated his male friends' resistance to intimate conversation: "Like other people, like my other friends, they'd just be like, whatever, go away or, I'll see you next week or something. She's just like, like wants to be with me all the time and talk to me for one, stuff like that." In drawing this contrast, he reveals his sense that his relationship with his girlfriend is a safe haven for intimacy, meeting an important emotional need. The emotional connection he feels with his girlfriend is also evident in his reflection on how he would "be lost" if they broke up, because "just sort of being together so long we've like become a part of each other, so . . . it [would] just [be] like, taking a piece out of a puzzle or something."[1]

Sexual Intimacy

Skeptics might wonder whether the boys in this study emphasized their desire for emotional connection because our interviewers (male and female) did not invite or encourage them to talk about explicit, unabashed sexual desire. However, the interview protocol contained pointed questions about sexual experiences in relationships. Many (though not all) boys displayed a comfort in talking with both male and female interviewers about their sexuality that we did not witness in girls' responses to similar questions in this study or in other research on girls' sexuality (Tolman, 1994, 1999, 2002; Tolman et al., in press). While their female classmates' descriptions of their sexual experiences were frequently shaded or muted with tones of danger, vigilance, and self-protection (Tolman, 1999; Tolman et al., in press), the boys conveyed a sense of freedom in speaking about their sexual experiences, as well as in anticipating future encounters with sexuality. Skater clarified an interviewer's more general question about physical experiences with a girlfriend, saying, "Do I get erections?" Later, he explained, "like I, I always wake up with an erection." Wayne, a 13-year-old White boy, told the interviewer about some of his sexual interactions with girls: "They've grabbed my ass . . . ah it's nice, it hurts. One of them told me that she wanted to suck my cock, she never did. . . . Well, I got a little excited, but then I was like wait, she won't." This is not to say that none of the boys expressed some nervousness or trepidation associated with sexual intimacy. For example, Sam described his anxiety during his one attempt to hold a girl's hand as "mind racing, heart pounding, wondering what she would do." But more typically, these boys approached this new aspect of their bodies and their first sexual and romantic relationships with curiosity, enthusiasm, and excitement.

Many of the boys described experiencing sexual desire, and in so doing also talked perceptively about how they were learning to deal with these feelings. They described developing boundaries for their sexuality that were both internally and externally motivated. They discussed their ideas of what sexual behaviors they thought were acceptable for themselves or boys their age. They also mentioned instances of halting sexual progression with girls, and generally seemed to do so with a sense of entitlement and confidence, that it was acceptable and possible to say no in the privacy and safety of interactions with girlfriends. For instance, Wayne explains:

> Oh, it was a nice relationship, she wouldn't—she wasn't easy, but she wasn't slow. She was just like the right speed. Like after a couple days, we like um— kissed her couple of times, and she didn't care, she was just like "yeah, it was pretty nice," too. But like she didn't just jump into everything wicked fast. And then she didn't not do it again.

While this girl's behavior was congruent with what he felt ready for, the question of her "speed"—and thus the unspoken matter of his not taking up a "speedy" or sexually predatory approach—lingers below the surface of his narration. For RZA, a 13-year-old White boy, the line he was not going to cross was sexual intercourse; like several of the boys, he reports not feeling ready to have sex because he is worried about disease and pregnancy, but he was otherwise open to a range of possibilities. "What's going to happen next? . . . Um, umm—it doesn't matter to me what . . . whatever she wants to do as long as it's not like sex or going all the way or something like that."

Defying conventional wisdom about adolescent male sexuality, a number of boys narrated a clear link between sexual intimacy and emotional intimacy and also their efforts to sort out the nature of the connection between the two. Significantly, this interplay became apparent when they were describing their private experiences with girlfriends or beliefs about romantic relationships. JJ, 14 years old and Latino, described how for him a French kiss meant that he and his partner were "going out . . . being girlfriend and boyfriend . . . that there was . . . it meant that there was love between us two (sigh)." One boy, Frank, illuminated his struggle to figure out what meaning sexual intimacy might have for the stewpot of emotional intimacy and relationship. He mused that kissing "shows love sometimes," which is what it meant to him when he kissed his girlfriend the first time, a time when kissing "was different because she was my girlfriend." However, at other times, kissing was not necessarily associated with feelings of love for Frank, as at a party after kissing a girl who was not his girlfriend, he said he "felt the same after it as [he] did before" because "it meant nothing."

Although boys, like Frank, often expressed a preference for sexual intimacy in the context of some form of emotional connection, the boys also said that emotional and sexual intimacy did not necessarily have to be linked. Many described having had sexual experiences while not in committed relationships. Sexual experiences outside of a committed relationship were acceptable even if one or both partners were in another relationship at the time. Wayne's response to a question about how he felt after kissing a girl several times who already had a boyfriend was "Well I wish I stayed a little longer but . . . other than that, nothing." RZA, who said that his closest relationship was with a girl who would "only kiss," explains that:

> Like I'd be going out with this girl and there'd be somebody like that that I kinda liked more or that I thought was prettier and I would call 'em, I'd be like, "I know I have a girlfriend, but I but I kind of like you more," you know? And like, when my girlfriend wasn't around, I'd go with that person.

And I'd do stuff with that person. I'd kiss that person. I'd do whatever with that person.

For Boo, having a sexual experience outside of a relationship gave him insight into the emotional bond he felt with his girlfriend, and the role of physical intimacy in that connection. When he kissed a different girl during the week he and his girlfriend were broken up, he said he "liked it in a way, 'cause it was different and I wanted to, but I didn't like it 'cause it made me kind of feel bad . . . because I missed the person I was going out with." He added that the experience had shown him that he was "really attached" to his girlfriend.

While many of these boys expressed a preference for both emotional and sexual intimacy in their romantic relationships, a few emphasized a driving interest in sex and an alignment with stereotypic notions of masculinity. Angel Negro de la Muerte,[2] a 13-year-old White boy, created an aura of bravado in the interview, peppering his stories with phrases like, "I'm the man" or "the SlickMaster," and reveling in covert expressions of "male supremacy" with his friends. He described himself in terms of his belief that most boys are driven by testosterone—"guys have sex on the mind 95% of the time, so like we we're really always expecting something to go down"—and looking for "Mrs. Right Now." However, when asked directly about his own experiences, he faltered and stammered, sounding less cocky and even disappointed. The experiences he described were mostly attempted forays into romantic relationships in which girls rebuffed him or were not physically close with him, to which his response was "don't don't play with my emotions like that." He seemed to have little actual sexual experience. A possible interpretation of this disjuncture between actual experience and hypermasculine posturing is that such boys are more vulnerable to this construction of masculinity because they have no countervailing experience. In other words, without the groundwork laid by experience, they narrate their masculinity into being in the face of a vacuum of actual evidence.

Public Performances: He's the Man!

In contrast to the private world of emotional and physical intimacy that characterizes these boys' romantic relationships stand their descriptions of the public world of their peer relationships, which played a significant and pervasive role in these initial experiences with sexuality and heterosexual relationships. While we did not hear stories of reckless sexual pursuit or predation or even privileging sexual experience for its own sake in the stories most of these boys told, the pressure that these boys felt to enact hegemonic masculinity for other boys was evident. The most frequently narrated route was through public displays of stereotypic male heterosexuality: the male who needs/wants sex and not relationships, commodifies and acquires sexual experience, dominates and objectifies girls in the service of his sexual interests and needs, and has no emotional vulnerabilities. We heard hints that in solidifying their status as heterosexual, boys were also accomplishing another key task: demonstrating that they were not homosexual. Boys told stories of what could be or was witnessed by other boys, as well as what they felt were the limits on what they could let their peers know about the real vicissitudes in their emotional and sexual experiences with girls and girlfriends. The public performances about which we heard were not about directly avoiding certain behaviors or monikers (i.e., Martino, 2000), but about creating public images that indicated they were interested in and actively seeking sex.

Much of the time, these boys' entrées into their romantic relationships occurred on school grounds, and often one of their friends brokered the relationship for the couple, rendering the activity in these relationships inherently public and transparent. In addition to their peers' awareness of the relationships that were beginning and ending, the school's staff were aware of dating behaviors of the students. Within this very public sphere, there was variation in how the boys negotiated the pressure to provide public evidence of the particular forms of heterosexual interaction that constitute hegemonic masculinity, sometimes participating in it, at other times resisting it, and sometimes managing to do both simultaneously.

The boys' interviews were peppered with stories, anecdotes, and asides that highlighted the ways they were expected to and had demonstrated their interest in sexual experiences with girls to their male peers. When LL Cool J, a 14-year-old Latino boy, was asked by his interviewer why a guy would want to have a girlfriend, he replied, ". . . to show other people . . . that he can have, let's say several girlfriends" which shows them "that you are macho or more of a man." James, a 14-year-old White boy, recounted his friends' response to seeing him kiss his girlfriend for the first time— "You were kissing. We saw you kissing. You're the man!"—illuminates not only the public nature but also the significance of public evidence of heterosexuality and "getting some." While in fact such an experience may have a private dimension, that is, that James was experiencing a moment of intimacy in kissing his girlfriend, the fact that it is performed in public insures that he is a "man."

Some boys described engaging in certain sexual experiences solely in response to feeling the pressure to do so. Doug, 13 years old and White, described how he got into a relationship with a girl in response not to interest on his part but to his friends saying, "'Oh you have to go out with her.' People saying 'you'd make such a perfect couple.' . . . If my friends left me alone, I don't know if I would have gone out with her so . . . I probably wouldn't have." He also described how he kissed a girl in front of his friends "to prove that it really happened." Similarly, Nervous Guy, a 13-year-old White boy, described a time when he felt pressured to play a truth-or-dare kissing game, because most of his friends were: "You gotta do something, so I did. And, like, it was terrible. I regret that, I guess, yeah." He described how he felt disgusted kissing a girl in this situation by the thought of "what's been in their mouth," describing it as "terrible," "disgusting," and "nasty, 'cause, like, I didn't want to." His description sounds like a violation: "I kept [laughing] tightening my mouth and she was, like, digging." Having gone home and washed his mouth out after what was his first kiss, he reflects that "it was kind of a rip-off, man. It was, like a big rip-off, like a disappointment. Like, 'cause it really didn't mean anything, it was just really dumb. [he pauses] In a way, that's just, like, rude to myself." Countering the script for what a "normal" boy would do in this situation are the actual, conflicted thoughts that he has about this experience: "I mean, I wasn't thinking, I guess, I was kind of having fun, I got like a picture in my mind, I was like 'No, no, no.'" The pressure these boys felt to meet the demands of their male peers made it hard to know and explore their own wants, desires, and limits and, for Nervous Guy, led to an unpleasant sexual experience which he then regretted.

A few boys narrated another function of having a girlfriend: to avoid being the target of homophobic harassment and humiliating or shaming labeling. JJ tells his interviewer that his friends would think he was gay if he turned down a girl who was willing to have sex. In a somewhat circuitous fashion, Angel Negro de la Muerte conveys the same sentiment, saying that he would be "socially destroyed" if he answered truthfully that he would have sex with another male for a million dollars. More generally, 15-year-old Ace Eagle, in response to his interviewer's question about why he thought boys his age wanted to have a girlfriend, replied simply, "So people don't think you're gay."

These boys also spoke about how displays of emotional vulnerability would leave them open to being a target of other boys' ridicule. Boo, who earlier in the interview had talked about how important mutual trust and caring in the context of an egalitarian friendship was in his actual relationship with his girlfriend, told a different story about relationships when asked what he thought boys were *supposed to be like* in a romantic relationship. He explained, "They're supposed to be like, they control it basically. Like they tell her what to do, or how to dress, or like who she can hang around or something." When the interviewer asked if there was any way that boys were not supposed to be, Boo emphatically responded, "They're not supposed to be sensitive, or like . . . open with their problems." Given his narration of his own experience as open and caring with his girlfriend, a key feature of these qualities is that other boys not be aware of them. According to him, if boys are seen to be sensitive then it "makes 'em seem like weaker." Boo warned that if a boy showed this side of himself and "other guys found out, they'd probably make fun of him."

When the Public and Private Worlds Meet (or Do Not)

How did these boys reconcile their desire for emotional intimacy and their curiosity about sexuality with the pressure to demonstrate their masculinity by proving to their friends that they could, or at minimum wanted, to "get some"? Faced with figuring out how to handle these competing desires and expectations in contradictory interstices where public and private spheres collided, the boys outlined incidents of tension throughout the interviews. These tensions were premised on fears, uncertainty, pressures, and anxiety about how to handle these conflicting messages, desires, and experiences.

The magnitude of these tensions is not something that the boys spoke about directly but became apparent in the tenor of their affect, thoughts, and behavioral responses and interaction with their interviewer. For example, RZA described the tension he experienced when feeling pressure to "be the man" and "get some" with a girl his friend planted as an "easy target" and his private desire of wanting physical intimacy to be a caring interaction with a girl. He explained:

> I was in my umm friend's house and it was me and this girl and him and we were all in the room together. And umm, he was being, he was being a little jerk. You know, he was like, oh, I'm going to leave you two alone and you

two can do whatever you want. So, he left the room. So we're sitting there, we're kissing, we're talking you know. We're like getting all like close, feeling and stuff like that. And I don't know what it was, I just didn't want to like do anything. And I just like got up and I said, I said I'm going to go get the kid. . . . And so I was like, no we can't do this right now. She's only thirteen.

RZA attended to, perhaps privileged, his own emotional response "I just like didn't want to do anything," rivaling the obvious expectation from his friend that he would take advantage of the situation to acquire publicly noticed sexual experience. For RZA, the absence of an emotional connection had more power than the expectation that he would want to take advantage of the opportunity to be with this girl sexually. Perhaps the added moral dimension, as he described and experienced it, of the girl being "only thirteen" enabled his choice to act responsibly and also in keeping with his actual feeling of not "want[ing] to do anything." Yet at the same time, he seemed to be aware that he was betraying his friend's expectation of how he should respond to this "gift" of easy sexual access.

Skater spoke in a fervent way to his interviewer about how his friend's presentation of him in the public domain as a boy who has had a lot of sex stands in opposition to how he would like to relate to a girl by "just be[ing] who I am." However, at the same time, he acknowledged the benefit of being recognized as a "player," in the public eye, meaning a boy or man who dates more than one female at a time and has sexual experiences with each. Skater recounted how he met a girl "through a friend, and like, she's telling like all her friends that I'm a certain way that I'm not really. That my friend told her, that I'm like. . . . You know what I mean . . . giving images of me, that's not true, so they like me more." Skater's way of dealing with his friend's false presentation of him was to try to have the best of both worlds: "Yeah, like, you kind of, you don't wanna ruin it, but I just act like myself, if she doesn't like it, then . . . oh well, I don't try to act like the person she thinks I am." The question that remains after this story is who Skater himself thinks or knows himself to be.

For James, having the reputation of being a player created a bit more trouble for him when he tried to maintain his relationship with his girlfriend, Melissa, while continuing his practice of going to the mall with his male friends to look at girls. Aware that this behavior made Melissa angry but also wanting to spend time with his friends, he attempted to resolve the conflict by lying to Melissa about where he was going. He explained, "I tell her I'm going somewhere else then I go to the mall. Like I'll say I'm going to my friend's house." While he was well aware that if Melissa were to find out he had been at the mall, she would become angry, he considered her anger over these mall outings to be "dumb"—"cause I don't touch them or talk to them, whatever. Like I'll look at them, like if I wasn't going out with her, I'd talk to them then, but I am so I wouldn't have." James told his interviewer that to him being a player did not make sense. He explained, "I think it's bad to be a player because . . . you cheat. Why go out with two different people? Why don't you just break up with one person and go out with the one person you really want to be with?" Nonetheless, James seemed to think it would be impossible to convince Melissa of this and she eventually broke up with him. Given that Melissa had on several occasions said to him "all boys are players," when the interviewer asked James whether there was a "way to convince [Melissa]" that *he* was not a player, James replied, "I don't know. I never tried." He seemed resigned that the conflict between his relationship with his male friends and that with his girlfriend was impossible to resolve. Not going to the mall with his friends or not participating in their sport of girl watching was not an option for him. Explaining his position to Melissa was also not considered an option for James.

For Andrew, however, a 13-year-old White boy, the public world of his immediate friends did not create the same kind of tension for him, as few of his friends were dating. While some girls had expressed an interest in him, he said he "just didn't feel like ready" to go out with any of them: "well, personally I've been asked and I refused, 'cause, you know, it's, it's like, you know, you don't really need it right now, it's like, it's not worth it, you know, I know some people that do, and that's fine with me and that's their choice, but I personally don't feel like dating right now." Perhaps buffered from the cultural push toward a particular form of masculinity by having friends who were not dating, and consequently not trying to get him to do so, he was able to respond to his own sense that he was not "ready" for romantic relationships with girls.

Moving toward a More Complex Understanding of Boys' Sexuality

The virulence of the notion that adolescent boys' romantic relationships are defined and driven exclusively by their sexual desires—their raging hormones—is so entrenched that it is thought to be a biological fact. The literatures on the psychology and sociology of men at the very least un-earth the complexity of emergent adult sexuality in the context of societal pressures to enact hegemonic forms of masculinity, which contribute to this social construction of male adolescence. Boys' sexuality sits as a kind of proverbial elephant in the room in critical analyses of the roots of male emotional "disability" in later adolescence and adulthood. The reality of new desires for sexual experience and intimacy in adolescence has not been well integrated into work on adolescent relationships in general, ro-mantic relationships in particular, or critical theory on the privileging of particular forms of masculinity. While we know that this small sample of boys cannot provide the full range of how boys are negotiating this new terrain of relationships and adult forms of sexual desire, their descriptions of the interplay of emotional and sexual intimacy, and even their explo-ration of how these two aspects of heterosexual experience do and do not go together, indicate that at least some boys enter adolescence with the ca-pacity to engage with romantic relationships in ways not limited to find-ing fleeting satisfaction of singularly focused and barely controllable sex-ual needs.

This study suggests that there is a lot more to boys' experiences of ini-tial heterosexual romantic relationships in early adolescence than acquir-ing belt notches. The stories told by these boys refute the notion that boys' bodies simply take over, edging out their minds and their hearts. They de-scribed their desires for and experiences of emotional intimacy with girls—their hopes for companionship, sharing, and trust in relationships, with their sexuality entering into their relational experiences in a variety of ways. On the one hand, interviews with these boys in general conveyed their greater freedom in sexual exploration and the open possibility that sexual experience did not have to be acquired within an emotionally close or committed relationship. On the other hand, many of the boys did value a connection between emotional and sexual intimacy and recognized a difference between their sexual experiences when emotions were or were not involved.

We were struck by the intensely private quality of boys' search for emo-tional connection. Questions or knowledge about this part of their lives was not willingly shared or displayed in view of their male friends. At the same time, their narration of the pressure that they felt to produce and visibly practice hegemonic masculinity in the public world of their male peers was as unequivocal as it was poignant. Given what they told us about their actual experiences, we are unsure how to relate these public performances to boys' actual identity development. The contrast with the kinds of descriptions that boys offered of authenticity in their real relationships was striking. Indeed, we found evidence in some cases of the kinds of tensions that one might anticipate such competing demands— their internal ones for intimacy, closeness, and connection and the external ones for enacting specific forms of masculinity—would produce. But such tensions were not discernable in all cases.

Some of the impoverished solutions that these boys came to left us with a sense of loss and impending loss. We heard boys tell about actual experiences that reflected our conception of, and hopes for, adolescent sexual health: the freedom to explore new sexual feelings, new relationships, and the interplay between sexual and emotional intimacy. We are concerned, however, about how this endeavor is being shaped by the mandates of masculinity with which they strive to comply, perhaps at this stage of their development, primarily in the service of avoiding negative consequences more than for establishing felt identities. The contradictions we heard these boys narrate either sounded painful to us or like they will become painful. We doubt the sustainability of efforts to demonstrate and maintain their masculinity in their relationships with other boys while at the same time being able to maintain authentic relationships with themselves, honoring their desires and interests in their heterosexual romantic relationships.

Their stories give us pause as we begin to speculate about the experiences these boys describe in relation to the difficulties with emotional connectedness and expressiveness described in the literature on older adolescent boys and men. We hope that this small study ignites discussion of developmental processes that begin with emergent adult sexuality in which boys can and do experience emotional intimacy that may be eclipsed, diminished, or even forgotten or lost over time. As we heard James do, boys may increasingly resolve the tension created by pressures to enact hegemonic masculinity in public performances of heterosexuality by giving up the intimacy, with its many forms of vulnerability, in favor of the emotionally bankrupt option that hegemonic masculinity demands.

While this resolution may appear to be, and in some cases may in fact be, a source of power or status for some young men, it requires a Faustian bargain that takes its toll on men's ability to have integrity in their relationships and to have psychological health (i.e., Kimmel, 1996; Real, 1997). As Niobe Way and her colleagues (2001) found in their study of different types of adolescent relationships, those adolescents who had more disengaged relationships (much more likely to be males) were more likely to have lower self-esteem and higher levels of depression. We were also struck by how boys tried to resolve their relational dilemmas in isolation, as talking about the fears and feelings associated with the complexities of negotiating heterosexual relationships while trying to secure one's status as masculine is anathema. This isolation is reminiscent of how adolescent girls constantly reinvent the wheel of resolving the dilemmas of their own sexual desire, at odds with societal conceptions of "normal" girls, as if these problems were only their own and out of relationship with other girls or women (Tolman, 2002).

We are keenly aware of the many unanswered questions that this study produces. For example, how do ethnic diversity, family history, and community expectations shape a boy's response to the hegemonic definition of masculinity? Are there competing versions of masculinity to which these boys also have access? How do boys who do not have homosexual interests experience heteronormative pressures? The tension we identified between boys' desires for emotional intimacy and the pressure to publicly demonstrate their masculinity and heterosexuality in specific ways that place authentic relationships with romantic partners in jeopardy raises a unique developmental conflict for boys' sexuality. Do boys' early romantic experiences—and whether they choose to emphasize their alignment with hegemonic masculinity or resist it in favor of more authentic relationships with their romantic partners—predict different pictures of adult masculinity and relational capacity? This study begs the question of what happens to boys who do not meet the dominant "standards" of masculinity, either by choice or not. This study begins to suggest that boys may benefit from interventions that help them develop critical perspectives on masculinity.

The development of boys' sexuality clearly has consequences for girls, who negotiate their own sexual and relational development in the context of their beliefs about masculinity and boys' sexuality (Tolman, 2002). This view of masculinity not only inscribes what is possible and off-limits in boys' relationships, it also regulates girls' behavior, sense of freedom and safety, and ability to explore and express their own sexual curiosity. While boys may not actually be taken over by relentless hormones, such beliefs effectively do result in girls being carelessly trampled in the fray.

The findings of this study suggest implications for interventions in early adolescence that create environments that fortify boys' capacities to develop and maintain authentic relationships in which intimacy, trust, and emotional honesty are possible. The boys in this study demonstrated their desire for these types of relationships, but the evidence also suggests the difficulties boys face and are likely to continue to encounter in sustaining these relationships while living up to a rigid and dissociated masculine ideal.

NOTES

This research was supported by a grant from the Ford Foundation. The authors would like to thank Judy Chu and Michelle Porche for their countless contributions to this project, and Kate Collins and Marta Allyson White for their assistance with preparation of the data. Special thanks also to the teens who participated in this study and to the staff and administrators at the research sites for their commitment and collaboration.
it afterwards.

1. One might argue that the predominance of these boys' expressions of desire for emotional connections with girlfriends was an artifact of being interviewed by women—i.e., they were simply telling the female interviewers what they believed women wanted to hear. However, the examples in this section, which represent the manner in which most of the boys talked about their relationships, were drawn from four interviews—2 with female interviewers and 2 with male interviewers.

2. Within the context of this particular school, Latino boys and girls are stereotyped as highly sexualized. It may be that Angel's choice of code name was an attempt on some level to emphasize his sexual prowess by associating himself with this group. In the interview, he also used Spanish words to emphasize certain sexual themes, for instance, explaining that being a "papasuelo," or pimp, is a "good thing amongst the guys here."

REFERENCES

Bergman, S. J. (1995). Men's psychological development: A relational perspective. In W. S. Pollack (Ed.), *A new psychology of men* (pp. 68–90). New York: Basic Books.

Brod, H. & Kauffman, M. (Eds.). (1994). *Theorizing masculinities.* Thousand Oaks, CA: Sage.

Chu, J. Y. (2000). Learning what boys know: An observational and interview study with six four year old boys. Unpublished doctoral dissertation. Graduate School of Education, Harvard University.

Connell, R. W. (1995). *Masculinities.* Berkeley: University of California Press.

Connell, R. W. (2000). *The men and the boys.* St Leonards, Australia: Allen and Unwin.

Epstein, D. & Johnson, R. (1998). *Schooling sexualities.* Buckingham: Open University Press.

Feiring, C. (1999). Gender identity and the development of romantic relationships in adolescence. In W. Furman, B. B. Brown & C. Feiring (Eds.), *The development of romantic relationships in adolescence* (pp. 211–231). New York: Cambridge University Press.

Furman, W., Brown, B. B. & Feiring, C. (Eds.). (1999). *The development of romantic relationships in adolescence.* Cambridge: Cambridge University Press.

Gurian, M. (1996). *The wonder of boys.* New York: Putnam.

Kimmel, M. (1994). Masculinity as homophobia: Fear, shame and silence in the construction of gender identity. In H. Brod & M. Kaufman (Eds.), *Theorizing masculinities* (pp. 119–141). Thousand Oaks, CA: Sage.

Kimmel, M. (1996). *Manhood in America.* New York: Free Press.

Kindlon, D. & Thompson, M. (1999). *Raising Cain: Protecting the emotional life of boys.* New York: Ballantine Books.

Lesko, N. (Ed.). (2000). *Masculinities at school.* Thousand Oaks, CA: Sage.

Mandel, L. & Shakeshaft, C. (2000). Heterosexism in middle schools. In N. Lesko (Ed.), *Masculinities at School* (pp. 75–104). Thousand Oaks, CA: Sage.

Majors, R. & Billson, J. M. (1993). *Cool pose: The dilemmas of black manhood in America.* New York: Touchstone.

Martino, W. (2000). Policing masculinities: Investigating the role of homophobia in the lives of adolescent school boys. *Journal of Men's Studies, 8(2),* 213–236.

Pollack, W. (1998). *Real boys: Rescuing our sons from the myths of boyhood.* New York: Random House.

Real, T. (1997). *I don't want to talk about it: Overcoming the secret legacy of male depression.* New York: Scribner.

Rich, A. (1980). Compulsory heterosexuality and lesbian existence. *Signs, 54,* 631–650.

Shulman, S. & Collins, W. A. (1997). *Romantic relationships in adolescence: Developmental perspectives.* San Francisco: Jossey-Bass.

Silverman, D. (2000). Analyzing talk and text. In N. K. Denzin & Y. S. Lincoln (Eds.), *Handbook of qualitative research,* 2nd ed. (pp. 821–834). Thousand Oaks, CA, Sage.

Simon, W. & Gagnon, J. H. (1986). Sexual scripts: Permanence and change. *Archives of Sexual Behavior, 15(2),* 97–120.

Tolman, D. L. (1994). Daring to desire: Culture and the bodies of adolescent girls. In J. Irvine (Ed.), *Sexual cultures: Adolescents, communities and the construction of identity* (pp. 250–284). Philadelphia: Temple University Press.

Tolman, D. L. (1999). Femininity as a barrier to positive sexual health for adolescent girls. *Journal of the American Medical Women's Association, 54(3),* 133–138.

Tolman, D. L. (2002). *Dilemmas of desire: Teenaged girls talk about sexuality.* Cambridge, MA: Harvard University Press.

Tolman, D. L., Spencer, R., Rosen-Reynoso, M. & Porche, M. V. (in press). Sowing the seeds of violence in heterosexual relationships: Early adolescents narrate compulsory heterosexuality. *Journal of Social Issues.*

Way, N. (1998). *Everyday courage.* New York: New York University Press.

Way, N., Cowal, K., Gingold, R., Pahl, K. & Bissessar, N. (2001). Friendship patterns among African American, Asian American, and Latino adolescents from low-income families. *Journal of Social and Personal Relationships, 18(1),* 29–53.

12

Adolescent Boys' Heterosexual Behavior

Joseph H. Pleck, Freya L. Sonenstein,
and Leighton Ku

Becoming sexually active is clearly an important event in adolescent boys' experience. In addition, adolescent boys' sexual and contraceptive behavior has clear ramifications for teen pregnancy and for sexually transmitted diseases. This chapter presents some of the work on adolescent males' heterosexual behavior conducted by The National Survey of Adolescent Males over the last 15 years. Specifically, we discuss findings based on two surveys of large, nationally representative samples of adolescent males aged 15–19, conducted in 1988 and in 1995. Our survey data make it possible to describe what adolescent boys are doing sexually, how their sexual behavior is or is not changing, and some of the basic dynamics underlying their sexual behavior. In particular, this chapter focuses on three research questions. First, we examine how rates of heterosexual intercourse and condom use have changed in recent decades among U.S. adolescent boys aged 15–19. This information is important for informing adolescent health policy and for increasing our understanding of the developmental experience of adolescent boys. There are several ongoing large-scale studies documenting levels and trends in adolescent girls' sexual and contraceptive behavior (Abma et al., 1997; Manlove et al., 2000). Prior to our work, however, no data on such trends were available for males. Our analyses of change in males' sexual behavior in recent decades first compares levels of heterosexual intercourse and condom use in our 1988 survey with an earlier national survey on this topic conducted in 1979. We then compare results from our 1988 cohort with our 1995 cohort.

The second research question we examine focuses on the validity of adolescent boys' self-reports about having heterosexual intercourse and using condoms. Some scholars are not confident about the accuracy of boys' self-report data regarding their sexuality. Anecdotal data suggest that boys may exaggerate their level of sexual experience. At the same time, in reporting whether or not they use condoms, boys may want to present themselves as behaving in a socially desirable way. Since public policy is grounded in part on research based on self-reports, it is important that their validity be assessed. We use a variety of methods for this purpose, including comparisons with external data, prospective prediction of behavior in a follow-up of the 1988 cohort, and a methodological experiment embedded within the 1995 survey.

Our third and final research question focuses on how boys' heterosexual behavior and condom use are linked to masculinity. The linkage may seem obvious, and has been assumed by policy makers. For example, a former Secretary of the Department of Health and Human Services called for action to address "a generation whose manhood is measured by the caliber of the gun he carries or the number of children he has fathered" (Sullivan, 1991). A governor has urged the policy community to send the message that "contrary to what many of today's young people think, making babies is no act of manhood" (Wilder, 1991). But what is the scientific basis for positing a linkage between masculinity and adolescent males' sexual behavior? This chapter discusses our work on the role of "masculinity ideology" in adolescent boys' heterosexual experience and condom use, in the context of prior approaches to understanding how a boy's sexual behavior may be linked to issues of masculinity. For this purpose, we focus our empirical analyses on the 1988 survey data.

Methods

Sample

1988 COHORT

The 1988 National Survey of Adolescent Males (NSAM) selected a national probability sample of 1,880 boys between the ages of 15 and 19 years from the noninstitutionalized, never-married U.S. male population. This survey used a multistage stratified sample, and also over-sampled African American and Latino males so that their numbers would be large enough to base valid population estimates for these groups. However, by employing sample "weights,"[1] these data can be used to describe the national population of U.S. males aged 15–19. The response rate among those eligible to be interviewed was 73.9% (Sonenstein, Pleck & Ku, 1989). Following the 1988 survey, further data were collected from this sample. In 1991, 1,676 men (now 18–22 years old) were re-interviewed. The follow-up rate from the 1988 survey was 89.1%, not including 11 men who died between 1988 and 1991.

1995 COHORT

In 1995, a new nationally representative sample of males aged 15 to 19 was drawn. A cohort of 1,729 males living in the conterminous United States, not including persons living in prisons or institutions, was interviewed (Sonenstein et al., 1998). Like the 1988 cohort, this new sample was developed using multistage stratified selection procedures, again with over-sampling of minority males and use of sample weights to describe the population. Among eligible males, the response rate was 75.0%.

Procedures and Measures

At each wave of data collection, in-person interviews were conducted at a confidential location and lasted about an hour. The interview protocol consisted of close-ended questions. For the most sensitive topics, a short, self-administered questionnaire was employed. The main focus of the interview was the males' experiences with and attitudes about sex and contraception, especially condom use. However, the interview also covered a broad range of other topics potentially related to sex and contraception, such as other risk behaviors, experiences in school, self-efficacy, and sociodemographics.

In addition, the interview also assessed masculinity ideology using the Male Role Attitudes Scale (MRAS). This eight-item measure includes seven items drawn from Thompson and Pleck's (1986) Male Role Norms Scale. MRAS items were selected to represent the three factorial dimensions of the Male Role Norms Scale: status, toughness, and anti-femininity. Eight items considered most relevant to an adolescent sample were selected, and wording was simplified to be more appropriate for this age group. Sample items included "A young man should be physically tough, even if he is not big" and "I don't think a husband should have to do housework." An additional item about the link between masculinity and sex, a topical area absent from the Male Role Norms Scale, was added from Snell, Belk, and Hawkins (1986). An index was derived from the eight items with a coefficient alpha of .56.

Results

How Adolescent Boys' Heterosexual Behavior Has Changed

1979–1988

Data from the 1988 NSAM can be compared with a prior large-scale study conducted by Zelnik, Kantner, and Ford's (1981) National Survey of Young Men in 1979 (NSYM). The National Survey of Young Men interviewed a national representative sample of 847 males who were aged 17–21 and lived in metropolitan areas. Zelnik, Kantner, and Ford's sample differs from the NSAM with males in the Zelnik sample being older, living only in cities, and including married males. However, the two studies overlap with both including substantial numbers of 17–19-year-old and never-married males residing in metropolitan areas (609 in the earlier study, 742 in the NSAM). A comparison of the 1979 and 1988 samples shows that the proportion of males who have ever had heterosexual intercourse rose from 65.7% to 75.5% over this period. Within racial subgroups, heterosexual experience rose from 71.1% to 87.7% among Blacks, and from 64.5% to 73.0% among non-Blacks (Zelnik, Kantner, and Ford's survey distinguished only Blacks and non-Blacks).

Use of condoms alone or with other methods also rose from 21.1% in 1979 to 57.5% in 1988 (23.2% to 62.0% for Blacks; 20.5% to 56.5% for non-Blacks). Our analysis tabulated condom use as including both the use of condoms by themselves as well as in combination with other methods. Almost all prior research on sexual behavior had coded condom use with other methods *only* as use of the other method. Use of female contraceptive methods alone dropped somewhat, but use of ineffective or no contraceptive method dropped markedly (50.9% to 20.8%) (Sonenstein, Pleck & Ku, 1989). Thus, while the proportion of adolescent males who were heterosexually active increased somewhat between 1979 and 1988, their use of condoms rose markedly.

1988–1995

NSAM data were also analyzed to examine how adolescent boys' heterosexual behavior changed between 1988 and 1995. Comparison of the 1988

NSAM cohort with the 1995 cohort of 15–19-year-olds indicated that the proportion of these males who were heterosexually active declined from 60.4% in 1988 to 55.2% in 1995. However, this decrease occurred only among White males (56.8% to 49.5%). Among African American males, the rates held constant at 80.6% and 80.4%, and among Latino males, 59.7% and 60.9%. Analyses by age further confirmed that young men were delaying first intercourse in 1995 as compared to 1988. As one indication of this delay, the percentages of 19-year-olds who were sexually active in the two surveys were almost identical: 85.7% and 84.0%; whereas the percentages of 15-year-olds who were sexually active dropped from 32.6% in 1988 to 27.1% in 1995. Condom use at last intercourse also increased, from 56.9% in 1988 to 67.0% in 1995. This increase in condom use was most evident among the younger males (e.g., in 15-year-olds compared to 19-year-olds). Increased condom use was evident in all ethnic groups: from 54.4% to 66.8% in White males, 65.5% to 73.9% in African American males, and 53.0% to 58.2% in Latino males (Sonenstein et al., 1998).

The Validity of Adolescent Boys' Reports about Their Sexual Behavior

The dramatic increases in adolescent males' condom use between 1979 and 1995, and the postponement of first heterosexual intercourse shown among White male youth in 1995 compared to 1988, are noteworthy, *if* males' self-reports about intercourse and condom use are valid. Many other researchers have questioned the validity of adolescents' self-report data about sex. Validity is primarily a methodological issue, but because of its centrality to our research, and to all research with adolescent boys using self-report methods, it is worthwhile exploring it in some depth. In this section, we briefly present several different approaches to address these validity concerns.

Consistency with External Data

The increase in condom use evident in the NSYM and the NSAM data between 1979 and 1988 is corroborated by women's reports for the same period. Women's reports about whether a condom was used at last sexual intercourse were more than twice as high in the 1988 National Survey of Family Growth (NSFG) as in the 1982 NSFG (Mosher, 1990). In addition, changes between the 1988 and 1995 NSFG surveys parallel those observed in the NSAM, namely, there was a marginally significant reduction in the sexual activity of 15- through 19-year-old females and significant increases in condom use at first intercourse (Abma et al., 1997). Further, national natality data showed that the rate of adolescent childbearing fell between 1991 and 1994 (Ventura et al., 1996), and gonorrhea rates declined from 1992 to 1995 (*Sexually Transmitted Disease Surveillance*, 1995, 1996).

Internal Consistency in the 1988 Survey

The NSAM interviews ask the sexual intercourse and condom use questions in two places in the interview: first, in an interviewer-administered survey (IAI), and then in the survey's "self-administered" questionnaire (SAQ), which participants were given to complete in private and on their own after the end of the interview. Upon completing the short SAQ booklet, participants were asked to place the booklet in an envelope that the researcher/interviewer immediately sealed to assure the participant of the confidentiality of his responses. In the 1988 survey, the consistency between responses about ever having sexual intercourse and about condom use between the IAI and the SAQ (kappa = .80) is quite high (Sonenstein, Pleck & Ku, 1989).

Prospective Prediction of Pregnancies, 1988 to 1991

We also examined the association between the sexual behavior that males reported in the 1988 survey with the pregnancies they reported in the 1991 follow-up survey. A composite measure of sexual risk-taking in 1988 was developed with 5 levels, ranging from "never had intercourse" to "had intercourse in the last 12 months with more than 5 partners, without condom use." With standard sociodemographic factors controlled, our 1988 risk-taking measure was a strong predictor of pregnancies between 1988 and 1991, as reported in the 1991 survey (Sonenstein, Pleck & Ku, 1993).

Social Desirability Analysis in the 1991 Follow-Up

Further, the 1991 NSAM included a "social desirability" scale (Paulhus, 1991). This scale assesses the tendency for respondents to give socially desirable answers via items concerning socially desirable behaviors which few people do (e.g., "I'm always willing to admit it when I make a mistake"), and socially undesirable behaviors that most people do (e.g.,

"There have been occasions when I took advantage of someone"). Our results showed that self-reported condom use is unrelated to this social desirability response set (Pleck, Sonenstein & Ku, 1993a), suggesting that reported condom use is not biased by social desirability influences.

Effect of Two Modes of Administration on Self-Reports in the 1995 Survey

Prior research suggests that the greater the level of privacy afforded by the data collection method, the more willing respondents are to report socially stigmatized behaviors. For example, reported rates of substance use are consistently higher with self-administered questionnaires (SAQ) than with interviewer-administered protocols. The more stigmatized the substance (e.g., heroin vs. alcohol), the greater the discrepancy in reported rates (Turner, Lessler & Devore, 1992). Variations in reported rates of a behavior according to the degree of confidentiality of the data collection method give a direct indication of the extent to which reports of that behavior are biased by social desirability effects.

Determining the validity of adolescent males' self-report data about their sexual behavior was so important that we tested this specifically in our 1995 survey. We randomly assigned respondents in the 1995 new cohort of 15–19-year-olds to two conditions: one group reported sexual behaviors with the paper-and-pencil SAQ used in the 1988 survey and its 1991 follow-ups, while the other group used a new methodology, audio computer assisted self-interviewing (audio-CASI). In the latter condition, males were given a laptop with headphones, which displayed and read aloud the questions, and recorded their responses on the keyboard. Because the SAQ requires handing a form to the interviewer with one's responses (which can be easily read), while audio-CASI involves entering responses on computer keyboard (requiring technical skill to retrieve), we hypothesized that respondents would experience audio-CASI as a more private method.

As expected, a variety of stigmatized behaviors were reported significantly more often with audio-CASI than the SAQ. For example, 5.2% of audio-CASI respondents report ever taking street drugs with a needle compared to 1.5% of SAQ respondents. Other significant differences occurred for being drunk at last heterosexual intercourse (34.8% vs. 15.3%), using drugs at last heterosexual intercourse (15.8% vs. 9.7%), ever having sex with a prostitute (2.5% vs. 0.7%), and ever having sex with someone who shoots drugs (2.8% vs. 0.2%).[2] Respondents also reported sharing needles with others, using crack/cocaine, and participating in violence-related behaviors such as threatening to hurt others and carrying guns, knives, and razors at significantly higher rates with audio-CASI (Turner et al., 1998). By contrast, differences were nonsignificant for behaviors not stigmatized among adolescents, such as drinking alcohol in the last year (65.9% vs. 69.2%). These differences give an indication that respondents indeed experienced audio-CASI as providing more privacy than the SAQ. Further, these comparisons suggest that, like the difference between in-person interviewing and the SAQ, a significant SAQ versus audio-CASI reporting difference for a particular behavior reflects how much social desirability bias influences their reporting of that behavior.

The percentages of sexually active males who reported using a condom the last time they had heterosexual intercourse were almost identical in the two conditions, 64.4% versus 64.0% (Turner et al., 1998). Reports of ever having heterosexual intercourse in the last five years were also relatively similar (and not significantly different) with the paper-and-pencil SAQ as when audio-CASI was used (49.6 vs. 47.8%). The small and non-significant difference in adolescent males' SAQ compared to audio-CASI reporting of sexual intercourse and condom use is thus another piece of evidence that these reports are not biased by social desirability influences. Considering this and the other data reviewed here, the available information suggests that the dramatic increases in adolescent males' condom use and the changes in sexual behavior between 1979 and 1995 observed in the NSAM are real.

Homosexual Behavior and Orientation

One reason that audio-CASI methodology was introduced in the 1995 survey was that the rates of male-male sexual contacts reported in 1988 seemed too low, with 2.1% reporting any type of contact (Ku, Sonenstein & Pleck, 1992). Prior surveys that asked adult males about their homosexual contacts during adolescence provided much higher prevalence estimates for this period than male adolescents reported in the NSAM. Because of its implications for the transmission of HIV and other STDs, it was particularly important to obtain better estimates of the frequency of same-gender sexual contacts.

In the 1995 cohort of 15–19-year-olds, 5.5% of males using audio-CASI reported having any (lifetime) male-male sex, compared to 1.5% of those using the paper SAQ, a highly significant difference. This comparison is again consistent with our interpretation that respondents experience audio-CASI as more confidential than the SAQ, and audio-CASI increases reporting of stigmatized behaviors. The decrease in SAQ-reported male-male sex among 15–19-year-olds from 2.1% in 1988 to 1.5% in 1995 could be evidence of a small decrease in rates of adolescent homosexual contacts. However, since the SAQ versus audio-CASI comparison indicates that SAQ reports are depressed by social desirability bias, it is also possible that heightened stigmatization of homosexual behavior among adolescent males accounts for the decrease.

The type of contact most frequently acknowledged with audio-CASI in 1995 was the act of being masturbated by another male (3.5%). Receptive oral sex was reported by 2.3% and receptive anal sex by 0.8% (Turner et al., 1998). In the 1988 data collected with a paper SAQ, the majority (52.6%) of those reporting homosexual contacts never used a condom (Ku, Sonenstein & Pleck, 1992). The 1988 data also revealed discrepancies between males' reports of male-male sexual contacts and self-reported sexual orientation. Orientation was assessed by the male's self-classification as 100 percent heterosexual, mostly heterosexual, bisexual, mostly homosexual, 100 percent homosexual, and not sure. Whereas 2.1% reported that they ever had some homosexual contact, 13.1% reported that they were other than 100 percent heterosexual. Further, a small number (0.3%) of those reporting themselves as 100 percent heterosexual acknowledged some male-male contact (Ku, Sonenstein & Pleck, 1992). Replication of these analyses with the 1995 data (not yet undertaken), using audio-CASI reports of male-male contacts and of sexual orientation, will likely contribute to our knowledge of the complex link between same-gender sexual contact and the construction of sexual orientation in recent cohorts of adolescent males.

Adolescent Boys' Masculinity Ideology

Perhaps NSAM's most important contribution to understanding adolescent boys' heterosexual behavior concerns a conceptual link that seems obvious: adolescent boys' heterosexual behavior has something to do with issues of "masculinity." This connection may seem self-evident, but in terms of empirical research, it was not well established prior to NSAM.

One strategy used in prior research involves simply comparing rates of sexual behavior for adolescent boys and girls. The ways in which boys' behavior differs from girls' were attributed to masculinity or the male gender role. However, this strategy is flawed as aggregate gender differences can result from biological as well as socialization differences between males and females. A second strategy employed in prior research employs the construct of "gender orientation" as an individual-differences variable. Gender orientation refers to the personality dimension assessed by measures such as the Bem Sex Role Inventory (BSRI, 1974) and Spence and Helmreich's Personal Attributes Questionnaire (PAQ, 1978) (for a comprehensive review, see Lenney, 1991). These scales ask respondents to rate themselves (e.g., strong-weak) on a variety of adjective dimensions that have been previously determined to be more characteristic of males or females based on U.S. populations. In the few studies investigating the link between these measures' masculinity subscale (M) and adolescent males' sexual behavior, however, *few* significant associations have been found. That is, variations in how "masculine" a male thinks he is are not linked to his pattern of sexual behavior. A few studies take the gender orientation approach further by distinguishing socially positive aspects of masculinity (e.g., rating oneself as strong) versus socially negative ones (e.g., aggressive). Although prior research provides considerable evidence that perceiving oneself as possessing socially negative masculine traits is associated with adolescent males' substance use, negative masculinity appears to be independent of adolescent males' sexual behavior (for a review, see Pleck, Sonenstein & Ku, 1993b).

Our research developed a third approach: linking adolescent males' sexual behavior with their gender ideology, that is, their attitudes and beliefs about gender (Pleck, Sonenstein & Ku, 1993b, 1993c, 1994a, 1994b). According to this approach, the way that gender as a social construct influences behavior is not by shaping personality traits, but by establishing normative beliefs about how males and females should act. The hypothesis deriving from this approach is that a male's sexual behavior is influenced by the extent to which he believes that males as a group *should* act "masculine," not by the extent to which he believes that he, as an individual, is "masculine."

Within the gender ideology approach, a further distinction needs to be made between gender-comparative beliefs and gender-specific beliefs. Almost all available scales for gender attitudes (which are often labeled attitudes toward women) use items that are gender-*comparative*. For instance, the first item in Spence, Helmreich, and Stapp's (1973) Attitudes toward Women Scale, which is the measure used most frequently to assess gender attitudes, is "Swearing and obscenity are more repulsive in the speech of a woman than of a man." Agreeing or disagreeing to this kind of item has been uncritically interpreted as reflecting an attitude only about how women should act. To assess masculinity ideology more precisely, the NSAM developed the Male Role Attitude Scale (MRAS) using gender-*specific* items. This attitude scale includes statements like "A guy will lose respect if he talks about his problems" and "A young man should be physically tough even if he is not big."

In the 1988 NSAM, whether a male held a more traditional or a less traditional masculinity ideology, as assessed by the MRAS, was significantly linked with numerous aspects of his relationships and his sexual and contraceptive behavior. Males with a more traditional ideology said they had a less intimate relationship with their current or most recent female partner. They more often endorsed the belief that relationships between women and men are inherently adversarial. They also had more heterosexual partners in the last year (Pleck, Sonenstein & Ku, 1993c; see also Pleck & O'Donnell, 2001).

Prior research about the factors influencing adolescent males' condom use has focused especially on their attitudes about condom use and their beliefs about male responsibility to prevent pregnancy. Not surprisingly, these factors usually do predict condom use (see review in Pleck, Sonenstein & Ku, 1991). This prior research, however, left unanswered the question of why some males have more favorable attitudes about condoms and male responsibility, while others have less favorable beliefs. Filling this gap, NSAM analyses established that males with more traditional MRAS scores had more negative attitudes about condoms and male responsibility to prevent pregnancy. In addition, these traditional males were less likely to believe that their partner would like them to use a condom, and were more likely to believe that causing a pregnancy would validate their masculinity. These findings supported a conceptual model that claimed that traditional masculinity ideology influences condom-related attitudes, which in turn influence condom use (Pleck, Sonenstein & Ku, 1993c).

These significant multivariate relationships were replicated within the African American, Latino, and White NSAM subsamples. In addition, these associations with the MRAS persisted even with sociodemographic variables controlled, thus ruling out the possibility that masculinity ideology and sexual behavior were linked only because both are a function of background characteristics like education and family socioeconomic status. Overall, NSAM documents in a more convincing manner than previous studies how boys' "masculinity" is linked to their heterosexual behavior and their use of condoms. These analyses not only establish that masculinity ideology is a significant influence on adolescent males' condom use, but also give insight into the process by which this influence manifests itself.

Discussion

Data from the National Survey of Adolescent Males provide a variety of insights into adolescent boys' heterosexual behavior and condom use. It provides important "social indicator" data about how adolescent males' heterosexual and contraceptive behavior have changed over the last 25 years. Our methodological work suggests that one can study adolescent boys' sexual experience via self-reports, with some confidence in the data's validity. Our findings about their increasing condom use and their delaying of first intercourse in recent years counters negative stereotypes about adolescent males as sexually irresponsible. Finally, NSAM helps us understand how adolescent male heterosexual behavior derives from cultural norms of masculinity by revealing how traditional masculinity ideology is linked to heightened risk of unintended pregnancy and sexually transmitted diseases, and to limitations in the quality of adolescent boys' heterosexual relationships.

Future research should investigate whether the increases in condom use and delay of first intercourse observed here in adolescent males through 1995 have continued. Partly as a result of our work, the National Survey of Family Growth has included males in its 2002 data collection (for the first time), and these data will be available soon. There is also a need for more studies on how masculinity influences adolescent males' sexual behavior. We are currently in the process of analyzing relationships between masculinity ideology and sexual behavior in our 1995 data. These relationships should also be examined in samples of younger adolescent males (Pleck & O'Donnell, 2001). The concept of masculinity ideology itself also needs development. For example, Chu, Porche, and Tolman (2001) observe that by focusing on beliefs about the importance of men's adhering to culturally defined standards for male behavior in general, rather than within the contexts of specific relationships, the concept of masculine ideology is somewhat decontextualized. Yet they also find that masculinity ideology, when it is assessed within specific relationships, is negatively associated with well-being measures, which is consistent with gender role strain theory (Pleck, 1995). Thus, our understanding of the lives of boys can be enriched by this and other developments in our understanding of the dynamics and influence of masculinity ideology in their lives.

NOTES

The National Survey of Adolescent Males has been supported by the National Institute of Child Health and Human Development (HD-27119, HD-30861) and by the Office of Adolescent Pregnancy Prevention (APR-00963). Part of the work reported here was also supported by the Cooperative State Research, Education and Extension Service, U.S. Department of Agriculture, under Project No. ILLU-45-0329 to Joseph H. Pleck.

1. For example, if Latino males are over-sampled by a factor of 2, each Latino counts as .5 of a person in descriptive statistics, e.g., calculating the proportion of all males who have ever had sexual intercourse.

2. In a given sample, the closer the percentages are to 0 or 100, the smaller the difference needed to be statistically significant. Conversely, a relatively large difference is less likely to be significant the closer the percentages involved are to 50.

REFERENCES

Abma, J., Chandra, A., Mosher, W., Peterson, L. & Piccinino, L. (1997). Fertility, family planning, and women's health: New data from the 1995 National Survey of Family Growth. *Vital Health Statistics, 23* (19).

Bem, S. L. (1974). The measurement of psychological androgyny. *Journal of Personality and Social Psychology, 42,* 155–162.

Chu, J. Y., Porche, M. V. & Tolman, D. L. (2001). Assessing adolescent masculinity ideology as framed with a relational paradigm: Scale development, validity analysis, and correlates with self-esteem. Unpublished manuscript.

Hofferth, S. L. (1987). Contraceptive decision-making among adolescents. In S. L. Hofferth and C. D. Hayes (Eds.), *Risking the future: Adolescent sexuality, pregnancy, and childbearing, Vol. II, Working papers and statistical appendices* (pp. 56–77). Washington, DC: National Research Council.

Ku, L. C., Sonenstein, F. L. & Pleck, J. H. (1992). Patterns of AIDS-related risk and preventive behaviors among teenage men in the U.S.A. *Public Health Reports, 107,* 131–138.

Lenney, E. (1991). Sex roles: The measurement of masculinity, femininity, and androgyny. In J. P. Robinson, P. Shaver & L. Wrightsman (Eds.), *Measures of social-psychological attitudes* (pp. 573–660). New York: Academic Press.

Manlove, J., Terry, E., Gitelson, L., Papilo, A. R. & Russell, S. (2000). Explaining demographic trends in teenage fertility, 1980–1995. *Family Planning Perspectives, 32,* 166–175.

Mosher, W. D. (1990). Contraceptive practice in the United States, 1982–1988. *Family Planning Perspectives, 22,* 198–205.

Paulhus, D. (1991). Measurement and control of response bias. In J. P. Robinson, P. R. Shaver & L. S. Wrightsman (Eds.), *Measures of personality and social psychological attitudes* (pp. 17–60). New York: Academic Press.

Pleck, J. H. (1994). *Social psychological factors influencing male contraceptive use.* Wellesley, MA: Wellesley College Center for Research on Women, Working Papers.

Pleck, J. H. (1995). The gender role strain paradigm: An update. In R. F. Levant & W. S. Pollack (Eds.), *A new psychology of men* (pp. 11–32). New York: Basic Books.

Pleck, J. H. & O'Donnell, L. N. (2001). Gender attitudes and health risk behaviors in African-American and Latino early adolescents. *Maternal and Child Health Journal, 5,* 265–272.

Pleck, J. H., Sonenstein, F. L. & Ku, L. C. (1991). Adolescent males' condom use: Relationships between perceived cost-benefits and consistency. *Journal of Marriage and the Family, 53* (4), 733–746.

Pleck, J. H., Sonenstein, F. L. & Ku, L. C. (1993a). Changes in adolescent males' use of and attitudes toward condoms, 1988–1991. *Family Planning Perspectives, 25* (3), 106–110, 117.

Pleck, J. H., Sonenstein, F. L. & Ku, L. C. (1993b). Masculinity ideology and its correlates. In S. Oskamp & M. Costanzo (Eds.), *Gender issues in contemporary society* (pp. 85–110). Newbury Park, CA: Sage.

Pleck, J. H., Sonenstein, F. L. & Ku, L. C. (1993c). Masculinity ideology: Its impact on adolescent males' heterosexual relationships. *Journal of Social Issues, 49* (3), 11–29.

Pleck, J. H., Sonenstein, F. L. & Ku, L. C. (1994a). Attitudes toward male roles among adolescent males: A discriminant validity analysis. *Sex Roles, 30* (7/8), 481–501.

Pleck, J. H., Sonenstein, F. L. & Ku, L. C. (1994b). Problem behaviors and masculinity ideology in adolescent males. In R. D. Ketterlinus & M. E. Lamb (Eds.), *Adolescent problem behaviors* (pp. 165–186). Hillsdale, NJ: Erlbaum.

Sexually Transmitted Disease Surveillance, 1995. (1996). Atlanta: Centers for Disease Control, Division of STD Prevention.

Snell, W. E., Belk, S. S. & Hawkins, R. C. (1986). The Stereotypes about Male Sexuality Scale (SAMSS): Components, correlates, antecedents, consequences, and counselor bias. *Social and Behavioral Sciences Documents, 16,* 9 (Ms. 2746).

Sonenstein, F. L., Ku, L., Lindberg, L. D., Turner, C. F. & Pleck, J. H. (1998). Changes in sexual behavior and condom use among teenage men: 1988 to 1995. *American Journal of Public Health, 88,* 956–959.

Sonenstein, F. L., Pleck, J. H. & Ku, L. C. (1989). Sexual activity, condom use, and AIDS awareness among adolescent males. *Family Planning Perspectives, 21,* 152–158.

Sonenstein, F. L., Pleck, J. H. & Ku, L. C. (1993). Paternity risk among adolescent males. In R. I. Lerman & T. J. Ooms (Eds.), *Young unwed fathers: Changing roles and emerging policies* (pp. 99–116). Philadelphia: Temple University Press.

Sorenson, R. (1973). *Adolescent sexuality in contemporary society: Personal values and sexual behavior ages 13 to 19.* New York: World Publishing.

Spence, J. T. & Helmreich, R. L. (1978). *Masculinity and femininity: Their psychological dimensions, correlates, and antecedents.* Austin: University of Texas Press.

Spence, J. T., Helmreich, R. L. & Stapp, J. (1973). A short version of the Attitudes toward Women scale. *Bulletin of the Psychonomic Society, 2,* 219–220.

Sullivan, L. (1991, May 25). U.S. secretary urges TV to restrict "irresponsible sex and reckless violence." *Boston Globe,* p. 1.

Thompson, E. H., Jr., & Pleck, J. H. (1986). The structure of male role norms. *American Behavioral Scientist, 29,* 531–543.

Turner, C. F., Ku, L., Rogers, S. M., Pleck, J. H. & Sonenstein, F. L. (1998). Adolescent sexual behavior, drug use, and violence: Increased reporting with computer survey technology. *Science, 280,* 867–873.

Turner, C. T., Lessler, J. T. & Devore, J. (1992). Effect of mode of administration and wording on reporting of drug use. In C. F. Turner, J. T. Lessler & J. C. Gfroerer (Eds.), *Survey measurement of drug use: Methodological studies* (pp. 177–220). Rockville, MD: National Institute on Drug Abuse.

Ventura, S., Martin, J., Matthews, T. J. & Clark, S. (1996). Advance report of finality natality statistics, 1994. *Monthly Vital Statistics Report, 44,* 11.

Wilder, D. (1991, March 28). To save the Black family, the young must abstain. *Wall Street Journal,* p. A14.

Zelnik, M, Kantner, R. & Ford, K. (1981). *Sex and pregnancy in adolescence.* Beverly Hills, CA: Sage.

13

Boy-on-Boy Sexuality

Ritch C. Savin-Williams

Sex between boys is sufficiently stigmatized in our culture as to be essentially ignored, subjected to misunderstanding, and stereotyped. Those who believe that such behavior does not exist frequently embrace antiquated assumptions that children are, or should be, sexless. Others acknowledge that a few boys may have sex with each other, although they dismissively attribute it simply to opportunistic play, rather than to consequential "sex." To them, same-sex behavior during childhood and early adolescence is negligible for the boys' future sexuality—and certainly should never be encouraged through open discussion. Others maintain the opposite—that it turns innocent boys away from heterosexuality to a life of promiscuous and dangerous homosexual sex (read: AIDS).

A slightly more enlightened view acknowledges that although some youths secretly participate in these unorthodox relationships for reasons beyond mere amusement, same-sex activities are customarily temporary and experimental. As noted developmental psychologist Eleanor Maccoby observed, although "a substantial number of people experiment with same-sex sexuality at some point in their lives," only "a small minority settle into a life-long pattern of homosexuality."[1] If true, then most same-sex encounters between boys are relatively insignificant, transitional encounters that are best disregarded. Absent from this discussion is the perspective that these boy-on-boy activities represent the expression of an enduring same-sex orientation that brings happiness, pleasurable gratification, and identity consolidation—an affirmation of a very important aspect of life.

Although some may deny that boy-on-boy sexual behavior takes place or believe that it is harmful and must be prevented, these views ignore developmental research and are not based on the real life experiences of children and adolescents. For example, one of the best predictors of adult homosexuality is child and adolescent same-sex sexual activity, suggesting its early origins.[2] Gay and bisexual young men frequently and vividly recall their first same-sex encounter and attribute immense significance to it for their developing identity, sexuality, and intimate relationships.[3] Furthermore, child and adolescent same-sex behavior occurs across the spectrum of sexual orientations and, as such, it likely impacts many more youths than those who eventually identify as gay or bisexual. Given the general cultural directive that such behavior should remain stigmatized, boys who engage in same-sex behavior might well be adversely affected by these negative views. This may be particularly true for boys who, in addition to participating in same-sex behavior, experience a preponderance of same-sex attractions and desires.

Boys are led, in this culture, to believe that their homoerotic attractions and longings for sex with other boys will diminish or evaporate once girls become available during adolescence. For some boys with transitional homoerotic desires and behaviors, this may be true, while for many others this sexuality is a central aspect of who they are. Whether these youths identify as gay or whether they engage in sex with other boys, their same-sex attachments are enduring. Parental and cultural proscriptions can shame, delay, or squelch these feelings—but they cannot extinguish them. Internal motivations to satisfy homoerotic desires often far exceed external prohibitions against them.

The exact number of boys who either identify as gay or simply engage in sex with other boys is almost impossible to determine, although it is certainly far more than the 1% to 3% who report they are gay or bisexual on representative, anonymous surveys of junior and senior high school students.[4] In fact, only a minority of teenage boys with same-sex attractions or fantasies reports that they are gay or bisexual or that they engage in sex with boys.[5] That males are more likely to experience same-sex attractions than they are to identify as a sexual minority is reflected in a recent national sex survey. Ten percent of all men reported at least one aspect of "adult same-gender sexuality." Of these men, nearly half found sex with another male appealing or were sexually attracted to males, but had no sexual experience with a male and identified as *heterosexual*. One quarter self-identified as heterosexual, had engaged in sex with a male, and reported no sexual attractions to males. The final quarter of men had a convergence of same-sex desire, behavior, and identity.[6] Similarly, in a recent study of college students, 5% of men self-identified as gay or bisexual. However, twice as many reported that they are mostly sexually attracted to males, and twice that number—nearly 20%—did not strongly disagree that they had sexual attractions to men.[7]

To fully account for the discrepancies in the domains of a boy's sexuality, far more than a chapter is needed. Nevertheless, using data first reported in my book, *". . . and then I became gay." Young men's stories,*[8] my goal here is to broaden an understanding of boys' lives through the narratives of young men who describe not just the who-what-where-when of their first same-sex encounters but also the *meanings* of these initial contacts.

The Study

Eighty-six young men between the ages of 17 and 25 were interviewed for the study. An age ceiling of 25 years was established to minimize the time lag between the experience of developmental events and their recall during the end of adolescence and the beginning of young adulthood. Young men were recruited through announcements in local university classes and flyers posted on campus bulletin boards and relevant public establishments (local bar, bookstore, cafe). Advertisements appeared in local gay newsletters and internet listservs.

Youths were, for the most part, articulate, educated college students who elected to participate in research described as attempting to understand the ways in which young men with same-sex attractions come to recognize their sexual identity during childhood and adolescence. At the time of the interview, 83% identified themselves as gay, 7% as bisexual, 5% as unlabeled, 5% as bi-gay, and 1% as questioning. These youths are not presented as necessarily representative of all youths with same-sex attractions. The sample included 13% Latino, 8% African American, 6% Asian American, and 2% Native American Indian youths. Few youths who were closeted to themselves or to others volunteered for the study. Those with diverse educational, socioeconomic, and geographical backgrounds were also inadequately sampled. As with other interview studies, nonverbally oriented and shy youths were also likely under-represented in the study.

Face-to-face interviews were conducted at a time and place of the youths' choosing and used a semi-structured interview protocol. Confidentiality was assured and consent for participation was secured. Tape recorders were considered too intrusive for the material requested, so verbatim notes were taken as the youths spoke. Youths were sensitive to this approach, pausing when the interviewer fell behind in note taking. These notes were immediately transcribed. Youths appeared comfortable with these arrangements and were willing to refer friends to the study.

Although questions about sexual development ranged from first memories of feeling different to the consolidation of a sexual identity, of interest for this chapter is one significant aspect of the developmental process—first sexual experience with another male. Sex was defined as genital contact on the part of one or both partners. To increase the probability of eliciting true memories, youths were encouraged at appropriate moments during the narratives to relate *specific* memories of their first same-sex experience and to anchor them in concurrent life events. Typical probes included: How old were both of you? Who was this person to you? Where did you meet? Who initiated the interaction and why? Where did this occur? What happened, sexually? How did you feel afterwards? How did this affect your sexual identity? Were there further contacts? For the most part, youths remembered exact markers and these details enhance their stories' credibility.

Context of the First Sexual Experience

At the time of the interview, slightly over half of the 86 young men had had sex with both a male and a female. Of those with at least one sexual experience, 84% first had sex with a boy. Six of the young men reported that they were "complete" virgins—no genital contact with a male or female—and two had had sex with a female but not a male. The average age of first sex with a boy was 14.3 years, considerably before first sex with a girl at age 15.7 years.

Of the developmental milestones assessed, none varied as widely as the age of first same-sex sexual experience. It could be as early as age 5 or as late as after 25—if the virgins in the study eventually have sex. Of the 86 young men, 54 (63%) had their first sexual experience during boyhood—before high school graduation. It is these 54 boys who are the focus of this chapter.

Age

Forty-three percent of the 54 youths had a prepubertal sexual experience with another male. The others reported first sexual contact during junior (30%) or senior (28%) high school. The average age of the first male partner was 14.2 years, slightly more than 2 years older than the interviewee was at the time of the experience. However, eliminating the five oldest partners resulted in an average age of first partner that was just slightly above that of the interviewee at the time of the encounter. In 76% of cases, youths had first sex with a peer within 2 years of their age. In 6 of the 54 pairings the boy was older than his first partner, although in no situation was he more than 2 years older. Of the 13 dyads in which more than 2 years separated the partners, 6 dyads were more than 5 years apart in age. A pubertal difference likely characterized three dyads.

One such pairing was 11-year-old David and his 15-year-old friend, Akiva, a friend of a friend. They first saw each other at Hebrew school and were immediately attracted to each other. The younger of two boys raised in a family that relocated from country to country because of his father's occupation, David had been called a "fag" since age 5. By age 9, he watched the men rather than the women in XXX movies, by 11 he bought male pornography "for" his female friends, by 12 he routinely had sex with other boys at his gym, and by 13 he came out to his parents. His first sexual experience was with Akiva.

> He sort of initiated the whole thing. At the present time Akiva has no clue of what he is but he certainly is very flamboyant. He came over with my friend to swim in our pool and in the process of changing clothes I noticed that he kept looking at me. My friend then left to go home and we were left alone. We were in my room and he said that he didn't know how to masturbate and so he asked me to show him, so I did him. He added if I would do a blowjob. I didn't give that to him but, of course, I wished I did afterwards. Neither of us really came and I was fully dressed the whole time.

The largest age difference was one pairing in which more than 30 years separated the two. A college junior at the time of the interview, Josh described his background as an "urban cafeteria Catholic." Josh's parents supported three children with blue-collar jobs in maintenance and transportation. Fascinated at age 11 by an advertisement for an all-male theatre cast, wrestling magazines, and televised football games, Josh identified as bisexual just before high school graduation and disclosed this information to a best friend during his college freshman year, and to his parents a year later. But during adolescence he struggled with the meaning of his same-sex attractions before he concluded it was "time" for him to have sex if he were truly going to be gay.

> Fifteen years old and he was 45. Oral sex. I met him at a gay theater. I came out thinking, finally I did it! I did it! I guess this is what is supposed to happen. I was nervous but I had a fake ID to get in. Looking back it made me feel really cheap. I didn't like it because of the circumstances. Not dirty, but it made it difficult to accept the whole gay thing until I fell in love in college.

> I've always liked older men and younger women. My first lover in college was 23. Probably the best kisser in my whole life! I can't tell you I'm disgusted with old men. I find them hot—well, maybe not over 45. He looked much younger in the dim lights of the theater!

Josh now identifies as gay and is involved in a long-distance relationship with a 30-year-old man he met while visiting his parents over the Christmas holidays.

The Partner

The first sexual partner was usually (70%) a friend—most often a best friend—from the neighborhood or school with whom the boy interacted on a daily basis. The first partner could also be a complete stranger (15%) or a family member (15%). No one had his first sexual experience with someone he was currently dating.

Two 9-year-olds playing truth-or-dare after practicing for their class Christmas play typify the common pattern of a friend being the first partner. "He kept showing me more and more of himself until he was finally naked. He finally said he dared me to touch him and I said 'don't be a faggot,' but I eventually did. I wished I had done more! Eventually I did because we did this every chance we got during the next 2 years."

Steven, a graduate student in engineering, also had first sex with a best friend 10 years earlier. Not out about his sexuality to his immediate or extended family, Steven was raised an only child in an upper-middle-class white, Protestant home on the West Coast. Aware of his attractions to boys since the fourth grade, Steven's first sexual experience several years later proved quite rewarding.

> We were both 13 and he was my best friend. We were sitting on my bed reading comic books and I started playing with his foot and he reciprocated. Neither of us came the first time, but he did the second. I masturbated to orgasm right after, however. So, just playing around having fun but there was some sense that what we were doing we were not supposed to do, but it was just so much fun. We did it a couple of more times that summer and from then on once or twice a year, and the last time that we did it we were seniors in high school. He is now married.

Finding romantic relationships during his conservative, private undergraduate college years proved unsuccessful. Now, Steven wants to be "monogamously married to a man in a suit and tie and with a Labrador retriever."

The initial partner could also be someone a youth had not met prior to their sexual activities. In these cases, he was often older than the youth. Josh's experience at the gay theater is one such example. These strangers were discovered in the neighborhood or at a gay organization, club, support group, or bar. Other meeting places included a shopping mall, bathroom, theater, church youth group, school club, summer camp, and athletic locker room.

Against the wishes of his father, Curt attended a music camp for gifted African American youths. Long regarded by his father as insufficiently masculine, Curt had always known that he was "interested in sex with boys." Recognizing his bisexuality prior to his first sexual experience, Curt was out to his mother, who once labeled someone with same-sex attractions as "a very horrible sick person who was perverted, a child molester, subhuman," but not to his father, who embraced similar views.

> I guess actually my first time was when I was 15 and at music camp. I'm not sure what this other guy is even today and he writes to me and said that he's had no sex at all since that time, but I think he must be leaning towards the gay side. Both of us were very curious. There was a hetero porn magazine that had been passed around from room to room and finally we had it. I think that maybe my gaydar was working even then because I somehow felt that he would be open to suggestion. So I suggested that we masturbate together. He didn't really want to but I did and he watched. The next night we

did it together, both of us masturbating separately. Then by the third night we began to fondle each other and then we had oral sex, which we did for the next 3 weeks, every night.

At the time of the interview, Curt was involved in a lingering, ill-defined romance with a fellow college freshman. After 3 months they ended their romantic relationship but have maintained the friendship and periodic sexual relations.

First-time sex partners could also be family members, usually a cousin but occasionally a brother. Two 6-year-old cousins were playing doctor

> with hard-ons and we took every chance to feel each other. Started basically petting each other, fondling each other's genitals. I was fascinated by the event. He initiated and I just went along. I had no idea about how he felt about the situation. I really didn't think it had any significance because we were just playing.

Growing up in south Florida, Catholic, and the only male child, Jose became aware very early that his attractions were directed toward males. For many years he assumed that it was just a phase but "this homosexual thing just wouldn't end!" He never dated girls and always felt different from his peers. Sex with his cousin Tony was one of his fondest childhood memories.

> I know that I was playing doctor at age 8 with my male cousin Tony, who was then 10. We made minor attempts at mimicking intercourse and I know that one time my mother caught us and said that it was wrong, but she didn't seem to get real angry. By age 13 we were still doing it.

> Later, in my house and my parents were gone at the time, we'd go out to the swimming pool and masturbate ourselves in the same room. I suggested at one point that we do something else and he agreed, so we tried out oral sex. We both came when we manually did each other.

It was not until his senior year in college that Jose self-identified as gay. He still has not come out to his mother, although she frequently asks probing and suspicious questions about his "male friends."

After initial sexual activities, most boys remained friends (72%), with half of the strangers becoming either friends or romantic partners. Most first-time same-sex encounters were experienced as positive, perhaps in large part because most were with best friends and were chosen rather than forced activities.

Motivations for the First Sexual Experience

Recollecting the reason for engaging in their first sexual experience proved challenging for many of the young men. They remembered that at the time their "excuse" was that they were having sex *primarily* because of curiosity or experimentation. However, many also recalled that they were more "into it" than their partner, and this greater enjoyment made it difficult to deny that they were participating out of lust or desire for sexual pleasure. Indeed, these two—curiosity and lust—inspired nearly 90% of all first sexual contacts. Only a few boys reported that their first sexual experience was motivated by a perceived obligation to their partner. Conspicuously absent were motives attributed to love or the alleviation of their virginity status.

Growing up Brazilian, Julio knew from an early age that neither his culture nor his Catholicism approved of his sexuality. Currently a high school senior, Julio first came out to his best friend in tenth grade. "I told him that I have fantasies about other men. I was very indirect initially but as we talked over the next couple of days I finally told him that I'm gay and he said that was fine with him." Julio is out to both parents, who are okay with it as long as "I love God and God loves me." Julio traced his first awareness of his same-sex sexuality to the sixth grade. Initially he was simply curious about his friends' activities, but he also noted that he had a "strange fascination" and a "compulsion" to participate in their games.

> The bunch of us who were about the same age and I heard several of the guys were sort of really into showing off their bodies. I found out about this, so on a campout I made sure that we sort of always ran around naked, and it was a particular boy. We had regular sexual contact and this is before puberty. It would involve some fondling and kissing, and it would never go to orgasm. I knew I loved it but I had no name for it, and this is sort of how I got to know all about sex education.

Not unlike many boys, 11-year-old Jack assumed that what he and his friend Sam were doing was similar to what most boys do to have fun. His liberal parents always affirmed sex, teaching him about sexual matters throughout his childhood. They did not, however, talk about sex between boys. Realizing that he enjoyed their "experiment" more than Sam did, Jack concluded that his motives might have a distinct basis. Soon after these sexual activities ended during adolescence, Jack came out first to himself and then to the girl he was dating.

> I know that he did not like it as much as I did. This one time that we got most active, neither one of us came. It was just that we did it for fun and neither one of us was particularly upset with it. We both knew that we still liked girls and we just assumed that all boys liked to do what we were doing. We sort of believed that what we were doing only existed in our minds. Kind of strange in a way because last week I was in this boy's wedding and I sort of felt like saying to everyone, "I remember when we did it; I had him first!"

A variety of boyhood sexual activities emerged from these child and early adolescent sex-play activities with friends and cousins that were motivated by curiosity and the desire to have fun, to experiment with their bodies, and to satisfy erotic desires.

Activities of the First Sexual Experience

The youth in the study perceived that the premiere sexual contact was usually initiated by the partner (50%) or was mutually initiated (20%). Orgasms were optional, achieved in one-third of initial sexual experiences. The low rate was due in large part to the prepubertal status of many youths and to the somewhat awkward or nervous circumstances of many sexual encounters. Sex with a first partner was occasionally a singular event but most often was an act repeated many times over several years. The initial contact frequently occurred in the home of one of the partners.

The most common sexual activities were mutual fondling (35%) and masturbation (35%). Oral sex (20%) was a distant third. Kissing was rare (2%), as was anal sex (9%). One youth noted that as 12-year-olds, he and his best friend did everything, but, "only sex. No kissing. He didn't want kissing." He and several other youths stated that kissing was too intimate, too indicative of the meaning that gay sex might have. Mouth-to-penis contact with your best friend was just having fun, but mouth-to-mouth contact stepped across a boundary into new territory—implying an identity or a lifestyle. At the time, Julio accepted without question the limitations imposed by his friends surrounding what constituted acceptable behavior.

> Another game we played was truth-or-dare. In one situation one of the dares was to become naked and we began touching each other, acting out heterosexual scenes, mutual masturbation, posing, and modeling. One boy said that there could be no sucking or fucking and so we didn't.

> It was just one of those things that we kids did. Sometimes we did contests of how fast one could reach orgasm and also how much. At the time I couldn't orgasm to ejaculation but there was this one guy who was 1 year older who was very well developed and he taught us all about it. This is how I found out about liquid orgasm.

Later, Julio realized that to have done what they did during games of truth or dare would have implied greater meaning. "As long as this was as far as it went then we couldn't be gay. Gays did things with orifices."

In the evolution of a relationship that began when both boys were 11-year-olds, Jack and his friend Sam's first sexual encounter did not include oral sex. Oral sex did, however, eventually become a central aspect of their sexual activities.

> We sort of spent time sleeping over at each other's houses and on this one occasion we slept in tents in his backyard. We were talking about girls, as we usually do, and then at some point we began to play strip poker and we would take flashlights and look at each other, very discreetly at first. That then evolved to we would lie on top of each other and read sort of racy kinds of things to each other. This is all, of course, heterosexual stuff. Then the next step was that we began to sort of rub together, you know, sort of rub each other's back while on top of each other naked. We never kissed.

> At some point we didn't know what else to do and we had heard from other boys about sucking. We didn't know exactly what was supposed to happen or what we were supposed to do, but we did have a rule that we agreed that neither one of us would pee in the other's mouth.

Two early adolescents experimented in their private school, attempting "anal sex but it wasn't successful because we didn't know how." A pair of 13-year-olds explored each other's bodies very closely after a Boy Scout meeting. "We did it twice in his room in his house, oral and anal. It was a good feeling."

Evaluation of the First Sexual Experience

In retrospect, the maiden journey was evaluated as "good" or "great" by 44 of the 54 youths, primarily because it fulfilled curiosity and lustful desires. When the sex was evaluated negatively, it was not due to the age or status of the partner or to the particular sexual behavior that occurred, but to the possible *meaning* of the sexual behavior. However, few youths expressed worry about the possibility of acquiring HIV.

When he was 16 years old, one youth reportedly experienced ecstasy after his first sexual experience. "I remember being nervous. Couldn't stop shaking, excited, but scared to death. Odd sensation feeling someone else. Never thought what it would be like. Took me by surprise. I was aware of my attractions before this but never acted on them." Although "everyone was doing it," several youths remembered that they were more "into" it than were their male partners. "I remember that I really enjoyed it. . . . This was before either one of us could even ejaculate and I remember that he kept on pulling on my penis and that it hurt. I told him it hurt but I wanted him to continue." Sometimes the partner wanted to curtail the sexual activities, much to the disconcertment of the interviewed youth. "Then when we got home he lost interest because he didn't want to do it anymore but I did. It was clearly more than just an experiment for me." Recognizing the precariousness of his sexual relations, Julio understood that he "couldn't show I liked it too much because then it would stop."

Although sex was perceived as great, fear of negative reprisals occasionally punctured the magical aura, causing some boys to feel guilt, shame, and anxiety. Early adolescents appeared particularly prone to guilt, prompting some formerly nonreligious youths to seek forgiveness from God. One junior high school boy wanted to join a neighborhood friendship group but first had to pass a ritual about which he was ambivalent. "The older guys built a fort and membership was we had to masturbate in front of them. I dropped my pants and came in a couple of strokes. They clapped, gave me a card, and taught me the motto. I should have felt great but I was extremely guilty about it after it happened. I prayed all night, confessed the next morning, and went to mass. I wasn't really religious before that."

Jose also recalled experiencing shame, which he termed his "Catholic guilt." Throughout the many years of sex with his cousin, Jose's adolescent enthusiasm was tempered by the knowledge that not all Catholics perceived his activities as morally acceptable.

> I felt guilty that I had done something wrong and I felt that we should go to confession. I know that I felt guilty because I would take these very long showers and I would brush my teeth. I knew that he and I were doing it for different reasons, him because it was sort of physical and sexual and me for different reasons. It meant more. I sensed something was wrong but once again I just told myself that it was just a phase. This is actually my mother's cousin. I still thought of myself as straight at this time.

Other youths, often as children, expressed a fear of getting caught and being punished by parents. One youth was part of a neighborhood gang that found sex a fun way to pass the hot summer days. Sex was not wrong, unless one was caught.

> We would put towels over the windows and then we would take our clothes off. We would masturbate each other as sort of play and we would get erections. I certainly remember having a lot of interest in this activity but I also remember that I didn't want to get caught with this kind of fun and play.

On the whole, however, a boy's first sexual experience was recalled as a "beautiful awakening," "ecstatic," and a "culmination of my sexual desires." When sex was characterized as an unpleasant experience, youths believed it was due to outside forces (parents, religion) condemning boy-on-boy sex. Childhood fears of getting caught merged into adolescent reservations about the consequences or *meaning* of the sexual behavior.

Meaning of the First Sexual Experience

Sexual activities were often experienced and interpreted in diverse ways depending on when they occurred during the life course.

CHILDHOOD

First sex prior to puberty typically incorporated same-age buddies or cousins and involved genital fondling and mutual masturbation. Youths were usually enthralled by these sexual encounters, committed to continuing them as long as possible, and convinced that sex had little significance beyond that of a whimsical, frolicking diversion. On reflection, the young men believed that childhood sex did not make them gay; it was simply an experiment or a desire for personal pleasure. The sexual orientation of the first partner was a matter of some speculation, with many doubting that he was totally straight.

Adrian's sexual history reflected several of these characteristics. Raised in a small Georgia town with three older siblings and his mother's parents, Adrian described his mother as a "very Donna Reed type" and his father as "I have no idea what he does, but he prepares market reports." Once he disclosed to his best friend, she "jumped up and down and hugged me." His siblings and parents were less thrilled, turning "red [mother], white [father], and blue [brother]." Adrian's first sexual experience was with his fifth-grade cousin. They "whacked off together in the same room under the sheets, but we didn't touch each other." At the time, it bore no meaning other than "Southern comfort." Adrian noted that they "fooled around" because it was "something that was fun and just something that we did, but this wasn't gay."

Few of these prepubertal boys understood the concept of "gayness" as an identity or a lifetime commitment. It would be several years, sometimes many years, before the boys associated early sex with adult sexual identity. However, despite the equation of first sex with physical pleasure, most boys were also aware that their sexual activities were "wrong" or "bad." This they knew because if parents discovered their activities, they would be punished.

EARLY ADOLESCENCE

The onset of puberty motivated boys to physically and mentally explore what they desired but had not acted upon. Although childhood sexual activity was often frivolous, except when it elicited fears of exposure and punishment, and was seldom interpreted as "homosexual," early adolescents with their developing cognitive abilities began to link sexual attractions with cultural definitions of sexual identities. This in turn created concern or worry about the *meaning* of their first sexual encounter. Several youths understood the connection between their desires and activities, identified as a sexual minority, and shared this information with others. Many more, however, did not.

During early adolescence, more "serious" forms of sexual behavior emerged, including anal activity. The partner was still primarily a friend, orgasms were more common, and sexual experiences were sought to satisfy lustful desires. In addition to increasing pleasure, orgasms could also generate guilt and shame, attenuating the resiliency of psychological defenses intended to deny or suppress the meaning of sexual activities. Although *being* gay was a burdensome reality against which they fought, the recognition that they were more "into it" than were their partners suggested to them that their *behavior* might be gay, with potent subsequent inferences for their identity and peer standing. Clearly, sex was more than a capricious, random event for many of these early adolescents.

The usual defense of an early adolescent to protect himself from understanding the implications of his first same-sex activity was to deny that it meant anything. One pair maintained their heterosexuality by saying to each other, "'If you were a woman I would do this to you.' Then we'd try to put it up the other's butt or suck on the other's nipple." Another defense was to intellectually minimize the act. After sex with his 12-year-old best friend, one youth recalled, "At the time I washed over it as much as I could, to make little of it as much as I could. At the time I avoided seeing it as being gay. It didn't have anything to do with myself being gay." Gradually, these and other defenses began to crumble.

Perhaps because of these internal conflicts about whether sex had implications beyond mere physiological arousal, more so than at any other age, first sexual experiences at early adolescence were evaluated as less positive. For example, the first encounter of the two 13-year-old Boy Scouts who became aware of each other's proclivities while peeing side-by-side after a meeting, was passionate and included oral and anal sex. The "good feeling" was diminished, however, by another concern. "Even then, the first time, I began to worry about what this meant. I knew what gay was and I couldn't be that."

By contrast, two early adolescents reported that the initial sexual encounter helped them *affirm* a gay identity or to disclose this fact to others. One boy realized that "by doing it with him I was saying goodbye forever to being straight, sort of a rite of passage. I was very nervous but I knew it was the right thing." For other youths, this clarity was achieved as same-sex experiences accumulated over time. After 2 years of sex with his 12-year-old neighborhood friend, a young man recalled, "This didn't make me gay because I already was, but it did make my sexual identity more concrete."

Interpretations of differences in meaning that distinguished boys who experienced sex with another boy during prepuberty from those who experienced it during early adolescence were also evident over time within individuals. For example, by early adolescence, Adrian was regularly "whacking off" in the basement with his best friend, Paul. Whereas in childhood his behavior had little meaning, by early adolescence its significance was becoming increasingly apparent.

> Paul and me talked a lot and then we whacked off in our separate beds. We did this at first in the dark but then we began shining flashlights on each other's dicks. On the third time, we put our hands on each other and we tossed each other off. This felt much better than when I did it by myself. We then went to blowjobs and this continued for about 2 years, every couple of weeks.

> We wanted to consider it as just experimenting, but I know we had our doubts. We both decided that no, this did not mean that we were gay. We were just exploring. I don't think either of us really believed this. He is now very closeted but I think he is gay. Later we would have phone sex.

Julio, as well, appreciated shortly after pubertal onset that sex with friends and his intense interest in male-male sexual activities meant something about a gay identity.

> I knew that this was on the path that I wanted and I knew that I was on it. I knew that others could sort of experience what I was and I knew that other people would think of it as being disgusting. I knew also that I always wanted to do more than other guys wanted to do except, of course, for this one guy.

Yet, Julio was also conflicted, similar to other early adolescents. He "was comfortable with my gay feelings but I didn't want to take on the identity. I didn't want to be a transvestite or a male prostitute because that was my image of what a gay person was. I didn't want to be a woman."

Puberty intensified the *possibilities of eroticism* by fashioning meaning to nascent sexual feelings present since childhood. The physical and emotional pleasure of desired sexual encounters could be exhilarating and reassuring, providing substance and understanding to that which was previously murky, or it could be noxious and threatening, reminding a boy of societal censure of his same-sex attractions. This duality, the onset of puberty crystallizing both exciting and frightening erotic possibilities, brought into sharp relief the nature of a boy's sexual desires. Relatively few, however, were inspired by their first boy-on-boy sex to proclaim, either privately to themselves or publicly to friends and family, their sexual identity. Perhaps with additional peer and family support and considerably less cultural negativity toward sexual minorities, the outcome would have been different.

ADOLESCENCE

For those who first engaged in same-sex sexual activities during high school, several striking characteristics were apparent. First, sex partners were less likely to be presumed heterosexual friends and family members and more likely to be strangers and gay friends. They often met in chance encounters in public places, thus increasing the likelihood of having only a single contact. Instigation of the sexual contact and orgasms were now more likely to be shared by both partners.

By adolescence proper, sexual contact increasingly implied to youths that their behavior had meaning for their sexual identity. It was less that high school students feared getting caught (childhood) or felt guilt or shame about their sexual activities (early adolescence). Rather, it confirmed that which they could not imagine during childhood, were terrified of and suppressed during early adolescence, and would come to accept during late adolescence and young adulthood. When superimposed upon known prohibitions against homoerotic desires, most adolescents recognized that their behavior was gay, although some held out a dwindling hope that sex with another boy did not necessarily mean that *they* as individuals were gay. After his initial sexual encounter with another male, one teen became emotionally upset because "This meant I was gay and thus I would become a fit target for all those gay jokes." Rather than being upset by this sexual revelation, another youth was relieved because "speculation and confusion" about his sexual inclinations had ended. He referred to his first sex as a "rite of passage by which I gained clarity about what was previously an abstraction." He had now been initiated into "gay life." For three youths, the significance of initial sexual experiences was heightened when they recognized romantic longings. Once this occurred, the implications of same-sex attractions became overwhelmingly poignant—an underlying gay predisposition.

Clarity, confirmation, and initiation into a gay life were enhanced if the first sexual experience occurred outside a youth's friendship network. In these more anonymous settings, a teen could test his sexuality, not among friends who might turn on him or not appreciate his struggles, but with a safe stranger within the context of a one-time act. If it did not work out, then he could always return to his former life without friends or family knowing about his experiment. The first partner's older age also served this purpose—someone more experienced and certain of his sexuality might better provide the acid test for a youth's uncertain gay sexuality. One such youth noted, "It was a really wonderful experience because he was so patient and gentle. I discovered it really was a confirmation, a solidification of who I am."

Brian visited one of the nation's gay meccas with the expressed intent of fortifying his same-sex sexuality and initiating himself into gay life. Raised the oldest of three children on a Northwest ranch, Brian's parents were officials of their tribal nation. Without the strictures of Western religion to hinder him, Brian most feared disappointing his Native American Indian elders. Desiring closeness with other boys since age 5 and realizing at 14 that his homoerotic feelings were not transitory, Brian tested whether his fantasies for boys would remain gratifying when expressed behaviorally.

> The first sexual occasion occurred when I went to San Francisco. This was when I was 15 years old. I was still very closeted. I saw advertised a gay film festival. And so I went with the purpose of trying to find other gay people. There was this one guy who was my age, so I went over to him and initiated a conversation. We went back to his place and we did mutual masturbation. This over the summer of my sophomore year in high school. He was also 15. He had been adopted by a lesbian couple, so he was very out. I felt that I could do it because it would be very anonymous and away from my home. We still actually have contact with each other. It felt very good. Later some guilt would set in. But he showed me the gay discos and the gay clubs.

Another youth used sex with a man to clarify his bisexuality. He dated several girls during high school and had sex with all of them. However, he was at a loss about what to do with his "homosexual tendencies." Finding no trusted and understanding male sex partners at his suburban high school, he searched an alternative newspaper in a nearby city to discover the hang-outs of gay men. After having anonymous sex, he concluded, "I knew I wasn't as sexually attracted to females as I wanted to be, but I loved being with them. And I knew how they made me feel, but they didn't make me feel what I wanted to feel when I was having sex with this guy."

Youths who initiated sex during their high school years were least likely to claim that these sexual activities had "no effect" on their sexuality. By this age, most knew what gay was and that sex with another male was one clear indication of being gay. Perhaps as well, by adolescence the sexual desires of most boys were so strong and so clearly oriented toward other boys that the meaning of their attractions could no longer be ignored. After sex, relatively few teens continued to profess heterosexuality. The purpose of the first sexual experience was thus less to engage in fun (childhood), lust (early adolescence), or romance (more of a young adult goal), but to clarify their sexuality, sometimes within the context of the anonymity of a singular, discrete event.

Effects of the First Sexual Experience on Sexual Orientation

Almost without exception, the young men reported that their initial sexual encounter did not make them gay. Over 70% evaluated the effect of boy-on-boy sex on their *sexual orientation* as "none." After recalling his first sexual experience, one young man explained, "This had no real impact on my sexual identity [orientation] because whatever caused me to be the way I am happened before this time." The other youths believed that their first time suggested to them that they might be, but did not *make* them, gay or bisexual. The awareness that they were not to blame for their sexual orientation often helped youths to come out earlier than those who believed that they were "damaged" by their behavior.

Only one youth, Wai, entertained the possibility that his initial sexual experience made him gay. Born in Hong Kong and raised with an older sister until he left home for a private school in Chicago, Wai recalled that shortly after pubertal onset, "I began to explore the whole issue of my sexuality. I was trying to make myself like girls but it just wouldn't work. I didn't go out on any dates [with girls] even though I kept thinking I ought to." Two months before the interview, Wai first disclosed to a friend. His first sexual experience 5 years earlier had turned his life around.

> We were 14, classmates, and we were talking on the phone and the conversation just sort of led to sex. I finally initiated the sex talk and just said why don't we do it and he agreed very readily. So, I went to his house and I was very shy. I didn't take off any of my clothes. He on the other hand came to the door naked. We hugged and kissed and felt each other. There was no orgasm the first time but he did teach me later how to masturbate.

I liked the feeling and I wanted to do it again and he said okay as soon as possible. Maybe this was the experience that made me gay. Maybe if the first person had been a female I would be straight today. Maybe I just wanted sex and because the first one was with a guy, this made me gay. It's what I thought then and sometimes I still think that now. It's not a problem because I like being gay and in the next life I'd like to be gay again.

Born of lust or disinterest, carefully orchestrated or a chance encounter, life altering or forgettable, the first sexual act was typically perceived as having no effect on a youth's sexual orientation. Rather, it constituted his sex education, helped him disclose his homosexuality to others, or corroborated that which he knew or suspected about his sexuality.

Discussion

Far too little is known or appreciated about the first sexual activities of boys with other boys. I believe suppression of public discourse and research on boy-on-boy sexuality is detrimental to the lives of boys of all sexualities. One example of how collective proscriptions against same-sex sexuality affect more than sexual-minority youths is the observation that most boys who are called "faggot" or "gay" are not truly gay in their sexual orientation, yet they suffer from societal damaging judgments and stereotypes of homosexuality. One such group may be boys for whom same-sex sexual encounters are experimental or opportunistic with seemingly little meaning or predictive power about their sexual orientation or sexual identity. Although heterosexual, they may be shamed by their behavior and made to feel inadequate, immoral, or inferior. The resulting psychic pain may turn to anger, the expression of which may be directed toward those they perceive as the truly "guilty" ones—boys who are most feminine in their behavior, personality, and interests. If they can reveal the *true villains*—the real "faggots"—then perhaps they can sufficiently divert the "heat" from themselves.

For other boys, however, same-sex desires and behaviors represent a central core of who they are. Some of these individuals will eventually identify as gay, bisexual, or a sexual minority, and participate in gay culture. To negate or misinterpret their feelings and needs can create unnecessary pain and shame that hinder their development of a vibrant, authentic sense of self. Similar to all youths, boys with same-sex attractions require affirmation that they are acceptable to family and friends. If they fear that their same-sex attractions may preclude them from this acceptance, they may become the boys who, despite childhood and adolescent same-sex behavior, decide that they *cannot be gay* and thus elect to blend into the fabric of American culture as heterosexual young men, with a secret. Little is known about how their lives are changed by their sexual experiences. Perhaps they are "liberals" who sublimate their homoeroticism by working for social justice for sexual minorities; or, perhaps, they are the violent victimizers of gay people, those most threatened and thus homophobic and recalcitrant for maintaining the oppression of sexual minorities. In either case, their inability or unwillingness to connect their sexual and intimate selves likely extracts a great sacrifice. Yes, they appear "normal," but in the process they lose an essential aspect of who they are.

To the extent that alternatives to heterosexuality are misrepresented, myths flourish, stigma abounds, and those who by their very nature are sexually unconventional are condemned. Few individuals concerned with the well-being of youths would advocate that being thus marginalized, especially during the vulnerable years of childhood and adolescence, is desirable. When oppression is unavoidable, survival is greatly enhanced by considerable personal and social support to counter normalization pressures. Although increased cultural visibility has recently been afforded to many aspects of sexual minorities' lives that offset these damaging stereotypes, normalize nonheterosexuality, and provide resources and support, we have been strikingly silent about the particulars of one aspect of their lives—their sexuality. The exception to this silence about boy-on-boy sexuality is the risk it represents for sexual diseases. We sometimes forget, however, that the very behaviors that can result in HIV infection can also lead to love, happiness, fulfillment, and identity integration and consolidation. These, too, deserve our attention. Whether same-sex behavior is a harbinger of curiosity, lust, sexual identity, or intimacy, we should seek to understand and appreciate it among our young.

NOTES

1. Page 191 in Maccoby's 1998 book, *The two sexes: Growing up apart, coming together* (Cambridge, MA: Belknap Press). No empirical support is given to substantiate either how many people experiment with same-sex sexuality or, of these cases, how many reflect a temporary versus a permanent sexual orientation.

2. The earliest research that found this strong relationship is A. P. Bell, M. S. Weinberg & S. K. Hammersmith, 1981, *Sexual preference: Its development in men and women* (Bloomington: Indiana University Press).

3. For one example, see J. Hart (Ed.), 1995, *My first time: Gay men describe their first same-sex experience* (Los Angeles: Alyson). However, these accounts often fall short because they are presented as narratives without comment, context, or analysis.

4. For a detailed examination of issues pertaining to the definition of the population of sexual minorities, see R. C. Savin-Williams, 2001, A critique of research on sexual-minority youths, *Journal of Adolescence, 24,* 15–23.

5. In Minnesota, 1.5% of boys identified their sexual orientation as gay or bisexual. However, three times that number reported same-sex attractions; only 5.1% of all students with homosexual attractions said that they are predominantly homosexual. Of the 1.6% of boys who engaged in same-sex behavior, slightly more than one-quarter described themselves as homosexual or bisexual; of the 2.2% who reported same-sex fantasies, less than one third described themselves as homosexual (G. Remafedi, M. Resnick, R. Blum & L. Harris, 1992, Demography of sexual orientation in adolescents, *Pediatrics, 89,* 714–721). In Massachusetts, 1.7% of boys identified themselves as gay or bisexual (R. Garofalo, R. C. Wolf, S. Kessel, J. Palfrey & R. H. DuRant, 1998, The association between health risk behaviors and sexual orientation among a school-based sample of adolescents, *Pediatrics, 101,* 895–902). In Vermont, 1.3% of boys reported a same-sex experience (R. H. DuRant, D. P. Krowchuk & S. H. Sinal, 1998, Victimization, use of violence, and drug use at school among male adolescents who engage in same-sex sexual behavior, *Journal of Pediatrics, 132,* 113–118).

6. Laumann and colleagues reported that 2.8% of men self-labeled as homosexual or bisexual, 4.5% found sex with another man appealing, and 6.2% were at least somewhat sexually attracted to men. Overall, 7.7% of the men reported same-gender sexual desire, 9.1% have had sex with another man since puberty, and 10.1% reported either same-sex desire or behavior (E. O. Laumann, J. H. Gagnon, R. T. Michael & S. Michaels, 1994, *The social organization of sexuality: Sexual practices in the United States.* Chicago: University of Chicago Press).

7. R. A. Lippa, 2000, Gender-related traits in gay men, lesbian women, and heterosexual men and women: The virtual identity of homosexual-heterosexual diagnosticity and gender diagnosticity. *Journal of Personality, 68,* 899–926.

8. Chapter 4, First Gay Sex, in which the data are presented according to the age when the first same-sex encounter occurred (1998, New York: Routledge). Valsin DuMontier interviewed one-third of the youths.

Part V

Schooling

14

Immigrant Boys' Experiences in U.S. Schools

Carola Suárez-Orozco and
Desirée Baolian Qin-Hilliard

Currently the children of immigrants[1] comprise 20 percent of the youth population in the United States. The majority of these children have Latino, Asian, or Caribbean origins—representing unprecedented cultural and linguistic diversity. The last fifteen years have witnessed growing scholarly attention to their adaptation. However, the issue of gender has been relatively unexplored in the literature on immigrant youth. Several scholars have identified a general pattern that is consistent with the national trend: immigrant girls tend to outperform boys in educational settings (e.g., Brandon, 1991; Portes & Rumbaut, 2001; Rong & Brown, 2001). Yet to date, very few studies have explored why this gendered pattern may exist. This chapter examines the experiences of schooling among immigrant youth, with a particular focus on immigrant boys' experience in school context.[2]

Gendered Trends among Immigrant Youth

Gender appears to be a significant force in shaping patterns of adaptation among immigrant youth. Portes and Rumbaut (2001) contend that "gender enters the picture in an important way because of the different roles that boys and girls occupy during adolescence and the different ways in which they are socialized." Although there has yet to be a large-scale empirical comparative study concentrating specifically on gender differences in immigrant children's academic engagement and achievement, a number of studies confirm the national trend that immigrant boys lag behind immigrant girls in academic settings across ethnic groups. Brandon's (1991) study of Asian American high school seniors shows that females reached higher levels of educational attainment faster than males. Rong and Brown (2001) find that African and Caribbean immigrant females outperformed their male counterparts in educational attainment. Waters's (1996) study of Caribbean American teens also suggests that it is far more likely for girls to graduate from high school than for boys. Similarly, Gibson (1993) finds that Mexican girls did better than boys in terms of grades and attitudes toward school.

Other researchers have found similar gender trends in academic engagement. In their recent report on second generation youth with various Latino and Asian origins, Portes and Rumbaut (2001) find that, compared to girls, boys are less engaged, have significantly lower grades, lower level of interest and work effort, and lower career and educational goals. Similarly, in her work with Latino high school students, Lopez (in press) finds that girls turn in homework more often, participate in more cultural activities, have a better relationship with teachers, and have a more optimistic future outlook at school compared to their male counterparts. In fact, Lopez points out that girls' high school experience is described as "institutional engagement and oppression" and young men's as "institutional expulsion."

In this chapter, we will report preliminary findings from the Longitudinal Immigrant Student Adaptation (LISA) study. We focus on the following two questions: Among immigrant students, what are the similarities and differences in schooling experiences (i.e., achievement and engagement) for boys and girls? What are the expectations of teachers for immigrant boys and girls? When differences occur among the students, how might we account for them?

Method

Currently in its fifth year, the Harvard Longitudinal Immigrant Student Adaptation study (LISA) was designed to deepen our understanding of immigrant youth's academic engagement and schooling outcomes. A total of 400 students, ages 9 to 14, stratified by gender and country of origin, from Central America, China, the Dominican Republic, Haiti, and Mexico were recruited within the first few years of immigration. Youth were recruited from fifty-one schools in seven school districts in Massachusetts and northern California. Participating schools provided access to students, teachers, staff, and school records.

Our study takes an interdisciplinary, longitudinal, and comparative approach. This project utilizes a variety of methods including structured student and parent interviews, ethnographic observations, projective and objective measures, reviews of school records, and teacher questionnaires and interviews. We adopt research strategies in the anthropological tradition to gain perspective on immigrant cultural models and social practices relevant to adaptation in the new setting. Youth are observed and interviewed in their schools, their communities, and their homes. These ethnographies allow us to gain the informants' points of view as well as identify locally relevant themes. Psychological methodologies including structured interviews, sentence completions, and narrative tasks are employed to carefully establish a data baseline on immigration histories and social and family relations, as well as academic attitudes and behaviors. Using triangulated data is crucial when faced with the challenges of validity in conducting research with groups with diverse backgrounds. By sorting through self-reports, parent reports, teacher reports, and our own observations, we are able to establish both concurrences and disconnections between what youth say they do, what others say they do, and what we see them do. The longitudinal design also allows us to calibrate changes over time. An interdisciplinary, multicultural team of over thirty bilingual and bicultural researchers enables us to gain entry into immigrant communities, establish rapport and trust with our participants, and develop culturally sensitive instruments. It also provides an interpretive community for understanding data and findings in context. In this chapter, we will report on preliminary findings that emerged from surveys, structured student and teacher interviews, field notes, and report cards.

Results

Academic Achievement

Findings from our study regarding academic achievement confirm the gender trend found for immigrant boys in general and Latino and Black males in particular (Dunn, 1988; Lopez, in press). Analyses of report card data reveal that the immigrant boys in our sample who attend middle and high schools in seven school districts obtain on average lower grades than do immigrant girls ($F = 5.52$, $df = 1$, $p = .02$). Boys have a significantly lower GPA than girls in language arts and lag behind girls in math, science, and social studies. In fact, across every single ethnic group in our sample—Chinese, Dominican Republican, Central American, Mexican, and Haitian—boys have statistically lower grades than do girls. Furthermore, girls are most likely to score in the highest grade range of B+ or better (24% of girls compared to 16% of boys), while boys are more likely to be represented in the lowest range of D– or lower (11% of boys compared to 8% of girls). Hence, immigrant girls tend to be the highest achieving students, and immigrant boys are more likely to be disengaged.

This trend of girls' outperforming boys at school also emerged from the teacher interview data. As part of the study, we asked seventy-four teachers in seven urban school districts on the East and West coasts who work with middle school and high school immigrant students about their perspectives on teaching immigrant students. As part of a series of questions, they were asked to respond to the question: "Have you noticed differences between how immigrant girls are doing and how immigrant boys are doing?" A total of 44% responded that boys did more poorly than girls either academically or socially. Only 13% thought that boys were doing better than girls on the whole. For example, a teacher working largely with Haitian students in the Boston area noted: "I would say that in general . . . the girls do better . . . because over the years that I have been here, most of the students who have gotten accepted to those Ivy League schools were girls for the most part." Immigrant girls succeed in schools in less strictly academic ways as well—a counselor working with Latino students in California told us: "Student body presidents and officers are almost always girls."

Academic Engagement

In recent years, a number of scholars have argued that academic achievement and adjustment are in large part a function of academic engagement. In order to perform optimally in the educational journey, the student must be engaged in learning. When a student is engaged, he is both intellectually and behaviorally involved in his schooling. He ponders the materials presented, participates in discussions, completes assignments with attention and effort, and optimally applies newfound knowledge in new contexts. Conversely, when academically disengaged the student "simply go(es) through the motions," putting forth minimum or, in extreme cases, no effort. Conceptually, we separate academic engagement into three dimensions—cognitive, behavioral, and relational. Cognitive and behavioral engagements are viewed as the manifestation of engagement, and relational engagement is viewed as a mediator of these engagements. As part of the LISA study, we developed an interview protocol that examined these dimensions of academic engagement. Structured interviews were individually administered in the student's language of preference by bilingual researchers.

Cognitive Engagement

Cognitive engagement was defined as the student's reported intellectual or cognitive engagement with schoolwork. This dimension includes both the elements of intellectual curiosity about new ideas and domains of learning, as well as the pleasure that is derived from the process of mastering new materials—do the students report that learning is inherently interesting to them? Cognitive engagement was assessed by asking students if they were currently interested in something, whether or not this interest was academically related, and whether they derived pleasure from learning new things, as well as by a composite score based on endorsing interest in math, science, language arts, and social studies courses. Our analyses showed that the cognitive engagement scores for boys were not statistically different from those for girls, and thus indicated no difference in cognitive engagement by gender.

Behavioral Engagement—Student Self-Report

Behavioral engagement refers to the degree to which students actually engage in the behaviors necessary to do well in school—attending classes, participating in class, completing assignments, and putting forth effort. We consider both general academic behaviors as well as subject-specific behaviors from both student and teacher perspectives. Behavioral engagement was assessed by asking students to report expended effort in math, science, language arts, and social studies courses, as well as attendance, lateness, and course-skipping frequency. They were also asked to rate a series of academic behaviors (e.g., turning in homework, paying close attention in class, putting forth best efforts in class and on projects) on a 4-point Likert scale. Findings demonstrate no gender differences in self-reported behavioral engagement. The only exception is that boys admitted to skipping classes more often than girls.

BEHAVIORAL ENGAGEMENT—TEACHER REPORT

Although boys did not report many differences in their own behaviors, analyses of the behavior checklists completed by teachers reveal another picture. Teachers were asked to rate a series of academic behaviors on a 5-point Likert scale ranging from "very poor" to "very good" for each participant in our study. Teachers reported that boys were more likely than girls to demonstrate "poor" or "very poor" attention in class, whereas girls were more likely than boys to demonstrate "good" or "very good" attention (see Table 14.1). Teachers also reported that boys were more likely than girls to demonstrate "poor" or "very poor" motivation and effort, whereas girls were more likely than boys to demonstrate "good" or "very good" motivation and effort. Similar patterns were reported for behaviors such as compliance with teacher requests: 13% of boys demonstrated "very poor" or "poor" behaviors compared to 9% of girls, whereas 61% of boys compared to 77% of girls demonstrated "good" or "very good" behaviors. Teachers also reported that girls were more likely than boys to demonstrate "very good" attendance, "very good" punctuality, and were more likely to complete homework. Boys were more likely to fall into the "very poor" ratings for each of these manifestations of academic engagement. Although teachers did not report significant differences between boys and girls in English reading or English oral expression, they did report that girls demonstrated better understanding of English. Furthermore, teachers reported that boys were more likely to have "very poor" or "poor" English writing skills (79%

TABLE 14.1
Teacher-Reported Levels of Behavioral Engagement, by Gender (n = 297)

		Boys (%)	Girls (%)	Chi-Square P value
Attention	Very Poor/Poor	24	13	0.002
	Good/Very Good	47	67	
Motivation/Efforts	Very Poor/Poor	30	11	0.0001
	Good/Very Good	44	68	
Behavior	Very Poor/Poor	13	9	0.002
	Good/Very Good	61	77	
Attendance	Very Poor/Poor	9	8	0.02
	Good/Very Good	71	79	
Punctuality	Very Poor/Poor	8	7	0.02
	Good/Very Good	68	79	
Homework	Never	7	1	0.0001
	Occasionally	21	12	
	Almost Always	27	38	
	Always	19	36	

of boys compared to 42% of girls). No significant gender differences emerged for the following academic behaviors: asking questions, relating to teacher, relating to peers, helping peers, or being referred to the principal. Overall, however, the teachers perceived the girls in a much more positive light than the boys. One teacher's response summarizes well the general outlook of many of the teachers:

> Girls, in general . . . tend to be more willing to buckle down, do their work, get all of their homework in. With boys, lots of times, there is more of a tendency to get distracted, to take as a role some anti-social types of behavior.

RELATIONAL ENGAGEMENT

Relational engagement is the degree to which students report meaningful and supportive relationships in school with adults as well as peers. We consider both the emotional and tangible functions of these relationships. Relational engagement was assessed by a composite score based on responses to a 4-point Likert scale (ranging from "very true" to "very false") on thirteen items, such as "Teachers care about me and what happens to me in class"; "I can count on my friends to help me in school"; and "If I have questions about school work, I can count on someone there to help me." Strikingly, we found that boys reported lower levels of relational engagement in school than girls ($F = 5.25$, $df = 1$, $p < .05$).

We also assessed relational engagement in our structured interviews. Our data indicated that boys tended to report more conflict with administrators and teachers at school than did girls. Boys were more likely than girls to report experiencing or witnessing their male friends' negative interactions with the security guard at school. Boys were also more likely than girls to perceive schools as a "prison." A boy from El Salvador told us:

> [At school] I don't like them taking electronic devices [pagers, cell phones] away, it's ridiculous; [our school] is a closed campus; it doesn't get windows; [it is] too old. They want to put cameras; we're going to be prisoners . . . not good when security wants to catch you. They are rude and rough with the students. The security often throws you to the ground, not to me, but I have seen it.

In response to the question "How do teachers and administrators treat most students?" a Dominican boy stated:

Bad. One time, a security guard threw my friend to the ground to search him because he saw my friend had a small knife in his pants' pocket. Another example is the teachers who are always screaming "go to class" and threatening you with suspending you from school. They say all these yelling at you. Everything is bad, if you talk, listen to music, etc.

Similarly, a Chinese boy, who later dropped out of high school, responded to the question "How do you feel about your school?" by saying:

Quite good. In terms of playing, quite fun to play. Easy to cut classes. I can walk out any time I want. Things I don't like? Of course the security guards. They always stop me and ask me many things, probably because of my appearance.

When asked "How do teachers and administrators treat most students?" he responded: "Not much. Teaching is just a job. Teachers just try to get by day by day and get salary at the end of the month, whether you learn things or not, it's not their business."

The interview data also suggested that boys reported more racism at school than girls. For example, when asked his feelings about his school, one Dominican boy told us:

The school environment is fine. The majority of the teachers are friendly, but some never leave the racism against Hispanics. What I like most is to share with people and to learn. What I don't like the most is the teachers' racism, and that some teachers do not care about the students. . . . A teacher that I asked to speak slow because I didn't understand much English, told me that is what I had come to the U.S. for and here English is spoken and he told me to go back to Santo Domingo.

Similarly, another boy reported,

Sometimes I didn't like some teachers. One teacher [Puerto Rican male] used to call me racial slurs in a joking manner. I used to hate those comments and told him so but he continued doing so. I got picked on by a teacher so much that once I was going to hit him. I got suspended for 8 days for it and he never got even reprimanded.

The immigrant boys in our study reflect on their lack of connection to and their hostile and racist experiences with their teachers and administrators. The boys appear to respond to these largely negative interactions with teachers by effectively "checking out" of the academic process.

Teacher Expectations

Consistent with Lopez's (in press) insightful ethnographic observations, teachers in our study report having different expectations for the boys than for the girls. A teacher in the Boston area admitted:

> I find the girls are far more focused when it comes to their education. Also keep in mind, teacher perceptions play a key role. We tend to know that if a girl is very quiet she is a very good student and we tend to nurture that type of individual far more. It may explain why a lot of girls tend to be successful.

Field notes taken by a researcher working with the LISA project in the San Francisco Bay area also reveal gender-based expectations from teachers:

> The teacher told me that before she started teaching she got "cultural awareness training" about the Mexican community in San Diego. She said: "they told me that Latino boys are aggressive and really, really, really, macho and very hard to teach. And they taught me that the girls are pure sweetness." I asked her if she thinks these "insights" are true. "Well, yes" was her response.

Teachers in our study readily admitted to favoring girls:

> Girls . . . are more hardworking, more than boys are. They are also neater with the work, more organized. . . . I usually favor girls more than boys, I also favor children that work diligently day after day, not necessarily the more intelligent ones. . . . Girls are more respectful than boys are.

Consistent with our survey findings regarding teachers' reports of behavioral engagement, the teachers told us in their interviews that they typically had more negative perceptions of the boys than the girls.

Discussion

Consistent with the literature, data from our study suggest that immigrant boys tend to demonstrate lower academic achievement and encounter more challenges in school than immigrant girls. From the student self-report data, we learn that boys do not report less cognitive or behavior engagement in school than girls. However, boys report being more disengaged relationally in the school than girls. They also tend to feel less support from teachers and staff and are more likely to perceive school as a negative, hostile, and racist environment. In addition, the teachers themselves report having more negative expectations of the boys than the girls. Thus, boys' poorer academic achievement and performance may not be due to less academic interest or capacity for learning ("cognitive engagement") or from less effort applied to schoolwork ("behavior engagement"). Rather, their poorer academic performance may be due to the combination of low social support ("relational engagement"), hostile experiences in school, and negative teacher expectations. In other words, negative social relations in school may be an important factor in explaining why immigrant boys are doing worse in school than their female peers.

Social Relations

A critical difference between boys and girls is in the realm of social relationships. Social relationships serve a number of crucial functions, including: providing a sense of attachment and support; inculcating aspirations, goals, and values; and conferring status and identity. In particular, relationships within schools provide several forms of support critical to academic outcomes, including: access to knowledge about academic subjects, college, the labor market, and how bureaucracies operate; as well as advocacy, role modeling, and advice (Stanton-Salazar, 2001). In a series of elegant studies of Mexican American adolescent social networks within schools, Stanton-Salazar found that although boys were more likely to report family cohesiveness and supportive parental relationships, their school-based relationships were less supportive. Boys were less likely to be "engaged with teachers and counselors . . . boys appeared to communicate less, which forced them to infer the meaning of an agent's words and actions, usually from a position of little trust" (Stanton-Salazar, 2001, p. 203).

As part of the LISA study, a separate interview was administered specifically to assess networks of relationships. Participants were asked to name the most significant people in their lives and people who were important to them in the following categories: family members (including extended family), peers, adults in schools, adults in the community (e.g., mentors, neighbors, church members, community leaders), and individuals still living in the participant's country of origin. In addition, they were asked about pertinent demographic data about these significant individuals (including racial and national background, language of communication, frequency and place of contact). Finally, using a modified Q-sort strategy, the participants were asked to name which of these individuals served which functions (e.g., "Which of these people helps you with your homework? Which of these people can you tell your troubles to? Which of these people tells you about what to do to get to college?").

Analyses of these data were quite revealing. Although there were no gender differences in the number of people named in the initial list of "most important people" in their lives, there was a significant difference in quality of these relations. Boys were more likely than girls to report they had no one to turn to for specific functions, including: help with homework (24% of boys vs. 15% of girls); problem-solving (17% of boys vs. 5% of girls); keeping secrets (15% of boys vs. 8% of girls); and borrowing money (7% of boys vs. 2% of girls). In addition, we found that girls were more likely to name supportive relationships specifically with adults in their schools than were boys (49% of girls had at least one supportive adult relationship in school vs. 37% of boys).

These findings support the other findings reported in this chapter. They suggest that gender differences in the quality of relationships in and out of school may help to explain the gender differences in academic outcomes. If boys are not receiving as much support (e.g., for school-related as well as non-school-related difficulties) and guidance in and out of school, and are more likely to experience overt acts of hostility and low expectations from their teachers, they may find it much more difficult to achieve academically than girls. Research with nonimmigrant youth has consistently found that teacher-student support as well as student-student support is critical for the academic achievement of both boys and girls (see Roeser, Eccles & Sameroff, 1998).

Peer Pressure

Another factor that may help to explain boys' poorer school performance may be related to peer pressure. Many researchers have noted that peer pressure to reject school is quite strong among boys. Furthermore, behaviors that gain respect with their peers often bring boys in conflict with their teachers. Some researchers point out that immigrant boys from certain ethnic backgrounds are more pressured by their peers to reject school, compared to immigrant girls. In her research with Punjabi youth, Gibson (1993) indicates that immigrant boys in general are more likely than their sisters to develop an "oppositional relationship" with the educational system or to see schooling as a "threat to their identity."

Field notes from the LISA study suggest that immigrant boys are more quickly recruited into the mores of their new social environments, which are often in deeply impoverished inner-city schools that do not foster cultures of high-achievement orientation. Observing an English as a Second Language middle-school classroom, a researcher on our team noted, "I didn't see much interaction between recently arrived immigrant girls and the Chicana (young women of Mexican origin that have been in the U.S. for two or more generations) students. In contrast, the immigrant boys seemed to be taken under the wing of the "backroom boys"—a term the researcher coined to describe disengaged boys who sat in the back of the classroom, often disrupting instruction. Another set of field notes revealed: "In contrast to the recently arrived immigrant boys, recently arrived immigrant girls sit to the front left of the classroom. They tend to huddle together, and are very quiet. They don't participate in class but they follow along . . . as a strategy of survival."

Statements made by a number of teachers reveal similar patterns of boys' more rapid integration into their social settings. A teacher working in a largely Latino high school in the Boston area noted:

> In terms of the guys, one of the hardest things I see is they need to become tough. Dialogue becomes something of the past. You have to save face, you have to argue it out. The lack of tolerance is much more pronounced. The readiness to fist fight, to take it out . . . it has a lot to do with the environment of our schools and cities.

Another teacher noted: "In Hispanic culture it's not too cool to be smart, carrying books . . . [This affects boys more than girls] because they don't want to be harassed." A teacher working with a diverse group of immigrant origin students told us:

> The males seem to have more leeway, more freedom to be with friends and so they kind of become a little bit more, too, maybe I shouldn't let anyone here hear me say that—too Americanized. . . . The ones who still retain their customs from their country . . . actually do better academically . . . [The

problem of adopting] "the clothing, speech, slang, and other mannerisms" [of the new culture is] not really so much with the young ladies.

Hence, as Portes (1998) has noted, social relations can generate positive as well as negative social capital. Peer pressure to be cool, tough, and possibly "American" may make it difficult for immigrant boys to do well in school.

Negative Social Mirroring

In addition to problems of support and expectations, there are other reasons, including negative social mirroring, that may help to explain why immigrant boys may perform more poorly in school than immigrant girls. Anthropological cross-cultural evidence from a variety of different regions suggests that the social context and ethos of reception plays an important role in immigrant adaptation. As John Ogbu (1978) and George DeVos (1980) have persuasively demonstrated, for youth coming from backgrounds that historically have been and continue to be depreciated and disparaged within the host society, academic outcomes are compromised. Boys from disparaged groups appear to be particularly at risk of poor academic outcomes. This is true, for example, for Afro-Caribbean youth in Britain, Canada, and the United States; for North African males in Belgium; Koreans in Japan; and for Moroccans and Algerians in France (Suárez-Orozco & Suárez-Orozco, 2001). These developing youth, like the children in our sample, are keenly aware of the prevailing ethos of hostility in the dominant culture.

We asked our sample of children to complete the sentence "Most Americans think that [Chinese, Dominicans, Haitians, Mexicans—depending on the child's country of origin] are . . .". Disturbingly, the modal response was the word "bad." Other responses included: "stupid," "useless," "garbage," "gang members," "lazy," and "we don't exist." When expectations of sloth, irresponsibility, low intelligence, and danger are reflected in a number of social mirrors including the media, the classroom, and the street, the outcome can be devastating for immigrant children's adaptation. Psychologically, what do children do with this negative reception? Are the attitudes of the host culture internalized, denied, or resisted? The most positive possible outcome is to be goaded into "I'll show you. I'll make it in spite of what you think of me." More likely, however, the child responds with self-doubt and shame, setting low aspirations in a kind of self-fulfilling prophecy: "They are probably right. I'll never be able to do it." Yet another worrisome response is that of "You think I'm bad. Let me show you how bad I can be." Immigrant boys' less positive attitudes toward school may be attributable not only to their different experiences at school but also to how they are perceived within a larger social context.

Family Responsibilities

Gender differences in family responsibilities at home may also play a role in explaining differences in academic outcomes between girls and boys. Research findings consistently suggest that, compared with their brothers, immigrant girls have many more responsibilities at home. Valenzuela (1999) finds that, compared with boys, immigrant girls participate more in tasks that require "greater responsibility" and "detailed explanations." Their roles include translating, advocating in financial, medical, legal transactions, and acting as surrogate parents. Eldest children in particular are expected to assist with such tasks as babysitting, feeding younger siblings, getting siblings ready for school in the morning, and escorting them to school (Valenzuela, 1999). Similarly, Lee (2001) finds that Hmong girls, in particular, are often expected to cook, clean, and take care of younger siblings. Olsen (1997) observes in her study that besides childcare and household chores like cleaning and washing, many immigrant girls, especially the oldest daughters, need to work to help the family.

Based on two waves of data collection, we found that although boys and girls did not report different levels of responsibility for translating, girls were significantly more likely to report responsibilities for cooking and childcare. Several teachers in our study expressed concern about excessive home expectations for immigrant girls. It is also possible, however, that developing a sense of responsibility at home may transfer to school settings. Jurkovic et al. (in press) found that while "filial responsibilities" sometimes compete with schooling pursuits, performing caregiving tasks also provided youth with an increased sense of personal and interpersonal competence. Hence, these responsibilities may provide unanticipated benefits to girls who shoulder greater household responsibilities.

Conclusion

Our data present strong evidence not only of poorer academic performance among immigrant boys than among immigrant girls, but also the reasons why such gender differences may exist. Our data suggest that immigrant boys may not struggle in school because they have less internal motivation or are less able to achieve in school (i.e., cognitive or behavioral engagement). Rather, they may struggle because of the social context that offers them little support, guidance, and encouragement to do well in school. The context of the school, home, and peers as well as the larger culture should be considered in any discussion of gender differences in academic outcomes among immigrant youth.

It is also important to note that there may be tremendous variation across and within immigrant groups. Not all immigrant girls thrive in school and not all immigrant boys struggle in school. For example, Lee (2001) finds that although Hmong adolescent girls tend to have higher motivation and achievement, they were also more likely than boys to drop out of high school. Similarly, Gibson (1988) finds that Punjabi boys took more advanced courses, had higher rates of college attendance, and earned higher degrees than Punjabi girls. A recent article in the *New York Times* reports that although Latino boys have a higher high school dropout rate (28%) than Latina girls (26%), Latina girls are found to leave school earlier than boys and are less likely to return (Canedy, 2001). This trend favoring boys seems to be particularly strong in cultures that are considered more traditional and have stricter gender role expectations and gender grading (Gibson, 1988; Qin-Hilliard, 2001; Sarroub, 2001). These findings underscore the need to look at variations within and across gender groups in school outcomes among immigrant adolescents.

In addition, it is important to note that, although the focus of this chapter was on gender differences, there were a lot of similarities detected between the immigrant boys and girls. For example, perceptions of school safety, attitudes toward Americans, beliefs about American attitudes toward their ethnic group, as well as responses on many projective narrative tasks revealed no gender differences. A number of common experiences— including shared immigration stress, schooling and neighborhood contexts as well as the ethos of reception—may account for the similarities in the experiences of immigrant boys and girls (Suárez-Orozco & Suárez-Orozco, 2001).

Future research should continue to consider gender differences in immigrant children's adaptation. We should also search for the commonalities, as well as the particular risks, challenges, and protective characteristics that are relevant to the lives of all immigrant youth. Interdisciplinary, multidisciplinary, triangulated research is essential to begin to understand the lived experiences, in and out of school, of the understudied population of immigrant youth. Given the high proportion of immigrant origin youth, their adaptation will have crucial implications for the nation we become.

NOTES

The data for this research is part of the Harvard Longitudinal Immigrant Student Adaptation (LISA) study conducted by Principal Investigators Carola Suárez-Orozco and Marcelo Suárez-Orozco. Desirée Baolian Qin-Hilliard, a researcher with the study, has collected data from Chinese informants and has been involved in instrument development and analysis. We wish to thank Vivian Louie and Lisa Machoian for providing theoretical advice and to Robin Harutunian for helpful editorial suggestions. We also want to thank Terry Tivnan, Josephine Louie, Nora Thompson, and Quentin Dixon for their analytic work. This project has been made possible by generous funding provided by the National Science Foundation, the W. T. Grant Foundation, and the Spencer Foundation. The data presented, the statements made, and the views expressed are solely the responsibility of the authors.

1. In discussing immigrant youth, we are referring to both the first generation (i.e., children who are born abroad) as well as the second generation (i.e., children born in the new land of foreign-born parents).

2. All differences reported between boys and girls are tested with Chi-square analyses. Only differences that reached statistical significance are reported in this chapter.

REFERENCES

Adams, P. L. (1990). Prejudice and Exclusion as Social Trauma. In Noshpitz, J. D. & Coddington, R. D. (Eds.). *Stressors and Adjustment Disorders.* New York: John Wiley and Sons.

Aronowitz, M. (1984). The social and emotional adjustment of immigrant children: A review of the literature. *International Migration Review,* 18, 237–257.

Athey, J. L. & Ahearn, F. L. (1991). *Refugee Children: Theory, Research, and Services.* Baltimore, MD: John Hopkins University Press.

Brandon, P. (1991). Gender differences in young Asian Americans' educational attainment. *Sex Roles,* 25, 45–61.

Canedy, D. (2001). Often conflicted, Hispanic girls are dropping out at high rate. *New York Times,* March 25, A1.

Chavez, L. R. (1992). *Shadowed Lives: Undocumented Immigrants in American Society.* Fort Worth: Harcourt Brace College Publishers.

Chu, J. (1998). *Relational Strengths in Adolescent Boys.* Paper presented at the American Psychological Association Annual Convention (106th), San Francisco, CA.

Cobb, S. (1988). Social support as a moderator of life stress. *Psychosomatic Medicine,* 3, 300–314.

Cohen, S. & Syme, S. L. (1985). Issues in the study and application of social support. In Cohen, S. & Syme, S. L. (Eds.). *Social Support and Health.* Orlando, FL: Academic Press.

Cornell, R. W. (2000). *Men and Boys.* Berkeley: University of California Press.

Das Dasgupta, S. (1998). Gender roles and cultural continuity in the Asian Indian immigrant community in the U.S. *Sex Roles,* 38, 953–974.

David, D. & Brannon, R. (1976). *The Forty-Nine Percent Majority: The Male Sex Role.* Reading, MA: Addison-Wesley.

DeVos, G. A. (1980). Ethnic adaptation and minority status. *Journal of Cross-Cultural Psychology,* 11, 101–124.

Dunn, J. (1988). The shortage of black male students in the college classroom: Consequences and causes. *The Western Journal of Black Studies,* 12, 73–76.

Espin, O. M. (1987). Psychological impact of migration on Latinas: implications for psychotherapeutic practice. *Psychology of Women Quarterly,* 11, 489–503.

Falicov, C. J. (1998). *Latino Families in Therapy: A Guide to Multicultural Practices.* New York: Guilford Press.

Flaskerud, J. H. & Uman, R. (1996). Acculturation and its effects on self-esteem among immigrant Latina women. *Behavioral Medicine,* 22, 123–133.

Fordham, S. (1996). *Blacked Out: Dilemmas of Race, Identity, and Success at Capital High.* Chicago: University of Chicago Press.

Fuligini, A. (1997). The academic achievement of adolescents from immigrant families: The roles of family background, attitudes, and behavior. *Child Development,* 69, 351–363.

Garbarino, J. (2000). *Lost Boys: Why Our Sons Turn Violent and How Can We Save Them.* New York: Anchor Books.

Garcia Coll, C. & Magnuson, K. (1997). The Psychological Experience of Immigration: A Developmental Perspective. In Booth, A., Crouter, A. C. & Landale, N. (Eds.). *Immigration and the Family: Research and Policy on U.S. Immigrants* (pp. 91–131). Mahwah, NJ: Lawrence Erlbaum Associates.

Gibson, M. A. (1988). *Accommodation without Assimilation: Sikh Immigrants in an American High School.* Ithaca, NY: Cornell University Press.

Gibson, M. A. (1993). Variability in immigrant students' school performance; The U.S. case. *Division G. Newsletter, American Educational Research Association.* Washington, DC.

Glasgow, G. F. & Gouse-Shees, J. (1995). Themes of rejection and abandonment in group work with Caribbean adolescents. *Social Work with Groups*, 4, 3–27.

Grant, L. & Rong, X. L. (1999). Gender, immigrant generation, ethnicity, and the schooling progress of youth. *Journal of Research and Development in Education*, 33, 15–26.

Griffin, S. T. (2000). *Successful African-American men: From Childhood to Adulthood*. New York: Kluwer Academic/Plenum Publishers.

Grinberg, L. & Grinberg, R. (1990). *Psychoanalytic Perspectives on Migration and Exile*. New Haven: Yale University Press.

Hernández, D. & Charney, E. (Eds.) (1998). *From Generation to Generation: The Health and Well-Being of Children of Immigrant Families*. Washington, DC: National Academy Press.

Hoffman, E. (1989). *Lost in Translation: A Life in a New Language*. New York: Penguin Books.

Hongdagneu-Sotelo, P. (1994). *Gendered Transitions: Mexican Experiences of Immigration*. Berkeley: University of California Press.

Hudson, R. J. (1991). Black Male Adolescent Development Deviating from the Past: Challenges for the Future. In Bowser, Benjamin P. (Ed.). *Black Male Adolescents: Parenting and Education in Community Context* (pp. 271–281). Lanham, MD: University Press of America.

Jordan, W. J. (1999). Black high school students' participation in school-sponsored sports activities: effects on school engagement and achievement. *Journal of Negro Education*, 68, 54–71.

Jurkovic, G. J., Kuperminc, G., Perilla, J., Murphy, A., Ibanez, G. & Casey, S. (in press). Ecological and ethical perspectives on filial responsibility: Implications for Primary Prevention with Latino Adolescents. *Journal of Primary Prevention*.

Kao, G. & Tienda, M. (1995). Optimism and achievement: The educational performance of immigrant youth. *Social Science Quarterly*, 76, 1–19.

Kleinfeld, J. (1998). *The Myth that Schools Shortchange Girls: Social Science in the Service of Deception*. Washington, DC: The Women's Freedom Network.

Kruhlfeld, R. M. (1994). Buddhism, Maintenance, and Change: Reinterpreting Gender in a Lao Refugee Community. In Camino, L. A. & Krulfeld, R. M. (Eds.). *Reconstructing Lives, Recapturing Meaning: Refugee Identity, Gender, and Culture Change*. Amsterdam: Gordon and Breach.

Landale, N. S. & Oropesa, R. S. (1995). Immigrant Children and the Children of Immigrants: Inter- and Intra-Ethnic Group Differences in the United States. *Institute for Public Policy and Social Research*. East Lansing: Michigan State University.

Laosa, L. (1989). *Psychological Stress, Coping, and the Development of the Hispanic Immigrant Child*. Princeton, NJ: Educational Testing Service.

Leadbeater, B. J., Kupermine, G. P., Hertzog, C. & Blatt, S. J. (1999). A multivariate model of gender differences in adolescents' internalizing and externalizing problems. *Developmental Psychology,* 35, 1268–1282.

Lee, S. (2001). More than "model minorities" or "delinquents": A look at Hmong American high school students. *Harvard Educational Review,* 71, 505–528.

Loeber, R., Farrington, D. P., Stouthamer-Loeber, M. & Van Kammen, D. B. (1998). Multiple Risk Factors for Multiproblem Boys: Co-Occurrence of Delinquency, Substance Use, Attention Deficit, Conduct Problems, Physical Aggression, Covert Behavior, Depressed Mood, and Shy/Withdrawn Behavior. In Jessor, Richard (Ed.). *New Perspectives on Adolescent Risk Behavior* (pp. 90–149). New York: Cambridge University Press.

Lopez, N. (in press). Interrupting Race(ing) and Gender(ing) in High School: Second Generation Caribbean Youth in New York City. In Mollenkoph, J., Kasinitz, P. & Waters, M. (Eds.). *The Second Generation in Metropolitan New York.* New York: Russell Sage Foundation.

Louie, V. (2001). Parents' aspirations and investment: The role of social class in the educational experiences of 1.5 and second-generation Chinese Americans. *Harvard Educational Review,* 71, 438–474.

Luthar, S. (1999). *Poverty and Children's Adjustment.* Thousand Oaks, CA: Sage Publications.

Mizell, C. A. (1999). Life course influences on African American men's depression: Adolescent parental composition, self-concept, and adult earnings. *Journal of Black Studies,* 29, 467–490.

National Center for Educational Statistics. (2001). *Dropout Rates in the United States: 2000.* Washington, DC: U.S. Department of Education.

Ogbu, J. U. (1978). *Minority Education and Caste: The American System in Cross-Cultural Perspective.* New York: Academic Press.

Olsen, L. (1997). *Made in America: Immigrant Students in Our Public Schools.* New York: The New Press.

Orfield, G. (1998). The Education of Mexican Immigrant Children: A Commentary. In Suárez-Orozco, Marcelo M. (Ed.), *Crossings: Mexican Immigration in Interdisciplinary Perspective.* Cambridge, MA: David Rockefeller Center for Latin American Studies/Harvard University Press.

Phinney, J. & Landin, J. (1998). Research Paradigms and Studying Ethnic Minority Families Within and Across Groups. In McLoyd, Vonnie C. & Steinberg, Lawrence (Eds.). *Studying Minority Adolescents: Conceptual, Methodological, and Theoretical Issues* (89–109). Mahwah, NJ: Lawrence Erlbaum Associates.

Pierson, L. H. & Connell, J. P. (1992). Effect of grade retention on self-system processes, school engagement, and academic performance. *Journal of Educational Psychology,* 84, 300–307.

Pollack, W. (1998). *Real Boys: Rescuing Our Sons from the Myths of Boyhood.* New York: Holt & Company.

Portes, A. (1998). Social capital: Its origins and applications in modern sociology. *Annual Review of Sociology,* 24, 1–24.

Portes, A. & Rumbaut, R. G. (2001). *Legacies: The Story of the Second Generation.* Berkeley: University of California Press.

Prince, G. S. (1968). Emotional problems of children reunited with their migrant families in Britain. *Maternal and Child Care,* 4, 239–241.

Qin-Hilliard, D. B. (2001). Understanding the adaptation and identity formation of Chinese immigrant adolescent girls: A critical review of the literature. Doctorate Qualifying Paper. Harvard Graduate School of Education, Cambridge, MA.

Roeser, R. W., Eccles, J. S. & Sameroff, A. J. (1998). Academic and emotional functioning in early adolescence: Longitudinal relations, patterns, and prediction by experience in middle school. *Development and Psychology,* 10, 321–352.

Rong, X. L. & Brown, F. (2001). The effects of immigrant generation and ethnicity on educational attainment among young African and Caribbean Blacks in the United States. *Harvard Educational Review,* 71, 536–565.

Rumbaut, R. (1977). Life Events, Change, Migration and Depression. In Fann, W. E., Karocan, I., Pokorny, A. D. & Williams, R. L. (Eds.). *Phenomenology and Treatment of Depression.* New York: Spectrum.

Rumbaut, R. G. & Cornelius, W. A. (1995). *Becoming American: Acculturation, Achievement, and Aspirations among Children of Immigrants.* Annual Meeting of the American Association for the Advancement of Science, Baltimore, MA.

Sarroub, L. (2001). The sojourner experience of Yemeni American high school students: An ethnographic portrait. *Harvard Educational Review,* 71, 390–415.

Shuval, J. (1980). Migration and Stress. In Kutasshm, I. L. (Ed.). *Handbook of Stress and Anxiety: Contemporary Knowledge, Theory, and Treatment.* San Francisco, CA: Jossey-Bass.

Smart, J. F. & Smart, D. W. (1995). Acculturation stress of Hispanics: Loss and challenge. *Journal of Counseling and Development,* 75, 390–396.

Smith, R. (1999). *The education and work mobility of second generation Mexican Americans in New York City: Preliminary reflections on the role of gender, ethnicity, and school structure.* Eastern Sociological Society Meeting, Boston, MA.

Spencer, M. B., Swanson, D. P. & Cunningham, M. (1991). Ethnicity, ethnic identity, and competence formation: Adolescent transition and cultural transformation. *Journal of Negro Education,* 60, 366–387.

Stanton-Salazar, R. D. (2001). *Manufacturing Hope and Despair: The School and Kin Support Networks of U.S.-Mexican Youth.* New York: Teachers College Press.

Steinberg, L., Lamborn, S. D., Dornbusch, S. M. & Darling, N. (1992). Impact of parenting practices on adolescent achievement: Authoritative parenting, school involvement, and encouragement to succeed. *Child Development,* 63, 1266–1281.

Steinberg, S., Brown, B. B. & Dornbusch, S. M. (1996). *Beyond the Classroom.* New York: Simon and Schuster.

Suárez-Orozco, C. (2000). Identities under Siege: Immigration Stress and Social Mirroring among the Children of Immigrants. In Robben, Anthony & Suárez-Orozco, Marcelo (Eds.). *Cultures under Siege: Social Violence and Trauma.* Cambridge: Cambridge University Press.

Suárez-Orozco, C. (2001). Psychocultural Factors in the Adaptation of Immigrant Youth: Gendered Responses. In Agosín, Marjorie (Ed.). *Women and Human Rights: A Global Perspective* (pp. 170–188). Piscataway, NJ: Rutgers University Press.

Suárez-Orozco, C. (in press). Psychosocial Factors in the Adaptation of Immigrant Youth: Gendered Responses. In Agostin, M. (Ed.). *Women and Human Rights: A Global Perspective.* New Brunswick, NJ: Rutgers University Press.

Suárez-Orozco, C. & Suárez-Orozco, M. (1995). *Transformations: Immigration, Family Life, and Achievement Motivation among Latino Adolescents.* Stanford, CA: Stanford University Press.

Suárez-Orozco, C. & Suárez-Orozco, M. (2001). *Children of Immigration.* Cambridge, MA: Harvard University Press.

Suárez-Orozco, C., Todorova, I. & Louie, J. (in press). "Making up for lost time": The experience of separation and reunification among immigrant families. *Family Process.*

Suárez-Orozco, M. (1998). *Crossings: Mexican Immigration in Interdisciplinary Perspectives.* Cambridge, MA: David Rockefeller Center for Latin American Studies and Harvard University Press.

Sung, B. L. (1987). *The Adjustment Experience of Chinese Immigrant Children in New York City.* New York: Center for Migration Studies.

Tatum, B. (1997). *"Why Are All the Black Kids Sitting Together in the Cafeteria?" and Other Conversations about Race.* New York: Basic Books.

Thorne, B. (1997). Children and Gender: Construction of Difference. In Gergen, Mary M. & Davis, Sara N. (Eds.). *Towards a New Psychology of Gender* (pp. 185–201). New York: Routledge.

U.S. Department of Education. (1995). *Conditions of Education 1995.* Washington, DC: National Center for Educational Statistics.

Valenzuela, A. (1999). Gender roles and settlement activities among children and their immigrant families. *American Behavioral Scientist, 42,* 720–742.

Vernez, G., Abrahamse, A. & Quigley, D. (1996). *How Immigrants Fare in US Education.* Santa Monica, CA: Rand.

Vigil, J. D. (1988). *Barrio Gangs: Street Life and Identity in Southern California.* Austin: University of Texas Press.

Waters, M. (1996). The intersection of gender, race, and ethnicity in identity development of Caribbean American teens. In Leadbeater, B. J. R. & Way, N.

(Eds.). *Urban Girls: Resisting Stereotypes, Creating Identities* (pp. 65–84). New York: New York University Press.

Weissbourd, R. (1996). *The Vulnerable Child.* Reading, MA: Perseus Books.

Wick, J. W. (1990). *School Attitudes Measure: Technical Manual.* American Testronics.

Wills, T. A. (1985). Supportive Functions of Interpersonal Relationships. In Cohen, S. & and Syme, S. L. (Eds.). *Social Support and Health* (pp. 61–82). Orlando, FL: Academic Press.

15

Understanding the Exceptions
How Small Schools Support the Achievement of Academically Successful Black Boys

Gilberto Q. Conchas and Pedro A. Noguera

On most measures of student performance, Black male students are typically over-represented at the bottom rungs of the achievement ladder.[1] Black males are more likely than any other group to be suspended and expelled from school (Meier, Stewart & England, 1989), and more likely to be classified as mentally retarded or suffering from a learning disability (Milofsky, 1974; Harry, Kingner & Moore, 2000). Black males are more likely to be tracked into remedial and low ability courses and more likely to be absent from advanced placement and honors courses (Oakes, 1985; Pollard, 1993). In contrast to Black males, Black females commonly perform at higher levels in math and science courses, and are significantly more likely to attend college (Pollard, 1993). Even class privilege and the material benefits that accompany it fail to inoculate Black males from low academic performance. When compared to their White peers, middle-class African American males lag behind both in grade point average and on standardized tests (Jencks & Phillips, 1998).

Research on the achievement of African American students, particularly boys, has typically focused on the ways in which their attitudes and lack of motivation contribute to lower academic performance (Ogbu, 1990). Yet, many Black students frequently report high educational aspirations (Fordham, 1996; Fine, 1991; Ogbu, 1987, 1990; Hauser & Anderson, 1991), even higher than White students of similar class backgrounds (MacLeod, 1995). In considering other factors that might contribute to Black students' lower academic performance, researchers have suggested that Black students place less value on schooling because they perceive their opportunities for mobility to be limited due to racial discrimination (Ogbu, 1987), that Black students tend to see themselves as victims and to adopt self-defeating behaviors that undermine their performance in school (McWhorter, 1999; Steele, 1991), and that rap music may be responsible for the decline in Black student achievement (Ferguson, 2000).

Other scholars have focused their research on the role that schools can play in enhancing or hindering the achievement of minority students. For instance, factors such as racial segregation (Orfield & Eaton, 1996), inequities in funding (Kozol, 1991), and the politics of school governance (Meier, Stewart & England, 1989) have been identified as conditions that contribute to lower performance among minority students. Factors within school such as tracking and ability grouping (Oakes, 1985), the lack of a culturally affirming curriculum (Lee, 2000; Boykin, 1983) and lower teacher expectations (Goyette & Conchas, 2002; Valenzuela, 2000) have also been found to influence minority achievement. In sum, these scholars tend to attribute low academic achievement among minority students to broader patterns of social inequality that are prevalent throughout American society and that become manifest in the sorting practices of schools.

There is a complex relationship between the aspirations and achievement of African American students. The complexity is even more pronounced among lower-class Black males who attend urban public schools. These students typically express a desire to succeed in school and in professional careers, but further probing often reveals considerable doubt that they will actually attain their goals (Conchas, 1999). Mickelson (1990) has attributed the apparent discrepancy between the aspirations and achievement of African American adolescents to the tension created by conflicting abstract and concrete goals. For example, the Black students Mickelson surveyed expressed an abstract desire to attend college and obtain professional careers, but further probing revealed they actually believed their futures would be less promising. Mickelson's (1990) research also suggested that the achievement of Black students is far more likely to be influenced by their concrete perceptions of opportunity than by the abstract aspirations they articulate to adults.

The research presented in this chapter explores the relationship between school conditions and individual attitudes and aspirations. Rather than focusing on low student achievement, this study draws on data from a study of high-achieving Black male students in three college prep career academies located within a large, urban public high school. We focus on the factors present within these small learning communities that seem to account for the success of its Black male students. By focusing on the exceptions, namely Black male students who succeed academically, we hope to illuminate how environmental and cultural forces, both within and outside of school, influence their academic aspirations and goals.

Race, Identity, and Academic Achievement

Cultural ecologists offer one possible explanation for the low academic achievement of Black males. They posit that African American youth adopt "oppositional behavior" in relation to schooling that undermines their academic performance (Fordham & Ogbu, 1986; Ogbu, 1974, 1989). According to the cultural-ecological paradigm, nonvoluntary minority students, or minority students whose cultural history involves forced "immigration" rather than voluntary immigration (e.g., African Americans) reject aspects of schooling that they equate with forced assimilation, due to the historical experience of racial oppression (e.g., slavery, colonization, and conquest) (Ogbu, 1978: 33). As members of caste-like subordinate groups, these students perceive the opportunity structure as constraining their possibilities for social and economic mobility in a racially stratified society (Ogbu, 1974, 1987). These researchers suggest that Black students, as well as other racial minorities, expect limited rewards for educational effort, and as a result, are more likely to give up and to adopt self-defeating behaviors.

While the cultural-ecological paradigm has been helpful in contextualizing and historicizing analyses of minority student performance, the model contains fundamental flaws and omissions. First and foremost, it neglects to explain the wide variations in minority student performance, both within and across "nonvoluntary" minority groups (Conchas, 2001; Conchas & Clark, 2002; Conchas & Goyette, 2001; Gandara, 1999, 1995; Gibson, 1997; Noguera, 2001; Suárez-Orozco & Suárez-Orozco, 1995). Second, it provides no analysis of how the experiences of minority students in school settings influence their academic achievement as well as their attitudes and perceptions toward school. The failure to analyze the schooling experiences of minority students creates the impression that they arrive at school with an anti-intellectual orientation (McWhorter, 1999; Steele, 1991), and reinforces the assumption that the causes of poor academic performance lie within the attitudes and culture of students.

A vast body of research has shown that the schooling experiences of minority students are central to understanding their academic outcomes. Minority students, particularly those who reside in low-income, urban neighborhoods, are more likely than White students to attend under-funded, disorganized schools (Anyon, 1995; Kozol, 1991; Noguera, 1996); more likely to be taught by uncredentialed teachers (Darling-Hammond, 1997; Gandara, 1999); and more likely to be tracked inappropriately into remedial courses (Oakes, 1985). Although there is considerable evidence that the school experiences of many minority students are significantly different from those of White students, many researchers have overlooked the role of school processes and the ways they influence the aspirations of minority students (Conchas, 2001; Conchas & Clark, 2002).

It has long been recognized that schools play a major role in the social-ization of children (Brookover & Erickson, 1969). For example, schools are sites where children learn how to follow instructions and obey rules, interact with others, and deal with authority (Apple, 1982; Noguera, 2001; Spring, 1994). Schools are important sites for gender role socialization (Datnow, Hubbard & Conchas, 2001; Dyson, 1994; Thorne, 1993), and in most societies, they are primary sites for instruction in the values, norms, and language associated with citizenship (Loewen, 1995; Spring, 1994). Schools are not the only places where children formulate views about race. However, as schools are often sites where children are most likely to en-counter persons of other racial or ethnic groups (Peshkin, 1991), they can play a central role in the formation of racial identities among children (Tatum, 1992; Troyna & Carrington, 1990).

In a departure from the cultural-ecologists, we believe that the struc-ture and culture of schools play a major role in reinforcing and maintain-ing racial categories and the stereotypes associated with them (Conchas, 2001; Conchas & Clark, 2002; Noguera, 2001). As schools sort and label children by perceived measures of their ability, and single out certain chil-dren for discipline and others for rewards, they convey implicit and ex-plicit messages about racial and gender identities. In schools where White or Asian children are disproportionately placed in gifted and honors classes, the idea that these children are inherently more intelligent may be inadvertently reinforced (Conchas, 2001; Conchas & Goyette, 2001; Goyette & Conchas, 2002). Similarly, when African American and Latino children are over-represented in remedial classes, special education pro-grams, or on the lists for suspension or expulsion, the idea that these chil-dren are not as smart or as well-behaved becomes more entrenched in children's minds as well as in the adults' minds (Conchas, 2001; Ferguson, 2000; Noguera, 2001; Stanton-Salazar, 2001). Such messages may be conveyed even when responsible adults attempt to be impartial in their handling of sorting and disciplinary activities. In essence, schooling practices either reinforce existing attitudes and beliefs about the nature and significance of race through the maintenance of racial hierarchies (Conchas, 2001; Conchas & Goyette, 2001; Noguera, 2001) or, on rare occasions, challenge and attempt to subvert these hierarchies.

Unless there are deliberate and concerted efforts to alter typical patterns of achievement, many African American males under-perform, drop out, or are pushed out of school. In schools where the failure of Black male students is the norm and where racial patterns of achievement have been fixed for long periods of time, students and the adults who work with them are more likely to perceive racial identity as determining academic performance (Meier, Stewart & England, 1989; Noguera, 2001). Though the official rhetoric may suggest otherwise, the implicit message at these schools is clear: Black males may excel in sports, but not in areas that require intelligence such as math or history (Majors & Billson, 1992; Noguera, 2001). The location of Black males—in remedial classes or waiting for punishment outside the principal's office (Ferguson, 2000)—and the roles they perform in school settings suggest that intellectual activities are incompatible with their socially constructed personas and out of bounds to them. Such activities are out of bounds, not just because Black males may refuse to participate, but because no adult expects or encourages them to transgress established racial norms.

Within this system, there often are a small number of Black males who adopt cultural codes and behaviors that make it possible for them to resist racial stereotypes and achieve academic success. These students are typically ostracized and labeled as "sell outs" by their peers, who may regard violation of established racial patterns or stereotypes as a form of group betrayal (Fordham, 1996; Girabaldi, 1992). Unless there are concerted efforts by schools to support and encourage such students and others to deviate from group norms that are based on racial stereotypes, it is highly unlikely that the insidious link between racial identity and academic performance can be broken (Noguera, 2001).

The point that cultural-ecologists and others who hold Black males solely responsible for their low performance in school ignore is that schools can take steps to significantly increase the possibility of academic success. There is considerable evidence that the vast majority of Black students, including males, would like to do well in school (Conchas & Clark, 2002; Kao & Tienda, 1998; Noguera, 2001). Additionally, there are schools where academic success for Black students is the norm and not the exception (Leake & Leake, 1992; Sizemore, 1988). Both of these facts provide a basis for hope that achievement patterns can be reversed if there is a willingness to provide the resources and support to create conditions that nurture academic success. Learning more about the conditions that are present in schools where Black male students manage to succeed may be the key to figuring out how to support the achievement and aspirations of larger numbers of Black students.

Our study examines the experiences of academically successful African American male students. Specifically, we attempt to understand how the experiences of Black males in and out of school influences their aspirations, and how they manage to succeed academically even as they are influenced by the negative images of Black males that are prevalent in American society. Our ultimate goal is to illuminate the steps that schools can take to enable larger numbers of Black males to experience academic success.

Methods and Setting

The data presented are derived from a two-year research project (1996–1998) that focused on the sociocultural mechanisms that contribute to school success for racial minority students in a large, urban, comprehensive high school in California. Racial minority groups in this school include Latino, Vietnamese, and African American students. This chapter draws from interviews and observations of the schooling experiences of 13 African American male students who were enrolled in one of three of the college-bound programs in the school. Nine of these males were from low socio-economic backgrounds and four were from middle socio-economic backgrounds. The data presented in this chapter also include interview data from 45 teachers and administrators at the high school.

Baldwin High School[2] is located in a large city in Northern California. The population of the city consists predominantly of minority groups. At the time of the study, Baldwin High served 1,700 students: African American (65%), Asian American (20%), Latino (13.8%), Native American (0.5%), and White (0.3%). More than a dozen different languages are spoken at the high school. For years, the high school has struggled with issues of safety, poor academic performance, and a high dropout rate—mainly among African American and Latino males. In 1998, a mere 11% of graduating students enrolled in college. At the time of this research, the majority of college-bound Black students were enrolled in several small academies located within the school. These academies included a Computer Academy, Medical Academy, Graphics Academy, Teacher Academy, Transportation Academy, and a well-established advanced placement (AP) program. The college preparatory curriculum was composed of standard college prep courses as well as 12 AP and honors courses. This chapter concentrates on the schooling experiences of the high achieving[3] Black males in the Medical Academy, Graphics Academy, and AP Program.

These three academies or schools-within-a-school housed a student population whose racial and ethnic composition differed from that of the "mainstream" school. The AP program served 64 students: Asian (66%), African American (15%), White (14%), and Latino (5%). The Graphics Academy enrolled 127 students: Asian (56%), African American (25%), White (10%), and Latino (9%). The Medical Academy housed 267 students: African American (55%), Asian (32%), Latino (10%), and White (3%). In contrast to the majority African American composition of the larger school profile, the ethnic diversity of each academic academy resulted in distinct school experiences for the Black male students in this study.

Results

Black Student Voices on Race and Schooling

The African American student population at Baldwin High School is richly diverse. Students from a wide range of socio-economic backgrounds—including single female-headed households, two-parent households, and situations where extended kin serve as legal guardians—attend the school. Despite social class differences, struggles to succeed in school are common for most of the Black students. The high achieving Black students in our study hold a critical view regarding the role of race, and of tracking, in creating these difficulties and in perpetuating the academic hierarchies in the school. They pay close attention to racial tensions that exist in the larger school culture when they compare their own academic achievement to that of other minority groups. When Lewis is asked about whether there are any racial issues in school, he responds:

> *Lewis:* Yeah, everybody, like at lunchtime, one group is with their own and on one side, up in the court area another group and another in front.
>
> *GC:* Can you explain this for me in more detail?
>
> *Lewis:* At lunchtime, the Blacks be in one spot in an area of the school, the Asians be on the other part, the Hispanics be on another part, it's just separated. Everybody knows where everybody's at and nobody go in their space, or if they do, they might have a problem. Teachers, too!

When asked to explain what he means by "Teachers, too!" Lewis replied: "They be separating at lunch too and be talking behind each others' backs." Lewis sees his teachers as participants in the racially polarized school culture. Our interviews and observations at the school confirmed Lewis's description. With few exceptions, the students and teachers were rigidly polarized along racial and ethnic lines.

Several students in our sample thought that teachers preferred Asian students, and commented that "people think that Asians are the smartest." Students claimed that they had observed and personally experienced teachers pushing Asian students to excel in their classes, while offering less encouragement to African Americans and Latinos. They reported that teachers favor Asian students in a variety of ways, praise them more often, and give them better grades. Renee, for instance, takes a strong position on this issue: "Teachers be having favorites. *They are racist.* They don't like Blacks. . . . The students are not that racist, but the teachers are different. They like Asian students better." The extent to which counselors and teachers buy into the "model minority" stereotype[4] seems to have a direct impact upon the educational environment and aspirations of Black students at the high school. The adults' biases affect how students perceive their status within the school's pecking order, and undermine students' confidence that their teachers are looking out for their best interests.

This pattern of preferring Asian students and of racial tensions in general, however, was perceived to exist only in the larger mainstream school and not the smaller academies. In fact, the positive social experience and the apparent lack of racial tensions between the teachers and students in the academies seemed to be the primary reason for the academic achievement of the Black students in the current study. The supportive atmosphere of the academies contributed to healthier and more positive learning experiences among the students.

Academically Successful School Communities

The Black males attending the academies reported that they experienced an intimate school-within-a-school community that created a spirit of camaraderie among students and teachers. Tyrone, a Medical Academy student, explains how the culture of his small learning community promotes positive peer relationships.

> I think it's the work. I mean you can go and ask somebody else if you don't know the work, because people in the Academy are into the health field and they are not too much concerned with all the racial issues that are going on in the school and world . . . when you get hit with a problem, Black, White, Mexican or Asian, you can go ask them, ask them if you think they know it . . . it's not about racial things; it's about getting your work done.

The majority of the African American males in our study share these views. "In the academy," writes James, "everybody wants to be friends . . . it's like a community where everybody wants to be your friends, so eventually everyone in the community are friends." In the words of academy students, "we are like a family [where] everyone knows each other."

The Academy model embraces a number of principles associated with successful school reform, including a strong school-within-a-school community and small class size (Conchas 2001; Conchas & Clark, 2002; Stern, Dayton & Raby, 1998). The structure of the academy allows students and teachers to get to know one another well and to feel included as part of a team. Teachers also have more time to cater to individual concerns and needs, and this has a direct impact on students' experiences. For Martin, the difference between the academy and regular classes is that in the academy, one is "inside a school-within-a-school, so, pretty much you get more attention than a regular teacher can give you. . . . Regular teachers have more kids than we have . . . basically block classes . . . and we get more attention and more things done in the Academy." J.R. echoes this sentiment: The "[Medical] Academy teachers give you more one-on-one and you have more time to focus on that teacher . . . we never got that much in 9th grade, 'cause she have too many students who's coming to her and she can't teach the whole class. Here, they have more time."

The strong school-within-school community makes it possible to avoid or lessen the racial and ethnic hostility found in the larger high school culture through the formation of strong inter-racial peer cultures. In contrast to the rest of the school, students in the academy are exposed to individuals from a variety of racial and ethnic backgrounds. Black academy students report they form genuine friendships with non-Black youths. These friendships make it possible for students to better understand each other and learn to appreciate cultural differences. For example, Mike states "students here make a big difference. . . . Like in the 9th grade, I didn't have no real Asian friends . . . but now I have several of them in each class and I get to learn about their culture and stuff, like what they do and eat, what they like." The interview data revealed that Academy students thrive on strong and positive forms of peer and adult relationships that cut across race and ethnicity. Integration within a smaller learning community appears to be key to future academic success.

Given a more intimate learning community, effective pedagogy and career-related curriculum also help to further engage the students. The smaller academy classes allow teachers to structure classes so students can work together on projects. Teachers view collaboration among students as essential and work long hours on pedagogical and curricular practices and activities. Teachers also want students to enjoy themselves. James, in the Medical Academy, describes the work that teachers assign as both fun and educational: "You see, the work the teachers give is fun, and we group in a group way to get to know each other and everyone take care of each other 'cause we do stuff for health." James confirms that the academy structure encourages youth to form positive social relationships. The main goal of the academies, according to teachers, is to establish pedagogical and curricular approaches that enhance and promote human interaction instead of exclusionary practices.

Peer Groups and the Promotion of Pro-School Ideology

The African American males whom we interviewed expressed a very strong and positive orientation toward school. The majority of these students think education "is key" to social mobility—for themselves and for all people of color in the United States. James explains this connection in the following way:

[S]chool is very important . . . when you see those who are out of school, and who work in good places, you always feel like you want to be in a place, a position, just like that. If you want to be in a position like that, then you need to go to school and learn . . . and go through all the steps . . . before you can get where they're at.

We learned from our sample of high achieving African American males that it is uncommon for these students to pressure one another to cut class or disengage from school. On the contrary, they seem to encourage each other's academic success. The three college prep academies create learning cultures in which young people work hard to maintain high academic standings. Students who claim that they would not usually work as hard in school report that "because everybody is working, [they] don't want to be the one[s] not working." Steve explains his relationships with other students in the academy:

I mean, we develop relationships where . . . they inspire me to do my work. . . . I mean, it's just like they're just there, it's an inspiration. When I have one of those days when I just don't feel like doing no work, if I see them doing their work, I start working. I think to myself, "man, I'm slipping in this class. I need to take . . . start doing my work."

The peer cultures in the three academies create environments that appear to inspire and encourage hard work among the majority of students. While the peer culture stresses high achievement, students are not left to fend for themselves. They encourage and assist one another with their assignments and support each other in times of need. The caring and work-oriented learning environments seem to encourage most students to feel they can overcome adversity with the help of their peers.

Family, Role Models, and Schooling

Along with positive peer cultures, the African American male students in our study cite three major issues as sources of their school engagement and motivation to succeed: (1) the importance of family and home life; (2) the significance of adult role models; and (3) the role of the school context. These three issues may also be closely related with Black males' early exposure to professional careers and future aspirations.

The high-achieving African American males with whom we spoke suggested that family and home environments are important for positive school engagement. The majority of these males view their parents as the most significant source of their school engagement. Many of these students said that they need good home "training" in order to do well in school. For these students, home training refers to how parents encourage and discipline them at home. Consider, for example, the following focus group testimony from Bill and Tyrone:

> *GC:* Why do some students do well in school and others do not?
> *Bill:* I think that basically, it comes from the home. . . . The training basically. . . . If you have good training and discipline, you show the household that you are a good student. . . . Where discipline is lacking . . . students . . . don't have . . . concern about school . . . and it's not a priority.
> *GC:* And what do you think?
> *Tyrone:* It is like Bill said, it starts at home.

Similarly, Martin says that his mother keeps him on track to do well in school. He, in turn, assists his little brother:

> *Martin:* The family is very important cause, like, my mom is strict, very strict, hard. . . . She be making sure I do my work, try to get around high school . . . I have a little brother and I take care of him, he be with me sometimes.
> *GC:* So your mom keeps you going straight?
> *Martin:* My momma told me this old saying, "Don't let nobody hold you back. You can have your friends, but if they go into one direction, you go the other direction."

The males in our study also expressed a need for and interest in receiving support that goes beyond the classroom and into the community. Several described Black men who serve as role models in school and in the community who have had a positive influence upon them. Mike, for example, notes that because of the prevalence of single female heads of households in Black communities, the need for adult male role models is urgent: "It's like the single parent stuff. . . . Like mothers have boys, but the boys should have a role model. In the academy we get some, but we need men role models, too."

Several of the low-income students in our study have an adult male role model at home and they talk about how their experiences differ from those of their friends, whose fathers are absent. For these youth, an adult male exposed them to professions and to the realities of society. For instance, Rick's father's constant guidance triggered his desire to become an engineer:

> *GC:* Rick, where did you learn the processes of becoming a musician or engineer?
>
> *Rick:* It's like through TV, you look at people who are working and you go to a big business and stuff and you see how they deal with the computers. . . . Then you go to like an engineering business and you see how they work with computers and then you tell the two major differences.
>
> *GC:* Did anyone have an impact on you learning this process?
>
> *Rick:* Well, I remember when I was small, my father cleaned a computer place and he took me everywhere he went when he went to work and stuff. I always sat down and watched what the engineers were doing.
>
> *GC:* Do you think other males like you get these experiences?
>
> *Rick:* Nah, not a lot of us. Most Black males have no role models, you know, but what we see on TV.

Rick understands the importance of mentors to expose African American males to various career options and to break stereotypes. The middle-class students in the sample agree that it is important for them to have adult male role models. While only two of the middle-class students lived with both of their parents, each of the middle-class students reported that there were adult males who provided them with support and who exposed them to college and the world of work. Dion, for instance, remarks how his uncle, an engineer, told him about the Graphics Academy at Baldwin as a way to engage in engineering and enroll in college:

> I was kinda looking for something more rigorous and I kinda wanted to look into the electronics field. My uncle T., he told me about the engineering and electricity field, he is an engineer. He told me to look into it and into the [Graphics] Academy. We also get mentors in here and go to college, good colleges.

There is no doubt that male role models both in school and in the home are essential to the academic success of African American young men.

Along with role models at home, the majority of students in our study also alluded to the school context as significant in the development of motivation. Students sense a link between the school context—including teachers, exposure to professions and college preparatory curriculum—and their achievement. The academy provides the conditions that are necessary for these youth to engage and do well in school. James, for instance, comments on the teacher's role in engaging students in the material:

> Teachers play a role . . . in helping make class interesting. You need good instructors to help you focus on your task . . . so you can get the job done. I think it's teachers. . . . I don't like teachers who just throw work at you and don't explain it, they don't have to go into a big sermon about it, but at least give you some guidelines on how to do the work. . . . Good teachers also encourage you to do your best, they try to motivate you, they give you space when you need it, they give you time to do the work and they make sure, you know, you get it done.

"Good" teachers, therefore, appear to make a difference for students in various academic settings.

In addition, the students with whom we spoke felt that teachers should provide a nurturing and caring learning environment. "I like my math teacher because he explains the assignments and he demonstrates on the board how to do it and he gives homework in repetition too and if you still don't understand it, he has time after school to tutor you," explains Tyrone. He adds that the academy teacher "helps you wherever you're struggling at and that's a big help for me 'cause math takes me a long time, so I go after school." All these issues help foster Black males' optimism toward school and future career success.

Optimism in Spite of Constraints

The Black males in our study recognize the structural constraints in society, but they are determined to succeed despite them. They express a confidence and determination not to allow racism and lack of opportunity to impede their social mobility. Most subscribe to the American Dream: they believe that through individual determination, they can overcome obstacles and be successful. For example, Tyrone thinks that "there's always gonna be obstacles, but if you got your mind made up, no matter how many obstacles there is, you're gonna get up and do it." This determination to succeed is closely related to the various institutional factors in the school and community that promote high academic achievement, confidence, and persistence.

Additionally, a positive racial identity appears to be closely related to academic achievement. Most of the young men in our study expressed great pride in Black people and their African ancestry. Regardless of how they interpreted their racial background and status, these African American students strive to embrace their common history. They do not adopt a "raceless" persona (Fordham, 1996) or shy away from their racial group or community. Rather, they embrace their identity and draw upon it as a source of strength. Some Black students report that they intend to enroll in Black colleges to maintain and better understand their identities. The following interview captures this poignantly:

> *Rick:* I feel proud of my background, that's why I want to apply to mostly Black colleges, down south and stuff, like Morehouse.
> *GC:* Why Black colleges?
> *Rick:* Because they are good for keeping me on track and who I am, you know, they make you feel more in control.

Family and church also appear to be places that had a positive influence on the boys' identities. Joe explains that his father makes sure that he understands racism and how the church is important as a place to embrace difference and as a resource against racism: "My dad always told us to be aware of racism and he told us about what might happen to us in the future. He says to always be proud and act who we are . . . I celebrate Kwanzaa and do a lot of things with my family. We go to an African-oriented church and we sing African songs and stuff." Likewise, J.R. states that his mom and the church help him with his identity, and that the school also embraces his community: "I am African American and don't feel bad. Some Blacks wanna think that it's not all that, but my momma and church keep us proud. At school, it isn't different. Some [students] are okay with it [being Black], others are not . . . [The English teacher] has us read Malcolm X and stuff." John also reports how his class exposes the students to African heritage and cultural awareness. "I really want to be into African heritage and where my ancestors came from. In class, we learn about our background."

Conclusion

Our research suggests that schools can play a major role in promoting the achievement of Black males, both lower and middle class, and that they can take steps to undermine the insidious linkage between racial identity and academic performance. In contrast with cultural-ecologists, this research suggests that school context may be more important than individual attitudes in furthering academic achievement. In fact, the conditions we have described within the academies at Baldwin High School—supportive teacher-student relationships, a positive peer culture, a rigorous curriculum—appear to nurture and support the motivation and aspirations of students. This does not mean that schools can completely mitigate the effects of larger structural forces that shape the lives of young people outside of school. Poor, Black male students who reside in economically depressed inner city neighborhoods are particularly vulnerable to a broad array of risk factors that schools cannot control or influence (Garbarino, 1999; Noguera, 2001). But at the minimum, schools should not contribute to these hardships or function as a source of negative social capital to undermine the hopes and dreams of the students they serve (Wacquant, 1998).

The perceptions and expectations that are held toward Black males profoundly affect their aspirations about college and future occupations (Noguera, 2001). A significant body of research suggests that by helping young people acquire a concrete sense of hope about their future, it is possible to positively influence their behavior. This appears to be true not only for academic achievement, but also for teen pregnancy (Luker, 1996) and juvenile delinquency (Garbarino, 1999; Skolnick & Currie, 1994). Put more simply, young people who think they are heading somewhere behave differently than young people who think they are headed nowhere.

Changing the culture and structure of schools such that African American males are regarded with respect, and provided with the support and resources needed to reach high educational goals, are the most important steps that can be taken to make high levels of academic achievement the norm among Black males. Building stronger relationships between schools and communities can also be important in providing support for Black male students. In several communities throughout the United States, churches and community organizations already play a major role in providing support to Black students (McPartland & Nettles, 1991; Noguera, 2001). These organizations affirm the identities of Black males by providing them with knowledge and information about African and African American history and culture, and instilling a sense of social responsibility toward their families and communities (Ampim, 1993; Myers, 1988; Noguera, 2001). Schools are often unable to provide this kind of support, and for that reason partnerships with community groups can be helpful.

Most importantly, we suggest that community involvement may serve to counter the negative images associated with Black males in society. Because of the broad array of hardships and obstacles they face, Black males have been described as an endangered species (Gibbs, 1988). Schools can and should play a major role in helping Black males to overcome these barriers. For that to happen, more schools will have to change so that one day those African American males who succeed will no longer be the exceptions.

NOTES

1. Although Black includes a diversity of people that are not native to the United States and cannot be lumped into a single category, we use this term interchangeably with African American.

2. Baldwin High School, along with student and teacher names, are all pseudonyms.

3. High Achieving refers to students who are engaged and doing well in school, enrolled in college preparatory courses, identified by teachers as academically successful, and who maintain a grade point average necessary for college admittance to the University of California or California State University systems.

4. The notion that Asian students constitute a model minority is widely held among educators and researchers. For a discussion of the origins of the stereotype and its impact on students, see *Unraveling the 'Model Minority' Stereotype* by Stacey J. Lee (1996).

REFERENCES

Ampim, M. (1993). *Towards an Understanding of Black Community Development.* Oakland, CA: Advancing the Research.

Anyon, J. (1995). *Ghetto Schooling: A Political Economy of Urban Educational Reform.* New York: Teachers College Press.

Apple, M. (1982). *Education and Power.* Boston: ARK.

Boykin, W. (1983). On the academic task performance and African American children. In J. Spencer (Ed.), *Achievement and Achievement Motives*. Boston: W.H. Freeman Company.

Brookover, W. B. & Erickson, E. L. (1969). *Society, Schools and Learning*. Boston: Allyn & Bacon.

Conchas, G. Q. (1999). *Structuring Educational Opportunity: Variations in Urban School Success among Racial Minority Youth*. Unpublished doctoral dissertation, University of Michigan, Ann Arbor.

Conchas, G. Q. (2001). Structuring Failure and Success: Understanding the Variability in Latino School Engagement. *Harvard Educational Review* 71(3), 475–504.

Conchas, G. Q. & Clark, P. A. (2002). Career Academies and Urban Minority School Success: Forging Optimism Despite Limited Opportunity. *Journal of Education for Students Placed At Risk* 7(3), 287–311.

Conchas, G. Q. & Goyette, K. A. (2001). The Race Is Not Even: Minority Education in a Post-Affirmative Action Era. *Harvard Journal of Hispanic Policy* 13, 87–102.

Darling-Hammond, L. (1997). Doing What Matters Most: Investigating Quality Teaching. New York: National Commission on Teaching and America's Future, Teachers College.

Datnow, A., Hubbard, L. & Conchas, G. Q. (2001). How Context Mediates Policy: The Implementation of Single Gender Public Schooling in California. *Teachers College Record* 103(2), 184–206.

Dyson, A. (1994). The Ninjas, the X-Men, and the Ladies: Playing with Power and Identity in an Urban Primary School. *Teachers College Record* 96(2), 219–239.

Ferguson, R. (2000). *A Diagnostic Analysis of Black-White GPA Disparities in Shaker Heights, Ohio*. Washington, DC: Brookings Institute.

Fine, M. (1991). *Framing Dropouts: Notes on the Politics of an Urban Public High School*. Albany: State University of New York Press.

Fordham, S. (1996). *Blacked Out: Dilemmas of Race, Identity, and Success at Capital High*. Chicago: University of Chicago Press.

Fordham, S. & Ogbu, J. U. (1986). Black Students' School Success: Coping with the Burden of "Acting White." *Urban Review* 28, 176–206.

Gandara, P. (1995). *Over the Ivy Walls: The Educational Mobility of Low-Income Chicanos*. Albany: State University of New York Press.

Gandara, P. (1999). Staying in the race: The challenge for Chicanos/as in higher education. In J. F. Moreno (Ed.), *The Elusive Quest for Equality: 150 Years of Chicano/Chicana Education*. Cambridge, MA: Harvard Educational Review.

Garbarino, J. (1999). *Lost Boys: Why Our Sons Turn to Violence and How to Save Them*. New York: Free Press.

Gibbs, J. (1988). *Young, Black, and Male in America: An Endangered Species*. New York: Auburn House.

Gibson, M. A. (1997). Conclusion: Complicating the Immigrant/Involuntary Minority Typology. *Anthropology and Education Quarterly* 28, 431–454.

Girabaldi, A. (1992). Educating and Motivating African American Males to Succeed. *Journal of Negro Education* 61(1), 4–11.

Goyette, K. A. & Conchas, G. Q. (2002). Family and Non-Family Roots of Social Capital Among Vietnamese and Mexican American Children. *Research in Sociology of Education* 13, 41–72.

Harry, B., Kingner, J. & Moore, R. (2000). *Of Rocks and Soft Places: Using Qualitative Methods to Investigate Disproportionality.* Conference paper presented at the Minority Issues in Special Education, Harvard University, November 17, 2000.

Hauser, R. & Anderson, D. (1991). Post High School Plans and Aspirations of Black and White High School Seniors: 1976–1986. *Sociology of Education* 64, 140–165.

Jencks, C. & Phillips, M. (1998). *The Black-White Test Scores Gap.* Washington, DC: Brookings Institute.

Kao, G. & Tienda, M. (1998). Educational Aspirations Among Minority Youth. *American Journal of Education* 106, 349–384.

Kozol, J. (1991). *Savage Inequality.* New York: Crown Books.

Leake, D. & Leake, B. (1992). Islands of Hope: Milwaukee's African American Immersion Schools. *Journal of Negro Education* 61(1), 24–29.

Lee, C. (2000). *The State of Knowledge about the Education of African Americans.* Washington, DC: Commission on Black Education, American Educational Research Association.

Lee, S. J. (1996). *Unraveling the 'Model Minority' Stereotype: Listening to Asian American Youth.* New York: Teachers College Press.

Loewen, J. (1995). *Lies My Teacher Told Me.* New York: New Press.

Luker, K. (1996). *Dubious Conceptions: The Politics of Teenage Pregnancy.* Cambridge, MA: Harvard University Press.

MacLeod, J. (1995). *Ain't No Makin' It.* Boulder, CO: Westview Press.

Majors, R. & Billson, M. (1992). *Cool Pose: The Dilemmas of Black Manhood in America.* New York: Simon and Schuster.

McPartland, J. & Nettles, S. (1991). Using Community Adults as Advocates or Mentors for At-Risk Middle School Students: A Two-Year Evaluation of Project RAISE. *American Journal of Education,* August.

McWhorter, J. (1999). *Losing the Race.* New York: New Press.

Mehan, H., Villanueva, I., Hubbard, L. & Lintz, A. (1996). *Constructing School Success: The Consequences of Untracking Low-Achieving Students.* Cambridge: Cambridge University Press.

Meier, K., Stewart, J. & England, R. (1989). *Race, Class and Education: The Politics of Second Generation Discrimination.* Madison: University of Wisconsin Press.

Mickelson, R. (1990). The Attitude Achievement Paradox among Black Adolescents. *Sociology of Education* 63(1), 44–61.

Milofsky, C. (1974). Why Special Education Isn't Special. *Harvard Educational Review* 44(2), 437–458.

Murphy, J. & Hallinger P. (1985). Effective High Schools—What Are the Common Characteristics? *NASP Bulletin* 69, January, 18–22.

Myers, L. J. (1988). *Understanding an Afrocentric World View: Introduction to an Optimal Psychology.* Dubuque, IA: Kendall Hunt.

Noguera, P. A. (1996). Confronting the Urban: The Limits and Possibilities of School Reform. *Urban Review* 28(1), 1–19.

Noguera, P. A. (2001). The Trouble with Black Boys. *Harvard Journal of African American Public Policy* 7, 23–46.

Oakes, J. (1985). *Keeping Track: How Schools Structure Inequality.* New Haven: Yale University Press.

Ogbu, J. U. (1974). *The Next Generation: An Ethnography of Education in an Urban Neighborhood.* New York: Academic Press.

Ogbu, J. U. (1978). *Minority Education and Caste: The American System in Cross Cultural Perspective.* New York: Academic Press.

Ogbu, J. U. (1987). Variability in Minority School Performance: A Problem in Search of an Explanation. *Anthropology and Education Quarterly* 18, 312–334.

Ogbu, J. U. (1989). The individual in collective adaptation: A framework for focusing on academic underperformance and dropping out among involuntary minorities. In L. Weis, E. Farrar & H. G. Petrie (Eds.), *Dropouts from School* (pp. 181–204). Albany: State University of New York Press.

Ogbu, J. (1990). Literacy and schooling in subordinate cultures: The case of Black Americans. In K. Lomotey (Ed.), *Going to School.* Albany: State University of New York Press.

Ogbu, J. U. & Batute-Bianchi, M. E. (1986). Understanding sociocultural factors: Knowledge, identity and school adjustment. In D. D. Holt (Project Team Leader Ed.), *Beyond Language: Social and Cultural Factors in Schooling Language Minority Students* (pp. 73–142). Sacramento: California State Department of Education, Bilingual Education Office.

Orfield, G. & Eaton, S. (1996). *Dismantling Desegregation.* New York: New Press.

Peshkin, A. (1991). *The Color of Strangers, The Color of Friends.* Chicago: University of Chicago Press.

Pollard. D. S. (1993). Gender, Achievement and African American Students' Perceptions of Their School Experience. *Education Psychologist* 28(4), 294–303.

Sizemore, B. (1988). The Madison Elementary School: A Turnaround Case. *Journal of Negro Education* 57(3), 243–266.

Skolnick, J. & Currie, E. (1994). *Crisis in American Institutions.* New York: Harper-Collins.

Spring, J. (1994). *American Education.* New York: McGraw-Hill.

Stanton-Salazar, R. (2001). *Manufacturing Hope and Despair: The School and Kin Support Networks of U.S.-Mexican Youth.* New York: Teachers College Press.

Steele, S. (1991). *The Content of Our Character: A New Vision of Race in America.* New York: Harper Perennial.

Stern, D., Dayton, C. & Raby, M. (1998). *Career Academies and High School Reform.* Berkeley: University of California at Berkeley, Career Academy Support Network.

Suárez-Orozco, C. & Suárez-Orozco, M. (1995). *Transformations: Migration, Family Life, and Achievement Motivation among Latino Adolescents.* Palo Alto: Stanford University Press.

Tatum, B. (1992). Talking about Race, Learning about Racism: The Application of Racial Identity Development Theory in the Classroom. *Harvard Educational Review* 62(1), 1–24.

Taylor-Gibbs, J. (1988). *The Black Male as an Endangered Species.* New York: Auburn House.

Thorne, B. (1993). *Gender Play.* New Brunswick, NJ: Rutgers University Press.

Troyna, B. & Carrington, B. (1990). *Education, Racism and Reform.* London: Routledge.

Valenzuela, A. (2000). *Subtractive Schooling: U.S.-Mexican Youth and the Politics of Caring.* New York: State University of New York Press.

Wacquant, L. (1998). Negative Social Capital: State Breakdown and Social Destitution in America's Urban Core. *Netherlands Journal of Housing and the Built Environment* 13(1), 25–40.

Watson, C. & Smitherman, G. (1996). *Educating African American Males: Detroit's Malcolm X Academy.* Chicago, IL: Third World Press.

Weinstein, R., Madison, S. & Kuklinski, M. (1995). Raising Expectations in Schooling: Obstacles and Opportunities for Change. *American Educational Research Journal* 32(1), 121–159.

16

From Preschool to Middle School

The Role of Masculinity in Low-Income Urban Adolescent Boys' Literacy Skills and Academic Achievement

Michelle V. Porche, Stephanie J. Ross, and Catherine E. Snow

Competence in literacy skills is a critical component of children's success throughout their schooling careers (Snow, 1991). Literacy research has shown that being read to and talking about books are important precursors to children's literacy development (Bus, van IJzendoorn & Pellegrini, 1995). Creating a regular routine with books has also been shown to be positively related to later reading skills and academic success (Teale, 1984). However, researchers suggest that the significance of reading for later achievement reflects not only the fact that it is an intellectual activity but also that it is "a profoundly social process, embedded in parent-child relationships, and that frequency and quality of children's book reading experiences are strongly related to the history of other interactive experiences that children share with their parents and other caregivers" (Bus, 2001, p. 41).

Our understanding of the phenomenon of boys' literacy experiences in particular starts from the premise that gendered messages and practices in literacy training can have a profound impact on boys' educational experiences in reading and language arts (as could also be said of girls' experiences in math and science with respect to expectations of femininity). More specifically, we rely on Gee's (2001) sociocultural perspective as a framework to explore boys' early literacy development and subsequent academic achievement. Gee argues for the existence of multiple literacies that include both written and oral languages and that are relevant to individuals or groups of individuals depending on social and cultural location and entwined in interactive processes with other people. Describing these literacies as "rooted in different socially situated identities" (p. 31), Gee proposes that researchers studying literacy and language development reframe their investigation to focus on the ways in which individuals and groups develop their literacy skills through the process of working with others to acquire, and participate in, sociocultural practices. Furthermore, Gee (2001) argues that literacy practices are embedded in particular ideological, political, and social contexts. In this analysis, we focus on gender as a particular context for understanding children's literacy development from a sociocultural perspective.

Overall, there is limited evidence in the literacy research that suggests sex differences between boys and girls in early skill and ability level. Snow, Burns, and Griffin (1998) reviewed a number of empirical studies of reading difficulties that, when viewed together, tend to discount clear gender differences, especially when larger representative samples are included. However, while there are few indicators of gender differences in reading skills and achievement for boys and girls, especially in their early academic years, there are numerous findings of boys' increased risk for special education placement, retention, and dropout as they proceed through adolescence (U.S. Department of Education. National Center for Educational Statistics, 2000, 2001).

Popular literature highlighting the plight of boys in school often attributes boys' literacy-related academic difficulties to the feminization of school curriculum in opposition to boys' masculine "hard-wiring" or to undue attention paid to girls that takes away needed resources for boys (Gurian, 1999; Pollack, 1998). If we were to believe these hypotheses, we might be rightly concerned about material inequities leading to academic disparities. However, it is important to note that, historically, formal education in this country has been an institution for boys. Only in the twentieth century, when girls were allowed to enroll in public education, was language arts designated as the academic ghetto for girls in order to ensure boys' domination of science, math, and vocational training (Rury, 1991). The argument that boys are "naturally" at a disadvantage for reading success may actually obscure a trend in which reading is interpreted as a feminine activity in our culture and thus is valued and promoted differently for boys (Askew & Ross, 1988; Kimmel, 2000). This may be especially the case for poor and working-class families where men in the community often have jobs that emphasize manual labor over literacy skills (see

Willis, 1977; MacLeod, 1987, 1995). Martinez (1998) argues that this focus on individual shortcomings in boys' reading abilities obscures the larger issue of how educators' constructions of gender may influence reading instruction.

The fact that boys are more frequently targeted for special education services may reflect concerns regarding behavior as well as ability, especially given the co-occurrence of reading difficulties with attention problems (Snow, Burns & Griffin, 1998). Similarly, the tendency for boys to be retained and/or to drop out of school (Meisels & Liaw, 1993) does not necessarily reflect a lack of cognitive ability, but may be symptomatic of boys' rejection of an academic path to success or choice to pursue employment instead of continuing education. It may also be the fulfillment of a teacher's low expectations. Experiments have shown that teachers can be swayed into believing the inferiority of students based on categorical affiliation (Rosenthal, 1987). In turn, teachers' gender bias can lead to poorer performance for boys in their early literacy development (Palardy, 1998).

Children internalize expectations about gender at an early age and these lessons have implications for their learning and academic trajectories. A study of expectant parents (Grieshaber, 1998) underscored the desire for male children to carry on the family name as well as male responsibility within the family. Even before they were born, these idealized sons were expected to play hard, be competitive, and enjoy the rugged outdoors, and hardly expected to display a bookish fervor for reading. Expectations of conformity to gender roles increase as children enter school. Recent calls for the integration of gender equity in preschool classrooms highlight the problems both boys and girls will face, academically and socially, if they remain immersed in gender-typed classroom environments (Marshall, Robeson & Keefe, 1999). Even as classroom materials for early education become less dominated by images of boys and more evenly inclusive of images of girls, stereotyped images of boys (e.g., as aggressive, argumentative, competitive) are still prevalent in early reading materials and even more so in books geared toward older children (Evans & Davies, 2000).

The progression of stereotypical masculine images that become more evident in children's books across grade levels parallels the process by which boys develop masculine identity. Studies suggest that as boys enter middle school there is greater gender intensification and differences in sex role attitudes increase (Galambos, Almeida & Petersen, 1990). It is conceivable that gender-bifurcated patterns of literacy training (Millard, 1997) may contribute to the discrepancy between girls' greater proclivity to reading and boys' apparent disinterest (Hall & Coles, 1997), and thus may have implications for boys' academic engagement and achievement.

This chapter investigates how gendered messages and practices in early literacy training may be linked not only to boys' literacy skills but also to their attitudes toward reading, literacy practices, and their academic achievement during middle school. We chose to focus on these questions while collecting data for a study on literacy. Among numerous visits to children at home with their families and at school with their teachers and peers, one particular interaction stood out. A young single mother of two boys, ages 5 and 3, took a break between book reading activities with her older son (the participant in our study) to remark on literacy practices with her boys. She told us that her younger son "doesn't really like to be read to" so she "doesn't do that with him." Although this boy was only three years old, he was given substantial leeway in making decisions that could have critical implications for his educational future. His mother did not consider his dislike of reading unusual or cause for concern. As we reflected upon this mother's offhand remark, we became increasingly interested in how the process by which young children become readers and begin to develop relationships with text might be influenced by gender.

Specifically, our analysis begins with an examination of differences between boys' and girls' early language and literacy ability and later reading engagement and achievement during middle school. Next, we consider three factors that may contribute to boys' literacy skills, their attitudes toward reading (e.g., their beliefs about reading, how they feel about reading), their literary practices (e.g., what they like to read, whether they choose to read in their free time), and their academic achievement. The first factor concerns the distinct patterns in preschool age boys' and girls' cognitive experiences of and sexposure to early book reading. The second factor relates to the social-emotional experiences of preschool literacy practices such as how mothers engage preschool boys and girls during reading activities. These activities might influence the child's conception of reading as a masculine or feminine activity. The third factor considers ways in which boys are socialized toward male gender roles that often emphasize physical over intellectual activities.

Sample and Procedures

Participants were drawn from a sample of ethnically diverse low-income middle school students who have participated in the Home-School Study of Language and Literacy Development at the Harvard Graduate School of Education since they were in preschool. This longitudinal research project was originally designed to study precursors to language and literacy development and the influence of the home and of the school on language and literacy development (Dickinson & Tabors, 1991, 2001; Snow, 1991; Snow & Tabors, 1993). As the participants have grown, the research focus has expanded to include investigations of social and psychological components of development that influence academic success.

All 83 participants in the original sample were Head Start eligible (i.e., having household incomes at or below the poverty line) when they began the study at three years of age and were initially recruited from preschool sites across the Northeast rather than from a single school. Out of the original sample, 22 boys and 32 girls completed the 7th grade testing and interview protocol, comprising the core analytic sample for most of the analyses conducted for this chapter. The majority of the participants identified as White (67%), while the remainder of the sample identified as African American (21%), Latino (5%), and bi-racial (7%). Of the original sample, 32% came from homes with single mothers and 39% came from homes where the family received Aid to Families with Dependent Children (AFDC). Over the years, many of the participants' circumstances improved due to changes in their mothers' employment, education, and marital status. Although the level of attrition is relatively high, a review of the sample by year showed that the group characteristics, including the racial composition, of the participants were relatively stable. However, African American boys dropped out in significant numbers, thus limiting our ability to draw any conclusions based on racial or ethnic affiliation.

Data from ten years of longitudinal study were evaluated, including: observational data from child-mother dyads engaged in literacy activities collected when the participants were 4 years old, qualitative interview data collected when the participants were in 6th and 7th grade, and standardized assessments of language and literacy ability and achievement during elementary and middle school. Our analyses focuses in particular on differences between boys' and girls' performance, from kindergarten through 7th grade, on various measures of language and literacy skills, as indicated by standardized tests as well as maternal reports and observations of home supports for early literacy. We also analyzed teachers' evaluations and participants' self-reports of literacy engagement during middle school. Depending on the year in which data were collected, our sample size ranged from 54 to 72 children. Our primary interest was to compare boys and girls on their ability, early literacy exposure, adolescent literacy practices and motivation for engaging in those practices, and subsequent academic achievement. Table 16.1 provides an overview of the measures used in this analysis and their administration schedule.

Results

Assessment of Gender Differences in Ability and Achievement

To assess differences between boys' and girls' language and literacy ability over the course of the study, we used the Peabody Picture Vocabulary Test (PPVT) (Dunn & Dunn, 1981), a popular standardized test of receptive vocabulary skill that has been shown to be strongly related to intelligence testing. In general, we found no significant difference between boys and girls, though boys scored slightly higher on the PPVT at each year of testing. Exposure to new words, especially vocabulary that is out of the ordinary, is a critical factor in children's language development (Tabors, Beals & Weizman, 2001). Vocabulary, as measured by PPVT scores, was highly correlated with exposure to "rare word" use in the home (measured during preschool home visit observations), thus boys' higher scores may reflect the fact that boys were exposed to more rare word use at home than girls ($t = 2.59$, p [less than] .01). Related analyses have shown mothers to engage with sons in significantly more science-type talk that includes rare words, which is related to better outcomes in boys' results of tests of science literacy (Tenenbaum et al., under review). It seems that mothers may provide rich language experiences for boys and girls in gender-specific domains and this may have implications for later gender differences in specific subject areas. Nevertheless, boys and girls in the sample appeared to be cognitively matched at early childhood in preparation for language and literacy development. In fact, boys even appear to have a slight advantage that may be related to the type of talk they are exposed to at home.

Although girls and boys were closely matched on measures of language and literacy ability throughout elementary school, gender differences, particularly in performance and academic achievement, began to appear

TABLE 16.1
Description of Activities and Assessments Used in the Analysis
by Participants and Years Administered

Activity/Assessment	Description of Activity/Assessment	Participants Administered	Year(s)
Peabody Picture Vocabulary Test— PPVT (Dunn & Dunn, 1981)	Standardized assessment of receptive vocabulary, as child identifies pictures that represent vocabulary words.	Child	Kindergarten, 2nd, 4th, 6th, and 7th grades
Book Reading	Task conducted during . home visits where mother reads to her child two books supplied by researchers (*The Very Hungry Caterpillar* and *What's Next Baby Bear*) and one book of the child's choice	Mother and child	Children age 4
Mother Interview	Interview conducted during home visits including questions about frequency of book reading and number of people who read to child.	Mother	Children were 3, 4, and 5 years old
Mealtime Recording	Conversation recorded by family during a meal time, analyzed for use of rare words.	Mother and child (could also include siblings and other family members)	Children were 3, 4, and 5 years old
Child Interview	Interview conducted during annual school visit including questions about literacy, frequency of book reading, and enjoyment of book reading, and child's educational future.	Child	Children were in 6th and 7th grades
Teacher-Child Rating Scale—T-CRS (Hightower et al., 1986)	Questions posed to teachers about students' motivation, work habits, and attention.	English Teacher	Children were in 6th and 7th grades
Rochester Assessment Package for Schools— RAPS (Connell, 1996)	Questions posed to students during annual school visit where students rated their effort, attention, and emotional engagement in school.	Child	Children were in 6th and 7th grades

in middle school. For instance, by the time they reached 7th grade, boys were less likely than girls to report liking to read and tended to have lower grades in English. Boys were also rated by their 6th and 7th grade teachers as being less well behaved and as acting out more than the girls ($t = -1.82, p < .08; t = 2.31, p < .03$, respectively), and as having more learning difficulties than girls ($t = 1.83, p < .07$), on average. The teachers' reports also suggest that boys were less motivated to achieve, had worse work habits, and were less able to concentrate and follow directions than girls. In addition, the participants' self-reports in sixth grade showed boys as being less engaged than girls ($t = -1.93, p < .06$). Studies with national samples similarly show that boys are less likely than girls to hold positive attitudes about recreational reading, even when controlling for reading ability, and that these differences begin to appear as early as first grade and increase as children get older (McKenna, 2001; McKenna, Kear & Ellsworth, 1995). As these performance and achievement trends did not appear to be related to ability, we sought to explore how early literacy exposure and later literacy practices might reflect the boys' ongoing socialization toward stereotypical masculine roles. Specifically, we examined: (1) cognitive experiences in preschool literacy practices, (2) socio-emotional experiences of preschool literacy practices, and (3) boys' experiences of gender socialization.

Cognitive Experiences of Preschool Literacy Practices

In an effort to explain differences in adolescent academic achievement, we tested for distinct patterns in preschool age boys' and girls' cognitive experiences of and exposure to early book reading. We found no significant difference in mothers' reports of preschool daughters' and sons' overall frequency of exposure to book reading; boys and girls were reported to have equal access to books in the home. However, there did appear to be differences in the cognitive feedback that mothers provided to girls and boys during activities in which mothers and their children read three books together, namely *The Very Hungry Caterpillar* and *What's Next Baby Bear?* and a third book of the child's choice. Specifically, analyses of mother-child interactions during home visits when the children were four years old revealed gender differences in two particularly important variables that are related to later literacy development. The first variable that emerged from these interactions, named "immediate talk," refers to talk directly related to the book as it is being read. The second variable, named "non-immediate talk," refers to talk that links topics in the book to the outside world and to past experiences, and draws on general knowledge. The use of non-immediate talk has since been found to be especially critical for fostering comprehension because it helps children begin to make sense of the story as it relates to their everyday lives (see De Temple, 2001).

Our analyses indicate that mothers of boys tended to provide less immediate and non-immediate comments during the book reading activities, as compared with mothers of girls ($t = -1.68$, $p < .10$). Mothers of boys also tended to request less immediate information and non-immediate information from their sons ($t = -2.00$, $p < .05$), produce fewer utterances, and engage in less overall book talk with their sons during the book reading activities ($t = -1.69$, $p < .10$). Likewise, boys appeared to be less verbal than girls during these activities ($t = -1.66$, $p < .10$). It is conceivable that these differences in the ways in which mothers engage and respond during early childhood reading activities may contribute to the differences we observed between the girls' and boys' literacy performance and achievement later in middle school.

Socio-emotional Experiences of Preschool Literacy Practices

A second factor that may contribute to the gender differences in literacy performance and achievement is the socio-emotional experience of early literacy practices. Specifically, we found that in addition to quantitative and qualitative differences in the children's cognitive experiences of preschool literacy practices, the mothers in our study tended to interact differently with girls and boys during the book reading activities that we observed when the participants were four years old.[1] Although virtually all of the mothers in the study reported regular and consistent book reading with their children and there was no significant difference between frequency of these practices for girls and boys, reports indicate that boys tended to be read to less often and by a lesser variety of people, as compared to girls. Analysis of transcripts from book reading observations in the home follow similar trends, with boys getting less exposure to talk about books, though these differences are not significant. The transcripts also provide greater evidence of a successfully integrated reading routine for girls than for boys. In sum, it seems that while all of the mothers in the study viewed reading with their children as important, they nevertheless appeared to place less emphasis on this activity for the boys than for the girls. We hypothesize that such differences may ultimately influence the importance boys place on reading, particularly if they come to view reading as a feminine activity.

In order to illustrate ways that children might be exposed to reading routines that are gender-specific, we present transcripts from parent-child dyads. For instance, during our preschool home visits when mothers were asked to read *The Very Hungry Caterpillar* to their child "just as they would normally do if the researchers were not present," several boys resisted the activity. For example, one boy said, "no because I already read that one before." Another boy had to be cajoled into sitting still as his mother recounted his protest about a school experience earlier in the week, "Mommy they read me that dumb old caterpillar book again." In fact, several mothers had to negotiate seating arrangements with their sons, with some boys stubbornly insisting on sitting or standing some distance away from the mother and the book, at the far end of the couch or on the floor or opposite mom with an upside-down view of the book. Even boys such as Ethan,[2] who enjoyed being read to, were playfully defiant during this activity.

> *Mother:* Do you want me to read this to you?
> *Ethan:* [laughs]
> *Mother:* I'm not reading it to your toes!
> *Ethan:* [laughs again—he is lying down with his feet toward mother]
> *Mother:* Come up here with me! Look at this!

Moreover, 6 of the 22 boys had difficulty even beginning the activity because they were distracted by the presence of toys brought to the visit for another activity (see Katz, 2001). One boy exclaimed, "I just wanna play with the toys, that's what I wanna do. I see the bag—let me grab it." The boys' resistance to the reading activity required redirection and negotiation from researchers and mothers: "Well, how about I read you this story first, okay?" Incidents such as these suggest the lack of appeal that this reading task, and perhaps reading in general, had for these boys, particularly when other activities were available.

In contrast, field notes indicated a readiness of many of the girls to participate, as they settled on their mothers' laps to hear the familiar tale of *The Very Hungry Caterpillar.* Girls were also more commonly and more dramatically praised during this activity as their mothers engaged in questioning about the book's plot and helped daughters to decode words:

> *Mother:* What do you think happened?
> *Monica:* He growed and he growed into a butterfly.
> *Mother:* Jeez, you are smart!
> *Monica:* He was a beautiful butterfly!
> *Mother:* How did you know that?
> *Monica:* Because I [laughs] have it at my school!
> *Mother:* Oh, you're smart!

> *Mother:* Go ahead, look at it and tell me what it says if you can. [as she points to the title]
> *Emily:* Caterpillar!
> *Mother:* The Very . . . [speaking slowly]
> *Emily:* Hungry Caterpillar.
> *Mother:* Very good!

Boys similarly received praise for pointing out the "little egg" and "watermelon" and so forth:

> *Mother:* And what is that? [as she points at the picture]
> *Greg:* A sun.
> *Mother:* Right. He started to look for some food. What is he doing?
> *Greg:* [tries to turn page]
> *Mother:* No no no no no. I didn't touch this yet.

> *Mother:* And one slice of . . . What is this? [points to picture]
> *Sean:* Um . . . [throws arms up and looks at researcher, then hesitates]
> *Mother:* Watermelon.
> *Sean:* Watermelon!
> *Mother:* Good!

However, such praise was sparse and appeared to reflect lower expectations, as shown in the second example in which Sean's mother soon provides him with the answer.

Through these visits that allowed us to watch mothers interact with their children at home, we were able to get a sense of the processes and experiences of book reading in the participants' everyday family routines. There was substantial overlap in boys' and girls' experiences that contributed to language and literacy development. But there was also evidence of subtle patterns of variation that foreshadow gender differences in attitudes toward reading and reading achievement later in life. As it turned out, the academically successful students in our study tended to be girls who practiced and enjoyed both school-related and recreational reading, and have done so from an early age.

Boys' Experiences of Gender Socialization

In addition to cognitive and socio-emotional experiences of early literacy practices, boys' socialization toward male gender roles also appeared to influence their literacy engagement and achievement in middle school. By middle school, one-fourth of the children in the sample had been retained and one-third of the children had received some kind of special services (ranging from reading tutoring to special education placement). However, boys in the sample were no more likely than girls to be at risk for school failure based on these particular markers. While fears for these children's futures are evenly spread between boys and girls, we were surprised by individual cases among the boys in the sample who were in trouble. For instance, whereas girls showing patterns of risk by middle school had exhibited consistent markers of concern throughout their time in our study, boys at risk in middle school included several of the brightest boys in the study.

For example, Ethan, who was especially advanced in his early language and literacy skills, and whose parents and teachers provided strong support and had high expectations for schooling, began to withdraw from academics in sixth grade. When asked whether he thought he'd go on to college, he replied, "I don't really want to. My parents are gonna try and make me." By seventh grade, his aspiration to become an actor was well established and he had already begun going on auditions. The only thing he saw standing in the way of his career was "only my parents . . . um, by saying, like, 'I don't think you should take this job,' you know, or you know, 'you're not paying as much attention on like schoolwork . . . as you are on your acting career,' you know." This boy, who once had engaged wholeheartedly in his school work, no longer saw much value in it.

Ethan, who was also identified by teachers and researchers as a boy of high academic ability and a precocious reader in early elementary school, explained his loss of interest in reading matter-of-factly, "basically (be)cause I used to read a lot and now I just, I just have more stuff to do, ya know I've got a more complex life, I guess." His standardized test scores on the PPVT measure consistently revealed that his cognitive abilities far exceeded that of other children in the study, even as his grades dropped and he was consequently referred to school counselors. There are a number of reasons for Ethan's downward academic trajectory, including his taking on a more conventional masculine role. What we witnessed in his development over ten years was a change in the value he placed on his literacy skills that corresponded to various clues about his development of a masculine identity. Being a better reader than other students in his class gave him high status in early elementary school, as he gained positive recognition and attention by his teachers. However, this did not benefit him—nor any other boy—in the same way in middle school when simply being smart was more a cause for ridicule than for popularity. As a teenager, Ethan's interview narratives focus on his independence from his parents, his isolation from classmates, and his tough stance against school authorities and peer bullies. The fact that he liked to "read a lot" and from a variety of genres had narrowed down to an interest in reading scripts for acting jobs.

In their seventh grade interviews, 6 of the 22 boys reported that they read "a lot," and when asked why, simply stated that it was an activity they did often. Similarly, the eight girls who reported reading "a lot" also equated it with liking to read a lot, but often provided more elaborate answers about why they liked to read: "I like adventures and stuff like to imagine things." "Because sometimes books are interesting and I just like finding out what the end is going to be." "It fills your mind with stuff, I don't know just gives you ideas." Whereas girls articulated the intellectual journey of reading, boys emphasized the action of reading. For example, in describing his enjoyment of reading, Peter explains:

> I like just to read, I usually read it aloud, or I'll read it on tape, and then I'll like read it to the tape and then I'll mark it, and then later on I'll listen to it over again, but I think reading's fun and it teaches you a lot. I'll like have, um, well I usually use my dad's karaoke machine, I'll talk into the microphone. And I'll read the whole of it and I'll record it. And later on I'll play it back.

By making reading a more physically active process, Peter transformed what is usually a solitary and calm activity into boisterous entertainment.

On the other end of the spectrum, both boys and girls who disliked reading were equally likely to describe it as "boring!" However, boys were more vigorous in their responses:

Casey: It's not fun.

Conrad: It's just too hard to read. It's boring. I'd rather play video games.

Jack: I hate it. It's boring. It like stinks. You sit there with your eyes halfway shut.

Justin: They're just boring. They just like don't make sense. They have no adventure.

Just having to talk about reading was a grim prospect for Jack:

Jack: Is this all you do is ask like a ton of boring questions?

Interviewer: Yeah. It's my job.

Jack: (speaking very slowly and imitating the voice of an old man) Why? I'd—rather—be—in—class—listenin'—to—my—teacher—when—lightning—strikes.

Another reason that boys gave for not reading, which the girls in our sample did not mention, is that it was one of many things in their lives for which they were too busy. Brian, who received strong home support for literacy and chose advanced books for his pleasure reading (*Narrative Biography of Frederick Douglas*), told us, "I hate reading. I don't like to read books. I don't have the time. I don't really take the time to read either." As they moved through adolescence, the boys seemed to feel that they needed to shoulder more serious responsibilities (such as preparing for employment), while leaving the activities of their childhood behind (such as formal schooling). As boys' lives begin to be filled with activities outside of school, class requirements seemed oppressive and uninspiring as Brad put it, "Well because now all I'm really reading is like school books and most of them are pretty boring so, like I spend time reading those so I really don't have time to read anything else." His reading of Hemingway's *Old Man and the Sea* was dry compared with *Bart Simpson's Guide to Life* and *Freddie Kruger's Tales of Terror*. Just as there appeared to be gender differences in reading practices, it also seemed that children developed reading preferences that are bifurcated by gender.

Although these boys typically regarded reading as a narrow pursuit that is academic in nature and necessarily dry, there was also evidence in their interview narratives that their attitudes toward reading could vary across different genres of reading materials such that reading mystery or horror stories could be thought of as fun and therefore not really "reading," especially when compared to reading assigned texts. In his 6th grade interview, James suggests a distinction between genres:

> *James:* I don't like to read.
> *Interviewer:* You just don't, you just really don't like to read?
> *James:* No, because usually the books that teachers give us to read are boring.
> *Interviewer:* Mmhm. What about reading on your own?
> *James:* That's a much different story.

When the interviewer pressed James to talk about how much he liked to read school books versus books he chose on his own, he still insisted that he didn't like to read much because the books he picked were "usually about four hundred pages!" James also pointed out that he was "not a very beginner reader," indicating some satisfaction with his skill level, as he talked at length about his delight with *Interview with a Vampire* (all the while playing with his fake vampire teeth).

In fact, we heard contradictions between their attitudes about reading and the practices of reading throughout the interviews with the boys. Even as boys expressed disdain for reading, they described books that they enjoyed reading, books that reflected stereotypically masculine adventure and horror stories. For instance, one boy described how "boring" reading was because it "has no adventure" and then talked in detail about the book he was currently enjoying:

> *Justin:* um *The Crossing* . . . um it's about this immigrant in Mexico. And he's going North to get a job. Because he's poor. And he lives in a cardboard box. And he has to cross, is it the Rio Grande? Yeah.

Another boy, Jack, told us that he "hate[s]" reading because it "stinks," but then went on to tell about how "I read a couple *Goosebumps*. Those are easy, I finish those in an hour." He also recalled finishing *It* by Stephen King, which would not necessarily be an easy read for this boy in special education placement. Even boys who claimed they did not like to read, and actually avoided reading books, were avid fans of sports magazines

(*Sports Illustrated, Skateboarding World*) and admitted to reading biographies of sports stars.

Clearly, the discrepancy between the boys' claims that they do not like to read and their apparent enjoyment of reading on some occasions is linked to some extent to the genres of their reading materials. However, the boys' contradictory responses also raise the question of whether heightened pressures to accommodate masculine stereotypes in middle school may lead boys to take on a tough guy attitude toward reading and other school-related activities. For instance, Paul, who was identified early on for special education services, described how difficulties with reading could lead to ridicule from classmates (undermining his dignity and thus perhaps his masculinity):

> Well, first of all, books you know, they got a lot of big words, some books have little words, but you have to get used to reading. I just don't, we don't read a lot in class. Because if I read in a class, everyone, they start laughing if you make a mistake on a word.

While boys may enjoy being the class clown to gain attention, and may be unconcerned with calling out a potentially wrong answer (Orenstein, 1994; Spencer, Porche & Tolman, under review), that is quite different from being laughed at or labeled as "dumb." Boys may be sensitive about the way they are perceived by peers regarding their identity as readers and therefore try to avoid being teased for making mistakes, like Paul, or picked on for being a good reader, like Ethan, or simply for reading too much or reading girls' books. Viewed from a sociocultural perspective, boys' positive engagement in literacy experiences is embedded in masculine socialization, so that their connection to reading is bound to masculine hobbies and activities. As Smith and Wilhelm (2002) found, boys reported more enjoyment and interest in reading books and magazines unrelated to school assignments, on topics such as sports, cars, adventure and so on. Reading was identified as valuable in the sense that it allowed the boys to gain immediate information, such as sports scores and other news, or to solve problems, such as providing hints for winning at video games.

Although the boys in our sample appeared to have different tastes in reading materials and possibly even a different orientation to reading, as compared to girls, they were nonetheless engaged in literacy practices in ways that reflected both masculine interests and the fact that other activities take priority over reading in their busy and complex lives. The risk for boys is therefore not lower reading ability but their narrow and formal interpretation of acceptable reading practices. The academic reading that the boys in this low-income sample reject is an activity that is essential for school success and adult reading proficiency (Snow, 2002). While educators might appreciate any kind of reading that a child does outside of school, limited exposure and resistance to a wider variety of materials connected to reading proficiency may undermine academic achievement (Worthy, Moorman & Turner, 1999), even as it firmly reinforces a masculine identity. As Brad explains, "I don't really like the classics and stuff but some of them are okay like *Robin Hood* and *Treasure Island*. But I mostly like, just like adventure and uh mysteries and horror stories." School success and transition to higher education is dependent upon proficiency in comprehension skills across subject areas. Boys, like Brad, who only want to read adventure stories, also deny themselves opportunities to improve their literacy skills; their masculine identity is not likely to be challenged by using this strategy, but neither is their intellectual ability.

Pathways and Meanings

The goal of this study was to learn about the development of children's reading practices in and out of school, and particularly ways in which early interpersonal literacy practices at home may contribute to later gender differences in reading practices and academic achievement among the participants in our study. In addition to highlighting differences in the interpersonal aspects of early literacy practices, an analysis of the interview data also revealed differences in the intrapersonal processes, such as the ways in which individuals respond to various genres of reading materials. For this low-income sample we found that boys and girls started out equally matched on language and literacy ability and early academic achievement measures. This suggests that boys are not innately poor readers any more than girls are innately good at reading. We also found that boys and girls received a similar frequency of exposure to early reading activities. Thus, based on evidence of stable cognitive ability, we would not expect differences in later academic achievement.

However, differences do appear beyond early childhood that seem to reflect gender socialization, which may be inadvertently linked to the *qual-*

ity of literacy experiences for boys and girls. For instance, a closer look at the early childhood data suggests the subtle beginnings of a divergence in approach to reading with girls compared to boys. During the preschool book reading activity, boys spent less time talking with their mothers about the books they were reading and mothers requested less information of them compared to girls. This pattern of talking about books may be related to boys' middle school interviews, in which they tend to elaborate less on the process of reading, compared to girls. This divergence may be exacerbated by the internalization of masculine and feminine ideologies which has been found to intensify in adolescence (Galambos, Almeida & Petersen, 1990). This would explain the growing disparity in literacy engagement and achievement for boys and girls as they move through adolescence.

As much as they can be enjoyable social activities between parent and child, early book reading experiences also establish a routine that prepares the child for later classroom practices meant to foster reading proficiency. Examples from preschool transcripts of boys and girls in this low-income sample suggest that early literacy practices for boys may include less encouragement and help with decoding, as well as less active questioning and discussion about text, that promotes understanding and prepares them for later academic success. Based on our study, mothers' experiences of reading with boys do not seem to provide the same sense of day-to-day routine or degree of challenge as with girls. In adolescence, the absence in school of reading material that is appealing to boys may also reinforce beliefs about reading as a feminine activity, especially if materials that appeal to girls (such as fictional narratives which include attention to the emotional lives and relationships of characters) are plentiful in the curriculum (Worthy, Moorman & Turner, 1999).

Contrary to recent popular discourse that attributes boys' academic struggles to attention paid to girls' issues, data from our study offer a much more complex and perhaps puzzling story of boys' trajectories of achievement. In our sample, statistical tests of measures of language, cognitive ability, and home support of early literacy show no difference between boys and girls. Standardized assessments of language and literacy ability continue to show no difference between boys and girls as they progress through school—both for students on successful and less successful (e.g., special education placement and retention) trajectories. However, by middle school, significant differences begin to appear in teachers' assessments of boys as being less interested in learning and in having more discipline problems. These emergent differences may reflect messages about masculinity that may not directly imply a lack of emphasis on literacy, but rather, promulgate encouragement of other activities that are more reflective of conventional masculine activities, for instance, play, sports, and action. As Eder, Evans, and Parker (1995) point out in their ethnography of middle school, popular boys tend to be those who participate in extracurricular sports activities, who are seen as tough and competitive. Reading, which is considered a more demure activity, may be seen by boys as being incompatible with this desired image. In a culture of adolescence that does not value academic achievement, and in a culture of masculinity that does not value reading, boys like Ethan, who are intelligent, may become discouraged in their academic pursuits, and boys like Paul, who are self-conscious about making mistakes, may, in their efforts to avoid being ridiculed, miss opportunities to develop their reading skills.

The early routines parents establish in reading to their sons may not communicate as strong an emphasis on literacy, and by extension, academic success in language arts, as that which girls receive. This is not to say that boys are not encouraged to do well in school. Rather, there are stronger expectations that they do well in academic domains that are traditionally masculine, such as math and science, or excel in vocational programs that provide job skills. Similarly, while boys may not have less exposure to reading, the choice of reading material that is narrowly geared toward masculine ideals and reinforces stereotypical masculine behavior seems less likely to enhance a balanced set of skills necessary for academic success.

Our educational system goes to great lengths to establish itself as gender neutral, yet responses to reading and math difficulties, whether conscious or unconscious, are quite different and may ultimately put boys and girls at risk in various academic domains. For instance, much attention is paid to the remediation of reading difficulties common for boys, such as dyslexia, but not to the remediation of math learning difficulties common for girls, such as dyscalculia. In both cases, the potential influence of gender role expectation should be considered seriously in our diagnoses and subsequent interventions in these arenas. Parents and educators seriously committed to the preparation of children's success in school and beyond do students a disservice by attending to their needs without consideration of the greater social context in which learning takes place. Gender is one of the most imposing aspects of this social context but remains relatively under-explored. Through increased investigation, gender may provide a lens with which to understand how and why learning may or may not take place and may serve as a starting point for engaging boys in reading activities that are vital to their success in an increasingly information-based society.

NOTES

Support for this research was provided by the William T. Grant Foundation. Thanks to Patton Tabors for her helpful suggestions in the preparation of this chapter.

1. Activities were planned with mothers because of their role as primary caretaker in each of the families we visited; in one-third of the families, they were the sole caretaker. We do not suggest that mothers should be judged as exclusively responsible for reading socialization. We would argue that fathers play as much a part in gendered messages for children through their presence and absence during literacy activities; however, we do not have observational data with male caretakers.

2. Pseudonyms are used to ensure confidentiality of participants.

REFERENCES

Askew, S. & Ross, C. (1988). *Boys don't cry: Boys and sexism in education.* Milton Keynes: Open University Press.

Bus, A. G. (2001). Parent-child book reading through the lens of attachment theory. In L. Verhoeven & C. Snow (Eds.), *Literacy and motivation: Reading engagement in individuals and groups* (pp. 39–53). Mahwah, NJ: Lawrence Erlbaum Associates.

Bus, A. G., van IJzendoorn, M. H. & Pellegrini, A. D. (1995). Joint book reading makes for success in learning to read: A meta-analysis on intergenerational transmission of literacy. *Review of Educational Research, 65,* 1–21.

Connell, J. P. (1996). *Rochester assessment package for schools.* Rochester, NY: Institute for Research and Reform in Education.

De Temple, J. M. (2001). Parents and children reading books together. In D. K. Dickinson & P. O. Tabors (Eds.), *Beginning literacy with language* (pp. 31–51). Baltimore, MD: Paul H. Brookes Publishing.

Dickinson, D. K. & Tabors, P. O. (1991). Early literacy: Linkages between home, school and literacy achievement at age five. *Journal of Research in Childhood Education, 6,* 30–46.

Dickinson, D. K. & Tabors, P. O. (Eds.). (2001). *Beginning literacy with language: Young children learning at home and school.* Baltimore, MD: Paul H. Brookes Publishing.

Dunn, L. M. & Dunn, L. M. (1981). *Peabody Picture Vocabulary Test-Revised (PPVT-R)*. Circle Pines, MN: American Guidance Service.

Eder, D., Evans, C. & Parker, S. (1995). *School talk: Gender and adolescent culture.* New Brunswick, NJ: Rutgers University Press.

Evans, L. & Davies, K. (2000). No sissy boys here: A content analysis of the representation of masculinity in elementary school reading textbooks. *Sex Roles, 42* (3–4), 255–270.

Galambos, N. L., Almeida, D. M. & Petersen, A. C. (1990). Masculinity, femininity, and sex role attitudes in early adolescence: Exploring gender intensification. *Child Development, 61,* 1905–1914.

Gee, J. P. (2001). A sociocultural perspective on early literacy development. In S. B. Neuman & D. K. Dickinson (Eds.), *Handbook of early literacy research* (pp. 30–42). New York: Guilford Press.

Grieshaber, S. (1998). Constructing the gendered infant. In N. Yelland (Ed.), *Perspectives of gender in early childhood* (pp. 16–35). London: Routledge.

Gurian, M. (1999). *A fine young man: What parents, mentors and educators can do to shape adolescent boys into exceptional men.* New York: Jeremy P. Tarcher/Putnam.

Hall, C. & Coles, M. (1997). Gendered readings: Helping boys develop as critical readers. *Gender and Education, 9* (1), 61–68.

Hightower, A. D., Work, W. C., Cowen, E. L., Lotyczewski, B. S., Spinell, A. P., Guare, J. C. & Rohrbeck, C. A. (1986). The Teacher-Child Rating Scale: A brief objective measure of elementary children's school problem behaviors and competencies. *School Psychology Review, 15* (3), 393–409.

Katz, J. R. (2001). Playing at home. In D. K. Dickinson & P. O. Tabors (Eds.), *Beginning literacy with language: Young children learning at home and school* (pp. 53–73). Baltimore, MD: Paul H. Brookes Publishing.

Kimmel, M. S. (2000). *The gendered society.* New York: Oxford University Press.

MacLeod, J. (1987, 1995). *Ain't no makin' it: Aspirations and attainment in a low-income neighborhood.* Boulder, CO: Westview Press.

Marshall, N. L., Robeson, W. W. & Keefe, N. (1999). Gender equity in early childhood education. *Young Children, 54* (4), 9–13.

Martinez, L. (1998). Gender equity policies and early childhood education. In N. Yelland (Ed.), *Gender in early childhood* (pp. 115–130). London: Routledge.

McKenna, M. C. (2001). Development of reading attitudes. In L. Verhoeven & C. Snow (Eds.), *Literacy and motivation: Reading engagement in individuals and groups* (pp. 135–158). Mahwah, NJ: Lawrence Erlbaum Associates.

McKenna, M. C., Kear, D. J. & Ellsworth, R. A. (1995). Children's attitudes towards reading: A national survey. *Reading Research Quarterly, 30* (4), 934–956.

Meisels, J. H. & Liaw, F. (1993). Failure in grade: Do retained students catch up? *Journal of Educational Research, 87* (2), 69–77.

Millard, E. (1997). *Differently literate: Boys, girls, and the schooling of literacy.* London: Falmer Press.

Orenstein, P. (1994). *Schoolgirls.* New York: Doubleday.

Palardy, M. J. (1998). The effects of teachers' expectations on children's literacy development. *Reading Improvement, 35* (4), 184–186.

Pollack, W. (1998). *Real boys: Rescuing our sons from the myths of boyhood.* New York: Random House.

Rosenthal, R. (1987). "Pygmalion" effects: Existence, magnitude, and social importance. *Educational Researcher, 16* (9), 37–41.

Rury, J. L. (1991). *Education and women's work: Female schooling and the division of labor in urban America, 1870–1930.* Albany: State University of New York Press.

Smith, M. W. & Wilhelm, J. D. (2002). *"Reading don't fix no Chevys": Literacy in the lives of young men.* Portsmouth, NH: Heinemann.

Snow, C. E. (1991). The theoretical basis for relationships between language and literacy development. *Journal of Research in Childhood Education, 6* (Fall/Winter), 5–10.

Snow, C. E. (2002). *Reading for understanding: Toward a Rand program in reading comprehension.* Santa Monica, CA: RAND.

Snow, C. E., Burns, M. S. & Griffin, P. (Eds.). (1998). *Preventing reading difficulties in young children.* Washington, DC: National Academy of Sciences—National Research Council.

Snow, C. E. & Tabors, P. O. (1993). Language skills that relate to literacy development. In B. Spodek & O. Saracho (Eds.), *Yearbook in early childhood education, Vol. 4.* New York: Teachers College Press.

Spencer, R., Porche, M. & Tolman, D. L. (under review). We have come a long way . . . maybe: New challenges for gender equity.

Tabors, P. O., Beals, D. E. & Weizman, Z. O. (2001). "You know what oxygen is?" Learning new words at home. In D. K. Dickinson & P. O. Tabors (Eds.), *Beginning literacy with language* (pp. 93–110). Baltimore, MD: Paul H. Brookes Publishing.

Teale, W. H. (1984). Reading to young children: Its significance for literacy development. In H. Goelman, A. A. Oberg & F. Smith (Eds.), *Awakening to literacy: The University of Victoria Symposium on Children's Response to a Literate Environment: Literacy before schooling* (pp. 110–122). Exeter, NH: Heinemann.

Tenenbaum, H. R., Snow, C. E., Roach, K. & Kurland, B. (under review). Talking and reading science: Gender and developmental differences.

U.S. Department of Education. National Center for Education Statistics (2000). *Trends in educational equity of girls and women, NCES 2000-030,* by Y. Bae, S. Choy, C. Geddes, J. Sable, and T. Snyder. Washington, DC.

U.S. Department of Education. National Center for Education Statistics (2001).

Dropout rates in the United States: 2000, NCES 2002-114, by P. Kaufman, M. N. Alt, and C. Chapman. Washington, DC.

Willis, P. (1977). *Learning to labor: How working class kids get working class jobs.* New York: Columbia University Press.

Worthy, J., Moorman, M. & Turner, M. (1999). What Johnny likes to read is hard to find in school. *Reading Research Quarterly, 34* (1), 12–27.

About the Contributors

Xinyin Chen is Associate Professor at the Department of Psychology, University of Western Ontario. His research focuses on the cross-cultural study of children and adolescents' socio-emotional functioning (e.g., shyness-inhibition, aggression, and social competence), peer groups and networks, and family influences. With his international collaborators, he has been conducting several large-scale, longitudinal projects in Canada, China, Brazil, India, and Italy.

Judy Y. Chu, Ed.D. (co-editor) is a lecturer at the Program in Human Biology at Stanford University. She is the lead investigator of Learning What Boys Know, a multi-site research project examining boys' relationships and boys' psychosocial development during adolescence and early childhood. She is currently completing a book on boys' relational ways of being.

Gilberto Q. Conchas is Assistant Professor of Education at Harvard Graduate School of Education. His research concentrates on the sociocultural processes within the school context that structure variations in educational opportunity for low-income Latino, Asian American, and African American youth. A sociologist by training, his work focuses on social equity and urban schools, and aims to illuminate student voices as a means to make meaning of their lives in urban communities and schools.

Michael Cunningham, a developmental psychologist, is Associate Professor at Tulane University where he holds a joint appointment in the Department of Psychology and the African and African Diaspora Studies Program. His primary research interests include examining adolescent development in diverse contexts, particularly how self-perceptions influence the development of proactive and reactive coping styles among African

American adolescent males. Currently, he is examining the influence of context-specific perceptions on academic achievement orientation in African American youth.

Tricia Harmon is a doctoral student in Human Development and Psychology at Harvard University Graduate School of Education. Her doctoral research focuses on intimacy and violence in heterosexual relationships during adolescence.

Elena D. Jeffries received her doctorate in clinical psychology from New York University in 2002. Her dissertation used qualitative and quantitative methods to explore experiences of interpersonal trust among ethnic minority adolescents from low-income families. She currently works as a full-time clinician at the University of Medicine and Dentistry Partial Hospitalization Program for children and adolescents in Newark, New Jersey.

Violet Kaspar is Assistant Professor with the Department of Psychiatry, University of Toronto, and research scientist with the Centre for Addiction and Mental Health–Clarke Site. Her research program is focused on determinants of children's mental health and adjustment, particularly experiences of trauma exposure and social stress in racial or ethnic minorities.

Leighton Ku is a Senior Fellow in Health Policy at the Center on Budget and Policy Priorities, Washington, DC. Between 1991 and 1998, he was a co-principal investigator for the National Survey of Adolescent Males.

Stacey J. Lee is Associate Professor in the Department of Educational Policy Studies at the University of Wisconsin–Madison. She is the author of *Unraveling the Model Minority Stereotype: Listening to Asian American Youth.* Lee is currently completing a book, *(Re)Interpreting America: Hmong American High School Students in the Midwest.*

Leah Newkirk Meunier is a doctoral student in the Human Development and Family Sciences program at University of Texas at Austin.

Harold W. Neighbors, Ph.D., is Associate Professor and Associate Director for Research Training with the Center for Research on Ethnicity, Culture, and Health (CRECH) in the Department of Health Behavior and Health

Education in the School of Public Health at the University of Michigan. He is also Associate Director of the Program for Research on Black Americans (PRBA) at the Institute for Social Research, where he leads the Program's Mental Health Work Group. His research interests include ethnic and cultural influences on assessment of mental disorder, and informal and professional service utilization by African Americans.

Pedro A. Noguera is Professor in the Teaching and Learning Department at New York University. His research focuses on the ways in which schools respond to social and economic conditions within the urban environment. His latest book is *Confronting the Urban: How City Schools Can Respond to Social Inequality* (Teachers College Press).

Joseph H. Pleck is Professor of Human Development and Family Studies at the University of Illinois at Urbana-Champaign. He is Co-Principal Investigator for the National Survey of Adolescent Males, which monitors national trends in U.S. young men's fertility behavior and contraceptive use. His current research focuses on young men's development of stable romantic unions and on fatherhood. His books include *Men and Masculinity, The American Man, The Myth of Masculinity, The Impact of Work Schedules on the Family,* and *Working Wives/Working Husbands.*

Michelle V. Porche, Ed.D., is a data analyst for the Home-School Study of Language and Literacy Development at Harvard Graduate School of Education. Her work on the project includes the investigation of the cognitive and socio-emotional factors related to school achievement for young children and adolescents, as well as the long-term effects of maternal involvement at school and home on young children's academic achievement.

Desirée Baolian Qin-Hilliard is a doctoral candidate in Human Development and Psychology at Harvard Graduate School of Education. Her doctoral research examines gender dynamics in Chinese immigrant children's educational and psychosocial adaptation. Qin-Hilliard is the co-editor (with Marcelo Suárez-Orozco and Carola Suárez-Orozco) of the six-volume series titled *Interdisciplinary Perspectives on the New Immigration* and *The New Immigration Millennium Reader.* Qin-Hilliard is also the co-editor (with Marcelo Suárez-Orozco) of a forthcoming book on globalization and education.

Myra Rosen-Reynoso is a Doctoral Research Fellow at the Institute for Community Inclusion, Children's Hospital, Boston, Massachusetts. She is also a Ph.D. candidate at the Lynch School of Education, Boston College.

Stephanie J. Ross, M.A., is Project Director on the Home-School Study at Harvard Graduate School of Education.

Ritch C. Savin-Williams is Professor of Developmental and Clinical Psychology at Cornell University in the Department of Human Development. He teaches courses on gender and sexual minorities and adolescent sexuality. Savin-Williams has written six books on adolescent development, including, ". . . *And Then I Became Gay": Young Men's Stories* and *"Mom, Dad, I'm Gay": How Families Negotiate Coming Out.* He is currently writing a book reviewing what is currently known about sexual-minority youth and a book on growing up female with same-sex attractions. Savin-Williams is also a licensed clinical psychologist, with a primary sexual-minority adolescent and young adulthood clientele.

Daniel T. L. Shek (Ph.D., B.B.S., J.P.) is Professor in the Department of Social Work at The Chinese University of Hong Kong. His research interests include Chinese adolescent development, mental health and mental disorders, Chinese families, psychological assessment, substance abuse, program evaluation, and social science research methods.

Catherine E. Snow, Ph.D., is the Henry Lee Shattuck Professor of Education and Principal Investigator of the Home-School Study at Harvard Graduate School of Education. Since 1978, her research interests have focused on the field of language and literacy development and its educational implications in a variety of populations, including low-income and bilingual children. She is a co-author of *Unfulfilled Expectations: Home and School Influences on Literacy and Preventing Reading Difficulties.*

Freya L. Sonenstein is Director of the Population Studies Center at the Urban Institute, Washington, DC. She is Principal Investigator for the National Survey of Adolescent Males. She is also Director of the National Survey of America's Families, and has published widely on child care, welfare reform, and family planning.

Renée Spencer, M.S.S.W., Ed.D., is Assistant Professor at the Boston University School of Social Work. Her research focuses on the role that strong relationships with adults play in adolescent psychological health and well-being and how relational theories inform the study of risk and resilience.

Howard C. Stevenson, Ph.D., is Associate Professor with tenure in the School, Community, and Clinical Child Psychology and Interdisciplinary Studies of Human Development Programs at the University of Pennsylvania. His research and consultation work identifies cultural strengths that exist within families and mobilizes those strengths to improve the psychological and educational adjustment of children and adolescents using communities and neighborhoods as the major vehicles of support and social change. As a clinical supervisor and therapist in family and child psychotherapy, Stevenson also focuses on developing community and family systems interventions to increase the academic and social adjustment of poor youth.

Meg Striepe, Ph.D., is Research Scientist on the Gender and Sexuality Project at the Center for Research on Women at the Wellesley Centers for Women.

Carola Suárez-Orozco is Executive Director of the David Rockefeller Center for Latin American Studies at Harvard. She is also Co-Principal Investigator of a five-year longitudinal interdisciplinary study of Central American, Chinese, Dominican, Haitian, and Mexican immigrant youth examining their adaptation to schools and U.S. society. Her research focus is on the intersection of cultural and psychological factors in the adaptation of immigrant and ethnic minority children. She is the co-author (with Marcelo Suárez-Orozco) of *Children of Immigration* and *Transformations: Migration, Family Life, and Achievement Motivation among Latino Adolescents.*

Darian B. Tarver is a doctoral student in the Department of Health Behavior and Health Education and a masters' student in the Department of Health Management and Policy in the School of Public Health at the University of Michigan. His research interests include youth violence and suicide prevention.

Deborah L. Tolman, Ed.D., is Professor of Human Sexuality Studies at San Francisco State University. She is also the director of a new research center at the Institute on Sexuality, Social Inequality, and Health. She has written extensively about adolescent sexuality, including her book, *Dilemmas of Desire: Teenage Girls Talk about Sexuality* (2002).

Barbara M. Walker is a Senior Research Associate at the University of East Anglia, Norwich, UK. Her research examines the development of individual and gendered identities among boys from a range of English backgrounds. Her interests also include boys' sexual health education, parent-school interaction, and ethnographic methodology.

Li Wang is a lecturer at the Department of Psychology, Peking University.

Niobe Way, Ed.D. (co-editor) is Associate Professor of Applied Psychology at New York University. Her research focuses on the social and emotional development of low-income urban adolescents and the ways in which the ecological contexts shape development. She has written extensively about the development of urban youth, including her books *Everyday Courage* (NYU Press) and *Urban Girls* (NYU Press).

Naima T. Wong, M.P.H., is a doctoral student in the Department of Health Behavior and Health Education at the University of Michigan. Her research interests include youth suicide and violence prevention.

Yuqing Zhang is Associate Professor at the Institute of Psychology, Chinese Academy of Sciences.

Shujie Zheng is a doctoral candidate at the Institute of Developmental Psychology, Beijing Normal University.

Marc A. Zimmerman, Ph.D., is Professor of Health Behavior and Health Education in the School of Public Health, Psychology, and the Combined Program in Education and Psychology at the University of Michigan. He is Director of the Prevention Research Center of Michigan and the Youth Violence Prevention Center. He is also Principal Investigator for the Flint Adolescent Study, a longitudinal study designed to investigate the protective factors associated with adolescent problem behavior. His primary research interests include the application and development of empowerment theory and the study of adolescent health and resiliency.

Index